SHAMANISM AND THE EIGHTEENTH CENTURY

SHAMANISM

AND THE
EIGHTEENTH CENTURY

Gloria Flaherty

PRINCETON UNIVERSITY PRESS   PRINCETON, NEW JERSEY

Library of Congress Cataloging-in-Publication Data
Flaherty, Gloria, 1938–
Shamanism and the eighteenth century / Gloria Flaherty.
p.   cm.
Includes bibliographical references and index.
ISBN 0-691-06923-9 (acid-free paper)
1. Shamanism—History—18th century.   2. Europe—Intellectual
life—18th century.   I. Title.
BL2370.S5F53   1992
91-21073   291—dc20   CIP

This book has been composed in Linotron Baskerville

Princeton University Press books are printed
on acid-free paper, and meet the guidelines
for permanence and durability of the Committee
on Production Guidelines for Book Longevity
of the Council on Library Resources

Printed in the United States of America by
Princeton University Press, Princeton, New Jersey

1   3   5   7   9   10   8   6   4   2

The following articles were preliminary
versions of chapters in this book:

"The Performing Artist as the Shaman of Higher Civilization,"
MLN 103 (April 1988): 519–39. Reprinted by permission of
The Johns Hopkins University Press

"Mozart and the Mythologization of Genius,"
Studies in Eighteenth-Century Culture 18, ed. John W. Yolton and
Leslie Ellen Brown (1988): 289–309. Reprinted by permission of
the American Society for Eighteenth-Century Studies.

"Goethe and Shamanism," *MLN* 104 (April 1989): 580–96.
Reprinted by permission of The Johns Hopkins University Press.

Harold Jantz

Contents

Illustrations

THE NEED to cope with the mysteries of birth, life, and death is endemic to all peoples in all cultures. In the primordial past, there were men and women who were singled out to help their fellows overcome the difficulties of existence in a world fraught with terrifying, cataclysmic events. Those shamans represented the integration of social forces that allowed the particular society to function properly. They cured illness when they could, and they soothed both patient and family when they could not. Their efforts on behalf of individuals resulted in the kind of communal well-being that produced continuity. They were revered by the members of their tribes, who thought they knew how to control awesome mysteries by interceding with the spirits that populated the universe.

The phenomenon of shamanism manages to persist today in various altered forms that are not always easily accessible to the average person. Sometimes even highly trained specialists have difficulty recognizing the degree of purity or decline in available shamanic vestiges. Nevertheless, the study of shamanism is currently being conducted in many diverse fields. Scientists, especially those in ethnopharmacology and psychoneuroimmunology, fields that have developed rapidly during the last few years, seek out shamanic healing practices involving herbs and other substances. Students of biofeedback write extensively on the role of imagery in maintaining as well as regaining health, while psychiatrists explore the psychological ramifications of belief in so-called wonder cures. The number of dissertations in anthropoloy alone is staggering, for again and again someone professing to be a shaman appears in a South American, Amerindian, Siberian, Near Eastern, or African tribe.

Shamanism also continues to receive attention from humanists. Literary specialists seek the origins of the basic genres in its rituals, and historians of art look at the cave paintings of Lascaux and Trois Fréres in comparable ways. Musicologists concentrate on the instruments and performance techniques employed so as to engage and manipulate the emotions of entire audiences. Biblical scholars produce similar kinds of thought-provoking studies.

The manner in which shamanism is generally treated today might lead one to think that the phenomenon came to light only in the middle of the twentieth century, with the renewed interest in drugs, sex, and the occult. Shamanism, however, has fascinated people since

Western culture began. That fascination has manifested itself in different ways at different times. That which is now called the New Age seems to be a version of something that has regularly recurred. The vocabulary and syntax may change, but the basic structure remains constant.

The focus of my research has been the European encounter with various forms of shamanism. Early travel accounts and ethnographic writings have often been plundered for their descriptions of shamanism, but the reception of that phenomenon has not been documented historically for the most important age of European exploration and colonization. The first part of this book provides that documentation. The second part treats the concurrent assimilation of such information into the European intellectual and artistic mainstream.

Many people aided me in bringing this project to fruition. There was the long line of students at Bryn Mawr College and the University of Illinois who not only bore with me but also helped stimulate my research over the years as this book was germinating and growing. There were colleagues who challenged the avenues I pursued, thereby pointing me to still other questions in need of answers. Their skepticism led me to the discoveries that make up this book. And there were many librarians who provided invaluable assistance. I am especially grateful to those at the Newberry Library, the University of Chicago, the University of Illinois, Bryn Mawr College, the Bayerische Staatsbibliothek in Munich, the Niedersächsische Staats- and Universitätsbibliothek in Göttingen, and the Zentralbibliothek der deutschen Klassik in Weimar. I should also like to recognize the efforts of the many pages in this country and abroad who invariably filled my book requests with speed and good cheer.

The need for a history of shamanism began to dawn on me as I was doing research on Goethe and theater while in the Federal Republic of Germany on a Fulbright Senior Research Award. The first part of this book was made possible through the magnanimous assistance of the Institute for the Humanities of the University of Illinois. The confidence these organizations had in me came at a crucial juncture in my career and was exceedingly important for my work.

Among the numerous people to whom I am indebted, three stand out. My special thanks go to Mamie Gray, our departmental executive secretary, who gave tirelessly of her energy and generously of her patience in order to initiate me into the wizardry of the computer. Without the endless encouragement of my mother, Jean Flaherty, this book would not have been possible. She provided much practical advice, and as always throughout my life, she bolstered my spirits and helped me keep the faith during the most trying times. My greatest debt is to Harold Jantz, to whose memory this book is dedicated. He taught me to read literature in spite of myself. He instilled in me a love for eighteenth-century studies. And he motivated me to follow my own scholarly instincts, even when they contradicted his.

SHAMANISM AND THE EIGHTEENTH CENTURY

Introduction

SHAMANISM is an ever-changing phenomenon that has been considered quite exotic, if not quixotic, throughout all history. In most cultures the world over, there are women as well as men who exhibit both the need and the ability to induce in themselves the kinds of experiences that take them to the brink of permanent madness or death. Those experiences include depersonalization and fragmentation, in addition to feelings of weightlessness, ascensionism or flying, and bilocation. There are as many words for these practitioners as there are tribes supporting such practices. In some areas of the globe, such a practitioner would be referred to as a *kam*, *bö*, *angekok*, *ojun*, or *tadyb*, while in others, he or she would be known as a *piayé*, *curandero*, wizard, soothsayer, faith healer, or shaman.[1] Despite the potentially painful "crashing" during subsequent reentry into everyday reality, shamans are supposed to be able to relate their experiences in ways that somehow touch the members of their tribes and do them some good.

Shamans are said to prognosticate through their visions, to manipulate and bend the future through their communications with the spirit world, and to provide catharsis through ecstatic rites grounded in drugs, alcohol, or the stimulations to the inner ear that come from jumping, running, or frenetic dancing to loud music and fluctuating lights within an enclosed space. Great shamans are masters of ventriloquism and legerdemain. They understand about speaking in tongues or voices, about laying on hands, and about diverting a subject's attention. They instinctively know when and how to employ music, dance, costume, and all the other components of theatrical performance.

Such practitioners and their followers have aroused the curiosity of intellectuals at least since the fifth century B.C., when Herodotus recounted the death-defying feats of the Scythian soothsaying poets Aristeas and Abaris. Herodotus also reported on the delight the Scythians took in sweat baths and in the long, deep inhalation of burning hemp.[2] Classical scholars throughout the ages have not only continued to study Herodotus, but they have also pointed out numerous other "shamanic" practices of antiquity. Some scholars have attributed the rise of the late Hellenistic novel to the trances of shamans, while others have seen in those trances the origins of theater and fairy tales. Still others have believed shamans responsible for the very creation of Greek mythology.[3]

Reports about shamans still practicing in remote parts of the world received increasing attention during the 1940s and 1950s when the social sciences were rapidly coming into their own as disciplines. The two names that stood out then and continue to stand out are those of Claude Lévi-Strauss and Mircea Eliade. While the latter analyzed those reports in order to interpret the shaman as an archaic religious ecstatic, the former compared shamans to modern psychiatrists, stressing their salutary effects for given audiences. Lévi-Strauss elaborated:

> The modern version of shamanistic technique called psychoanalysis thus derives its specific characteristics from the fact that in industrial civilization there is no longer any room for mythical time, except within man himself. From this observation, psychoanalysis can draw confirmation of its validity, as well as hope of strengthening its theoretical foundations and understanding better the reasons for its effectiveness, by comparing its methods and goals with those of its precursors, the shamans and sorcerers.[4]

With the 1960s, interest in shamanism took on another guise. Poets such as Jerome Rothenberg, who edited the anthology *Technicians of the Sacred*, asserted that it was precisely the new Western interest in the oral, tribal cultures of the Third World that had been responsible for such a massive popular return to intuition and instinct. Rothenberg went on to claim that the Beat poets, along with Rainer Maria Rilke, Arthur Rimbaud, and the various generations of Dadaists, with their attempts to combine words, music, dance, and event, all represented "neoshamanisms."[5] In explaining the manipulation of the creative imagination, Rothenberg wrote:

> Our ideas of poetry—including, significantly, our idea of the poet— began to look back *consciously* to the early and late shamans of those other worlds: not as a title to be seized but as a model for the shaping of meanings and intensities through language. As the reflection of our yearning to create a meaningful ritual life—a life lived at the level of poetry—that looking-back related to the emergence of a new poetry and art rooted in performance and in the oldest, most universal of human traditions.[6]

Artists who created multimedia events, such as Joseph Beuys, were also adapting shamanism to their purposes around this time. Beuys was rescued by Tatars when his Luftwaffe aircraft was shot down during World War II. Those people used fat and felt to induce healing, so Beuys adapted the like as his early sculpting materials. He went on to experiment with using sound, especially music, as an equally valid medium for sculpture. As Beuys himself explained, "When I appear as a kind of shamanistic figure, or allude to it, I do it to stress my belief in other priorities and the need to come up with a completely different plan for working with substances. For instance, in places like universities, where everyone speaks so rationally, it is necessary for a kind of enchanter to appear."[7] Many of the drawings Beuys entitled *Shaman* were contained in an exhibition sponsored by London's renowned Victoria and Albert Museum, which also brought out an impressive catalogue of them in 1983. Some of those drawings were studies for so-called shamanic happenings, the most startling of which must have been *Coyote*. It constituted the three days Beuys spent in the carefully delimited space of a New York art gallery together with a live coyote, a cane, much straw, fifty copies of the *Wall Street Journal*, a triangle, and a tape-recording of chaotic turbine sounds. Wrapped in an enormous felt blanket and wearing the trilby hat he insisted was shamanic, he was carried in and out on a stretcher and transported to and fro in an ambulance.[8]

By the mid-1970s, French intellectuals had so often invoked the word "shaman" in their debates as to make it a kind of theoretical buzzword. Roland Barthes, focusing on the subject of voice in "The Death of the Author," for example, had written that "in primitive societies, narrative is never undertaken by a person, but by a mediator, a shaman or speaker, whose 'performance' may be admired (that is, his mastery of the narrative code), but not his 'genius.'"[9] Barthes did not, however, detail what he understood or meant by that still rather elusive word "shaman."

Jacques Derrida, like so many of his compatriots searching for answers, went back to ancient as well as eighteenth-century texts to explain the essence of performance, among other things. His conclusion was that Plato "is bent on presenting writing as an occult, and therefore suspect power. Just like painting, to which he will later compare it, and like optical illusions and the techniques of *mimesis* in general. His mistrust of the mantic and magic, of sorcerers and casters of spells is well attested."[10] The role of Socrates as a *pharmakeus*—sorcerer, magician, shaman—was apparently definitively illustrated for Derrida by the passage in the *Symposium* where comparison is made to the shamanic power of Marsyas, the flute-playing satyr.[11] The section in Plato where Socrates is addressed by Alcibiades is worth quoting at length:

> And are you not a flute-player? That you are, and a far more wonderful performer than Marsyas. For he indeed with instruments charmed the souls of men by the power of his breath, as the performers of his music do still: for the melodies of Olympus are derived from the teaching of Mar-

syas, and these, whether they are played by a great master or by a miserable flute-girl, have a power which no others have; they alone possess the soul and reveal the wants of those who have needs of gods and mysteries, because they are inspired. But you produce the same effect with the voice, and do not require the flute: that is the difference between you and him. When we hear any other speaker, even a very good one, his words produce absolutely no effect upon us in comparison, whereas the very fragments of you and your words, even at second-hand, and however imperfectly repeated, amaze and possess the souls of every man, woman, and child who comes within hearing of them. And if I were not afraid that you would think me drunk, I would have sworn as well as spoken to the influence which they have always had and still have over me. For my heart leaps within me more than that of any Corybantian reveller, and my eyes rain tears when I hear them. And I observe that many others are affected in the same way.[12]

More recently, the Milwaukee Center for Twentieth-Century Studies has developed "shaman" into a shibboleth for its program. There the word became intimately tied to postmodernism, a concept purportedly derived from Arnold Toynbee and given currency by Ihab Hassan. Michel Benamou has gone so far as to contend that performance, if not shamanism itself, is "the unifying mode of the postmodern."[13] Neither Toynbee, nor Hassan, nor Benamou has, however, shown any historical accountability for the use of that vocabulary. Not one of them has offered a precise explanation of just what is meant, within which context. The result is that we are left with nothing but confusion.[14]

As these lengthy introductory remarks indicate, the word "shaman" has come to mean many things to many people. Disentangling the multitude of often contradictory strands without diminishing or destroying any of them has been a far larger job than I originally suspected. Since the word is associated with the beginning, I started my disentanglement efforts with it and proceeded from there. Until well after the middle of the eighteenth century, the shaman was being described with the words *giocolare* in Italian, *jongleur* in French, *Gaukler* in German, and wizard in English, the last of which is presumably stem-related to the preceding.[15] Of all the many words in many languages and dialects designating the phenomenon, the one that came from the Sanskrit (*šramana/šrama*) and was transmitted through the Siberian Tungus to early explorers is the one that happened to become the generic term before the end of the eighteenth century.[16] Those explorers were mostly native Germans, were trained in Germany, or acknowledged German as the up-and-coming language of scientific discourse. From 1714 on, England was ruled by the German-speaking Hanoverians, whose support of exploration and research led to many cross-Channel cooperative ventures. As a result, the nouns *der Schaman*, *die Schamanka*, and *das Schamanentum* were in use during the eighteenth century; the verb was *schamanen*.

That "shaman" gained acceptance as the generic term so long ago should not really be surprising, since enlightenment, like power, has always had two meanings. Both enlightenment and power have long been sought on various planes and in many ways. As male-dominated scientific professionalism burgeoned—something Michel Foucault has pointed out—whatever was rationally inexplicable, such as the power associated with the herbal knowledge of the wise women, the witches or shamankas, was condemned.[17] It did not, however, disappear. It remained operative, yet went underground, and it provoked continuing research and reflection.

My immediate objective is to discuss how shamanism was reported by observers and perceived by the public, and how it became assimilated into the intellectual mainstream during the eighteenth century. I do so with a still greater purpose in mind. I should like to corroborate the work of those colleagues who have cast doubts on the basic assumptions, periodicity, and value of what has been long called the *siècle des lumières*, the *Aufklärung*, or the Enlightenment. The eighteenth century was too deeply involved with the occult to have us continue to associate it exclusively with rationalism, humanism, scientific determinism, and classicism. Manifestations of irrationalism, supernaturalism, organicism, and romanticism appeared uninterruptedly throughout.[18] It was precisely the tension between those who limited themselves to enlightenment of a purely rational sort and those who included serious consideration of what was derogatorily called the night-side of nature that informed the very way in which Western European knowledge was advanced. That relentless tension helped revolutionize human thought, and affected the shape the world was to take.

Emphasis shifted to inductive methods with an insistence on firsthand observation, objective analysis, and mathematical measurement. That shift in itself, however, produced the kind of intellectual attitude that encouraged inquiry about whether the superstitions of the present might not turn out to be the scientific data of the future. While many eighteenth-century intellectuals upheld mechanistic approaches to nature, others staunchly worked at developing the old-fashioned organic ones, sometimes even mentioning historical figures like Paracelsus and his curiosity about the teachings of the wise women. As Thomas S. Kuhn argued in 1962 in *The Structure of Scientific Revolu-*

tions, alternative approaches to science are never ignored simply because a consensus-formed paradigm delimits what are considered the normal bounds of investigation: "Discovery commences with the awareness of anomaly, i.e., with the recognition that nature has somehow violated the paradigm-induced expectations that govern normal science."[19] Scientific revolutions occur, according to Kuhn, when the paradigm has been deserted and the science it defines is no longer practiced. Then a new paradigm emerges to take its place. The history of science does not evolve linearly, he contends, because such changes have been reversed and could be reversed again. The main example he gives is Albert Einstein's explanation of gravitational attractions, which "has returned science to a set of canons and problems that are, in this particular respect, more like those of Newton's predecessors than of his successors."[20]

Those who continued to probe the anomalies and espouse holistic approaches in the eighteenth century might not have convinced the contemporary scientific establishment of the veracity of their findings, but they did help keep alive age-old questions about the relationship of the mind and the body. They pursued many other unfashionable topics as well. They recognized the whole globe, with all its inhabitants, natural resources, and potential for investment as well as political power, as a rich source of knowledge. The conquistadores, travelers, and missionaries of past centuries were supplanted in the eighteenth century by botanists, zoologists, topographers, geographers, geologists, engineers, physicians, apothecaries, linguists, ethnographers, anthropologists, historians of religion, and a fair share of adventurers. As a result of what they continued to uncover, old disciplines changed radically, and new ones emerged rapidly.[21]

Funding for expeditions was generally available, though certain international contacts, in addition to excellent credentials, were necessary. The solitary explorers as well as the large teams depended on European financial support. There was money from religious orders, such as the Capuchins and the Society of Jesus; there were grants from the British Association for Promoting the Study of Africa; and there were the munificent coffers of the Russians, especially Catherine the Great, who wanted to gain information about a vast realm that sorely needed consolidating if it were ever to be exploited.[22]

As was to be expected, such support, whether in the form of references or hard cash, came with certain strings attached. Those strings often limited the dissemination of findings, if not the actual freedom of inquiry. The "Instructions of Her Imperial Majesty" to one expedition outlined not only the topics to be treated but also the means of treatment. Catherine wanted to know specific things about the inhabitants of her empire, so she ordered the explorers to "observe their dispositions and different corporeal qualifications; their government, manners, industry, ceremonies, and superstitions, religious or profane; their traditions, education, and manner of treating their women; useful plants, medicines, and dyes; food, and manner of preparing it; habitations, utensils, carriages, and vessels; manner of life and economy." She also wanted to know how they hunted, made war, and domesticated animals. But all that was not sufficient. The empress ordered the expedition to collect tribute by using psychology and bribes rather than out-and-out force. The explorers were to abstain from manslaughter as much as possible since, she thought, friendly, humane tactics would not only keep the natives quiet, but would "make them incline to trade, to be industrious in hunting."[23]

The instructions the king of France gave to Jean François de Galaup La Pérouse were similar, yet much more detailed. In addition to prescribing the exact longitudes and latitudes the voyage was to take, those instructions specifically ordered the gathering of intelligence about the presence of the Russians, British, Spanish, and Portuguese in the areas traversed. Each of the two frigates was to keep double journals about such matters as well as about the natural surroundings and their inhabitants. Native ability to assimilate European customs and methods of agriculture was to be noted, since the ultimate goal was a mercantile one: control of raw materials and, eventually, manufacturing. The natives were also viewed as potential consumers, so their clothing as well as arms and other artifacts were to be collected, labeled, classified, and catalogued. The draftsmen onboard were to make drawings to facilitate general comprehension of the observers' scientific descriptions.

The royal instructions incorporated questions posed by the medical and scientific societies as well. Native bodies were to be examined carefully, and their parts, especially the forehead and the forearm, were to be measured. The pulse rate was to be compared with that of Europeans, as was "the age of puberty in both sexes, the menstrual flux, pregnancy, child-bearing, suckling, proportion of males and females."[24] Everything influencing disease, health, and healing was to be noted. Of special interest was the materia medica available to the natives. Examinations were to include both tasting and smelling. As far as the application of such substances was concerned, the instructions read: "Observe the remedies used in warm countries to counteract peculiar disorders, and even describe the superstitious processes which are frequently the only medicine of barbarous nations."[25]

Many eighteenth-century scientists complained bitterly about the assumptions that underlay the explorations. Some, like George Forster, thought of European mercantilism as science gone awry. It seemed to him an all-too-literal application of what Francis Bacon had written about taming, shaping, and subduing Mother Nature, as, for example the passage in which Bacon stated, "I am come in very truth leading to you Nature with all her children to bind her to your service and make her your slave."[26] This protest against the patriarchal, totalitarian thrust of science in the Enlightenment persisted into the twentieth century, when Max Horkheimer and Theodor W. Adorno wrote "The Concept of Enlightenment." They also blamed Bacon for encouraging the development of a method for learning, from nature itself, how to use it in order to dominate it as well as other men.[27]

The eighteenth-century writers who contributed to the persistence of such protest were open to the study of theoretical inconsistencies and irregularities because their scientific attitude was different. So too were the methods they had learned to apply. They had, in many cases, received their academic training—usually in classical philology, history, and medicine—at the university considered politically safe enough to become the repository for, among others, artifacts from the South Seas expedition of Capt. James Cook. The University of Göttingen, founded in the middle of the eighteenth century by the Hanoverians, the royal house of England, seems to have had the reputation of imbuing its students with reverence for Mother Nature as well as with intellectual curiosity and scientific know-how.[28]

Those men who set out to explore this planet, from the frozen Arctic and arid Siberian wilderness to the variegated continents of the New World, and then on to the warm South Pacific islands and hot African deserts, did the job they were sent out to do. They submitted measurements. In most instances, copious sketches and illustrations accompanied their maps and diagrams.[29] They also sent back artifacts—costumes, weapons, utensils, musical instruments—as well as seeds and specimens of the fungi, herbs, and other plants indigenous to the particular geographical place. Equally important were the lengthy descriptions and reports of matters pertaining to the life-style of the native inhabitants with whom the explorers had contact.

Most eighteenth-century observations of shamanism were written from the point of view of the interested yet disbelieving Western European. They almost all follow the same pattern. The observers sought out matters as outlined in their formal instructions, and they subjected those matters to what they believed were empirical tests and rational analyses. Sometimes, hearsay of varying levels of trustworthiness was included. Whether treating shamans in Siberia, Lapland, Greenland, or the Americas, the reports attempted to come to terms with the ritual of the healing or soothsaying séance. They treated its theatricality by mentioning both its acoustical and its visual aspects. The shaman's costume, with its symbolic spangles, teeth, and feathers, was stressed as much as the tambourine, with which the shaman was said to fly to the various levels of the heavens in order to recapture lost souls or gain victory over evil spirits. Greatest attention was usually given to the trance state: not only to attaining it and recovering from it, but especially to its genuineness. Again and again, the reports contained phrases like "dead to the world," "as if dead," and "paroxysm of unconsciousness and powerlessness." Those who lived in an age that feared apparent death—*Scheintod*, that condition in which the body's vital signs are negligible or seem nonexistent—could hardly begin to conceive of such an imbalanced mind-body relationship.

Such reports from the field were quickly published, sometimes in installments as soon as they arrived in Europe, and other times simultaneously in two or three languages. Their reception clearly evidences what new historicists consider the imaginative contribution of successive interpreters, each one based on its predecessor in such a way as to develop a chain of interrelated texts forming a particular view of reality.[30] The image of an extended filtration process would, however, be preferable to that of a chain in order to describe what was operative among the texts I uncovered concerning shamanism. The information they contained was picked up by eighteenth-century scholars, mostly comfortably ensconced academicians, who analyzed it and shared it with other colleagues, who thereupon filtered it and passed on what they considered important to yet other colleagues. Those colleagues then read those filtrations in order to provide their interpretations to the European reading public, which never seemed bored by news about the other parts of the world: Alaska, Siberia, China, India, Arabia, Turkey, Guiana, Louisiana, and so on. The next filtration—or what some might call "cribbing"—came from the compilers of dictionaries and encyclopedias. Then there was still further filtering by the popularizers, who often exploited the enormous market for folio-sized picture books or for children's books. Of course, there were also many of those who have been identified as travel liars.[31] The genealogy of their cribbings or lies will probably always remain hard to trace.

Whatever the level of scientific objectivity or truth, the average literate eighteenth-century European rarely failed to hear about the latest publications dealing with travel, exploration, geography, and ethnography. Such publications were the talk of the cafés, the themes of articles in the moral weeklies, the sources for the latest dress fashions, and the subjects of new operas. They also became the topics of works by bishops as well known as Richard Hurd and by thinkers as famous as Montesquieu and Voltaire. They formed the basis for formal university lectures by philosophy faculty members as renowned as Immanuel Kant. They were even the means whereby a physician-dramatist of the stature of Friedrich Schiller inadvertently caused the students at the University of Jena to rise up and riot in support of the study of universal history. Other dramatists were also smitten with travel reports, as were many novelists, composers, people of the theater, and critical theorists. One essayist who brought out a handbook for prospective voyagers agreed that the proliferation of travel literature had become comparable to a contagion of epidemic proportions.[32]

Although there were many matters about the "other" parts of the world that interested eighteenth-century Europeans, the seemingly ubiquitous phenomenon of shamanism, with its self-induced cure for a self-induced fit, thoroughly captured their attention, their interest, and, above all, their imaginations. They were absolutely fascinated by tales of explorers who had had to acclimate themselves to the languages and customs of the inhabitants whose lands they were measuring and mapping. Those explorers were known to be at the mercy of strange aboriginal people and their inexplicably effective means of healing and solving problems. The mockery that might have initially existed ceased as soon as European lives were saved. The reports that the survivors sent back to Europe, often a mixture of bravado and truth, served to whet the appetites of their contemporaries, who persisted in demanding yet more information.

The emergent publishing industry recognized a profitable market and managed to keep it well supplied. In addition to the works dealing with current exploration, science, and anthropology, there were many compilations and reissues of older travel accounts. Books unearthing purportedly historical information about other cultures were published as well.[33] Some authors assumed the poses of detectives whose aim was to reconstruct the past by finding clues in the available literature.[34] Others depicted the scholarly pursuit of the truth about shamanism as an adventure into the unknown otherness, and they tried to convey their own sense of peril or excitement to their readers.[35]

There were as many books speculating about origins, especially of the American Indians and their medicine men, as there were those proclaiming the arrival of a new time of intellectual liberty that permitted public discussion of matters once forbidden to all but a select few.[36] Geographies almost always included mention of seemingly outlandish local mores. Other books capitalized on the growing interest in exoticism among readers with long accounts of shamanic practices involving drugs, convulsions, and urine baths. Such books even became

the subject of plays, the most notable being the one by August Friedrich Ferdinand von Kotzebue about Mauritius Augustus de Benyowsky.[37] The market was virtually overrun with books encouraging
Europeans themselves to go exploring, or better yet, to enjoy such
adventures vicariously through reading.[38] One booster even vindi-
cated Russia as a remarkably hospitable land where travel was not only
cheap but comfortable.[39]

As the eighteenth century wore on, more and more pedagogical
travelogues appeared.[40] The ones designed principally to bring moral
edification often singled out what would have made the shaman a terrifying figure to young, impressionable readers, presumably so they
would choose to behave in such a way as to demonstrate gratitude for
their Christian religion and their enlightened European upbringing.[41]
Those narrating the grueling existence of Europeans in captivity in
foreign lands could be equally frightening for adults. The debunking
that went on about native practices encouraged publication of a number of exposés about European magic and enthusiasm, which invariably included comment about fraudulence elsewhere in the world.[42]

Expensive, deluxe books that comprised beautifully illustrated,
though not always accurate, descriptions of aboriginal peoples provided news about clothing as well as evidence of physiognomic differences.[43] They stimulated their readers' imaginations by focusing on
the accoutrements as well as the activities of the shaman. Albums of
portraits and collections picturing costumes and rituals remained in
high regard among readers for years to come.[44] Thus, information
about shamanism—whether fact or fiction—became all-pervasive and
extraordinarily intense in the eighteenth century.

While some Europeans continued to ridicule what they considered
puerile trickery and ignoble credulity, others began taking shamanistic practices very seriously. Shamanism seemed to them to epitomize
a grand confluence of ageless human activities the world over. As
Lester S. King recently wrote in *The Philosophy of Medicine: The Early
Eighteenth Century*, "The relations of magic, animism, mysticism, and
advanced religious thought, and the stages of naive, mature, and sophisticated science are all intertwined."[45] Intellectuals of all pursuits
and persuasions studied and discussed shamanism. Theologians and
philosophers investigated not only its relationship to superstition and
the history of religion, but more importantly, its relationship to enthusiasm and the kind of spirit possession that necessitated exorcism, all
of which were experiencing a resurgence.[46] Physicians studied shamanism to learn how the imagination might be used to alleviate pain
or at least make it tolerable. They also hoped to discover explanations
for psychopharmacological matters, especially about the smoking of

some kinds of plant substances and the drinking of a brew concocted from certain mushrooms. Comparisons to somnambulists, charmers, and miracle workers were frequently made, as were references to lunatics. Eighteenth-century ethnographers and anthropologists regarded shamanism as possibly representing one of the major links that connected the inhabitants of Asia and America across what was soon to be named the Bering Strait.

Classical archaeologists and philologists, whose work went far beyond that of Johann Joachim Winckelmann, could not refrain from thinking about the many ways shamanism, as practiced by aborigines alive in the eighteenth-century world, conformed to various Greco-Roman mysteries. They recalled information about remotest antiquity and its frenzied, lewd revelers. Epimenides and his long sleep could not be forgotten, nor could Orpheus and the belief in the transmigration of souls. Pythagoras and his trip to Hades, where he saw Homer and Hesiod doing penance, also had to be considered.[47] On the other hand, eighteenth-century musicians related their reading about shamanism to what they knew of oriental music, specifically Turkish music, and how it was applied to whip soldiers into battle-ready frenzy. Sometimes, the legendary assassins and Near Eastern gardens of sexual delights were mentioned.

Aestheticians as well as students of literature and theater also profited from the steady stream of information about shamans. An increasing number began to think more often in terms of the creative personality, the human imagination, and the arts of performance, on which so much in shamanism seemed to hinge. They contemplated the implications of daring and brinksmanship. They recalled Plato's Ion and actors getting carried away by their roles. They reconsidered the recently rediscovered Longinus, the emotional transport he thought the sublime produced, and the shamanic examples he cited to support his thesis. Or they concentrated on the legacy of the recent past, reviewing the magical worlds created by Ariosto, Spenser, and Shakespeare. Among critical theorists, focus shifted from the work of art to the person or persons who made that work come alive. The genius did not persuade the people in his audience with rational arguments. He somehow mysteriously transmitted his creative trance to them so as to transport them out of ordinary, everyday reality into other cosmic regions, where they themselves could experience the profound mysteries of birth, life, death, and regeneration.

The reception of shamanism in Western Europe has not been given historical treatment for many reasons, the most troublesome being not only its complexity but also the partisanship it engenders. For some, the very subject contradicts the tenets of rationalism and should not be broached at all.[48] Others strongly disagree. Those scholars who believe something more profound is involved are, however, often ridiculed for their concern about matters that do not fall within the boundaries of what Kuhn would call normal scientific inquiry.[49] Still others prefer to relegate the study of shamanism to the domains of anthropology or religion. Furthermore, shamanism has not been deemed a subject worthy of history because it has often been viewed as existing only in cultures the West believed antedated its own invention of history. The possibility that something so closely associated with primitive stages of human development might have had a lingering effect on Western arts and sciences is difficult for many to entertain. Questions about the trustworthiness of observations, eyewitness accounts, documents, and sources add as much to the complexity as do the degrees of change from archaic purity to civilized decline that shamanism has undergone over the centuries in various areas of the world.[50] The influence of contacts with more advanced cultures also remains exceedingly difficult to calculate. 7

Since this book inaugurates attempts to view the reception of shamanism within the historical context of Western Europe, it seemed advisable to present the diverse materials I uncovered in as straightforward and pragmatic a manner as possible. Therefore, two parts are necessary. The first provides a chronological exposition that attempts to reconstruct the historical stages in which that information was gathered and made public.[51] It lets the successive texts show how shamanism entered the European consciousness generation by generation as something foreign, yet increasingly familiar.

Part 1 identifies the reporters on the subject and then locates them in a particular theological, economic, or scientific context. Once their general orientation has been established, I focus on the intellectual background and training responsible for their approach to what would have been, for them, the new and the unknown. I discuss the texts they read in preparation for their work, as well as those they cited as authorities, in order to gauge how the perception of shamanic otherness was evolving into certain thought patterns, ranging from the diabolic to the exotic and eventually the artistic. As a result, we see how observations in the field were informed by the reading of earlier texts, which were then, in turn, incorporated into the new publications. As the filtration process continued, those texts invariably converged with others in the minds of early writers who produced interpretations without doing any fieldwork at all.

Throughout the first part, I give attention to the problems that enlightened science had in dealing with the various vestiges of shamanism—that is, some scientists' inability to come to terms with what Kuhn considered the anomaly that challenges the paradigms of normal science. As more and more assumptions, sometimes even unacknowledged ones, were called into question, the framework for discussion about shamanism broadened, and shifts in methodology occurred. Those shifts brought still other perceptions with them conditioned by the expanding study of European mythology and folklore as well as Renaissance Neoplatonism and magic. Increasingly, shamanism interested physicians who sought viable remedies for their patients rather than logical, scientific explanations for their peers.

Part 2 of this book was only made possible by part 1, which unearthed and clarified enough documents to support the contention that information about shamanism was so widely available that it could, indeed, be simultaneously assimilated. Here I take as examples Denis Diderot, Johann Gottfried Herder, Wolfgang Amadeus Mozart, and Johann Wolfgang von Goethe, who, each in his own way, absorbed material from the shamanic discussion that was raging and used what he took to give shape to his own special field of endeavor.

The initial reason I chose to concentrate on these four major figures was the relationship between the philosophes in Paris and the German courts. As my research progressed, a rather intricate web of interrelationships emerged. The news Diderot and Friedrich Melchior Grimm wrote about in the *Correspondance littéraire* circulated from Gotha to Weimar and then to St. Petersburg, and also on to intellectual circles in university towns like Göttingen. Herder, who became personally acquainted with Diderot in the 1770s, was very interested in the latter's stopover in Germany during his journey to Russia. Many of Diderot's ideas and suspicions were shared by Johann Georg Zimmermann, friend of Catherine the Great and physician to George III, Frederick the Great, and the Goethe family. All were attracted by the seemingly limitless artistic capabilities of Mozart. Grimm, who remained well connected to France, Russia, and the German lands throughout his life, even tried to facilitate Mozart's career at various junctures.

My concluding chapter concentrates on Goethe's *Faust* because it brings together ideas on knowledge and power, in the occult as well as the enlightened sense. The new reading I suggest is based on viewing the figure of Faust in both the first and second parts of the Goethean drama as another, more advanced stage in the evolution of the shaman. He is no longer the magician whom earlier European folklore damned because he sold his soul to the devil in order to gain knowledge about the forces controlling nature. Goethe's Faust may have the many flaws of a human being, but he is the best scholar-scientist-healer-artist-ruler the advanced culture of the West can offer. He epitomizes for the modern world the kind of civilizing influence Orpheus represented for the ancient world. Goethe's masterpiece is the ultimate creative appropriation of the information about shamanism that had inundated the West in the eighteenth century.

Part One

FROM FABLES TO FACTS:
THE EUROPEAN RECEPTION
OF SHAMANISM

CHAPTER ONE

The Paradigm of Permissibility, or, Early Reporting Strategies

THE AGE of discovery brought forth a prodigious supply of information about the multifarious vestiges of shamanism all over the world. The methods used to gather this information can at best be termed elusive, and the means of disseminating it, eclectic.[1] The reporters usually strove for as much accuracy as circumstances in the field would allow, but their observational skills were mostly undeveloped. As could be expected, they saw and evaluated things solely on the basis of European religion, politics, and social customs, which then blended with their own personal desires for fame and fortune.

Their reports appeared almost at the same time as did those works investigating alchemy and magic as possible means for discovering the hidden secrets of nature. All those reports and works happened to coincide with the rising tide of European fear of witchcraft.[2] The ensuing craze produced mercilessly widespread persecutions and many obstacles for those attempting to articulate what they thought they observed about what seemed to be not quite normal. If their reports did not treat shamanism as a form of diabolic demonology, they were listed on the *Index librorum prohibitorum*; they were refused license to appear in print; or, even worse, they incurred accusations of heresy. Such difficulties encouraged the development of a theologically acceptable paradigm or safe pattern of discourse that served as a model to be copied.[3] As long as the devil was clearly disavowed, questions could be broached about matters otherwise considered too delicate or forbidden. While many writers conscientiously adhered to this paradigm of permissibility, there were others who merely used its rhetoric, oftentimes with no other objective than titillating their readers with stories of exotic or lascivious rituals. Still others developed evasive strategies that did not compromise their intellectual integrity.[4] Some very serious investigators who refused to adulterate their findings never did get to see their works published during their lifetimes. Only several centuries thereafter did they appear.[5] Among them were some reports still valued today by ethnobotanists and pharmacologists about the unguents, anesthetics, and other medications used in shamanic healing.

An explanation for miraculous cures had been sought since the earliest travelers to the New World recorded their experiences—if not before. Time and time again faith was singled out as the most significant factor. One traveler to the Americas in the sixteenth century, Alvar Nuñez Cabeza de Vaca (fl. 1535), totally astonished himself when the treatments demanded of him by some natives succeeded to such a degree that even a corpse purportedly came back to life. His success was attributed to imitating indigenous medicine men while also saying the Lord's Prayer and making the sign of the cross over the patients. In other words, he combined an appeal to their faith with his own Christian belief.[6]

The arrogance of eurocentric male Christendom was evident in most early accounts of shamanism. Their authors unabashedly referred to native peoples as stupid brutes who believed in evil spirits and worshiped heathen idols because they had no sense of the true god. Paul Einhorn (d. 1655), for one, tried to articulate what he had learned about Baltic superstitions. He often expressed his amazement at the acknowledged high status of women in those geographical areas, and, in trying to give reasons for it, he related pregnancy and fertility to the innumerable songs about "the mothers," whether the revered mothers of the forest, the garden, or the sea.[7] Einhorn, a Christian missionary, did not overlook the sexual aspects of heathen religious practices. He explored the importance of what he interpreted as their saturnalias, stressing that all kinds of carnal activities were accompanied by lascivious songs and deeds, in addition to veneration of the highly honored god Comus. He also recognized a tendency to go underground, something that was becoming increasingly prevalent among the believers in shamanism who had been assaulted by European missionaries and conquerors. While explaining how the Baltic peoples managed to outwit those sent to convert them to Christianity, Einhorn displayed his own knowledge about the literature of travel to the New World and Asia as well as the remote parts of Europe. Despite whatever efforts might have been made, Einhorn reported that the local peoples retained their faith in the power of "their soothsayers, augurs, and priests of the idols."[8]

Another description of early seventeenth-century Livonians along the Baltic coast exemplified how lip service could be paid to reason while at the same time denigrating the quality of local wizardry: "They are by nature obtuse and dull, inclined to Necromancy and Sorcery, but in the performance of an Exorcism, so palpably ridiculous, that I wonder how they have obtained that repute they have in the World among those, who ought to be wiser than to believe such groundless Fictions."[9] So strong was the hold of shamanism on the minds of the

Baltic peoples that writers at the end of the eighteenth century were still remarking about it and about the precariousness of the entire Christianizing effort.[10]

Nicolas Witsen (1640–1717), who was eventually to become mayor of Amsterdam, was yet another on-site witness to shamanistic practices in the seventeenth century. He spent his youth traveling rather widely throughout the imperial Russian lands. His innate curiosity, coupled with his natural research instincts, made him so well known at the Muscovite court that Peter the Great sought him out there and later in Amsterdam. It was Witsen who happened to facilitate Peter's introduction to the members of the political as well as the scientific community of Western Europe, among whom was the famous physician, Hermann Boerhaave (1668–1738).[11]

Witsen's account of his travels and studies, *Noord en Oost Tartaryen*, was first published in 1692 in what apparently was such a rare, limited edition that not even his good friend and colleague Gottfried Wilhelm Leibniz (1646–1716) knew about it.[12] Included in that account were descriptions of the various forms of idolatry and superstition that Witsen found still extant. After displaying his familiarity with classical antiquity by mentioning Pythagoras and metempsychosis, and after making comparisons with other inexplicable aspects of the accepted past, he spent a great deal of effort on the shamanic practices he managed to observe or learn of during his travels. Everything he reported about them naturally remained within the accepted paradigm of permissibility. Writing in Dutch, he used the Germanicized word *Schaman* and explained to his readers that it meant a priest of the devil.[13] He found the kinds of services such priests rendered to the various tribes of aborigines intriguing. About one tribe, he reported the following:

> They come to their heathen priests or holy men in order to be helped out of need when ill or otherwise discomforted as if to a source of information. These then go for advice to the idol, and they make the people believe one absurdity or another. For example, according to ear- and eyewitnesses, in order to become healthy, they will slaughter the best horse and consume the meat with the entire family in one day. The hide, feet, and head are hanged at the church tower in honor of the idol. In so doing, they pray to it for themselves. (634)

Witsen's great desire to communicate what he had learned about the phenomenon of shamanism had led him to include an illustration of a shaman from the Tungus in full ceremonial regalia and wearing a hat with reindeer antlers, long recognized as symbolizing death and regeneration (plate 1).

Plate 1. A Tungus Shaman or Priest of the Devil.

Another tribe's practices prompted him to offer a strikingly comprehensive description:

Thus must the sorcerer with his magic know what to say, or advise about who has done such, or what is going on. In the same way as this swearing and the stabbing of knives occur, so, too, do they practice magic, or, rather, make predictions. They chop down the branches of trees, which they then lay on the water, or, in the winter, set in the middle of the ice, around which they do their work. And then they take in their hand a heavy cutting knife or an arrow, making much clamor by jumping and screaming while drumming on a little drum. Afterward the soothsayer then also stabs himself bravely in his body. Many Samoyedes stand around him screaming similarly. The sorcerer, hurting himself in this manner, falls in a faint while jumping, and after having lain for a time, just as if rising out of a sleep, begins to prophesy about all the preceding matters. This is the most respected kind of divination. Smaller things are divined and examined with fewer efforts, although not without practicing magic in their manner, but rather without the chopping down of trees, that is, only inside a tent or in the smoke from the fireplace. One finds some Christians who ask advice from them as often as from the devil, and through that try to retrieve their lost or stolen goods. (896)

Those practices were corroborated by such people as John Perry (1670–1732), an architect and engineer, whose relatively long-term residence among the Russians resulted in *The state of Russia under the present Czar*, a work that was thereafter translated into many languages. In Perry's opinion, the corruption, ignorance, and idleness of the so-called Christian clergy prevented the czar's enlightened attempts to introduce social as well as religious reforms. Consequently, superstition of all kinds was widely prevalent, as was sodomy and other such habits.[14]

Similar circumstances on the other side of the globe were attested to by Lionel Wafer (ca. 1660–ca. 1705), a buccaneer and physician who spent several years in the Americas. In 1699, he published *A New Voyage and Description of the Isthmus of America*, a work that saw several editions in various languages before 1750.[15] His attention was particularly drawn to matters having to do with curing and healing. He therefore described how the natives very successfully treated wounds with herbs they chewed in their mouths to the consistency of paste.[16] Their methods of bloodletting also concerned him. Most startling to him, however, were the various shenanighans of their shamans, or, as he preferred to call them, conjurers. It was they who predicted and prognosticated as well as cured. He thought of them as being "very expert and skillful in their Sort of Diabolical Conjurations." He described a séance or "pawaw" that he himself had experienced:

We were in the House with them, and they first began to work with making a Partition with Hammocks, that the *Pawawers*, for so they call these Conjurers, might be by themselves. They continued some time at their Exercise, and we could hear them make most hideous Yellings and Shrieks; imitating the Voices of all their kind of Birds and Beasts. With their own Noise, they joyn'd that of several Stones stuck together, and of Conch-shells, and of a sorry Sort of Drums made of hollow Bamboes, which they beat upon; making a jarring Noise also with Strings fasten'd to the larger Bones of Beasts. And every now and then they would make a dreadful Exclamation, and clattering all of a sudden, would as suddenly make a Pause and a profound Silence. But finding that after a considerable Time no Answer was made them, they concluded that 'twas because we were in the House, and so turned us out, and went to work again. (290–91)

Once more they had no luck, so they double-checked the area and found some of the explorers' items of clothing. They removed them because of their negative aura or influence, and "Then they fell once more to their *Pawawing*; and after a little Time they came out with their Answer, but all in a Muck-sweat; so that they first went down to the River and washed themselves, and then came and deliver'd the Oracle to us" (291).

Healing was an important issue for the French explorer Louis Armand, baron de La Hontan (1666–ca. 1713) as well. The account he gave of his travels in America contained an entire section called "Diseases and Remedies of the Savages." In addition to describing the procedures—the dancing and the howling like animals—he remarked on the background and calling of the shamans, or, as they became known in the French literature, jugglers: "A *Jongleur* is a sort of *Physician*, or rather a *Quack*, who being once cured of some dangerous Distemper, has the Presumption and Folly to fancy that he is immortal, and possessed of the Power of curing all Diseases, by speaking to the Good and Evil Spirits."[17]

The reactions to shamanism that such voyagers and explorers supplied were supplemented in the course of the sixteenth and seventeenth centuries by the observations of missionaries and hostages or prisoners. Again and again they linked the present to the past by making comparisons to still earlier travelers, such as Giovanni da Pian del Carpine (d. 1252) and Marco Polo (1254–1324). Their reports went through several editions in different languages and also appeared in the major collections of voyage literature.[18] Pian del Carpine wrote in general terms about purification rites, oracles, divination, and sorcery among the Tatars he observed during his expedition to the northeast in 1246.[19] Marco Polo related his perception of the healing séance he witnessed in China. He described how chanting and increasingly frenetic dancing induced in the practitioner a deathlike trance that purportedly allowed for communication with the spirit world so as to reveal the cause of and the cure for the particular affliction. The curiosity coupled with objectivity that he mustered explains why later centuries so often credited him with having keen powers of observation:

But when they are ill they make their *physicians, that is* magicians come to them, these are the devil-charmers and those who keep the idols (*and with these the province is well supplied*), *and ask them to foresee concerning the sick.* And when these magi are come *they ask about the manner of the sickness*; then the sick persons tell the ills which they have, and the magi, *very many of them being gathered together*, begin immediately to sound *their* instruments *of music* and *to sing and to* dance and leap *in honour and praise of their idols; and they continue this dancing, singing, and playing all together for a long time* until some one of these magicians fall all on his back on the ground or on the pavement *or on the bed* and *with* great foam at the mouth and seems dead, *and then they dance no more.* And *they say that* it is that the devil is *entered* there inside his body, *and* he stays *thus a great while*, in such manner that he seems dead. And when the other magicians *his companions*, of whom many were there, see that one of them is fallen in such way as you have heard, then they begin to speak to him and they ask him what sickness this sick man has *and why he has it.* And that one *remaining in ecstasy* answers. Such a spirit has smitten him because he did him some *great evil and* displeasure, *and he names some one.* And the *other* magicians say to him, We pray thee that thou pardon him *the fault* and that thou *accept and* take from him for recompense of his blood those things which thou wishest *to have, all at thy will.* And when these magicians have said *these and* many *other like* words and have prayed much the spirit who is in the body of the magician who is fallen down, *then that spirit* answers. And if *it seems to the demon by the signs of the sickness that* the sick man must die *in that sickness of his*, he answers like this and says, This sick man has done so much wrong to such a spirit and is so bad a man that the spirit will not *be pacified by any sacrifice* [*or*] pardon him for anything in the world. *Within so many days he will die.* This answer have those who must die. And if *he shows that* the sick man must be healed *of that disease*, then the spirit which is in the body of the magician answers *these magicians* and says, *He has offended much, but yet it shall be forgiven him. For* if the sick man wishes to be healed let them take two sheep or three, and let them also make ten drinks *or twelve* or more, very dear and good *to drink and with good spices.* And they say *again* that the sheep may have black heads, or they describe them *marked* in another way *just as they please to say.* And he says that he make sacrifice of them to such an idol and to such a spirit—*and he will name him*, and that so many magicians and so many ladies, *pythonesses, that is* of those who have the spirits and who have the idols, may gather *with them*, and that they *all must* make great praises *with great singing and with great lights and with good odours* and great feasting to such an idol and to such a spirit; *and that in this way the god will be appeased toward the sick man. And thus the spirit answers them when the sick man must be healed.* And when these have had this answer, the friends of the sick man instantly *perform all that the demon commanded and* do so as the magicians tell them *to do*.[20]

Marco Polo did not fail to mention the supportive role of the attending believers, whose antics were thought to help propitiate the offended spirit.

Such descriptions were confirmed by Jesuit missionaries who had begun writing each other by the second half of the sixteenth century about their observations in the field. What they wrote constituted a strangely engaging mixture of all kinds of information expressed with the necessary rhetoric and, of course, forced into the required paradigm. Their reports, whether translated or not, were known to circulate in most European countries in secular as well as clerical circles.[21] They were published annually in France from 1632 to 1673 and were brought together as *Lettres édifiantes et curieuses* between 1702 and 1773.[22] They were even considered worthy enough to be collected, edited, and translated more than once in eighteenth-century England. The editors roundly rejected Roman Catholicism along with what they considered its vices and viciousness, but warmly praised Jesuit approaches to learning about non-European peoples and their customs. Those editors went so far in presenting testimonials to Jesuit methodology that one wonders about the role the Society might have played in publishing such collections in England. Unlike the explorers, scientists, and opportunists, the well-educated, intellectually alert fathers actually settled permanently in the new environment, clothed themselves in native dress, usually that of penitents, ate indigenous foods, and strove to learn the local language in order to record it for posterity as well as to communicate with their charges.[23]

The Jesuits added several new aspects to the paradigm that allowed for the observation and discussion of shamanism. They continued to blame the Devil with his demons, and they supported the theory of degeneration, which held that such heathen practices represented a corruption of the true notion of deity. They went on to explain, however, that the extremely vivid imagination of the aborigine was neither tempered by a strong intellect nor controlled by a moral sense. Consequently, it was all too easily stimulated and manipulated. The shamans used many techniques to do so. In reporting how they interfered with the Christianization process, Jacques Marquette (1637–1675), for example, singled out their use of insults and verbal threats.[24] Others remarked about the choice of location and how it could instill sheer terror. The shamans somehow knew that the effect of certain rituals could be considerably heightened if they were held in caves or very cramped places where sights, sounds, and odors would take on non-worldly qualities.[25]

In some geographical areas, the primeval forest with its inherent mystery seemed to supply the special places. A traveler in Canada transmitted to a missionary one of the standard descriptions of a conjuring séance: "They withdraw into some thick Part of the Wood into which the Sun Beams can scarce make their Way, there the Savage appointed to be the Soothsayer turns and winds his Body into the most extravagant Postures, making such monstrous Grimaces as might fright any but the Devil, putting out his Tongue and foaming hideously, which he never gives over till there is a Signal, that the Devil is ready to answer; the whole Wood quakes and cracks and all the Company hears the Voice and gives entire Credit to it" (301–2).

Yet another aspect that became common in the shamanistic paradigm during the seventeenth century was the comparison to Greco-Roman antiquity.[26] The Jesuits contributed mightily because they wanted to share the experiences of their religious zeal with brothers in Europe. In order to communicate and, in some instances, to recruit colleagues, they relied on the common denominator in their educational background: the writings of the authors of classical antiquity. They described the practices of contemporary natives in terms of ancient mythology, poetry, and philosophy. Sometimes they gave specific names, but mostly an allusion sufficed.

A Jesuit in India provided a good example of the latter in his attempt to depict the frenzied performance preceding the ecstatic trance, a topic that was to receive great attention as the eighteenth century proceded. He wrote: "The Priests of the Idols have abominable Prayers to address themselves to the Devil, when they consult him upon any Event; but Woe be to that Man the Devil makes choice of as his Organ. He puts all his Limbs into an extraordinary Agitation, and makes him turn his Head after a most frightful Manner. Sometimes he makes him shed Abundance of Tears, and fills him with that Sort of Rage and Enthusiasm, which was formerly among the Pagans, as it is still among the *Indians*, the Token of the Devils Presence, and the Prelude to his Answers."[27]

The trance struck many early observers as genuine at some times, but not at others. Whichever the case might have been, the observers were astonished that the natives always became mystified. Most difficult for the enlightened European to understand were the demonstrated lack of discernment and the blind acceptance of obvious fraudulence. The Jesuits, most of whom recognized the staging, the role-playing, and the general theatricality of shamanic rituals, repeatedly admitted their amazement. In one instance, we read, "I do not pretend to deny, but that the Priests of the Idols, in Imitation of the Oracles really deliver'd by the Devils, do sometimes artfully counterfeit Persons possess'd, and give such Answers as they are able to those that consult them; yet, after all, that Dissimulation, is, as I have told you, only an Imitation of the Truth."[28]

Yet another aspect was added to the shamanic paradigm when some Jesuits likened such native dupery to a kind of illness. The superstitions of paganism, they contended, were diseases infecting the soul and could only be cured by a strict regimen of Jesus Christ, the everlasting panacea. Christians were portrayed not only as enjoying perfect spiritual health but also as commanding "bigger medicine."[29] The Jesuits nevertheless maintained great respect for the lesser medicine of the natives who had over the eons learned to heal everything from animal and insect bites to wounds and broken bones. The natives even seemed to be far in advance of their European contemporaries when it came to dealing with epileptics and victims of near-drowning accidents.

The conversion of heathen barbarians in the New World similarly engaged Franciscan Recollect friars. They, too, concentrated on shamans, deploring the ubiquitous trickery of their medicine and the strange power they managed to exert over the minds and hearts of fellow natives. Louis Hennepin (1640–1701) was one such friar, who related his explorations of the upper Mississippi valley. His account contains a summation of what he had observed about shamans in the field that typifies the Franciscan evaluation of the phenomenon in the latter part of the seventeenth century:

> There's no nation but what have their Jugglers, which some count Sorcerers: but 'tis not likely that they are under any Covenant, or hold communication with the Devil. At the same time, one may venture to say, that the evil Spirit has a hand in the Tricks of these Jugglers, and makes use of them to amuse these poor People, and render them more incapable of receiving the Knowledge of the true God. They are very fond of these Jugglers, tho they cozen them perpetually.
>
> These Impostors would be counted Prophets, who foretel things to come: they would be look'd upon as having almost an infinite Power: they boast that they make Rain or fair Weather, Calms and Storms, Fruitfulness or Barrenness of the Ground, Hunting lucky or unlucky. They serve for Physicians too, and frequently apply such Remedies, as have no

manner of virtue to cure the Distemper. Nothing can be imagin'd more horrible than the Cries and Yellings, and the strange Contorsions of these Rascals, when they fall to juggling or conjuring; at the same time they do it very cleverly. They never cure any one, nor predict anything that falls out, but purely by chance: mean time they have a thousand Fetches to bubble [i.e., cheat] the poor people, when the accident does not answer their Predictions and Remedies; for, as I said, they are both Prophets and Quacks. They do nothing without Presents or Reward. 'Tis true, if these Impostors are not very dexterous at recommending themselves, and bringing themselves off, when any person dies under their hands, or Enterprizes do not succeed as they promis'd, they are sometimes murdered upon the place, without any more Formality.[30]

The importance of shamanism for European medicine had long been recognized. So, too, had the parameters of permissible inquiry. As early as the sixteenth century, Giambattista della Porta (ca. 1535–1615) was denounced for dabbling in the occult and ordered to Rome to justify his curiosity about the witches' salves. He succeeded by explaining his scientific work and his campaign against the shamans and other charlatans who preyed on simple folk. In *Natural Magick*, first published in Latin in Naples in 1558, revised in 1589, and then translated into the major European languages, he described the relationship of the shaman to the peculiar behavior of women when subjected to certain substances:

To let nothing pass that Jugglers and Impostors counterfeit, They set a Lamp with Characters graved upon it, and filled with Hares fat; then they mumble forth some words, and light it; when it burns in the middle of womens company, it constrains them all to cast off their clothes, and voluntarily to shew themselves naked unto men; they behold all their privities, that otherwise would be covered, and the women will never leave dancing so long as the Lamp burns: and this was related to me by men of credit. I believe this effect can come from nothing but the Hares fat, the force whereof perhaps is venemous, and penetrating the brain, moves them to this madness.[31]

In order to investigate its applications without incurring the wrath of the authorities, subsequent practicing physicians were smart enough simply to apply the emergent paradigm of permissibility and use the commonly accepted rhetoric. After stating that it was the Devil himself who provided what it took to transform human beings into werewolves and the like, Jean de Nynauld, a doctor of medicine, went on, for example, to discuss those substances, among which were belladonna, aconite, and opium, in his *De la lycanthropie, transformation, et extase des sorciers* (Paris, 1615). He attempted to analyze their chemical components as well as gauge their potential potency with regard to human physiology. Their application directly to certain regions of the body suggested a relationship to sexuality that he was only obliquely willing to pursue.[32]

Nynauld was more interested in the profoundly deep, almost death-like sleep that such narcotic substances induced: "To such an extent that whoever uses it seems insane when talking, listening and speaking, or falls into a deep sleep, remaining without feeling for a few hours or days. One must not forget that in such matters the devil is at work, playing his usual role" (26). To him that kind of reaction indicated a possible means of suspending the perception of physical pain. His stress on the controlled application of drugs would seem to indicate that he was striving to discover the basic principles of anesthesiology. In so doing, he repeatedly called on the most famous among the legendary shamans—Pythagoras, Simon Magus, and Faust—in order to shed the light of science on the murky subjects of hallucinations, visions, and feelings of bilocation or transport.

Publications synthesizing observations and interpretations of the various means of curing proliferated during the early seventeenth century. Most of them comprised information from age-old writings about the mysteries together with that from contemporary travel reports and writings on witchcraft, magic, and alchemy. A good example of such a synthesis is Robert Burton's (1577–1640) well-known work, *The Anatomy of Melancholy* (1621). He reviewed Renaissance reports about ecstatic trances in which the practitioner sometimes lay for days "like a dead man, void of life and sense."[33] Upon recovery, the man would tell of his strange visions in a way Burton found very similar to the witches' accounts of their dancing and cavorting after long aerial journeys. All such cases, he thought, were attributable to "a corrupt, false, and violent imagination" (1:255). To support his argument, he wrote that the force of the human imagination was so great that an otherwise healthy patient, informed by a well-respected physician that he was sick, would usually be influenced by that diagnosis and actually become sick. Burton then stated: "Sometimes death itself is caused by force of phantasy" (1:256). Corroborating what a Jesuit missionary to China had related, he found that the cause of an illness could just as well be its cure. Consequently "spells, words, characters, and charms" remained universally effective among the common people (1:256).

The shamans had many other means of appealing to the imagination. Following Roger Bacon, who had pointed out the so-called artistry of their impostures, Burton attempted to expose their cheats and tricks, as so many were to continue to do in the course of the seventeenth century. He wrote:

> They can counterfeit the voices of all birds and brute beasts almost, all tones and tunes of men, and speak within their throats, as if they spoke afar off, that they make their auditors believe they hear spirits, and are thence much astonished and affrighted with it. Besides, those artificial devices to overhear confessions, like that whispering place of Gloucester with us, or like the duke's place at Mantua in Italy, where the sound is reverberated by a concave wall. (1:427)

The legendary shamans were so talented in manipulating the imaginations of their subjects that never, or rarely ever, were their many miraculous feats found out for what they really were. Unlike their less famous colleagues, the shamans were successfully able to do many things:

> build castles in the air, represent armies, etc., as they are said to have done, command wealth and treasure, feed thousands with all variety of meats upon a sudden, protect themselves and their followers from all princes' persecutions, by removing from place to place in an instant, reveal secrets, future events, tell what is done in far countries, make them appear that died long since, etc., and do many such miracles, to the world's terror, admiration, and opinion of deity to themselves, yet the devil forsakes them at last, they come to wicked ends. (1:205)

The lesser shamans, such as the witches of Lapland and Lithuania, might not have functioned on a grand, global scale, but, Burton insisted, they could "cure and cause most diseases to such as they love or hate, and this of melancholy amongst the rest" (1:205). Sometimes they supplemented the curing words with knots, amulets, or philters. Depending on the gravity of the case, they prescribed datura, bhang, or other substances stimulating opiumlike reactions of mirth or ecstasy (2:247). While Burton was interested in scrutinizing all such means of healing, he was very careful to group together the superstitious idolaters, heretics, enthusiasts, and diviners, and disavow them, along with those "men, that attribute all to natural causes, that will acknowledge no supreme power" (3:319).

Protestant theologians, concerned with relating heresy, witchcraft, and idolatry to popery, were similarly attracted to the current voyage literature. They read whatever was available, made selections relevant to their particular cause, and, with many learned references to the likes of Marsilio Ficino (1433–1499), Pico della Mirandola (1463–1494), Agrippa von Nettesheym (1486–1535), Paracelsus (1493–

1541), and other renowned Renaissance investigators of the unknown, brought out collections of extracts or summaries.

Samuel Purchas (1577–1626) provided one of the most often cited texts in the English language. His carefully selected compilation, entitled *Purchas His Pilgrimage, Or Relations of the World and the Religions Observed in all Ages and Places Discovered, from the Creation unto this Present*, first appeared in 1613 and went through many revised editions during the author's lifetime. Aiming to prove that the Anglican version of Christian monotheism was the truest and consequently the greatest, he reviewed innumerable recorded data about religious beliefs, including those of contemporaries all over the globe, ranging from the American enchanters in the West to the Samoyede witches in the East. Purchas clarified his editorial stance when he admitted in his dedication to the archbishop of Canterbury that there were "how many hundreds of their Treatises, Epistles, Relations and Histories, of divers subjects and Languages, borrowed by my selfe; besides what (for want of the Authors themselves) I have taken upon trust, of other mens goods in their hands." He compared such travel data with what was generally known about the Persian magi, the Scythian diviners, the Tatar sorcerers, and the Chinese soothsayers.

He was one of the earliest to concern himself with the very words that could be used to describe what seemed to be such a universal phenomenon. Throughout *Purchas His Pilgrimage* so many different words were used that a thesaurus more or less resulted. Among the English words were priest, sorcerer, mage, magician, practicer of wicked arts, charmer, diviner, soothsayer, augurer, demoniac, witch, enchanter, minstrel, poet, singer, idolater, and oracle. Although certain of those words did gain greater currency, the word shaman won out as the generic term in English as well as the other European languages in the course of the eighteenth century.

In addition to his philological concerns, Purchas was strongly drawn to certain quasi-historical and mythological figures. He found Zoroaster as appealing as did many others of his epoch. Like them, he associated Zoroaster with a great ability to perform "cunning in charms," even though he believed the magi represented the very worst kind of superstitious idolatry and sorcery possible (312–13). In discussing the Tatars and Cathayans, Purchas pointed out that the consumption of "spiced drinkes" was followed by much laughing, singing, and frolicking (362). He even unwittingly referred to the sexual basis of such rites.

Although he couched it in the paradigm as amended by orthodox Protestants, Purchas provided the English reading public with one of its earliest seemingly acceptable descriptions of a shamanic séance. He based it on an account from 1557. The importance of the tambourine, mask, and costume was readily apparent. Purchas wrote:

And first the Priest doth begin to play upon a thing like to a great sive, with a skinne on the one end like a drumme; his drumme-sticke is about a span long, and one end is round like a ball, covered with the skin of an Hart. Also the Priest hath as it were a white garland on his head, and his face is covered with a peece of a shirt of male, with many small ribbes, and teeth of fishes and wilde beasts hanging thereon. Then he singeth, as wee use here in England to hollow, whoope, or shout at Hounds, and the rest of the Company answere him with this Outes *Igha, Igha, Igha*, to which the Priest with his voice replieth. And they answere him with the self-same words, so many times, till in the end, he become, as it were, madde, falling downe as he were dead, having nothing on him but a shirt, and lying on his backe, I perceived him yet to breath, and asked why he lay so: they answered, Now doth our God tell him what we shall doe, and whither we shall goe. (364)

According to the account, the shaman got up, lay down again, and then rose to start singing once more. He pierced himself with a sword heated in the fire and enacted a long, drawn-out ritual seeming to deal with death and regeneration.

Later on in his compilation, Purchas, who was determined to discredit Catholicism as well as deconstruct the ancient mysteries, compared the Amerindian curers in Virginia with the papists. Both, he maintained, stomped and chanted to rattles, applied such things as incense, succumbed to strangely vehement gestures, and, "using extreme howlings, shouting, singing, with divers anticke and strange behaviours over the Patient, sucketh bloud out of his stomacke, or diseased place" (638).

The morality as well as integrity of Roman Catholic priests and monks came into question when Purchas dealt with reports of "women-men" in California and Peru. Such biologically male creatures wore female dress, performed women's work, and satisfied "the sodomitical lusts" of other men (652). Often they committed "the detestable sinne against Nature" in the very name of religion: "Every Temple or principall house of adoration kept one man or two or more, which went attired like women, even from the time of their childhood and spake like them, imitating them in everything. Under pretext of holiness and Religion, their principall men, on principall daies, had that hellish commerce" (730).

The 1626 edition of *Purchas His Pilgrimage* was greatly enlarged to include relations about still other parts of the world. Among them were the domains of the Muscovite emperors. Purchas selected sections emphasizing the similarity of Russian sorcery to that everywhere else. In addition to their imprecations, exorcisms, and blood-sucking, the practitioners "did many strange things by Magical Illusions" (974), so that their believers both feared and revered them. The strength of the belief in such "devillish illusions" (sic, 978) was worrisome to many civic and political leaders because they thought it impoverished the people materially as well as spiritually. Christianity was still only a very delicate veneer.

Even the emperor himself was reportedly consulting with sorcerers—something that was not altogether unusual at the time, given the propensity of others, especially the Habsburgs, to do the same. In Purchas, we read that the Russian emperor

> caused many Witches, Magicians, or *Wars* presently to be sent for out of the North, where there are many between *Colmogro* and *Lappia*. Threescore of them were brought post to *Musco*, where they were guarded, dyeted and daily visited by the Emperors great Favourite *Bodan Belscoy* to receive from them their Divinations or Oracles on the Subjects given them in charge by the Emperour. (Note that a great blasing Star and other prodigious sights, were seene a moneth together, every night over *Musco* that yeare.) (983)

The shamans of the north had long attracted the attention of missionaries as well as others trying to come to grips with the occult. So much information had been made available about the Finn-Lapps that Johann Scheffer (1621–1679), a native of Strasbourg who had emigrated to Sweden, saw fit to produce a kind of protoethnographic compilation of summaries in 1675. The title was *Lappland* in the German version, *Lapponia* in the Latin. The chatty subtitle, so typical for the age, clearly indicated that superstitions, magical arts, and problems in conversion to Christianity would be treated.[34]

Scheffer did not disappoint the readers of his subtitle. The hefty chapter he devoted to such matters clearly reflected the status of scholarship on the subject in the closing decades of the seventeenth century. He must have read just about everything available in the library of the university at Uppsala and, while acknowledging the paradigm that had become accepted among Protestants as well as Catholics, seems to have been personally involved in an engrossing intellectual pursuit: figuring out and explaining something that had eluded generations before him. He began his chapter by flatly stating as a fact that the sorcerers of Lapland and Finland had always been capable of great accomplishments. Their reputation was such that one was forced to wonder whether or not the Persian Zoroaster had somehow been their teacher.

Their powers, Scheffer continued, might not be so strong or so widespread in modern times because of the introduction of Christianity. Nevertheless, he maintained, shamanism still remained generally operative. There was something inexplicable about certain families. They were drawn to sorcery because they somehow intrinsically had closer ties to the spirit world. It was their children therefore who inherited the highly prized office of shaman. But, according to Scheffer, that was not the only way to become a shaman. There were other youngsters who experienced the calling to shamanism through illnesses that greatly heightened their spiritual perception. They, too, then had to endure the hardships and privations of the strenuous initiation process.

Scheffer described at length the shaman's many appurtenances, including the metal spangles, rings, bells, and chains. The tambourine was of special interest, so Scheffer spent many pages on it. He discussed the materials composing it, its shape and its structure, and the hieroglyphic decorations adorning it, and he provided various illustrations of it (plate 2). He also told of Lapps who resisted conversion to Christianity by adapting to the surrender or confiscation of their instruments. Sometimes they fashioned new ones, but mostly they learned to make believe—and that out of public view. Scheffer's treatment of the purported power of the tambourine shows how he was baffled, yet fascinated. Why some were believed to be better endowed, he could not explain. There were other, related things he was incapable of explaining. Although he mentioned that the touch of a female virgin was considered to desecrate the tambourine and rob it of its power, he did not choose to broach the issue of sexuality.

The uses to which the tambourine was put were thought to be four-fold. In addition to the divining and the prognosticating, there was the propitiating of spirits and the healing of fellow tribesmen. How such things were accomplished was even more important. A dual illustration depicted one shaman on his knees hitting the tambourine with a drumstick and another lying prostrate with the tambourine upside down on top of him (plate 3). Scheffer accompanied the illustration with enough descriptions of shamanic ecstasy to convince even the most stalwart disbelievers that something rationally unexplainable did indeed happen. The inducement through chanting, dancing, and drumming came up repeatedly, as did the eventual onset of ecstasy with the fainting or falling down "as if dead," which was then followed after some time by the revival and reporting of experiences had during the trip.

Scheffer graciously mentioned that those attending such séances were convinced that the shaman's soul freed itself from its physical confines so as to journey wherever necessary to find solutions to the

DE SACRIS MAGICIS & MAGIA LAPPONUM. 137
Facies ejusdem tympani aversa.

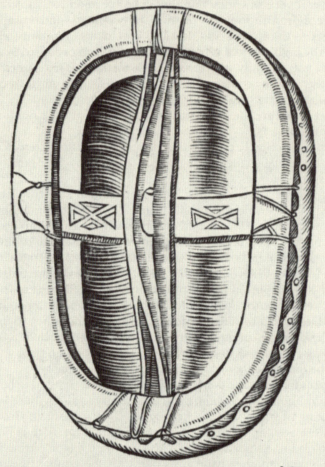

tes pulſantes, non unum tantum, cum uxore, quod Olaus tradit, verum plures, non modo viros, ſed & fœminas, cantiones deni-que ab omnibus prolatas, pulſante pariter, & cæteris, comitibus ipſius.   Quin imo cantiones diverſas, quarum quæ pulſanti eſt in ʋſu, *loiike*, quæ comitibus, *Duura* nuncupatur. | Sequitur nunc
S   de

Plate 2. Inside of Shaman's Drum.

DE SACRIS MAGICIS & MAGIA LAPPONUM. 139

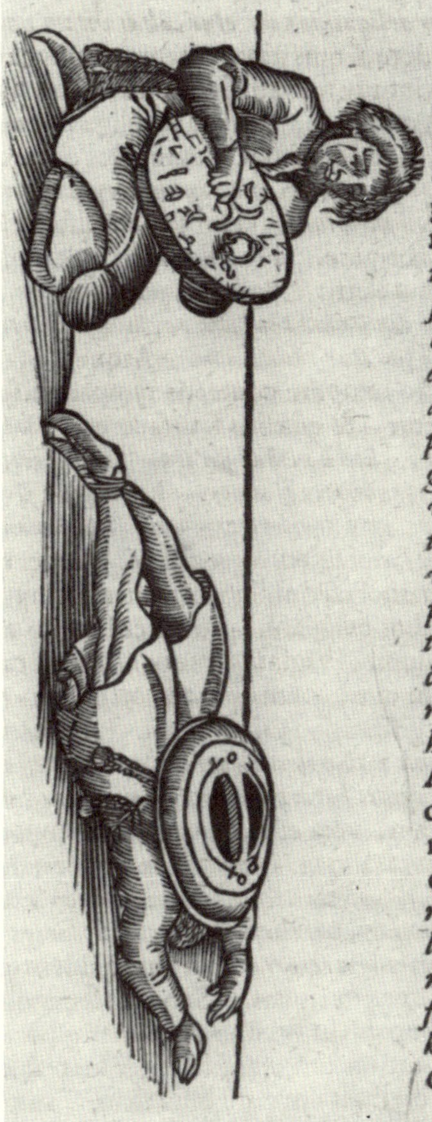

Addit hoc loco Samuel Rheen, folere cæteros, viros pariter fœminasque nil ceffare de fua cantione, fed quamdiu alter jaceat, ipfam repetere, ne fors memoria ejus excidat negotium, cujus caufa fuerit dimiffus: Verba ejus ipfius. *I medler tiid maofte the, fom tillftædes æhro, man ochquinnor, continuera med fin faong, alt till des trumbs lageren opvvaknar affin foempn, huar med de fkola paominna honom, huad hans begieren vvar, eller huad han vville vveeta.* Hoc eft: *Interea cæteri, qui funt præfentes, viri pariter ac fæminæ, continuo pergere in cantatione fua coguntur, donec ex fomno fuo experrectus fuerit tympanifta, ut fic ei revocent in memoriam id, quod habere vel fcire defideraverit.* Addit Anonymus, nifi hoc fecerint, tympaniftam bona fide mori, neque unquam è fomno evigilare: *The andre nærvvarande mofte fiunga, fao længe han ligger affvvimat, och paominna honom, hvvad han begærade foer, æn han afsvvimade, ellieft komer han fig alldrig foer.* h. e. *Cæteri præfentes canere neceffe*

S 2   *habent*

Plate 3. Shaman Drumming and Shaman in Trance.

problems in question. In order to help him and remind him of the problems, they continued the chanting, singing, and dancing, while conscientiously protecting his body from insects and any other assaults that might prevent the easy reentry of his soul. To prove he had actually flown away, and thus establish his credibility, the shaman upon reviving was supposed to present his audience with an object or token of something he claimed to have found on his trip beyond the rainbow. Then he consummated his mission by providing whatever information had been requested of him.

Long before the conclusion of the seventeenth century, some thinkers of the Enlightenment attempted to discredit shamanism as well as the paradigm that had evolved for dealing with it. Their aim was to give rational explanations debunking all religious mysteries, including those of Christianity. The conformities that had already been shown between ancient and modern paganism were now to be applied to the practices of what were considered contemporary European religious enthusiasts such as convulsionaries, Quakers, Jansenists, and Catholics. There was a twofold result, as Frank E. Manuel pointed out in his still valuable study from 1959, *The Eighteenth Century Confronts the Gods* (38). Those practices were viewed as impostures, and their followers were thought to be spiritually, if not mentally, ill.

Although many works exemplify this position, Bernard Le Bovier de Fontenelle's (1657–1757) *Histoire des oracles* (1686) stands out because of the level of erudition and method of handling, or, as the case may be, mishandling, evidence. It epitomizes the approach of those intellectuals who, without leaving the comfort of their studies in Paris, London, Berlin, or Naples, saw fit to denigrate the established religions of Europe while exploiting the explorers' reports so as to theorize about contemporary aboriginal religious practices in a witty and ultrasophisticated way.

Fontenelle's work was at least thrice-removed from the actual facts available at the time since it was a freely adapted, admittedly popularized translation into French of a learned book about the heathen oracles published a few years earlier in Latin by Anthony Van Dale (1638–1708), himself an immensely learned armchair observer. Fontenelle's popularization had so struck the fancy of the adventurer and talented novelist, Aphra Behn (1640–1689), that she rendered his French into English as *The History of Oracles, and the Cheats of the Pagan Priests* and had it published in 1688. Her "Epistle Dedicatory," together with Fontenelle's own preface, clearly warned prospective readers about the kind of intellectual stance to anticipate.

The book tried to demystify seemingly strange mythological or ancient historical occurrences by giving what were considered rational explanations. The part dealing with the origin of the oracles was the most explicit. There we read that Mount Parnassus must have had a hole emitting exhalations of the kind that caused human beings as well as beasts to experience strong feelings of exhilaration. During such delirious experiences, some people must have talked without knowing, and, by chance, they happened to speak what was later recognized as truth. As a result, the hole became a place of veneration.

Van Dale, Fontenelle, and Behn, all of whom were obviously aware of the innumerable accounts of other parts of the world, stressed not only climate but also topography as important for the evolution of oracles. Like many of their contemporaries, they were especially interested in the effect on human beings of caves, caverns, and close spaces. In *The History of Oracles*, we find, for example, the following statement: "And besides caverns of themselves affect one with a certain horror, which does not a little advance superstition; and in things that are only to make impressions on the imaginations of Men nothing is to be neglected."[35]

The sanctuaries that evolved were always situated so as to take advantage of the topographical features of the area. In addition to the alterations of light, there were acoustic considerations. The voices of the Pythian priestesses had always been reported as being so strained as to seem superhuman. And there were the intoxicating vapors that announced the arrival of the gods (110). The ways initiates were selected and prepared for descent into the den of Trophonius, the famous Boeotian oracle, were subjected to similar analysis. The result was approximately the same—that there was always a rational explanation to be found (130).

What Van Dale, Fontenelle, and Behn perceived as the degeneration of the oracles they attributed to four factors: (1) the basically corrupt nature of the practitioners themselves, who perpetrated all kinds of tricks; (2) the raillery of the ancient Greek philosophers, who valiantly tried to come to terms with such matters; (3) the subsequent benign neglect of the Roman conquerors, who simply remained uninterested; and (4) the rise of Christianity. Having read so much in the various current reports about the vivid imaginations of aborigines and the strong imagery in their languages, Van Dale, Fontenelle, and Behn tied the degeneration of the oracular tradition to the decline of poetry as a universal means of communication. They all thought that verse and rhyme helped contemporary primitives as much as it had peoples of earlier ages to remember what was necessary for survival: "It is very strange indeed that *Poetry* should be elder Brother to *Prose*, and that Men did not at first light upon the most natural and easie way of expressing their thoughts" (208).

It was in the eighteenth century that intellectuals began contemplating arguments to ratify this notion. The surfeit of travel reports stimulated many to think that poetry did, indeed, precede prose as the primordial means of communication. In the next chapter, I shall treat subsequent accounts of shamanic practices and, among other things, show how the connection to the creative and performing arts remained a common denominator.

CHAPTER TWO

Eighteenth-Century Observations
from the Field

IN THE EIGHTEENTH CENTURY, explorers became increasingly concerned with the very methods they were using to observe other parts of the world. First and foremost, they looked at themselves. They had, indeed, been strongly encouraged to do so by a steady line of professors who insisted that they must know themselves well before they could ever hope to understand any totally foreign, non-European culture. True knowledge of mankind would otherwise never be theirs, according to the wide-ranging and commonsensical handbook of one such teacher. He advised that "everyone should inspect his own heart; before he attempts to inquire into the character of others, he should observe his own inclinations and inconsistencies, watch himself on all occasions, know his failings, analize the operations of his soul, and then proceed to observe others with the utmost attention, even in trifles."[1]

The prefaces and dedications the scientific voyagers provided repeatedly gave biographical information about social background, personality, level of education, and specific training or preparation for the particular expedition. What began to emerge from these sometimes rather glorified confessions was a profile of the professional explorer.[2] He was depicted as a courageous as well as learned risktaker, absolutely dedicated to the service of science and humanity. One surgeon confessed that his duties prevented him from doing anything but hastily jotting down his impressions and observations. He consequently provided a biographical sketch, claiming his readers deserved to know what kind of character he had, so that they could fill in the gaps themselves: "A knowledge of the man becomes necessary, therefore, not only to enable us to appreciate his merits as a writer, but to qualify us for understanding many passages of his writings, or at least for entering fully into his sentiments and feelings."[3] External matters conditioning the explorers' way of seeing were usually also pointed out. They let their readers know about the framework within which they worked or, at least, the kind of instructions their patrons gave them, oftentimes even printing the charges verbatim. They related the questionnaires they were supposed to follow and other pre-established categories conceived to facilitate easy classification.[4]

The concern for rational analysis among the travelers led to examination of still other sides of their multifaceted endeavors. They often openly admitted their own points of view and commented on past European perceptions that could or could not be corroborated by what was currently observable in the field.[5] Adapting the kind of method Michel Eyquem de Montaigne (1533–1592) expostulated in his essay on cannibals (ca. 1580), they sought out eyewitnesses and informants, circulating advertisements among the natives.[6] Those scientists collected actual artifacts as well as information about the uses thereof. Sometimes they traded for them, so as to learn something of trading as well as something of the artifacts' value. Other times, they used stealth to obtain items sacred to the natives, including human remains, especially skulls. Such items were no longer mere exotic holdings in the trendy cabinets of curiosities in Western Europe. They began to be included in university museums, where collections were actively used for purposes of scientific examination and inquiry.

Record keeping was important to most explorers, so there was usually some prefatory remark about the method used. While some explorers kept diaries and logs according to dates or places, others arranged their notes topically. They often also mentioned the various ways they double-checked to determine whether there was any falsification or chicanery in what they obtained or experienced. In reflecting on the dangers of dealing with peoples of different and untested ethical stances, one author, who would seem to have experienced natives putting things over on him, urged caution coupled with vigilance: "To see mankind, we must strip them of their masks; without this precaution, all that we behold is but a sort of magic deception, where the rogue and the man of honour play the same part, and are equally undistinguishable in the scene."[7]

Reporting the information also posed methodological problems that somehow needed to be confronted. The prefaces again and again disclaimed connections to the ever-popular literature of imaginary voyages. They bore testimonials that the facts were as genuine as the explorer, within the limitations of his given profile, had been able to gather and as unadorned as he was able to articulate. While far from becoming dry and dull, the language of ethnographic discourse was energetically cleansing itself of European-type poetic flourishes and carefully separating itself from historical reportage. The eighteenth-century accounts could not, however, be totally divorced from what preceded them.[8] Many still honored or, at least, paid lip service to the paradigm of permissibility, which allowed for the detailed description of what Europeans considered unsavory customs.[9] As respect for that paradigm waned in the course of the nineteenth century, many writers of ethnographic studies deemed themselves too attuned to public delicacy to report anything that might prove offensive to their readers in Europe. They preferred, as they usually wrote, to draw the veil or close the curtain over such matters, which meant they thereby wiped them out altogether.[10]

In the eighteenth century, explorers often prepared for their expeditions precisely by consulting earlier accounts for maps, directions, and tips about survival tactics. The seemingly demonstrable importance of such consultations led to the publication of a number of bibliographies that gave prospective voyagers quick access to resources that might be of value to them.[11] The inquisitive who went into the field often recalled such works en route, so as to test what they themselves found, or they looked at them afterward, so as to provide readers with a basis for easy comprehension of what were totally foreign habits and mores. Occasionally such consultations underlined changes that had taken place in the meantime.[12] When possible, the explorers supplied lists of words, charts, maps, measurements, and illustrations. As the desire for pictorial depiction grew, so too did the recognition of artistic quality.[13] Draftsmen, illustrators, and artists became full-fledged members of expeditions. In this respect as well, the general tendency toward ever-greater professionalism became evident.

The increasing concern for objectivity and scientific exactitude, however, stimulated concern for matters, like shamanism, that did not seem to fit traditionally accepted methodologies or suppositions. Those matters could no longer merely be condemned, ignored, or hidden in the closet. In recognizing them, however, scientific investigators had to recognize the limitations of their own present methods and admit that they could not provide rational explanations for everything. They thereby learned that science was a process rather than a product.

The writings of explorers who uncovered and recorded information about shamanism show that the testing of assumptions and methods was already in full swing in the early eighteenth century. A classic example is *Travels from St. Petersburg in Russia, to Diverse Parts of Asia*, the work of John Bell (1691–1780), a Scottish surgeon. In the preface, he mentioned his medical training and recalled his youthful desire to see foreign countries. He also stated that he had kept careful notes in a diary while en route from 1715 to 1738. The reason he gave for publishing the notes as late as 1763 was the steady encouragement of a friend. They were certainly not to be considered fiction, for he had "through the whole, given the observations, which then appeared to me worth remarking, without attempting to embellish them, by taking any of the liberties of exaggeration, or invention, frequently imputed to travellers."[14]

Shamanism figured in Bell's work for a definite reason. The ambassador on the expedition had "resolved to inquire strictly into the truth of many strange stories," so wherever they went, he had all practitioners summoned to demonstrate their charms. Bell reported that female as well as male conjurers were locally called shamans. Usually they demanded tobacco, brandy, and presents before they even began to collect their equipment, consisting of "the shaytan; which is nothing but a piece of wood, wherein is cut something resembling a human head, adorned with many silk and woolen rags, of various colours; then, a small drum, about a foot diameter, to which were fixed many brass and iron rings, and hung round also with rags."[15] Bell described what he observed at the charming sessions relatively objectively before giving any kind of evaluation or personal comment. The answers of one female shaman, he wrote, "were delivered very artfully, and with as much obscurity and ambiguity, as they could have been given by any oracle" (1:208). Bell even went on to report something about her appearance that contradicted the popular European perception of the witch as an ugly crone: "She was a young woman, and very handsome" (1:208).

Sometimes Bell had an ulterior motive in assuming the guise of absolute objectivity. He wanted to reveal the fraudulence of the shaman and to point out the credulity of the people who took the shaman's actions for reality. Bell's treatment of the shamanic séance he witnessed among the Buryat-Mongols in southern Siberia contained all the aspects observers in the field had grown accustomed to take into consideration. In addition to the famous reputation of the shaman in question and the expectations it purportedly roused among the Europeans, there was an indication of the time, place, participants, and observers, as well as a description of the performance, a discussion of its outcome, and a general evaluation. Because the séance failed to satisfy the Europeans' expectations, they could not welcome it into the realm of phenomena and grant it stature as worthy of scientific examination, never mind verification. They could only view it as theater, and at that, not very good theater, just a kind of sideshow. Though Bell went on at great length, the entire passage is worth reading in his own words:

> As these shamans make a great noise in this part of the world, and are believed, by the ignorant vulgar, to be inspired, I shall give some account of the behaviour of this one, in particular, by which it will appear that the whole is an imposition.

He was introduced to the ambassador by the commandant, accompanied by several chiefs of his own tribe, who treat him with great respect. He was a man of about thirty years of age, of a grave aspect and deportment. At his introduction he had a cup of brandy presented to him, which he drank, but refused any more.

After some conversation, he was desired to exhibit some specimen of his art; but he replied, he could do nothing in a Russian house; because there were some images of saints, which prevented his success. The performance was therefore adjourned to a Buratsky tent in the suburbs. Accordingly, in the evening, we went to the place appointed, where we found the shaman, with several of his companions, round a little fire, smoking tobacco; but no women among them. We placed ourselves on one side of the tent, leaving the other for him and his countrymen. After sitting about half an hour, the shaman placed himself crosslegged upon the floor, close by a few burning coals upon the hearth, with his face towards his companions; then he took two sticks, about four feet long each, one in each hand, and began to sing a dismal tune, beating time with the sticks; all his followers joined in the chorus. During this part of the performance, he turned and distorted his body into many different postures, till, at last, he wrought himself up to such a degree of fury that he foamed at the mouth, and his eyes looked red and staring. He now started up on his legs, and fell a dancing, like one distracted, till he trode out the fire with his bare feet. These unnatural motions were, by the vulgar, attributed to the operations of a divinity; and in truth, one would almost have imagined him possessed by some demon. After being quite spent with dancing, he retired to the door of the tent, and gave three dreadful shrieks, by which, his companions said, he called the demon to direct him in answering such questions as should be proposed. He then returned, and sat down in great composure, telling he was ready to resolve any question that might be asked. Several of our people put questions in abundance; all which he answered readily but in such ambiguous terms that nothing could be made of them. He now performed several legerdemain tricks; such as stabbing himself with a knife, and bringing it up at his mouth, running himself through with a sword and many others too trifling to mention. In short, nothing is more evident than that these shamans are a parcel of jugglers, who impose on the ignorant and credulous vulgar. (1:253–55)

It is quite significant that Bell, like so many Europeans who dealt with this subject, chose to use the word juggler. Magicians, diviners, and tricksters as well as minstrels and musicians were often so described, not only in English but also in French and German.

Daniel Gottlieb Messerschmidt (1685–1735), who earned a doctorate in medicine in 1707, also had specific objectives in mind when he set out to explore Siberia in the early 1720s. One of the first learned men commissioned by Peter the Great, Messerschmidt aimed to observe topography and natural history as well as social customs, local languages, and monuments. Most important to him, however, was learning about indigenous illnesses, especially the epidemics, the kinds of medical treatment to which the natives subscribed, and the techniques as well as materia medica their healers had at their disposal.[16]

Because of Messerschmidt's predisposed methodological thrust, he was forced to confront shamanism. He could not bring himself even to wonder about possible medical applications of idols.[17] Nor could he give very much credence to any of the séances he himself witnessed. His self-image as the superior, European scientific professional clearly emerged from the account of what happened on March 19, 1721:

> After we were there a short while, a chap arrived and offered himself. He said he was willing to divine or prophecy. So, the doctor let him come hither. He had along a shaman's drum in which there was fastened a wooden shaitan covered with rags. Before he was to begin his art, he wished to smoke a pipe or some tobacco. After he had done such, he began while seated to rub the back of the drum with his shaman's spoon or drumstick just as if he wanted to smear it with fat. Simultaneously he hummed a little softly or quietly and murmured. With his left hand, however, he held onto the shaitan, which had been fastened to the drum. In the meantime, the doctor was asked what he demanded to know. The answer: the shaman should tell where the doctor wanted to go and what he otherwise knew of him. Thereupon the shaman rose, began to beat the drum harder and harder with the drumstick, made a clamor that became increasingly stronger, jumped upwards, leaped about like a crazy person, and grabbed with one hand into the hot ashes lying in the fireplace. In sum, the chap behaved very boisterously. When he had passed a quarter of an hour thusly, he suddenly stopped stock-still and stared with his eyes aloft and stood motionless for a long while. (67)

Messerschmidt, who interpreted all this as nothing but lies and trickery, saw no scientific value in it whatsoever. Such happenings could not, in his opinion, be replicated under controlled conditions. So sensitive were Messerschmidt's general findings that the Academy of Sciences had him surrender his research materials and remain silent about them. While he himself did not publish them, they were made available to others associated with the academy.[18]

The development of an objective methodology also concerned Philipp Johann Tabbert von Strahlenberg (1676–1747), a Swedish officer who spent thirteen years of captivity in Siberia and who accom-

panied Messerschmidt during the first year of his expedition.[19] Strahlenberg's approach combined anthropological investigation with linguistics and archaeology, as indicated by the full title of his report,
which was originally written in German and then translated into English in 1736.[20] As had become the custom, Strahlenberg used prefatory remarks to provide his readers with information aiding their
comprehension of his work. He assured them that he had transcribed
not one thing from others, nor had he added inventions of his own.
He even apologized for once in a while being forced to rely on informants as eyewitnesses, but quickly added that he only gave credence to
those whose integrity had been thoroughly checked (iii).

Strahlenberg devoted his entire eighth chapter to religious beliefs.
He explained that, of the three classes, the pagans were infinitely more
numerous in those northeastern regions than the Mohammedans and
Christians (288). Efforts to convert the pagans had, he continued,
largely failed because they knew no Russian, had neither writings nor
books, and lived in widely dispersed dwellings. Strahlenberg compared their beliefs with what he thought of as the superstitious idolatry of the Lapps and Finns (326). Nevertheless, he attested, his many
encounters with the native inhabitants of Siberia had never brought
him any personal harm or loss. As a matter of fact, he went on to make
comparisons that almost always showed the natives in a favorable
light: "And tho' these *Heathens* are stupid and ignorant in the Knowledge of God; yet they are naturally honest, and good moral People,
who hardly know what Perjury, Thieving, Fornication, Drunkenness,
Tricking, and other such Vices, are. And it is very rare to find any of
them Charged with the like, except those who live among the *Russian
Christians*, and learn these Vices of them" (289).

Francis Moore (fl. 1744) might have been active in a different part
of the world, but he had a similar sympathy for native peoples trying
to withstand what to them must have been the incomprehensible onslaught of Europeans with superior science and technology. His experiences exploring the areas surrounding the Gambia River in Africa
stimulated him, for example, to condemn the slave trade outright as a
creation of mercantile interests.[21] Moore's preface to *Travels into the
Inland Parts of Africa*, the report he published in London in 1738, made
the usual claims to truthfulness, explaining that embellishments and
"beautiful Works of Imagination" had been totally excluded in order
to let the real facts shine through (vi). He confessed in all honesty,
however, that he had consulted the ancient geographers and historians of the Nile for whatever information he could derive from
them (vii).

In addition to putting past scholarship to the test of present reality,

Moore supported the increasing tendency to observe sexual mores, especially as they related to cosmogonical, theurgical, and other such beliefs. His report about Mumbo Jumbo therefore turned out to be more provocative than what he wrote about witchcraft and superstition. Moore explained that Mumbo Jumbo was a tutelary spirit of the kind of sexually high-powered male who could easily keep the females in awe and subjection (40). He reported that he himself had once been paid a visit:

> On the 6th of May, at Night, I was visited by a *Mumbo Jumbo*, an Idol, which is among the *Mundingoes* a kind of a cunning Mystery. It is dressed in a long Coat made of the Bark of Trees, with a Tuft of fine Straw on the Top of it, and when the person wears it, it is about eight or nine Foot high. This is a Thing invented by the Men to keep their Wives in awe, who are so ignorant (or at least are obliged to pretend to be so) as to take it for a Wild Man; and indeed no one but what knows it, would take it to be a Man, by reason of the dismal Noise it makes, and which but few of the Natives can manage. It never comes abroad but in the Night-time, which makes it have the better Effect. Whenever the Men have any Dispute with the Women, this *Mumbo Jumbo* is sent for to determine it; which is, I may say, always in Favour of the men. (116)

The sexual aspects of aboriginal life were also treated by Georg Wilhelm Steller (1709–1746), a medical researcher whose participation in the superbly outfitted second Kamchatkan expedition of Vitus Jonassen Bering (1681–1741) led to the publication of *Beschreibung von dem Lande Kamtschatka, dessen Einwohnern, deren Sitten, Nahmen, Lebensart und verschiedenen Gewohnheiten.*[22] In addition to describing the various sex acts the natives engaged in, and with what purported kinds of partners, Steller reported what he learned about their shamanism (*Schamannerey*) and included three illustrations of a fully outfitted practitioner demonstrating his skills (plates 4, 5, 6).[23]

Steller wrote that the natives believed the world had been created by a not very smart male god named Kutka, whose wife, Chachy, was a superior kind of sorceress. Although Steller thought the stories he heard about them were either ridiculous or revolting, he nevertheless managed to provide examples. One such example had to do with Chachy's ability to find and reattach the male genitals that Kutka, a notoriously insatiable sodomite, lost when a mussel he was raping slammed shut (263). Another told about his definitive castration when caught in a still more blatantly adulterous act. Yet another story had to do with the great god of heaven descending during a thunderstorm so as to enter the body of the female shaman (*Schamannin*) and bequeath

a ein Schamann im Rücken

Plate 4. Shaman from the Rear.

Plate 5. Shaman from the Side.

Plate 6. Shaman from the Rear.

her the gift of prophecy and divination, which she then shared with her people during séances at night in cramped quarters by the light of very small, flickering fires (277–78).

Lasciviousness was so all-pervasive, Steller wrote, that it made the natives incapable of understanding anything except what was physical or what happened to appeal to their imaginations. This, plus their constant, seemingly idiotic laughter about everything, even their own pagan beliefs, led him to conclude that they lacked an inherent sense of shame as well as any respect for the awesomeness of the divine.

The absence of theological and moral culture did not, Steller insisted, preclude openness to new ideas. Though living in a raw climate that was not at all conducive to change, he reported, almost all the inhabitants had, at least, been baptized between 1740 and 1770.[24] The main problem was that the Christian missionaries were able to provide so little educational follow-up that the natives simply blended their old beliefs together with the new, creating strange mixtures that often became sects in themselves. With that observation, Steller noticed something that was to come up again and again throughout the eighteenth century: the strategies the natives perfected in order to be able to take their shamanic practices underground.

Stephan Krascheninnikow (1713–1755), a botanist who also went along on the Bering expeditions, felt he had observed enough to include information about shamans, or sorcerers and conjurers, in his reflections, which appeared in the Western European languages approximately twenty years later, during the 1760s. The German version was prepared by Johann Tobias Köhler, a professor at the University of Göttingen, while James Grieve, a medical doctor, was responsible for *The History of Kamtschatka, and the Kurilski Islands, with the countries adjacent* (1764).

As a scientist, Krascheninnikow was particularly interested in obtaining and analyzing the substances the various shamans used to induce ecstasy in themselves as well as to anesthetize their believers. He noticed that they brewed infusions of certain mushrooms, which happened to be the same kind the natives normally used in order to kill flies. The effect of such infusions on the human body was not lethal, but it was drastic:

> The first symptom of a man's being affected with this liquor is a trembling in all his joints, and in half an hour he begins to rave as if in a fever; and is either merry or melancholy mad, according to his particular constitution. Some jump, dance, and sing; others weep, and are in terrible agonies, a small hole appearing to them as a great pit, and a spoonful of water as a lake: but this is to be understood of those who use it to excess;

for taken in small quantity it raises their spirits, and makes them brisk, courageous, and cheerful.[25]

Anyone intoxicated from drinking the liquor of that mushroom was urged to save his urine in a vessel. It was supposed to be as effective as the original, if not more so. Krascheninnikow did not fail to add that one of the cossacks in his party tried it and nearly died.

Krascheninnikow, like Steller and so many others of his generation, was only too happy to give rational explanations for what he observed of shamanic behavior. From the supposed superior vantage point of the Western European, he cold-bloodedly demystified the ceremonies that a shaman so willingly shared with him and his colleagues. He wrote:

> In the year 1739 I had an opportunity of seeing, at the lower *Kamtschatkoi* fort, the most famous *Shaman Carimlacha*, who was not only of great reputation among these wild people, but was also respected by our Cossacks, for the many extraordinary feats that he performed; particularly that of stabbing his belly with a knife, and letting a great quantity of blood run out, which he drank: however this he performed in such an awkward manner, that any one, who was not blinded by superstition, might easily discover the trick. At first, sitting upon his knees, and beating some time upon his drum, he struck his knife into his belly, and then, from below his furred coat, he drew out a handful of blood, which he eat, licking his fingers. I could not help laughing at the simplicity of the trick, which the poorest player of legerdemain would have been ashamed of. One might see him slip the knife down below his fur, and that he squeezed the blood out of a bladder which he had in his bosom. After all this conjuration he thought still to surprise us more by shewing us his belly all bloody, pretending to have cured the wound which he had not made. He told us, that the evil spirits appeared to him in different forms, and came from different places; . . . they tormented him so much, that he was almost out of his senses. (230)

Like Steller, Krascheninnikow surmised that something inexplicable was afoot among the natives. The intrusion of the white Western Europeans with their scientific determinism was encouraging the shamans to drop out of sight quietly, yet quickly. The believers who remained publicly visible refused to talk about their practices, keeping them from their observers as a great mystery.

Poul Hansen Egede (1708–1789), son of a missionary, spent his whole life witnessing how the people of Greenland reacted to conversion efforts.[26] Though obviously not so conscious of methodology as some other colleagues in the field, his report corroborated what they wrote about the natives' strong sexual orientation, their association of regeneration with woman, and the seriousness with which they took their shaman, who was called an *angekok*. The report was translated from the Danish into German and published in Copenhagen in 1790 as *Nachrichten von Grönland, Aus einem Tagebuch, geführt von 1721 bis 1788*.

The shamanic séances the very young Egede confessed to attending without his father's permission always occurred at night in a carefully circumscribed, dimly illuminated space. He recorded all sorts of inexplicable happenings. Once the angekok, who was securely tied up, freed himself and then for hours played his tambourine with his drumstick while the onlookers chanted. At a later séance, strange voices seemed to be coming from inside the angekok. He thought wierd the time when an angekok convinced a girl she had no shadow so that he could be the one to blow her up a new one. But the time Egede considered the wierdest of all was when the natives persisted in asking him every once in a while whether or not he was frightened to death. They had asked him so often, he began to feel that he ought to be. Egede's father, who must have subscribed to the idea that boys will be boys, tracked down his absent son, broke in at just the proper moment, and encouraged him to pray to the true God to keep himself from being intimidated by the purveyors of such minor demons.

During the 1730s, Egede went so far as to agree with the natives that he should become an apprentice to a certain angekok. After a few lessons, however, the preparations struck him as too absurd, so he withdrew. He resisted the natives' attempt to convert him to their way and remained true to the faith of his father, intensifying his own personal dedication to debunking indigenous beliefs. In 1736, Egede wrote how someone in a religious discussion group he was conducting pointed out another man as "an angekok who can fly to the heavens and the moon" (95). With much zeal and no tact, Egede challenged the startled angekok to perform: "I asked him to make such an aerial journey before our eyes, then we would grant that he was a great angekok" (95). No such acknowledgment was forthcoming, for the angekok claimed that the sun was too strong for flying during that particular time of the year. He was most likely one of the ones who hedged because he sensed it was high time to head underground.

Such reports from Greenland document how the involvement of missionaries and explorers confused the natives and profoundly influenced their perceptions. One angekok complained bitterly to Egede about no longer being able to make a fully successful trip to the heavens. Only half of him took off, while the other half remained lying on the ground. His soul got there, but his body remained earthbound. He blamed the Christian sermons for ruining him and rendering his powers impotent.

Other angekoks slyly absorbed whatever was necessary from the new teachings in order to survive, and it was that strange mixture of beliefs that they mouthed when questioned. There was, for example, an angekok who agreed that heaven was indeed the most magnificent, splendiferous place. He was very happy to tell the missionary trying to convert him that he knew it was so because he had checked it out on a recent trip. After ascending straight up for a very long while, he had located the Christian heaven and found it populated with innumerable reindeer as well as people (214). Another one spoke of a virgin in a distant country who had given birth to an angekok so fantastically powerful that he could resurrect the dead as well as heal all kinds of illnesses. That man blamed persons like Egede's father for killing the great angekok, who, however, was so well endowed that he revived and flew off to heaven on his own power (36). Yet another had learned from a missionary about hot, internal parts of the earth where souls experienced a kind of immortality, so he planned to leave the frigid climate he was in and journey in that direction (121–22).

Explorers often unwittingly helped finish the process that religious missionaries like Egede had begun. The ultrarational scientific method they applied to shamanism might have demystified it on European terms, but on native terms, it brought about a different reaction. It forced believers to go into hiding, or at least to get out of public sight. Above all, it taught the natives to avoid so generously sharing their true beliefs and ceremonies with the Europeans.

Johann Georg Gmelin (1709–1755), a professor of chemistry and botany at the University of Tübingen, spent ten years exploring in Siberia as part of the second Bering endeavor.[27] The four volumes of observations he published as *Reise durch Sibirien, von dem Jahr 1733 bis 1743* appeared in Göttingen in 1751–1752, where they were warmly received by the scientific community. The title page even carried a poetic tribute by the world renowned physician and professor of botany on the faculty there, Albrecht von Haller (1708–1777): "Where Russia's wide realm coincides with the ends of the earth, And, where the East's border dissolves into the extreme West; Where no inquisitiveness penetrated; where strange species of animals Served still unnamed peoples; Where unknown ore spared itself for future artists, And never examined plants became green, There lay a new world, hidden by nature, Until Gmelin discovered it."[28]

Gmelin acknowledged encountering widespread shamanic practices throughout Siberia and explained that the various tribes called the practitioners different names. Germanicized words, such as *Kam*,

Schaman, Schamanka, and *Ajun*, he supplemented with German ones, such as *Zauberin* (sorceress), *Gaukler* (illusionist), *Hexe* (witch), *Taschen-spieler* (conjurer), *Betrüger* (deceiver), and *Schelm* (rascal). In addition to collecting words and rendering them comprehensible to Western Europeans, Gmelin applied other current scientific methods. He interviewed shamans he accosted, noting with dismay that they were for the most part totally illiterate. He often included exacting measurements in his descriptions of their ritual clothes (2:11). He observed other equipment as well and obtained whatever he could. His explanation for the behavior of those shamans who removed symbolic tidbits from the item before handing it over was simply that they wanted to be able to continue to cheat their fellows (1:288).

That is also how Gmelin interpreted the many shamanic séances, usually command performances, he witnessed. To the standard report format of where, when, who, and why, he added specific details revealing the ventriloquism, the sleight of hand, and the fancy as well as not-so-fancy tricks. He recognized the heavy theatricality of such séances, what with mask, costume, drum, dance, and song. The language he used to describe what he thought he saw came from theater, not from religion or science. There was the cantor and the chorus in addition to the prologue, the warm-up; the comedy, the entire séance; the farce, the shaman's antics; and the stage, the space defined by the audience seated in a circle (2:352–53). Gmelin even went so far as to imply that the shamans were mediocre performers who got so carried away with their roles that their movements seemed to consist of "distortions of the body like our mad people are in the habit of making" (1:275). Another shaman ran "back and forth as if raving; soon he sat down again, made horrible faces and physical contortions, rolled his eyes, now and then closing them, as if he were out of his mind. After he had performed this comedy about one half hour, another fellow took the drum from him, and the sorcery was over" (1:284). The degree of madness induced by the performance and its infectiousness seemed greatest in this instance: "Thereupon all three began raging as if they were mad, and screamed and jumped as if they wanted to quarrel with each other. The woman continued drumming, and, if one would have wanted to believe them, there was at that time a whole army of devils amid us" (2:85).

Gmelin was a resourceful enough scientist to get a trusting shaman to reveal how he accomplished his feats. The shaman told all, whereupon the scientist, instead of thanking him, demanded that the shaman confess his dishonest objectives publicly and openly. His refusal was interpreted as an attempt to protect the thriving business he had (2:87; see also 3:444). As word spread among the natives about the inquiries Gmelin made, many of the local shamans totally avoided appearing in his presence. Their followers always supported such temporary absences. For example, there was the remark, "We would have gladly seen something of their magic, but the people were clever enough to say that there was no kam around" (1:276).

The high level of frustration that the very rationalistic Gmelin felt was reflected in the frequency of his admissions that he tried so hard to bring enlightenment to the Siberian aborigines who believed in shamanism. Again and again he wrote that he had pointed out to them that they were being deluded by perpetrators of hoaxes. What appalled him personally was their fathomless gullibility and hopeless ignorance. Gmelin, for all his intelligence, learning, and experience, never came to suspect that something else, something far greater, might have been operative. That was for others to do.

Among them was Joseph François Lafitau (1681–1746), a Jesuit who spent many years as a missionary in Canada. He harbored misgivings about the scientific method promulgated by explorers like Gmelin, because it seemed to exclude too much or to deny the undeniable.[29] Lafitau preferred to look at things according to their own assumptions, which meant he first had to discover what those assumptions were. He himself was not only a keen observer but also a pragmatist who thought the unknown could only be apprehended through the known.[30] He referred constantly to classical antiquity, for his academic training had given him a thorough grounding, one he even applied for some time as a teacher of classics in France. While disavowing the intentions of die-hard rationalists like Fontenelle, Lafitau improved their comparative method by adding a little humility and a lot of fieldwork. His scientific instincts were so sharp that he made a number of contributions. The discovery of ginseng on the North American continent is, for example, credited to him. His work as a linguist, studying and attempting to systematize Indian languages, went hand in hand with his anthropological studies of native cultures.

Lafitau's study, *Moeurs des sauvages ameriquains, comparées aux moeurs des premièrs temps*, appeared in two volumes in 1724, the year before *Principi di scienza nuova* by Giambattista Vico (1668–1744), a professor of Latin eloquence who was well-read in the literature of travel, especially the Jesuit relations.[31] As far as the basis of religion in America was concerned, Lafitau wrote, it was comparable to that of the barbarians who first inhabited Greece and subsequently moved into Asia. It was "the same as that of the followers of Bacchus in his military expeditions and as that which served afterwards as the basis of all pagan mythology and of the Greek myths."[32] Lafitau, like Vico, drew comparisons between living races and mythical primordial peoples.[33] He pointed out specifically what the Americans had in common with the ancient Scythians, about whom Herodotus had written so much. They, too, indulged in sweat baths for purification purposes, and they, too, were accustomed to drinking such an inordinate amount of intoxicating beverages that not even contemporary Germans, Flemings, and Swiss were able to compete with them. Their priest, who served them also as a healer, was, in Lafitau's opinion, like the Mercury, the Anubis, or the Hermes of the ancients, or Orpheus, Eumolpus, Thamyris, and the other diviners. Emphasizing that different nations in various historical periods used different words, he referred to *Prêtres, Prêtresses, Mages, Devins, Hierophantes, Druides, Médicins, Saiotkatta, Agotsinnachen, Arendiouannens, Agotkon, Piayés, Boyés, Pagés, Charlatans*, and, most often, *Jongleurs* (1:237 [371–72]).

Lafitau, who wanted to determine the basic assumptions of his native charges for purposes of determining the proper program to ensure their firm conversion to Catholicism, paid great attention to their rituals and the ways they otherwise came to terms with the mysteries of life and death. He wrote that sexuality was as important as fertility in Amerindian beliefs. Those beliefs even attributed the origin of human beings on earth to a divine female who was banished from heaven as punishment for allowing herself to be seduced sexually. Lafitau scanned the roles of indigenous women, comparing what he uncovered with what he knew about ancient women, including the Greek maenads and the Roman vestal virgins. The power of virginity was strong enough to warrant such great veneration in most tribes that there were special words designating it and scrupulous ways of guarding it (1:218 [339]). The physical, totally sexual orgies of the Indians Lafitau compared to what he knew about antiquity, only to conclude that the main intent was not wanton promiscuity, but something having to do with the mysteries. As additional support for his argument, he mentioned Isis and then Ceres, the sheaf of grain, and the winnowing basket. He also noted that the natives attributed certain sexual traits to plants, which lost their efficacy for healing if not applied by chaste hands. Married Indians, who understood the secrets about using plants for purposes of curing, admitted to Lafitau that they no longer had any power and dared not try to do any healing.

That healing had to be left to the *Jongleur*, that is, the shaman. Lafitau reported as much as he could find out about the shamanic calling, the initiation, the duties, and the kinds of treatment the shamans used. In discussing the long, arduous initiatory process, he drew comparisons to the stages of preparation required before the descent into Trophonius's cave. The many tests and expiations were designed to liberate the soul from those carnal matters caused by the senses, thereby enabling it to communicate with the gods. Lafitau, unlike Fontenelle, was concerned less with the man-made fraudulence of the illusions than with their effectiveness as pedagogical means for conveying universal truths. He emphasized that it was those very illusions that allowed the initiate to approach death or Proserpine's abode, experience the most hidden secrets of nature, worship the divine powers close by, and then, seemingly miraculously, return to everyday reality (1:220–21 [342–43]).

Among the Indians, the young boy was isolated early on from his family and apprenticed to an old shaman. That proselyte was forced to deny his body by consuming concoctions of tobacco juice and by fasting. He was also made to suffer multiple skin lacerations so as to learn how to desensitize himself. The final ceremony, which paired him with his familiar spirit, occurred at night and was structured to instill fear and dread (plate 7). It always succeeded, for the proselytes thereafter revived physically once given nourishment, but "they have difficulty in curing their wounded imagination of the impressions made on it by the daemon to whom they are so servilely attached only, so they say, because they experience often terrible effects of his tyranny" (1:223 [349]).

Such experiences bestowed not only insight into the mysteries but also the ability to communicate with the spirit world. These extraordinary people enjoyed high status among their fellows, who regularly sought them out for purposes of consultation and medicine. Once more, Lafitau stressed the conformity with remote antiquity:

> In all the times of paganism, the diviners have been regarded as sages who had the knowledge of things divine and human, knew the efficacy of plants, stones, metals, all the occult virtues and all the secrets of nature. Not only did they sound the depths of hearts but they foresaw the future. They read in the stars, in the books of the destinies and carried on with the gods an intimate intercourse of which the rest of mankind was unworthy. Their seeming austerity of life and conventionality and the fact that they were above criticism and censure rendered them respectable to all who came to consult them as oracles and mouthpieces of the divinity. (1:237–38 [372–73])

Applying the paradigm of permissibility and its rhetoric, Lafitau pointed to the primordial origins of shamanism and argued against Fontenelle that it would be illogical and unscientific to discredit such a widespread and deep-rooted phenomenon merely because there were a few swindlers who premeditatedly cheated in order to enrich themselves. That kind of person, he continued, could be found in all human endeavors. Lafitau refused to agree that mankind could have

Plate 7. Initiation of a Caribe Shaman.

been so stupid as to allow itself to be duped for so many centuries. There simply had to be something genuine or worthwhile about shamanism.

Lafitau's search for that truth included probes of human psychology that considered its possible relationship to mythology. The Amerindian shamans, he wrote, like the ancient pythonesses, sibyls, and diviners, had fantastic control over their own bodies. They could will themselves into a trance, and, despite all the enthusiastic abandon, they could chant and dance with great precision. At the very height of their violent frenzy, they could speak comprehensibly enough to make pronouncements, albeit the customary vague ones. Somehow they were capable of curing themselves of the very madness they had induced in themselves. Whatever they did, they served as agents of a kind for their compatriots. Lafitau summarized:

> The shamans have some innate quality which partakes still more of the divine. We see them go visibly into that state of ecstasy which binds all the senses and keeps them suspended. The foreign spirit appears to take possession of them in a palpable and corporeal manner and so to master their organs as to act in them immediately. It casts them into frenzies of enthusiasm and all the convulsive movements of the sibyl. It speaks from the depths of their chests thus causing the fortune tellers to be considered ventriloquists. It raises them sometimes up into the air or makes them greater than their real stature.
>
> In this state of enthusiasm their spirit seems absorbed in that which possesses them. They are no longer themselves, like those diviners of whom Iamblichus speaks, in whom the outside spirit operated in such a way that not only did they not know themselves but they had no feeling and did not feel any hurt during that time so that one could touch them with fire without burning them, pierce them with blazing spits, then rain axe blows on their shoulders and cut their arms with razors. (1:243–44 [383–84])

Lafitau put his finger on something very important when he attributed such shamanic power to the fertility of the human imagination. The shaman was so imaginative that he could intuit the inner workings of his patient's imagination while simultaneously knowing how to manipulate it so as to provide remedies (2:209–10 [375–76]).

The Amerindian shamans also seemed to have a profound knowledge of "natural medicine," which interested Lafitau as well (plate 8). He discovered that they controlled their diet to great effect, and he ascribed their "better flesh than ours" to their eschewal of salt (2:205 [368]). He was particularly interested in the uses they made of certain herbs, in addition to ginseng, chica, tobacco, cohoba, and hemp (plate 9). The way they cured wounds was, in his opinion, so superb as to be

Plate 8. Healing Session and Funeral Rites.

Plate 9. Florida Council Meeting and Making Chica.

called "the masterpiece of their medical science" (2:204 [365]). The most common remedy they used was sweating, and, as to be expected, he recalled for his readers what Herodotus had written about the methods used by the ancient Scythians.

Lafitau acknowledged Amerindian medicine as relatively uncomplicated, directly connected to tribal life, and within the reach of all. His favorable comparison of it with the practices of his contemporaries in Europe understandably earned him their wrath:

> Some plants whose virtue they [Indians] knew, rather through long usage than through subtle reasonings, were the natural panaceas with which men were cured. We could still be cured by them if we had not lost their secret by wishing to over-refine them and if we had not complicated medicine with an indefinite number of barbarous terms which make it obscure and make a sort of impenetrable enigma of a science which should be within the reach of everyone because it concerns everyone. It is extremely important to everyone that what serves to maintain the harmony of life and health should not be in the hands of just a few people whom their profession authorizes to acquire reputation through sad experiments and by killing people with impunity. This is said, however, without meaning to insult the doctors of our day who are really skillful, have made their art much better and made great improvements over their predecessors. (2:202 [362])

While opposing the rise of professionalism and scientific specialization, Lafitau staunchly upheld diagnosis as God's gift of insight or divination.

CHAPTER THREE

Interaction, Transformation, and Extinction

THE SECOND HALF of the eighteenth century is known as the era of academic expeditions. Methodology was a particular concern of the European scientific societies and academies that sponsored them. Many of the explorers continued to seek conformities or to demystify shamanism by application of rational criteria. But more and more tried to observe, record, collect, and contemplate, if not explain, what they came across or solicited in the field. Measurements, and statistics in general, became increasingly prevalent, as did comments about psychological and linguistic factors. The words the individual tribes used for naming or describing the practitioners of shamanism were assiduously recorded and discussed.

Some explorers became interested in the imagination, emotions, and mental attributes of believers as well as of shamans. In addition to finding and studying native drugs and intoxicants, they tried to determine the purposes of aboriginal rituals and ceremonies. They inquired about the shaman's selection, or calling, and also about his training. When they questioned his reputation among his fellows, they confronted the kinds of problems that had affected mankind throughout the ages. One such problem had to do with the confusion caused by conversion efforts of various orthodox religions and the overlapping beliefs that resulted. Another involved tribal unity. The shaman seemed to be the main supporter, having knowledge of the sacred places and ancient myths as well as the ability to intercede with the spirits. Yet another was the problem of extinction. It was to rise in scientific importance in the late eighteenth century as the native peoples on the American continents as well as in Siberia were relocated or "removed" to make way for colonists and settlers.

Young, humanistically educated scientists thought—perhaps somewhat romantically—of what was lost when the Trojans, the Celts, and the Nibelungs disappeared from the face of the earth, so they rushed to the Americas and to the expanses of the Russian empire to record for posterity the current status of the vanishing peoples. Those scientists might not yet have mastered such concepts as assimilation or genocide, but they definitely understood what extinction meant. And they worried about it.

Their energetic response to seeking and preserving the truth was of course modified by unavoidable economic factors, unless they themselves happened to be wealthy aristocrats who could easily afford to pay the bills for their own expeditions—which sometimes was, indeed, the case. Many such financially as well as intellectually liberated explorers went on to question the ordinary criteria of what was supposed to be considered real. Their very questions once in a while happened to transcend the limits of the Newtonian mechanical or quantitative approach to nature. Some even went so far as to probe the occult as a possible source of knowledge.

The accounts of such intellectual pioneers in the second half of the eighteenth century contributed mightily to the development of greater freedom to ignore, if not dismiss, the paradigm of permissibility and the traditionally accepted categories. As a result, more applicable methods emerged, producing new disciplines as well as major changes in old ones.

The study of man as a social being was beginning to develop along various lines that then became independent sciences with their own specific kinds of methodology. The study of man as a physical organism with a mind and soul also changed. Medicine began to include consideration of the workings of the human imagination and the needs of the soul, in addition to examining skulls and other anatomical features.

Johann Peter Falk (1732–1774) was one "academic" explorer who traveled through the Russian provinces in the late 1760s.[1] His findings appeared in a two-volume topographic survey published by the Imperial Academy of Sciences in St. Petersburg. If he treated the customs of the various nations, he did so because he believed that climate and environment influenced social behavior. The Votyaks, when they subscribed to shamanism, considered forested mountains sacred, and, Falk stressed, even after they became Christians they remained so superstitious that they refused to use their baptismal names. They also continued to purchase their wives.[2]

One of the main goals of Falk's survey was to provide a kind of demography. He checked census figures and missionaries' conversion statistics, which disclosed matters pertaining to nation or tribe, religion, and amount of tribute paid to the empress. For example, he wrote about the Cheremiss that 8,618 people renounced their "shamanistic idol worship" for Christianity in 1747. By 1785, baptized Christians numbered 54,039, with only 1,673 shamanic heathens remaining (2:453–54).

Falk cited his sources conscientiously, and he discussed at length those travel accounts that his findings supported. Despite the objective slant he tried to project, his eurocentric attitudes were evident throughout. They are very noticeable in his treatment of Teleut shamanism. Among the aspects it manifested that he found special were the magical powers of the priest, known as the kam, and the selection of women as well as men to that office by inheritance. With regard to shamanic ecstasy, Falk stressed the importance of drumming: "The kam, who goes around dressed very foolishly, understands how to drum so that the gods appear to him and answer his questions, grant or deny his requests—but also so that the devils cannot endure his drumming and take leave" (2:560).

Ivan Ivanovich Lepechin (1740–1802), a Russian physician who became an adjunct of the Imperial Academy of Sciences after having studied in St. Petersburg and Strasbourg, was much more open to the unknown "otherness" of the eastern provinces when he explored them in 1768 and 1769. His intention was to gather information about history and economics as well as about flora and fauna. He always did so with an eye to the possible implications for medicine.

Among the many empirical methods Lepechin used was a kind of on-site interview. He constantly questioned natives, especially peasants and simple people, about their ways of preserving health and curing sickness. He wanted to identify the herbs and roots they used, and to learn about the methods of preparation as well as the proportions and the applications. The plants the natives considered magical or sacred received equal attention. Instead of mocking or shunning the natives, he attempted to figure out why certain plants were thought to immobilize wizards, sorcerers, and devils, or to make unclean spirits weep.[3]

Lepechin discussed the remarkably high esteem in which the shamans were held. Regardless of the orthodox religion to which the natives confessed publicly, in private they firmly maintained their belief in the shamans' great power to heal. Some natives sought out a shaman to treat the least discomfort or trouble, sometimes traveling more than 500 versts (approximately 530 kilometers) to reach the particular one they wanted to consult (2:45).

Lepechin described in detail the sacrifices and the curing sessions he had occasion to witness. One especially difficult obstetrical case among the Bashkirs was attended by a young shaman whose grandfather had reputedly enjoyed great shamanic power. All present, both men and women, feasted sumptuously before beginning their dance to scare away the evil spirits. While screaming and making much noise, they swayed and stepped frantically. After they had done that for some time, the shaman requested the spiritually strong to declare themselves and come forth to help him do battle. They did as he instructed. Around midnight, he suddenly made a ferocious face that struck Lepechin as being more comparable to that of a demon than that of a person. The shaman glared at the windows before shooting a gun, grabbing a sword, and running outside at top speed. When he returned, he reassured the expectant father that the evil spirits would no longer bother his wife. To demonstrate the truth of his victory, he pointed to the bloodstained places where the now-defunct spirits had been sitting. Lepechin attributed the patient's death the next day to too much tumult, excitement, and stimulation during a very difficult delivery (2:45–46). In addition to such gripping descriptions, Lepechin provided many statistics and collections of words. Copious illustrations, especially of plants, concluded each of the three volumes of his invaluable journal.

Illustrations of native customs became a standard feature of travel accounts because so many of the explorers worried about the limitations of verbal language to describe what they beheld or experienced. There are many illustrations, as well as a fairly objective account of various still-extant aspects of shamanism, in a three-volume publication by Petrus Simon Pallas (1741–1811), a renowned naturalist whose explorations of the entire Russian empire were warmly supported and thereafter amply rewarded by Catherine the Great.[4] It appeared as *Reise durch verschiedene Provinzen des Russischen Reichs* in 1771, 1773, and 1776 under the auspices of the Imperial Academy of Sciences in St. Petersburg.[5]

Pallas not only used prefatory remarks to convey his intentions and objectives; he also inserted supplementary qualifiers in his text. He countered potential complaints that he covered the same territory as Gmelin had more than a quarter of a century earlier by explaining that he had a decidedly different thrust. Like Gmelin, though, Pallas advertised among the natives for shamans to perform before him. His working schedule involved being en route during the good weather of summer and safely ensconced throughout the severe winter. Those months of encampment allowed him to review and refine his observations, articulating them with greater clarity.

Pallas found the psychology of the native peoples particularly engrossing. Their shamans, he wrote, exerted enormous control over them by repeatedly telling them stories that instilled fear and terror. They portrayed illusionary events as the truth of everyday reality, having learned to do so by analyzing their own dreams and by giving them suspenseful structures. The distinctions between dream and wakefulness were blurred, and whoever disbelieved or disobeyed was threatened with divine retribution. The Ostyaks, for example, had such hypersensitive imaginations that the least notion could intimidate them and fill them with shivers of dread (3:62). Other peoples dwelling in northern climates, especially those of the Arctic, were known to evidence similar nervous reactions. The Samoyedes, in particular, had a most peculiar kind of physical excitability, which Pallas believed came "in part from the excessive straining and irritability of the nervous system due to the effects of the northern climate and its required life-style, and in part from an imagination ruined by superstition" (3:76).

Pallas had also observed some, but not as many, highly irritable types among the Buryats and the Tatars of the Yenisei. He reported that such hypersensitivity manifested itself in differing degrees in different nations. Some people would react to the slightest provocation: "Each unexpected contact, for example, on the sides or on other sensitive parts, sudden shouts and whistling, or other frightful and quick manifestations bring these people beside themselves and almost into a kind of fury" (3:76). Others, much like the berserkers of Norse mythology, would fall into incontrollable rages, get hold of axes, knives, or other lethal instruments, and go after the people who had disturbed their tranquillity. Any substitute would do if the culprit could not quickly be found. Pallas further reported, "If they then cannot give vent to their rage, they beat about themselves, scream, shake violently, and are completely like madmen" (3:77). One remedy for pulling them out of such fits was to force inhalation of burning reindeer hair. That smoke induced lassitude followed by sound slumber for at least twenty-four hours, which Pallas considered a form of healing that uncovered still more clearly the roots of the problem. Conversations with a fellow explorer confirmed the prevalence of this psychological phenomenon among the Yakuts. Travel accounts describing cases among the Tunguses and Kamchatkans seemed to corroborate Pallas's suspicion that it was indeed very old and very widespread.

Such heightened sensitivity seemed to Pallas to be a prerequisite for the shamanic vocation. The exceedingly delicate nervous system of the shaman was attributed to the many seizures he suffered in childhood, and it was often described as feminine. The shamanka, however, did not escape early physical and emotional miseries because of her physiology. On the contrary, her behavior usually was reported as reclusive, strange, or hysterical. About one, Pallas heard, she had lived "as a girl for a long time in a kind of foolish melancholy" (3:223).

Pallas confirmed Gmelin's contention about the ubiquitousness of shamanism in Siberia, remarking that, despite various gradations of difference, there were great similarities among the many nations.

Pallas, who used the word shaman (*Schaman*) as a generic term for its practitioners, stressed that those nations resorted to a variety of words, among which were *Böh* and *Uduguhn* (1:359) as well as *Kamnö* (2:682), *Tadyb* (3:75), and *Kahm* (3:345). Usually he also included the personal names of the practitioners he met or saw perform.

Their costumes and appurtenances were as fascinating to Pallas as to his predecessors. He mentioned the awe such items in themselves inspired in the faithful, and he tried to tackle an explanation of their ritualistic significance. While able to deal with the materials and the styling easily enough by describing them, he had difficulty coming to terms with the iron spangles, bells, feathers, pieces of fur or animal skin, idols, and other ornaments, especially the real or symbolic antlers of the headgear (3:182). In what might be called the exasperation of a scientist loyal to the Germanic tradition, he wrote that the shamans wore "a rather French-looking outfit" when they practiced their magic (3:402). He also could not explain why those vestments were treated with such great reverence, nor why they were carried amid much pomp and circumstance to the place where the shaman would don them over his bare skin (3:222).

The shaman wore his garb, according to Pallas, in order to fulfill four major functions: holding ecstatic séances, conducting general sacrifices, manufacturing idols, and curing the sick. The séances, usually held after dark by the light of flickering fires, or perhaps of the moon, entailed so much chanting, drumming, and dancing that convulsive, trancelike movements arose in the shaman, who then seemed to transfer them to the participants. The sacrifices, which occurred at various times, only required the presence of the shaman when the spirits needed propitiating. After a reindeer, a sheep, or another animal was ceremoniously slaughtered and butchered, the bloody innards as well as the bones were cast toward the west, the hide was kept for idol making, among other things, and the flesh was appreciatively consumed by all (3:62–64). Shamans had various means at their disposal to cure the sick, ranging from séances and sacrifices to idol worship and "natural medicine."

Like other explorers of his generation, Pallas reported that the natives were becoming increasingly reluctant, if not defensive, about letting themselves be observed. Throughout his travels, he retained the arrogant stance of the Western man of science. He found abominable the belief in the transmigration of souls, and he often disavowed animistic views. Nevertheless, he showed some sympathy and even a certain amount of personal warmth for the practitioners who had allowed themselves to be Christianized, or at least baptized, only in order to be able to continue performing a task so apparently necessary for the survival of their particular society in such a harsh climate.

Pallas laughed at the jokes and tricks the Russian travelers often played on the simple yet naturally hospitable natives. But he did not at all approve in principle of desecrating what was locally held sacred. As a matter of fact, Pallas thought that was unduly cruel. Consequently, he recorded what he knew about indigenous objections and concurrent attempts to take shamanism underground. Among the Ostyaks, he learned that they not only hid the paraphernalia of their practices, but that they also posted guards to watch over them and to conceal from the Russians all approaches to them (3:60). Elsewhere Pallas was told that a talented shaman, who went by the Christian name of Stepan, was so shrewd that he would have gladly kept his powers hidden, "if my people had not by chance discovered his magic tambourine, which he had hidden in another yurt" (3:347).

As Pallas was conducting his investigation of shamanism in the Tungus, some Cossacks informed him that the most renowned local practitioner claimed to have been spiritually impotent since some professors traveling in the region took away his magic raiment (3:223). Pallas himself, however, was not above doing something similar in the name of science, of course, when a shaman failed to present himself docilely on command: "Because one did not find him at home, and I could suspect that he probably would have liked to make himself invisible in order not to conjure before me, I at least had his magic equipment fetched" (3:345). The confiscated items did, however, lead to illustrations that at least provided later centuries with a record of primordial customs as they were still being practiced—and also perceived—in the late eighteenth century (plate 10).

Some explorers had already pointed out the theatrical as well as the poetic aspects of shamanism. For the most part, their purpose was to demystify or debunk. Pallas had nothing of the sort in mind. He merely wanted to present an evaluation of what he truly thought he saw. The antics displayed during some séances he found comparable to the burlesque pantomimes known in Europe (3:64). Other rituals he considered more like farces or medicine-man shows (3:176, 182), while still others had more refined dramatic elements, which meant he thought they came closer to what was performed by Europeans enlightened by the precepts of Franco-Roman neoclassicism. Pallas, for all his eurocentrism and male chauvinism, did have a keen ability to recognize the origin of fables or literary fictions.[6] He contended that the shamans were both the originators and the conservators of the stories, the heroic tales, and the chivalric romances that provided the

Pallas Reisen Tom. III. Tab. V. pag. 345.

Plate 10. Shaman in Three Poses.

common experiential basis as well as the strength the natives needed to remain alive and tribally unified.[7]

Similar contentions were made by Johann Gottlieb Georgi (1738–1802) in *Bemerkungen einer Reise im Russischen Reich* and in *Beschreibung aller Nationen des Russischen Reichs, ihrer Lebensart, Religion, Gebräuche, Wohnungen, Kleidungen und übrigen Merkwürdigkeiten.*[8] Georgi was yet another of the "academic explorers" whose fieldwork in the remote Russian provinces was deemed exemplary during the late eighteenth century. The connection of shamanism to the origin of the arts seemed obvious to him, and he often remarked on it. Like the oracles of antiquity, he wrote, contemporary shamans and shamankas spoke in an extraordinarily flowery and unclear language so that what they said could be applicable in all cases, whatever the outcome. Actually, he added, it was necessary that they did so because their believers, who had only hieroglyphs, no alphabet, themselves only knew how to communicate by sharing images and sensations. The litany was one favored form because its rhythms and tones affected the body directly, without appeal to the higher faculty of reason. It simply turned the natives on. Georgi cited their particular kind of nervous system as the cause: "People of such makeup and such irritability must be rich in dreams, apparitions, superstitions, and fairy tales. And they are, too" (1:14). Georgi's disbelief in shamanic practices was all but canceled out by his utter amazement at the shamans' phenomenal poetic gifts, which he considered not only naturally effusive but also astonishingly sophisticated.

Like many of his contemporaries, Georgi zeroed in on the psychological makeup of the shamans and their believers. He agreed with his fellow explorers that climate, topography, and general environment greatly affected the nerves, with all their variegated fibers. Again and again, he wrote about having observed or heard about hypersensitivity and excitability among the natives. An unexpected event, a stray word, a sudden glance caused fits of fainting or paroxysms of frenzy among them.[9] In the methodological preface to the *Beschreibung*, in which he dutifully listed current scholarship as well as reporting the nature of his contacts with shamanism, he analyzed the shamanic personality in an attempt to produce a profile. His analysis was a far cry from that of those who wrote merely of tricksters and cheaters: "I have frequently witnessed the ceremonies of shamanic idol worship among the various heathens. Their priests and priestesses are part enthusiasts, part deceivers, and also part right good people who surpass their brethren in intelligence. As a rule, they can be easily won over by friendly treatment and small presents" (1:x; see also 377).

To the list of designations for the shaman, Georgi added *Muschan, Moschan, Maschan, Juma, Jömma, Toteba,* and *Totscheba* (1:33, 42, 71). He discussed their minor duties, the various rituals they performed, and the sacred places they protected. Like many who preceded him, he singled out the drum, the idols, and the bespangled, highly ornamented costume, occasionally providing foldout illustrations (plate 11). He also mentioned the mystical circumstances involved in the donning of the costume. Since verbal description struck him as so often insufficient, he included, in the large folio volume of ninety-five illustrations that accompanied his report, eight examples of shamans and shamankas in full regalia, with descriptive captions in Russian, German, and French (plates 12–19).

Georgi used the special section summarizing shamanic heathenism in the *Beschreibung* to explain the standard features of the séance, especially the convulsive movements and the transport. He was convinced that most shamans sincerely believed they had traffic with spirits. About the soul's trip itself, he gave more details than did most of his colleagues. He wrote that after some grimacing, "they fall down powerless because their soul leaves them and visits the gods of hell in their dwellings, mountains, forests, abysses, et cetera, and confers with

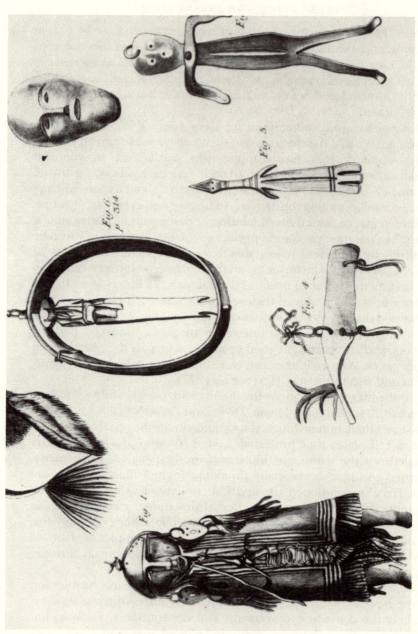

Plate 11. 1. Idol 2. Idol of the Sun 3. Human Figure 4. Reindeer 5. Swan 6. Idol of Dead Shaman 7. Wand.

Plate 12. Shaman in Kamchatka.

Plate 13. Shamanka from the Krasnoyarsk District.

Plate 14. Rear View of Krasnoyarsk Shamanka.

Plate 15. Tungus Shaman.

Plate 16. Rear View of Tungus Shaman.

Plate 17. Bratsk Shamanka.

Plate 18. Rear View of Bratsk Shamanka.

Plate 19. Mongolian Shamanka or Soothsayer.

them. The souls make this journey on bears, hogs, eagles, and the like. All of them assert afterward to have seen the spirits in visions as bears, lions, owls, eagles, swans, beetles, spiders, dragons, et cetera, as lustres or as shadows" (3:394).

The death of a shaman was another subject to which Georgi gave more attention than did most explorers. It seemed strange to European readers who based the *ars moriendi* on faith in Christ to learn that heathen shamans not only were hard to murder, but they also, for the most part, died very courageously. Georgi attributed their fearlessness to the benefits they expected to reap after lifelong efforts spent reconciling good and evil spirits. While alive, they were highly venerated, so they thought that after dying they would be counted among the sainted ancestors and constantly be offered sumptuous sacrifices (3:383).

Their fellow tribesmen also believed in an afterlife, but could never be so sanguine as their role models. Any corpse revolted them because they feared its return to life would bring additional torment. Rites enacted as part of burial ceremonies usually involved dramatically chasing death and the dead away so as to prevent any further contamination: "They jump over fire and crawl between posts, whereby the shaman makes striking movements with a rod in order to hold death back. Then they fumigate themselves and their shelter or abandon it and, on account of the feared memory of the deceased, never name them. Relatives with such names change them, which causes not slight harm for history" (3:382). The natives interpreted death as a transformation of the here and now into an underworld that was much the same. It was equally sad, so therefore no more desirable: "Under the earth reign the earth spirits, who try to inflict much harm on the dead" (3:383).

Although Georgi did not pretend to be a historian of religion, he thought the findings of his fieldwork clearly showed that shamanism was an archaic system of religious beliefs in which males usually dominated females in spite of the females' tendency to be at least equally effective at healing, divining, and prognosticating. The explanation he offered contained some vestiges of the degeneration theory but is no less worthy of attention:

The shamanic religion belongs to the religions of the ancient world. It is the oldest in the Orient and the mother of the Lamaist, Brahmanic, and other heathen sects. In India, its priests were to some extent philosophers, therefore it does not lack connection. With its adherents among our nations, it largely degenerated into contradictory idol-worship and blind superstition through the lack of texts and schools, through wars, migrations, inconstant manners, mutilated traditions, and the misrepresentations of dumb or deceiving priests. (3:375)

Inevitably governed by the attitude that sought conformities between the present and the past, Georgi even went so far as to state outright that shamanism was not only the epitome of natural religion but was also related to the teachings of Moses:

> Despite all the obscurity and confusion in shamanic heathendom, especially in its actual mythology, one cannot fail to recognize general concepts of natural religion and diverse elements from the Mosaic. The sacrificial fire, the offerings and displays of victims, the worship, the opinions about the uncleanliness of women due to natural changes, and many other things are quite certainly from the Jewish religion. (3:395; see also 1:xi)

Again and again Georgi referred to the various religions, whether Lamaism, Nestorian Christianity, or others that believed in the transmigration of souls and the eternal return, as "daughters of shamanism" (4:413).

Georgi was too astute an observer to overlook the subtle as well as not-so-subtle forms the natives adopted in order to continue their ancient practices without threat of punishment from those who seemed to know how to make "bigger medicine"—whether clergymen, physicians, or adventurers with firearms. Many of those natives admitted allowing themselves to be converted just to bring an end to the missioners' harassment. Georgi, ever the seeker of truth, examined information about the widespread practice of forced conversion to Christianity. What he found indicated that there were innumerable heathens who were Christians in name only (2:230). When he surveyed what the Lamaists and Mohammedans had accomplished, he came to the same conclusion (4:433). The natives, who realized their very survival was in jeopardy, did what needed to be done. They became secretive, less hospitable, and more crafty. For all their faults, Georgi's accounts of his travels in the Russian empire accomplished more by identifying questions than by answering them.[10] The process his work came to exemplify was one that revealed the interconnections among religion, psychology, medicine, anthropology, philosophy, and the arts.

Georg Forster's (1754–1794) background and training made him a promulgator of those interconnections. He was the son of the scientifically astute yet bad-tempered Johann Reinhold Forster (1729–1798), who inducted him at a very early age into the life of exploration and experimentation.[11] As a nine-year-old child, Georg accompanied his father, who had accepted the commission of Catherine the Great to inspect certain provinces of her empire. The time they spent there enabled Georg to learn Russian, among other things. When Johann Reinhold had a falling-out with his patron, he promptly gathered up his son and left for England, where a professorship in science awaited him. During that time the adolescent Georg had the chance to improve his understanding of scientific approaches as well as to gain mastery of the English language. Since his father once again became dissatisfied with his appointment, they left for London, where they sojourned awhile before being sought out to join Capt. James Cook's (1728–1779) second voyage around the world. Georg, about seventeen years old at the time, was offered a professorship in Kassel when he returned four years later. He cultivated collegial relationships with leading scientists, especially Georg Christoph Lichtenberg (1742–1799) in Göttingen, whose research more or less mediated between the mechanistic approach and organic ones. In 1784, Georg accepted a professorship at Vilnius.

The writings that resulted from Georg Forster's many travels were acknowledged during his own lifetime as eminently readable presentations of new and strange information. His objectivity seemed genuine, and he always set the scene in a way Europeans could understand. He quantified whenever possible, but in most cases he was forced to resort to the energetic use of the descriptive language that he so easily commanded. It was even said that he seemed to have a knack for making his readers long to travel to the places he described.

Comparisons of his writings with those of his older colleagues reveal certain similarities. Georg Forster not only commented on his own methodological concerns but also demonstrated his astounding knowledge about the entire corpus of travel literature. He repeatedly cited the works of religious as well as mercantile travelers, such as Pian del Carpine and Marco Polo. Statistics, whether census, conversion, or tribute figures, were mentioned again and again to show how the Christianization process had led to the transformation and decline of certain nations. For example, he reported that the aboriginal population of Greenland had declined from thirty thousand to ten thousand within about fifty years. He offered similar numbers for the Eskimos on the coast of Labrador.[12] He openly attributed the general decrease of such populations to the Christian missionaries, who had no sense of what was important for the survival of the natives. Totally disregarding the paradigm of permissibility, he wrote that the Amerindians had been self-sufficient people who needed neither lords nor priests in the European sense. They simply selected their best warrior to lead them when threatened by enemies on the warpath. The Amerindians, he continued, had no concern for formal religions or architectural structures. They prayed naturally at waterfalls, or wherever they noticed the invisible power of the universe at work. They had an instinctive sense of the holy. Nevertheless, they did consider it important to carry effigies of their tutelary spirits along with them.[13]

Georg Forster was equally critical of the European armchair intellectuals, who, never venturing out into the wide world, insisted on issuing pronouncements about the living conditions and customs of so-called savages. He bemoaned in print their sophisticated European witticisms, their generalizations about racial distinctions, their theories of religious degeneration, and their assertions about the dispersion of peoples after the Great Flood.[14] What bothered him most was their clouding of the issues. He claimed they did so because they had only cribbed what they wrote and, without having seen for themselves, applied the principles of Newtonian scientific methodology. Georg Forster—significantly, given the long tradition of reworking the reports of actual travelers—warned his readers to discriminate between the mere compilers and the real explorers.

When it came to substantive matters, the psychological makeup of native populations was something Georg Forster, like his colleagues, could absolutely not overlook. He wrote how amazing it was that those people managed to populate the globe and stay alive, never mind produce some complex social systems. He offered proof that certain Asiatic tribes had moved eastward to Alaska and then down the western coast of the Americas, and he argued that primitives were not at all so primitive as his contemporaries in Europe thought. There never was such a thing as a "noble savage" to scientific fieldworkers like him. Georg Forster blamed that concept on the armchair observers he so despised.[15] To jolt his fellow Europeans out of their complacency and superiority, he mentioned the Normans, who had moved in the other direction to Iceland and Greenland in the ninth century, and on to America in the eleventh.

Georg Forster zeroed in on the highly developed tracking and sensing abilities of native peoples, something that had not gone unnoticed by others in the field. That such abilities truly existed could easily be substantiated whenever necessary. He himself had marveled at it many times. The reason or explanation, however, was another matter. He singled out the natives' active, fertile imaginations, which he thought were molded by the climate and topography in which they lived. The natives were, he wrote, definitely products of their environment, much as contemporary Europeans were of theirs.

Along with many other explorers in the eighteenth century, Georg Forster's experiences among other peoples and cultures made him think that the arts as known in eighteenth-century Europe had their origins in rather simple folk beliefs and rituals. He mentioned the shamanic séance and the concomitant ecstasy that was interpreted as a spiritual journey to strange and wondrous otherworldly places. In his essay on pygmies, he went so far as to attribute the origin of all literary fictions to the travelers who ventured beyond the confines of their own cultures into the world. The main modern example he gave of the transmission of such fictions was Jonathan Swift's (1667–1745) satire of 1726, *Travels into Several Remote Nations of the World* by Lemuel Gulliver, who happened to be first a surgeon, then a captain of several ships.[16] It even contained an account of Glubbdubdrib, an island of sorcerers and magicians, where contact with the spirit world was a common and open occurence (3:vii and viii).

One of Georg Forster's more telling essays was entitled "Schwärmerey, eine Mutter der schönen Künste." About two pages long, it summarized what he could speculate on the basis of his real-life observations. He went on to state that folk belief was the very matrix of the more advanced arts and that enthusiasm—whether religious ecstasy, sexual bliss, or turning on with drugs or through vestibular stimulation—was what gave the creative imagination the wings it needed to soar.[17]

The shamanic origins of artistic creativity and their implications for human psychology were also of interest to Mathieu de Lesseps (1774–1832), a member of the French royal consular service and one of the few survivors of the famous lost expedition of Jean-François de Galaup La Pérouse (1741–ca. 1788). Having received instructions from Louis XVI as well as questionnaires from both the Academy of Sciences and the Academy of Medicine, La Pérouse entrusted much of what he had discovered between his departure from France in 1785 and his arrival in Kamchatka in 1787 to Lesseps, who then returned to Paris overland, thereby escaping the watery end met by his fellow explorers. The two-volume record of that yearlong journey, *Journal historique du voyage*, was published in 1790 at the royal printing office.

Like many Frenchmen who followed in the tradition of Fontenelle, Lesseps stressed reason and the methods he thought it suggested. Clarifying sources was important, so he usually explained whether he had been an eyewitness or whether he had relied on informants. Debunking cheats and illuminating their pretended revelations was even more important. Whenever he had the chance, he mentioned what he considered to be their impertinence and absurdities. Occasionally he assumed a historical stance. Once he queried somewhat historically, yet also philosophically:

As for the change that took place in the case of the shamans of Kamchatka, is it not exactly the story of all our charlatans? Approximately the same impostures, the same prevalence, and the same downfall. What thoughts come to mind on this subject! For example, that peoples as simple as they are ignorant, such as the Kamchatkans, have sometimes been dupes of their sorcerers' deceptions is not at all surprising, and they are excusable. But with so much unskillfulness and credulity to have become aware of and ashamed of their error—this, it seems to me, merits amazement and congratulations. For in the final analysis, do we not see every day in the most enlightened nations of Europe the appearance of various types of shamans who are just as perfidious, and just as dangerous? Only among the latter, each has apostles, disciples, and a significant number of martyrs. (1:130, note r)

He thought pointing out general conformities was justifiable, although he obviously did not think he was revealing his own French assumptions when he compared the inspirations and convulsions of the Siberian shamans to those of "that sect of Quakers" in England (1:183).

The shamanic séance, Lesseps wrote, represented a vulgar, terribly crude form of spectacle that duped spectators by stimulating them to sing along or otherwise participate. Such spectacle was art only in the sense of artifice, for reason had no place in it, and the distance between illusion and reality was entirely lost. The spectators were so taken in by the strange costumes, "decorated with bells and thin plates of iron" (2:279), and by the extravagant mummeries as to believe they were actually experiencing what their shaman merely described (1:128–29). The shaman managed to do so, Lesseps explained, by getting them involved and keeping them so busy that they had no inclination whatsoever to attempt to verify his preposterous cheats (1:181–83). With what he had absorbed from the Franco-Roman neoclassical code as his standard, Lesseps disavowed the absurd fictions, fables, fairy tales, and folk stories that grew out of shamanic beliefs. He thought they were all simply too bizarre and too lacking in reason (2:280–81).

Assuming the superior position of the French politician and man of the world, Lesseps wrote that the psychology of the aborigines, whose lives somehow depended on such childish games, had to be mentioned, if not explained. They were not only intellectually underdeveloped but also somehow racially constructed to be docile. They even allowed themselves to be converted for the sake of convenience rather than stand up to missionaries who were bent on destroying their precious idols and other ritualistic items. Like many eighteenth-century explorers, Lesseps helped document the native strategies that moved shamanic practices underground. He expressed worry about the innumerable secret cults that were confusing matters of religion as a result of such strategies (1:179, 181).

Despite the various objections Lesseps voiced about taking shamanism seriously as a subject worthy of scientific examination, he nevertheless contributed mightily to the late eighteenth century's understanding of the phenomenon. He discussed what orthodox believers labeled the "fear theory" of religious origins (2:302). He wrote of shamanic duties and described séances (2:278–79). He reviewed the various methods of curing, ranging from the magical to the surgical (2:94). Most important, he referred to the practitioner as a sorcerer, a gypsy, an artist, a magician, a prophet, and, most often, a *Chaman* (1:128–29), the late eighteenth-century French adaptation of the generic term German explorers had long been using.

Although there were exceptions, the attitudes toward discovery and exploration held by peoples of Germanic origin were very different from those of the French. Since the time of the Renaissance and the Reformation, the Germans had been developing a strong propensity toward individualism. The French often exhibited allegiance to preordained notions that belonged to a given code of accepted knowledge or behavior, while the Germans, including the Anglo-Saxons, with whom they shared common roots as well as current rulers in the Hanoverians, tended to be freer, examining particulars so as to determine principles from them. That tendency to work inductively was clearly demonstrated by Martin Sauer, who served as secretary to the expedition of Joseph Billings (ca. 1758–1806), whom Catherine the Great commissioned from 1785 to 1794 to explore the northeastern reaches of Russia stretching to the northwestern American coast. Sauer's work, *An Account of a Geographical and Astronomical Expedition to the Northern Parts of Russia*, appeared in London in 1802.[18]

Its objectivity was actually enhanced by Sauer's honest admission not only that he had a distinct personality, but also that he came from a particular cultural background. His European readers could not have helped being charmed by his reporting how the natives successfully taught him to ride their reindeer. His gratitude manifested itself in the comment, "above all, I was enchanted with the manly activity of my guides, their independence, and contentment" (46). Sauer acknowledged, yet eschewed relying on, the designation "noble savage" because of its origin among the armchair commentators, preferring to call the aborigines he encountered "great Nature's happy commoners" (46). Nor did he find them to be dim-witted brutes, as some explorers had written. They were, for the most part, healthy, hardy, normal people: "They are extremely hospitable and attentive to travellers, especially to such as behave with a degree of good nature, and very inquisitive and intelligent; for they ask questions freely, and answer any without embarrassment or hesitation. They are anxious to secure friendship and a good name, and seem to study the dispositions of such as may be of service to them, to whom they are liberal in presents, and even in flattery" (124). Sauer's personality also shone through the comments he made about the landscapes that were nothing less than awesome for someone reared in a relatively tame European countryside: "The romantic desolation of the scenes that frequently surrounded me, elevated my soul to a perfect conviction that man is the lord of creation" (47).

In reporting the status quo of native cultures, Sauer was forced to mention that Christianity had had a disastrous influence. Along with the zealous Russian missionary priests, themselves often illiterate and savagely superstitious, had come diseases, wars, and the thorough humiliation of the once almost omnipotent shamans. Their masks and musical instruments were taken from them, and their precious idols were burned. Furthermore, they were publicly mocked and scorned. In one instance, Sauer wrote, "we began to make our observations; but found that all their old customs were abolished, and that the race was almost extinct" (61). Sauer's personality being what it was, he particularly sought information about native perceptions of their own vanishing. While some had already forgotten even what their grandfathers and fathers had called their tribes, others had mythologized captivity and escape as well as migration. Among the Yakuts, he wrote, there was the story of Chief Omogai Bey who pulled up stakes and led his people into new lands to escape from the yoke of more powerful intruders. After some time, he was joined by a man named Aley who managed not only to avoid the conquerors but also to become a laborer of such overwhelming strength and skill that he quickly advanced to overseer and then manager. The chief became increasingly jealous, especially when "he observed, that all his tribe esteemed Aley to adoration; for they supposed him to possess supernatural powers, and attributed his continual good fortune and success to the immediate influence of his spirits. This made him uneasy; and with a view of securing his possessions and his name, he offered Aley his daughter in marriage. Aley now avowed himself a Shaman, and assumed the powers of divination" (110). The story ended when Aley explained he wished to wed the chief's adopted daughter instead. His wish was granted, and the couple brought forth twelve healthy sons who helped repopulate the tribe.

The importance of the shaman as a preserver of tribal unity came up time and time again among the native peoples Sauer encountered. He empathetically transcribed a report about the fate of indigenous beliefs made by one forcibly Christianized informant:

"Our Sorcerers (said he) were observers of omens, and warned us of approaching dangers, to avert which sacrifices were made to the demons: we were then wealthy, contented and free." He continued his discourse thus as nearly as I could translate: "I think our former religion was a sort of dream, of which we now see the reality. The Empress is God on earth, and her officers are our tormentors: we sacrifice all that we have to appease their wrath or wants, but in vain. They have spread disorders among us, which have destroyed our fathers and mothers; and robbed us of our wealth and our happiness. They have left us no hopes of redress; for all the wealth we could collect for years would not be sufficient to secure one advocate in our interest, who dares represent our distress to our sovereign." (308)

Sauer was so taken by what shamanism had meant that he devoted a section to the specifics of its practices (119–21). That section reiterated much of the information provided by earlier explorers about the tambourine, the costume, the unintelligible chanting, the paroxysms, and the trance. Like only a small number of his predecessors, Sauer went on to describe, if not fully explain, the sexual customs associated with shamanism. He wrote that the Alaskans were wont to dress boys like women and keep them as "objects of unnatural affection" (160). Among other tribes of northwestern America, he had learned that mothers were so fond of their male children as to bring them up in an effeminate manner, thereby protecting them from the dire effects of war and the chase. Those mothers, wrote Sauer, were even "happy to see them taken by the chiefs, to gratify their unnatural desires. Such youths are dressed like women, and taught all their domestic duties" (176).

Somewhat similar configurations of practices came to the attention of explorers in other areas of the Americas as well. Many were noted by William Bartram (1739–1823) in *Travels through North and South Carolina, Georgia, East and West Florida, the Cherokee Country, the Extensive Territories of the Muscogulges or Creek Confederacy, and the Country of the Chactaws*, which was published in Philadelphia in 1791 and reprinted in London the following year.[19] The celebrations of the Cherokees, he wrote, whether for ritualistic purposes or for mere diversion, generally involved sexuality and fecundity. Like many of his colleagues, Bartram mentioned their underlying theatricality: "Indeed all their dances and musical entertainments seem to be theatrical exhibitions or plays, varied with comic and sometimes lascivious interludes: the women however conduct themselves with a very becoming grace and decency, insomuch that in amorous interludes, when their responses and gestures seem consenting to natural liberties, they veil themselves, just discovering a glance of their sparkling eyes and blushing faces, expressive of sensibility" (369). The Creeks, on the other hand, were much less modest: "To accompany their dances they have songs, of different classes, as martial, bacchanalian and amorous; which last, I must confess, are extravagantly libidinous" (504).

Bartram emphasized how important music was to the Amerindians he had had a chance to observe. What he thought was their general recreational music he described as being at best "a hideous melancholy discord" (503). Their devotional or religious music, however, was of a much higher quality, in his opinion. Although he would not indulge in the black drink the natives offered him, he was truly moved by what he heard at some nocturnal séances, for "the notes are very solemn, and at once strike the imagination with a religious awe or homage to the Supreme" (451). After one séance, he explained that the music had appealed emotionally to the participants so strongly that it transmitted the kind of interpersonal harmony supportive of tribal unity:

> The tambour and rattle, accompanied with their sweet low voices, produce a pathetic harmony, keeping exact time together, and the countenance of the musician, at proper times seems to express the solemn elevated state of the mind: at that time there seems not only a harmony between him and his instrument, but it instantly touches the feelings of the attentive audience, as the influence of an active and powerful spirit; there is then a united universal sensation of delight and peaceful union of souls throughout the assembly. (503)

Certain places also inspired awe in the Indians, which made Bartram think that such locales, too, were part of the underpinnings of tribal identity and unity. While some were known to be associated with the spirits, others were said to be burial grounds, and still others seemed to be depositories for things holy. Bartram reported coming across one of the last: "This secluded place appears to me to be designed as a sanctuary dedicated to religion, or rather priest craft; for here are deposited all the sacred things, as the physic pot, rattles, chaplets of deer's hoofs and other apparatus of conjuration; and likewise the calumet or great pipe of peace" (453).

The sacredness of certain well-defined spaces was something the Italian Giuseppe Acerbi (1773–1846) could not help noticing during his journey into the frigid zone, or what he thought of as the grand, wild North. During a stopover in England, he brought his thoughts together in English as *Travels through Sweden, Finland, and Lapland, to the North Cape in the Years 1798 and 1799*, which appeared in London in two volumes in 1802.[20] In addition to various magic mountains, there were the smaller localities where paraphernalia, like the tambourine or runic drum, could be hidden from Christian missionaries. Acerbi also pointed out that the presence of a woman, whether menstruating or not, was commonly thought to desecrate such places. His sympathy for customs of that sort derived from his own purportedly scientific stance, about which he did in all honesty warn his readers in the preface to the first volume. He wrote that objective evaluations of such far northern customs and conditions could be made "by those only who have a just and masculine taste for nature" (1:x).

Despite its sexism and scientific limitations, Acerbi's account provides invaluable information about the status of shamanism in the late eighteenth century. Comparisons of his account with what writers like Purchas, Scheffer, and Egede had written at least partially serve to unravel what must have been happening during those two centuries when conversion efforts were so strong.

Acerbi reported that shamans no longer allowed themselves to be identified. When questioned, the natives always seemed indifferent to their tribe's ancient practices, claiming a strong belief in Christianity, the prescriptions of which they, at least publicly, followed to the letter (2:156–58). Eventually Acerbi realized that they had learned to assume such a pose whenever they felt they needed to be on guard. They were willing to employ any ruse to conceal their uninterrupted idolatrous practices (2:294).

Acerbi gave steady attention to those practices. First, there were the magic verses or runes, which had withstood the onslaught of Christianity and also modern science. The people continued to believe that such verses were "possessed of secret virtues" and had a high degree of efficacy when employed for purposes of healing (1:321). Rather than ban them or destroy them, Acerbi, who had strong historical instincts, suggested they be valued as "inestimable monuments of antiquity" (1:321).

Second, polytheism needed attention as a historical phenomenon. It seemed to be a result of the fierce climate and rugged environment in which the northern aborigines lived. But Acerbi proceeded to challenge the degeneration theory, concluding that "polytheism must have been the most ancient religion among mankind" (2:294). He drew on Norse mythology, which explained that magic had been brought from the east by Odin, whose shamanic powers, including those of his eight-legged steed Sleipnir, were generally acknowledged.

The female sex, which Odin himself occasionally saw fit to assume, also had to be mentioned, if only because the witches of Lapland had by the late eighteenth century become nearly synonymous with the occult. The steady transformation of such matters into the higher levels of European consciousness was something Acerbi could not avoid noting. There were, he wrote, simply too many modern as well as ancient stories about magic and magicians (2:308).

A third matter Acerbi treated was the shamanic drum, which he thought was the compendium of all paganism. He wrote that it was considered holy, and that most families possessed one to help themselves overcome minor problems. Only problems of a very grave nature warranted summoning the official shaman or *Noaaid* for a séance, during which his spirit purportedly ventured forth to the magic mountain to find a cure or a solution (2:310). His song of incantation was called the *Juoige*, which Acerbi considered "the most hideous kind of yelling that can be conceived" (2:311).

Acerbi's account of shamanism was typical of the late eighteenth century. He tried to pull together information related to various disciplines so as to produce a synthesis. He considered the arts as seriously as he did pharmacological matters and psychological factors. And he never lost sight of the general historical framework. Giving credence to hidden spirit-infested worlds was, he insisted, for better or worse, not only universal but also seemingly perpetual among simple folk as well as among artists. Acerbi went on to claim that scientists had since time immemorial suspected such hidden worlds might represent as yet unexplained natural phenomena. The summation he offered toward the end of his account seems to be an appropriate one for bringing this chapter to an end: "In England we even find witchcraft supported by royal authority, by James I. and countenanced by the great Lord Bacon. The belief in spirits, not less absurd, even the vigorous mind of Dr. Johnson was not exempt from. But these ridiculous, mischievous, and cruel delusions, are happily banished almost from the habitations of the most ignorant, and we already begin to wonder at the credulity of our ancestors" (2:313).

CHAPTER FOUR

Shamanism among the
Medical Researchers

MEDICAL RESEARCHERS became increasingly conscious of the implications of their activities during the eighteenth century. While specialties like obstetrics, pediatrics, psychiatry, and pathology were forming, questions were being asked about the nature of medicine as well as about its significance for society. Most important was the question whether medicine itself was a science, an art, or a combination of both.[1] For those who voted for the last, the proportions were of great concern. Human beings had already been recognized as not curable by means of mathematical abstraction, which mitigated against interpreting medicine as a pure science in the Newtonian sense. There were simply too many considerations to be factored in, including emotions and the imagination, as well as diet and drinking habits.

The role and status of midwives, barbers, apothecaries, surgeons, and physicians came up regularly, as did the need for training and apprenticeship. Again and again, the herbalism and other home-grown strategies of the wise women were denigrated in favor of the "science" that could be offered by the academically prepared male doctors who had had to dissertate on some abstruse theoretical issue before being set loose on society. Although professionalism seemed to be emerging triumphant, there was a residual suspicion that something other than mere academic learning was necessary to provide medical success—that is, comforting the afflicted, or at least trying to give people longer, less burdened lives than their predecessors had had. Public health loomed large, and matters that involved mental as well as physical well-being were avidly discussed. Sanitation, hygiene, and other kinds of preventive medicine were foremost among them, but rehabilitation of the mildly incapacitated as well as management or containment of the hopelessly ill were not neglected.

Reports by travelers that described shamanic healing of all kinds of illnesses captivated the medical researchers as much as they did everyone else. Many physicians staunchly disavowed such reports, comparing them to earlier tales of European witchcraft, or facilely labeling them childish hocus-pocus.[2] Other physicians, however, suspected that something having to do with self-preservation had to be operative among the aborigines, and they began to query just what that might be. Those with the curiosity and courage to pose such questions helped inhibit the rapid rise of medical professionalism, on the one hand, and, on the other, helped encourage further study of things wierd and seemingly supernatural. Like Bacon, Burton, and the long line of medical researchers involved in studying the relationship of the mind to the body, they felt compelled to consider any kind of folk healing as well as quackery. Whatever the motivation or consequence might have been, their increased attentiveness to shamans and shamanism was quite striking during the closing decades of the eighteenth century.

Jerome Gaub (1705–1780), a member of the Royal Society of London as well as of the learned societies in Edinburgh and St. Petersburg, had been called to the University of Leiden as a lecturer in chemistry at the request of Hermann Boerhaave in 1731. Several years later he gained an appointment as professor of medicine there, delivering an inaugural lecture entitled "On the Vain Expectation of Prolonged Life Promised by Chemists."[3] Gaub earned his reputation through the many books he wrote in search of a middle ground between mechanistic and psychological approaches. He also published essays on psychosomatic medicine that became very well known during his lifetime.

Among the topics Gaub treated in his many publications were what the philosophers and physicians had written on the mind-body problem, the unproved, yet acknowledged harmony of the psyche and the soma, and the mechanism creating interaction, especially among the emotionally disturbed. He also treated the role of imagery on the rational and irrational parts of the brain, as well as the corporeal effects of anger, anguish, terror, joy, and hope, and the therapeutic possibilities they offered. Two important topics that did not escape him were the general healing powers of nature and the very limited role of academically trained physicians in managing peoples' habits or altering their life-styles. Gaub repeatedly emphasized that the emotions made up such an important part of the human being that they should never be suppressed.

On the other hand, Gaub remained very concerned about those people who, whether through conscientious study or raw instinct, could successfully play on the emotions of their fellow creatures. He repeatedly deplored the activities of "windy quacks, nostrum venders and barber surgeons."[4] Yet he admired their ability to manipulate simple folk so as to achieve the desired physiological aims. His analysis of such manipulations stressed the naturally regenerative power of hope, as well as the ability of the quack or shaman to instill such positive thoughts in any given patient. Gaub's description is worth quoting at length:

It is this faith that physicians so greatly wish for, since if they know how to procure it for themselves from the ill they render them more obedient and are able to breathe new life into them with words alone, moreover they find the power of their remedies to be increased and the results made more certain. From this same source quacks, travelling venders of medicine, uroscopists and urine-boilers, who play tricks with charms, amulets and sympathetic powers, seek fame and fortune. For when they display their prodigies and confidently promise recovery to the ill, with high-flown words and rash boasts, credulity is seized by wonder and wonder leads to hope, which then buoys up a mind enfeebled by an obstinant tedious ailment and want of help. The arousal of the bodily organs is sometimes such that the vital principles cast off their torpidity, the tone of the nervous system is restored, the movements of the humors are accelerated, and nature then attacks and overcomes with her own powers a disease that prolonged treatment has opposed in vain. Let those fortunate enough to have more rapidly recovered by means of these empty arts than by means of approved systems of healing congratulate themselves, I say, on having regained their health, regardless of the reason![5]

Gaub's sterling academic credentials would seem to make him an unlikely researcher into what the eighteenth century considered the occult. Nevertheless, he mentioned various mountebanks, wizards, and old women who provided cures he could attest to but for which he could not provide rational explanations. One of the curers he rather angrily designated as "a certain well-known Hecuba."[6] Although Gaub showed little or no respect for such women, he remained mightily interested in what they knew about anesthetics and mind-altering substances. His interest contributed much to the birth and evolution of psychopharmacology.

Gaub encouraged his colleagues to engage actively in the search for "new drugs capable of affecting the mind."[7] Reactions to wine, opium, and hashish were well known, but Gaub sought more information about a particular "seed from a plant of Malabar called *ganscho*, the fumes of which are supposed to induce a delightful intoxication when breathed in through the mouth and nose, inspiring soldiers with mettle and priests with ecstasy."[8] With the right connections, such plant substances, which were actually Indian hemp or *Cannabis activa*, could be had.

What Gaub found so difficult to obtain were the kinds of concoctions and ointments the sorceresses, or shamankas, used in order to "fall into a profound stupor, invariably accompanied by the same vision of having been transported after a long aerial journey into a distant place, where they intermingle, cohabit, and dance with others of their ilk, all of this being so firmly impressed on their fancy that no argument after they awake can convince them that it was an empty dream."[9] Gaub, like his fellow researchers, longed to know what proportions of aconite, belladonna, hemlock, and whatever else would be necessary in order to make the consumer take flight.

Such concerns were shared by the Swiss-born Johann Georg Zimmermann (1728–1795), who worked under Gaub in Leiden after having received a doctorate in medicine from Haller in Göttingen. Zimmermann's rapid rise to international fame resulted not only from his good connections but also from the books he wrote early in his career. Instead of being theoretical treatises for specialists, they were about what he had learned from his actual experiences as a practicing physician, and they found a ready reading public among those acquainted with travel reports, which Zimmermann himself avidly consumed.[10] Firmly believing in the power of the mind to conquer the body, or at least to overcome pain, Zimmermann developed certain techniques of what now might be called bedside empathy. He thought they instilled in the patient hope, or at least positive feelings, images, and ideas.

Zimmermann took up such matters in the two-volume work he published in Zurich in 1763–1764, *Von der Erfahrung in der Arzneykunst*. He argued that medicine was not an exact science like mathematics, nor could it ever become one, because so many intangibles were involved (1:3). Faith and hope he considered the most difficult to keep under control, for on the one hand, they could stimulate the inherent regenerative powers of the body, and on the other, they could encourage the imagination to create the kind of fictions that produced superstitions and allowed for charlatanry.

The power such charlatans, whether quacks or shamans, had enjoyed since time immemorial derived from their uncanny ability to wield the intangibles in order to confuse reason and gain mastery over the imagination. Once submissive belief had been attained, most of the battle was won (1:37–38). The patient would feel relaxed and reassured that intercession with the spirits or the forces of nature was more than possible; it was, indeed, taking place. Although Zimmermann thought academically trained physicians could accomplish much by accounting for the psychology of the sick as well as of the healthy, he cautioned: "A physician becomes a charlatan when he is only audacious instead of possessing learning and genius" (1:36).

In Zimmermann's opinion, most medical writings comprised a mixture of error and truth because their authors had accepted so much on authority without double-checking it (1:114). They could provide memorized erudition, but very little genuine scientific learning. That only came from experience, which he defined as follows: "Experience in medicine comes from well-made and well-conceived observations and experiments that produce skill in the art of guarding against illnesses, recognizing those known to occur, soothing, and healing" (1:46).

Experience was also what produced the perfection of the human faculty of perception, or what currently might be termed diagnostic skill. Zimmermann called it medical genius and wrote that it combined the personal sensitivities needed for comprehending the hidden signs given by one's fellow man with the creative imagination of the artist and the well-honed intellect of the research scientist (2:2–4). No amount of reading or study could guarantee it. Furthermore, the most learned, academic physicians were usually not any good in actual practice. They had less sense for things human than did common conjurers and quacks. Writing a good ten years before the outbreak of what became known as the "genius movement" in the German-speaking lands, Zimmermann explained:

> Endowed by nature with true genius, the physician will synthesize the most diffuse observations, reduce a variety of causes into a single symptom, base his report in each case on essentials, and alter his methods according to circumstances. In order to advance from the known to the unknown, he must indeed continue to think on as he sees the invisible present itself as visible, and he must conclude what will be out of that which is, often guessing and often beginning his work before he has guessed. Genius proceeds slowly on dubious paths, spiritedly and quickly on known and dangerous ones. (2:23–24)

Hippocrates came up repeatedly as an exemplary medical figure. Of all the many talents of the ancient Greek, Zimmermann singled out his astounding knowledge of philosophy. He surpassed Plato, who, Zimmermann wrote, excelled only at organizing and discussing what others had reported, rather than making his own observations. Philosophy was important to Zimmermann because he believed it alone could prevent the kind of superstitions that arose when simple folk could not understand the causes of their afflictions and ailments, or anything else that complicated their lives: "Philosophy alone heals superstition. Wherever there is no philosophy, it is haunted. There are the witches; there are the spirits; there are the goblins; there the devil prevails all over. There is superstition" (2:90–91). Such had been the case, Zimmermann continued, since remotest antiquity. And such remained the case even in the purportedly enlightened France of the eighteenth century, where convulsives and those possessed by spirits were rampant. There were also, he added, many similar recorded incidences in the southern German lands, Vienna reporting many cases of what was termed female possession.

So successful was Zimmermann in his medical practice as well as his publishing that in 1768 he was appointed private physician to the elector of Hanover, who happened to be the king of England, George III. In 1775, Zimmermann got to know the renowned author of *Die Leiden des jungen Werthers*, Johann Wolfgang Goethe, with whom he had numerous discussions about medicine and psychiatry. He thereafter became a close friend of the Goethe family as well as its main medical consultant. While he treated and comforted the dying Cornelia Goethe Schlosser, they did what they could to help him with his own deeply troubled, emotionally unstable children. Catherine the Great was another eighteenth-century luminary interested in Zimmermann. He declined her enticing offer to move to St. Petersburg. On the other hand, he readily accepted the offer to attend Frederick the Great during his terminal illness in 1786, thereafter writing several books on the subject.[11]

Those books were, indeed, quite influential in shaping the historical reception of the philosopher-king. Yet it was the book Zimmermann published in 1756 and then amended and enlarged in the 1780s, *Über die Einsamkeit*, that won him a lasting reputation. In it, he examined the causes of the inclination to solitude, and surveyed its effects. He found the human imagination particularly susceptible since it all too easily drew false inferences from real sensations. Prolonged solitary withdrawal from society led to the kind of distemper that produced delusive images and frantic visions. The result was personal fancy, religious enthusiasm, or political fanaticism.[12]

The greater behavioral extravagances of women seemed to derive from their biologically determined imaginations and intuitions. Like Diderot and others, Zimmermann revealed the dangers of convents and other similar institutions. The emotional instability resulting from such solitude was compounded by the enormous pressure of a lifestyle that required abstinence from all natural sensual gratification (2:105–6). Ecstatic females, whether nuns or witches, so often spoke of their experiences as the blissful consummation of their marriage to the divine that Zimmermann attributed them to unrequited earthly love. The denial of the natural led to the unnatural or even the supernatural. He explained, for example, "Solitude is much more productive of visionary insanity in the minds of women, than in men. What in men is nothing more than fancy, is in the other sex augmented to frenzy; therefore Plato regarded women as the origin of all superstition and fanaticism" (2:133).

Men who sought solitude in order to mortify their bodies and thereby liberate their souls also experienced strange reactions. As a matter of fact, Zimmermann wrote, "Solitude is the parent of the Fakirs of India, and every other sect of mystics, to whatever religion they may belong" (2:106). Monastic seclusion, known to derive from melancholy, produced even darker melancholy and then madness.

One cure involved returning to society. Others involved indulging in happy activities. Here as well as elsewhere Zimmermann resorted to a theatrical example. He told of a despondent man who sought a cure for his unbounded melancholy by consulting one of the most famous physicians in Paris. That physician recommended he go "'to the Italian Comedy: your malady must be very obstinate if it does not yield to the magic powers of Carlin the Harlequin.' 'Alas!' replied the patient, 'I am Carlin, and while I excite the mirth of all the world, I am myself the victim of the most gloomy despondency'" (2:142).

Theater and the performing arts were equally important therapeutic measures, according to Johann Peter Frank (1745–1821), another internationally renowned physician with connections to the medical faculty at the University of Göttingen. After having taught there in the 1780s as a professor of philosophy and public health, he held a professorship in clinical medicine at Pavia before moving on to Vienna and then Vilnius. Frank devoted an entire section to the benefits of public entertainments in his *System einer vollständigen medicinischen Polizey*, which was first published in six volumes in the last quarter of the eighteenth century, was enlarged to eight volumes in the early nineteenth century, and was translated into many languages.[13]

To remain socially productive, Frank wrote, human beings required recreation suited to their character and tastes. Boredom brought the great danger of inertia and functional incapacity, so the state would do well to realize diversions were absolutely necessary. Formal theaters, opera houses, and concert halls were appropriate for large cities, where municipal governments should ensure public safety by examining architectural designs, and maintain clean air by installing ventilators (3:728). The length of such performances was very important and had to be gauged according to such matters as the endurance capabilities of the spectators' circulatory systems as well as their known attention span (3:734).

In acknowledging the palliative as well as the curative value of music, Frank mentioned the superhuman talents of Orpheus, compared them to those of some similarly enchanting contemporary performers, and then discussed the significance of shamanism for a down-to-earth program designed to support universal welfare. Since the earliest times, he wrote, people have tried to control the behavior of their fellows by murmuring certain mysterious charms, spells, incantations, and songs. Others claimed dancing and singing allowed them to metamorphose into various animals or travel through the many heavens (4:523).

Frank, another obviously well-trained, intellectual, and thoughtful physician who happened to be a devoted consumer of current travel reports, related European witchcraft, superstition, possession, and emotional aberrance to what he had read about shamanism in Gmelin and Pallas, among others. Frank wrote, for example,

> The history of the most ancient peoples teaches that they were accustomed to put all their trust in soothsayers, fortune-tellers, and necromancers and that these generally bragged about their particular intimacy with the demons by means of whose assistance they enjoyed all their extraordinary prerogatives. Each one who has been classified as a kam, that is, priest, among the Tatars can, after all, conjure. About such a kam they say that he sometimes sits whole nights in the field in order to study thoroughly what he should order his believers. Such a priest as this can neither read nor write; and the symptoms through which he is recognized as being qualified for this office consist in physical contortions such as our madmen are given to. (4:538–39)

Insisting that such magical beliefs warranted scientific attention, if only to be exposed as hoaxes, he spent a number of pages on a review of the many kinds of prognostications and activities that ranged from rainmaking, fecundating, and metamorphosing to healing, hexing, and scaring to death (4:545–65). He thought such things persisted because so many academically trained physicians allowed them, in order to cover up their own woefully inadequate scientific knowledge (4:598–99).

Frank summarized the evidence he either collected himself or read in the available literature, and he concluded, "The raptures, the soothsaying, and that sort of goings-on are always based on similar causes, namely, deception or illnesses" (4:626). Sometimes such altered states were, he added, induced by the consumption of certain unhealthy substances, such as coffee, tobacco, or drugs. The main objective, however, was curing, when not merely maintaining health. Frank repeatedly drew the attention of his readers to aborigines the world over. The methods the shamans used to gain native obedience and to influence their treatment of children, their diet, and their education were important to him. He mentioned the invisible world thought to have control over human fate, emphasizing, however, that he remained a nonbeliever. He stated that he could understand why the barbaric Germans and Celts were so superstitious, but he could not conceive

how the ancient Greeks, long held as exemplary, followed such imagis-
tic magical practices, especially the kind Pindar wrote that Aesculapius
himself perpetrated (6.1:27).

Both patients and physicians were the targets of the reforms Frank
hoped to introduce. While practicing preventive medicine and public
hygiene, they all needed to apply common sense and compassion to
effect changes in the basic laws involving such social problems as
unwed motherhood, illegitimacy, and unlicensed prostitution. Contemporary medical education was so devoid of practical experience
that he likened it to "dreams out of the domain of an imaginary tran-
scendental medicine!" (6.1:389). Improvement could only come from
forcing students to obtain the necessary scientific basis, to practice dis-
section, to gain clinical knowledge, and to observe the life-styles of real
people before they became patients. Frank stressed science, experience, and social accountability. Nevertheless, what he wrote about
gaining complete trust, keeping secrets, recognizing spiritual needs,
and manipulating intangibles like fear, pity, and hope would indicate
that much was being assimilated from the shamans, who had often
failed individual patients but who had at least managed to keep mankind from becoming extinct.

Christian Wilhelm Hufeland (1762–1836), who belonged to a well-
known Weimar medical family, had the same educational concerns as
Frank and Lichtenberg, both of whom he warmly acknowledged as his
teachers by dedicating publications to them. After Hufeland himself
became a professor at the University of Jena in 1793, his lectures were
often attended by five hundred students or more, wanting to hear
about the relationlship of human psychology to physical illness and
the almost divine, yet truly dangerous, role of the physician in re-
establishing psychosomatic harmony or health. Hufeland's association
with the day-to-day culture of Weimar, one of the great eighteenth-
century depots for gathering and dispensing information about exploration, sensitized him early in life to the kinds of curing that went
on elsewhere in the world. Whenever he had chance, he examined
them and studied their possible implications.

In a book arguing that pathology was the basis of all medical science, *Ideen über Pathogenie und Einfluss der Lebenskraft auf Entstehung
und Form der Krankheiten als Einleitung zu pathologischen Vorlesungen*
(1795), Hufeland took up the subject of immunity to disease. People in
higher civilizations, he contended, had lost what must have originally
been an inherent natural ability to ward off certain kinds of illnesses.
Their counterparts in the wild still had bodies that were immune to
highly toxic poisons that would instantly kill the sturdiest Europeans.
That difference Hufeland ascribed to diet, clothing, exercise, quality

of air, and general living habits as well as state of mind. He did not, however, offer an answer to the question why the natives could freely use various narcotics for medicinal purposes without seeming to become addicted to them.

Hufeland's *Die Kunst das menschliche Leben zu verlängern* (1797), the title page of which contained a motto by Goethe, one of his local patients, tried to distinguish the art of medicine, which had to do with health, from macrobiotics or the science of longevity, which had to do with prolonging life, regardless of its quality, for the maximum amount of time possible. In the theoretical part, which opened the volume, Hufeland presented a historical survey beginning with the ancient Egyptian mysteries and touching various professions. While relatively long lives were usually enjoyed by poets, painters, philosophers, and those who dwelled in worlds they themselves could control, physicians and those who had to struggle to survive in the real world usually died young. The worst statistics were those for the Negroes carried away from Africa for purposes of enslavement in the West Indies, where one out of five or six died young, and for the all-too-numerous foundlings of Europe. In Paris, Hufeland wrote, only 180 out of 7,000 were recorded as remaining alive beyond infancy. That alone made him as well as others wonder about the philosophical, but more especially the moral, bases of those men who, like Jean Jacques Rousseau (1712–1778), cavalierly relegated their natural children to foundling hospitals.

The practical part of Hufeland's book discussed how Europeans shortened their lives by following current fashions. He wrote about their pampered style of rearing children, their overindulgence in stimulants like coffee, their forcing celibate life-styles on sexually vigorous people, their disregard for public as well as personal hygiene, and their constant assaults on the imaginative faculty that prevented the body from naturally maintaining its balance.

Hufeland also suggested ways Europeans could learn to lengthen their own lives as well as those of their offspring. The hygienic and anatomical reasons for not encasing infant bodies in swaddling bands seemed rationally obvious to him, as did the beneficial effects of a natural mother's milk, rather than that of a wet nurse brought along by happenstance. Daily washing of one's body as well as one's underclothes was a must, something any so-called savage would do naturally and without prompting. Europeans, Hufeland repeatedly insisted, had to be convinced that they all should learn how to swim. They also had to be taught how to apply techniques of resuscitation to accident victims. Furthermore, Europeans had to learn to find the kind of academically trained physicians who would be for them the kind of friend or intercessor that the shaman was for the aborigines in other parts of the world. As Hufeland wrote, "If one has, however, found an able and honest physician, one should trust him completely. This reassures the patient and makes the curing procedure immeasurably easier for the physician" (664–65).

Many such issues had been taken up in previously published essays that Hufeland gathered together in the collection *Gemeinnützige Aufsätze zur Beförderung der Gesundheit und des Wohlseyns* (1797). In his preface, he warned prospective physicians that, as noble and divine as the profession of medicine was, they could expect so much frustration and loneliness that the many intoxicants in their purview might become too great a temptation.

Such substances and whatever else was listed in the apothecary books would, he wrote in the essay "Gefahren der Einbildungskraft," prove ineffectual against many ailments, especially those stemming from the imagination. About that kind he admitted, "Indeed, I do not know a more frightful and a more real illness" (101). Physical debilitation could result from charms or spells because they kept the imaginative faculty from blocking "the dangerous disposition to sickness" (114). The still-unexplained power of the imagination over the body was so strong that people in Europe as well as elsewhere in the world were known to die on command, out of fright, and after prophecy.

Hypochondria, the vapors, and nerves might have replaced bewitchment, enchantment, and diabolic possession as the prevailing fashion, but, Hufeland insisted, they shared the same source, common symptoms, and a comparable prognosis. To him, the mere recognition of similarities between what once was considered supernatural or paranormal and what had become medically comprehensible demonstrated the great advancement that had been made in science: "It is really a pleasant task to compare the symptoms of diabolical illnesses with the symptoms of today's nervous illnesses, and the earlier conceptions with those of the present, in order to learn to revere the progress of science and human culture as well as to get an idea about the influence of genuine enlightenment" (119–20).

A similar comparison formed the basis for Hufeland's explanation of lycanthropy, which allied ecstasy and physical bliss to the imagination. He wrote about past ages, for example,

At that time there was a multitude of people who on occasion caught the peculiar fit of imagining themselves to be wolves. Actually it was a veritable ecstasy, in which a finer organization of the eighteenth century would, perhaps, have heard angelic voices. People living among wolves back in those days heard the wolves howl, took on wolfish natures themselves, and in their thoughts engaged in all kinds of wolfish dealings. When they regained consciousness, they related everything they had done in their dream precisely as though it had really happened. Forsooth, with some of them it went so far that they not only had visions but actually ran away. (120–21)

In "Mesmer und sein Magnetismus," Hufeland discussed the methods being used to explore the imagination and its workings. Mesmerized subjects exhibited behavior he found similar to that of ecstatics, convulsives, and all those wildly high on certain narcotic substances: "One saw the most violent involuntary twisting of the limbs, half asphyxiation, distension of the torso, and confused glances. Here, one emits the most penetrating shrieks; there, one wants to burst out laughing; and over there, another dissolves in tears" (153–54). Hufeland cited many experiments to show that such reactions were caused by an imagination actively engaged rather than by the forces of animal magnetism. Music could induce them as well as intensify and modify them. The flashing of mirrors was also effective. But there was more than enough proof that the imagination in and of itself could not only bring on such fits but transmit them to others: "One knows for sure how great its power is with numerous other assemblies, how, for example, an intensity of courageous feeling or panic-stricken terror can spread from one individual across a whole army, how in this way even nervous afflictions can become infectious" (183).

Hufeland concluded that the application of imagination and the cultivation of measures using imagination might help modern medicine perform some scientific wizardry and effect what would be otherwise impossible cures. Such continuing experimentation, however, should be allowed "only in the hands of an intelligent physician" (185). The vocabulary of Hufeland's concluding sentence would seem to indicate that he had no quarrel with the beneficial accomplishments of shamanism as long as they could be explained scientifically and monitored by the academically trained, male members of the medical establishment: "By the way, there is certainly one observation that suffices to honor the German nation: as soon as magnetism began to become jugglery it could no longer obtain on German soil, and when it returned there, it very quickly gained a more solid and more philosophical appearance" (187).

Factors contributing to the emergence of that establishment proliferated in the eighteenth century. Wilhelm Michael Richter (1767–1822) provided a good example of one of them: the evolving historiographical methodology that interpreted current ethnographic and anthropological reports to suit its own male-oriented purposes. Richter, who was born in Moscow and sent to the *Gymnasium* in Reval, received his doctorate in medicine in 1788 from the University of Erlangen, after having studied in Göttingen and Berlin as well as in France, England, and the Netherlands. When he returned to Russia in 1790, he practiced his specialty of obstetrics and gynecology, accepted a medical professorship at the University of Moscow, and became a rather prolific writer.

The work in question, *Geschichte der Medicin in Russland*, was published in three volumes in Moscow from 1813 to 1817. Only later was it translated into Russian. Richter's preface bemoaned the lack of historical information on the subject, while at the same time mentioning the inaccessibility as well as the untrustworthiness of sources as reasons for that lack. Documents were either hidden away in monasteries or written by foreign travelers whose motives were suspect (1:v–vi). Consequently, the multilingual Richter confessed to spending many years on basic archival research as well as poring over the innumerable available travel accounts.

Richter began by writing that healing efforts were as old as humankind itself. Forced by nature to experiment with the unknown and the untested, primordial creatures had used their powers of observation to determine what succeeded and what did not. Little by little, by watching animals and fellow creatures, they learned to distinguish foods and healing substances from poisons. Richter offered as verification reports of aboriginal reactions from the new as well as the old world. Without so much as a fleeting reference to a *magna mater*, a shamanka, or a wise woman, he attributed the invention of medicine, nursing, and all healing powers to the sustained caring activities of the primitive paterfamilias:

> During the infancy of the human race, it was the fathers of families among all peoples who practiced the art of healing, although in an extremely empirical, coarse, and incidental way. The necessity of nature forced them into social union, not only to apply as medicine that which they learned from oral tradition about what their ancestors coincidentally had found useful, but also that which the new, heretofore unfamiliar experiences and observations of present occasions begot. *Therefore no one single individual invented the science of medicine.* It arose gradually through many observations, and its range expanded according to circumstances. (1:3–4)

Moving from mythological into historically recorded times, Richter quickly surveyed the contributions of ancient Greece, which, he wrote, saw to the transmission of the mysterious medical arts from Asia to

Europe. He, like many of his contemporaries, equated the Russians with the Scythians, so the implication was that medical knowledge had inherently been theirs since the beginning of the human race (1:13–14). Their patriarchally organized life was what Richter claimed led to their good health and well-being, for fathers or heads of households instinctively knew how to make hurts go away, to cure slight indispositions such as colds, and to provide constant nurturing during more serious afflictions. That claim was supported with citations to Marco Polo and others who had written on the customs and conditions of the sturdy peoples they had met (1:41–44).

Richter then turned to the Russian Orthodox Christian clergy, which, he wrote, did its healing and caring from purely charitable motives. He relegated to oblivion all aboriginal attempts to keep individuals healthy and tribes from dying out. Discrediting popular "mention of magic charms and conjurations and so forth" (1:93), he contended that certain males who managed to organize themselves had emerged as a scientifically oriented group of priestlike healers.

One of the most ardent rebels against such contentions was Johann Heinrich Jung (1740–1817), who received a doctorate in medicine in 1772, after having studied in Strasbourg at the same time as Goethe. Jung was an older man whose religious awakening at the age of about twenty-two precipitated his career change. While intellectually as well as emotionally dedicated to all sciences directly benefiting humankind, such as medicine, agriculture, forestry, and veterinary medicine, he gained so much fame from the novel he published in 1778, *Heinrich Stillings Jugend*, which the best-selling Goethe saw through the press, that he thereafter became known by the hyphenated name Jung-Stilling. The many sequels he produced, in addition to the devotional books, helped support his popular reputation, which rested solidly on his surgical contributions, especially his cataract operations, as well as his various academic appointments.

Jung-Stilling found as much fault with the objective rationalists of the French Enlightenment as he did with the subjective, perpetually emotive geniuses of the Sturm und Drang. The former had let reason run rampant, while the latter suffered, in his opinion, from sick imaginations. Preferring a life governed by Christian values, Jung-Stilling contended that all of them had lost the healthy human balance. He believed that balance derived from the soul's communication with its counterparts; consequently he went on to posit a spirit-inhabited world hidden from common view.

A summary of those ideas appeared in his treatise on spirits, *Theorie der Geister-Kunde, in einer Natur-Vernunft-und Bibelmäsigen Beantwortung der Frage: Was von Ahnungen, Gesichten und Geistererscheinungen geglaubt und nicht geglaubt werden müsse.*[14] First of all, the invisible spiritual world would never be perceived, much less studied, he wrote, if the mechanistic approach to investigating nature were considered the only valid one (43, 61). In a plea for broad methodological experimentation, he suggested recognizing those approaches that were less mathematically oriented and stretching them to their outermost limits. He himself worked "according to my theocratic system of independence" (43), which, he reported, not only made most phenomena comprehensible, but also provided solutions for many riddles that had long stymied scientists.

Jung-Stilling's "system" helped him explain that communing with the spirits required "a lively, very sensitive nervous system and an active imagination," in addition to constant concentration on supernatural matters (53). He warned, however, against interpreting as divinely initiated everything that seemed paranormal:

> It is an equally important major duty for each Christian that he set to work very carefully and not consider it as divine whenever something extraordinary is noticed here or there, like men, women, girls, or boys either falling into rapture or otherwise becoming enthused in some fashion or another and landing in an exalted state. At first, such people often utter magnificent things based in the word of God; then they gain adherents, and many are converted due to that; subsequently, however, the enemy of everything good mingles himself in. (113–14)

Sorcery resulted when wicked, godless people were involved, for they managed to reach only evil spirits. However, since the resurrection of Christ, himself a kind of shaman or miracle worker, such sorcery had been severely limited by rational relegation to the realm of superstition. Its practitioners could have no effect on the Christian soul, although they might cause physical afflictions that had not yet found scientific explanations (147).

In explaining the effects of Christianization on the European psyche, Jung-Stilling brought together mythology with anthropological speculation about primordial versions of shamanism. The ancient heathens, he wrote, had had druids—that is, conjuring priests and priestesses who worshiped idols and who regularly associated with the spirits in order to intercede for their compatriots. Of the many sacrificial celebrations, the one during the first night of May on the Brocken in the Harz Mountains was the most exuberant. In addition, the duties of these priests consisted of saying benediction, conjuring, bewitching, and disenchanting, and, particularly, concocting medicines and curing illnesses (148). Increased conversion efforts motivated the natives to conduct fewer and fewer celebrations out in the open. Charlemagne's dogged application of armed force to wipe out all abiding traces of heathenism saw to it "that they did, indeed, publicly attend Christian worship, but privately continued their heathen practices for a long time" (149).

Of all the practices, what came to be known as witchcraft remained in operation the longest. There was no one else the natives trusted as much, nor to whom they could go to seek recourse. In the absence of scientifically trained physicians, the witches served not only as the binding forces of social life but also as healers and curers. Since they thought such medical power depended on appeasing offended spirits with sacrificial celebrations, they continued to conduct them well into Christian times despite the threat of death at the stake. Citing published testimony from the trials, Jung-Stilling explained how latterday practitioners applied mixtures of multifarious narcotic substances to induce the kind of ecstasy that purportedly flew them to the witches' sabbath, or whatever the celebration might have been. One defendant, who claimed she had experienced nothing but sensual gratification and sexual bliss with the reigning billy goat and whatever else offered itself, had been witnessed lying in front of her own hearth all night with a rod between her legs.

The main conclusion Jung-Stilling drew from such testimony was that sexually deprived females of whatever age suffered definite physical reactions from consuming certain drugs because their imaginations already tended in that direction (150–51). Despite his pronounced mystical bent, his analysis was quite similar to that of his contemporaries in medicine. So was the way he treated matters having to do with prophecy, bilocation, magnetism, and somnambulism. His treatment of visions revealed continuing sensitivity to the personality profile of the purportedly archaic shaman. He wrote that a vision was totally meaningless, for

> it proves nothing further than a very active imagination and a natural disposition to consider images to be something real. Hysterical persons and hypochondriacs are inclined to visions. They get them with or without transports; but such people also easily develop their capacity for premonitions, so that they simultaneously come into contact with the spirit world; there then everything merges, and much knowledge and experience is needed to distinguish a vision from the genuine appearance of spirits. (171)

Jung-Stilling's emphasis on the medical implications of Christian mysticism might have made him suspect among most contemporary hard-core scientists, but his questions about the underlying assumptions of the mechanistic principles of Newtonianism and scientific determinism catapulted him, for a while, at least, to the forefront of the European Romantic movement, which in its earliest stages wanted to hear only about history, organicism, and psychology. Those were the people with the quality of mind to appreciate his thought-provoking yet eerily strange amalgam of artistic sensitivity, philosophical Pythagoreanism, ethnographic background-reading, anthropological speculation, psychological knowledge, scientific learning, and medical experience.

_____ **Part Two** _____

BACK TO FICTIONS AND FANTASIES:
THE IMPLICATIONS OF
SHAMANISM FOR THE ARTS
IN EUROPE

CHAPTER FIVE

The Impact of Russia on
Diderot and
Le neveu de Rameau

IN THE COURSE of the eighteenth century, information about shamanism continued to inundate Western Europe in such massive waves that
intellectuals had no alternative but to come to terms with it right at the
very moment of its arrival. Some Europeans were quick to apply to
standard aesthetic theory the prodigious ideas they managed to assimilate from travel reports.[1] Others agonized over them, transforming
them into works of art that, in several instances at least, were ac-
claimed masterpieces of their kind. Still others absorbed them so as to
invent public personalities for themselves and select trajectories for
their own careers. A few who had been carried along with the upsurge
of exciting new information eventually became terrified by what they
saw happening. The implications of this irrational phenomenon
seemed too far-reaching and not easily enough controllable to them.
Denis Diderot's (1713–1784) involvement with Catherine the Great
(1729–1796) and her Russian empire best exemplifies this reaction.[2]

Catherine, a German princess from Anhalt-Zerbst, was sent to Russia by her matchmaker, Frederick the Great, who in seeking allies
against Austria resorted to marriage politics. Catherine survived the
trip and an unhappy marriage and emerged as one of that century's
canniest political leaders. She thought of California as Russia's Peru,
with similarly rich resources to be had merely for the taking. She also
predicted in a letter to the first woman president of any scholarly society ever, Princess Catherine Romanov Dashkova (1744–1810), that the
Russian language, "uniting as it does the strength, the richness, and
energy of German with the sweetness of Italian, will one day become
the standard language of the world."[3]

Empress Catherine did, indeed, have her work cut out for her. First,
she wanted to have her vast realm inhabited—that is, colonized—with
Europeans. Her feelings of racial superiority clearly came through in
this matter, for she sought primarily Nordic types from Scandinavia,
the Baltic coast, and Germany. She offered potential colonists not only
land but also freedom from military service. Neither religion nor so-

cial class was, however, important to her. Jews, as well as those peasants who had left for other countries, were to be welcomed back to the Russian motherland as long as they promised to tend the land.

Second, Catherine wanted information about her huge realm in order to exploit it economically and to unify it. Consequently, she saw to the creation of what became known as the Free Economic Society. It funded the academic expeditions that set out to study the Empire of All the Russias between 1768 and 1774. Most of the explorers on these expeditions were associated with the German scientific movement. They traveled according to routes prescribed by the Academy of Sciences in St. Petersburg and were instructed to take cognizance of the questionnaires those academic specialists supplied. The required maps, measurements, and observations were faithfully submitted, as were the reports about a phenomenon that Catherine had been trying to wipe out, first passively and then more and more actively. That phenomenon was shamanism.

Shamanism represented to Catherine the Great a composite of all the dark, obscurantist forces conspiring against the advance of reason that the Enlightenment so warmly encouraged and so loyally supported.[4] Catherine, who was determined to change the image of her empire once and for all from irrationally Asiatic, or female, to rationally European, or male, associated the purveyors of shamanic beliefs and their followers with drug addicts, homosexuals, convulsionaries, religious enthusiasts, and political fanatics—that is, dissidents or assassins.[5] Like the early Spanish conquistadores in the Americas, she had no qualms about having them exterminated as quickly and efficiently as possible.[6] Her more scientifically oriented citizens, however, tried to sidestep such issues by sending the reports they made and the artifacts they collected to politically safe havens such as the German lands, especially the sleepy little university town of Göttingen.

Catherine applied the tactics of revisionism and wrote opposing whatever connected her realm with shamanism. Her three-hundred-page *Antidote* refuted the Abbé Jean Chappe d'Auteroche's (1722–1769) *Voyage en Sibérie* (1761), which, among other things, damned Russia as a nation confounded by its shamans.[7] There is much evidence in Catherine's opus showing how she thoroughly despised the emotionality and geniality of incipient Romanticism. She even criticized the Encyclopedists for including in their work articles on shamanism and other paranormal subjects, which she considered part of the dangerous contraband of the current passing fashion. Especially troubling was the article "Théosophes," which, she thought, revealed for public consumption matters that would best have been left concealed.[8] It reported on people who viewed human reason as pitiably limited rather than as supreme. In addition to reading body signs as masks of the soul, those people revered presentiments, hunches, and clairvoyance: "They claimed to be illuminated by an inner element, supernatural and divine, which burned in them and extinguished itself at intervals—elevating them to the most sublime knowledge when active, or causing them to fall into a state of natural idiocy when it ceased to act" (253). For them, "enthusiasm is the origin of all great things, good or evil" (254). The article further maintained that faith was the basis of all magic: "Innate natural faith makes us like the spirits; it is the principle behind magical workings, the energy of the imagination and all its marvels" (257). Of all the theosophs, Paracelsus stood out for following the compulsions of his enthusiasm. He spared no effort in his attempt to gather occult knowledge from all sources, whether the mines of Germany or the frontiers of Tatary. He and some of his colleagues had been known to attain that state of frenzy and rapture by using opium or other mind-altering substances (260). Whatever their specific fields, they all contributed to the irrationality that persisted in duping mankind with false religions, secret mystery societies, and artworks designed to provoke ecstasy.

Catherine combated such irrational practices in a multitude of ways. Her correspondence with the world-renowned physician Zimmermann often outlined her strategies. The article on theosophists, she explained on April 17, 1785, had stimulated her to try her pen at comedy writing.[9] In 1786, she published *Der sibirische Schaman, ein Lustspiel,* in addition to *Der Betrüger* and *Der Verblendete,* all of which were reissued two years later in Berlin and Stettin by the archrationalist Friedrich Nicolai (1733–1811) as *Drey Lustspiele wider Schwärmerey und Aberlauben.*[10] On April 22, 1787, Catherine thanked Zimmermann for his favorable review. Her words underscored the all-pervasiveness of the phenomenon:

I am very pleased about your positive opinion of the shaman in Siberia, for I am fond of the piece. But I fear no one will read it. These absurdities are stubborn and now fashionable. Most German princes know that it belongs to the proper tone of things to give appropriate models for all these impostures. They are tired of healthy philosophy. I recall that in 1740 even less than philosophical minds took pains to be philosophers, and now, reason and public spirit have disappeared. The new errors have made more people crazy among us than ever before.[11]

She once again took up the subject with Zimmermann on July 1, 1787. In addition to clearly identifiable charlatans like Cagliostro, she wrote, there were many, many others. She had herself during her Crimean journey encountered people who, for whatever purposes, danced and shouted themselves into a trance: "These are close to being inspired and not far away from the shamans of Siberia and Germany."[12]

In five acts, *Der sibirische Schaman* resolves a love intrigue while debunking the current European susceptibility to shamanism. The Bobins, natives of Siberia, bring their daughter Prelesta to St. Petersburg to find her a match more suitable than her beloved Iwan Pernatow, whom they consider too poor. They are accompanied by Amban Lai, who has become their family shaman because he purportedly wields remarkable healing powers, having even once saved Mrs. Bobin's life. The first act details his background in a manner one would expect from reading the explorers' reports. He was born on the border with China, lost both parents at an early age, and was reared by a native of the Tungus who, noticing his inclinations, apprenticed him to an old shaman: "So do the Mongols and other Siberian peoples call their priests."[13] Catherine uses dialogue as well as dramatic reports to inform the audience of Amban Lai's fraudulence. When people quiz the maid, she describes his cheats and tricks. In one instance, she happily shows off her superiority by commenting that he either knew how to make the master and his wife blind to his misdeeds, "or, they themselves wanted to deceive themselves so" (21).

Act 2 depicts various kinds of shamanic posturing. Amban Lai, who claims to have achieved the 140th degree, acknowledges his employer's approach before collapsing into unconsciousness. Mr. Bobin then has an opportunity to comment on his condition: "Whenever he is enraptured in his thoughts, it is like he is beside himself. He calls this condition the most fortunate and strives to reach it as often as possible" (24). Bringing him back to his senses requires a means that appeals to his imagination directly and strongly. Since it is not readily found, the stage directions instruct the actor to mime being tickled all over and then to shake his head like a Chinese doll before barking like a dog, miaowing like a cat, crowing like a rooster, and clucking like a hen. A comparison to the wailing and contortions of the bewitched in Siberia is given an ample footnote explaining that Amban Lai resembles "people who believe or pretend they are enchanted and, like the so-called possessed in other countries of Europe, make strange gestures and contorted postures, purport to foretell future things in a torrent of senseless words, also sometimes imitating the noises of various animals and calling out the name of him who spooked them, or as they say, ruined them" (29). With the tambourine now in hand, the shaman chants various vowels to its beats as he runs, hops, and leaps throughout the room. Then he collapses as if dead to the world while his adherents finish a short ballet around him. When he awakens, he removes his shaman's garb and begins speaking in sometimes sublime, other times muted tones, or he remains profoundly silent. The explanation of trying to achieve nonbeing or nonexistence with which the act closes deeply impresses the witnesses who have gathered (34).

The next two acts have the shaman apply his antics to particular circumstances. They also show how easily he builds a thriving business among the presumably sensible citizens of St. Petersburg. So many young men gather around to learn from him that one of the servants perceptively queries, "Isn't he even supposed to want to found a school for shamans?" (84). Amban Lai has difficulties with the lovesick daughter, however, for she believes her beloved has willingly betrothed himself to another.

Reason triumphs in the fifth act when the true lovers are reunited and when all the shaman's crimes are revealed. After discussing his right to a trial by peers, the last dialogue points out the common denominator of all those who buy what he has to sell: "They are indeed quite similar to the shamans. Like them, they follow imaginary rules, in the beginning deceiving themselves, and thereafter also those who believe in them!" (110).

Catherine's work was generally well received among intellectuals. The French spared neither ink nor paper in preparing panegyrics about her. Voltaire (1694–1778), who had great respect for her, exclaimed: "What times we live in! France persecutes the *philosophes*, and the Scythians show them favor!"[14] He could hardly believe that one woman had accomplished so much in so little time. Elsewhere, he wrote that he never really wanted to see Rome, but his desire to visit Russia—that was something else again: "I die of regret not to see deserts changed into proud cities, and 2,000 leagues of territory civilised by heroines. World history can show nothing comparable. It is the finest of revolutions." The Russomania that resulted ushered in a golden age of Franco-Russian diplomacy that lasted until the French Revolution threatened the very underpinnings of sovereignty and the divine right of kings.[15]

Diderot's interest in things shamanic paralleled his involvement with Catherine, which started in the early 1760s and persisted until his death in 1784, when she finally became the rightful owner of all his books and manuscripts. What might have begun as a business venture or survival tactic on his part burgeoned into an intellectual adventure of a magnitude that even a mind as agile as Diderot's could not contain. Catherine sent him monetary advances, but so enthralled was she at the time with his writings, atheistic utterances, and rationality that she got him elected to her academies in St. Petersburg.[16] She even went so far as to invite him to visit her. All the while, Diderot could not help reflecting on the weird-seeming similarities between the products as well as the processes of shamanic trance in Siberia and all the theories set forth by generations of Western thinkers since Plato. Also, at the same time, Diderot began drafting *Le neveu de Rameau*.[17]

Information about shamanism was so widely available that Diderot could have learned about it from any of a number of sources. Like many of his contemporaries, he had an insatiable thirst for fictional as well as factual reports, and he read widely in current anthropological writings. Rather than take that tack, however, I prefer to concentrate on one specific publishing enterprise with which he certainly must have been familiar, since he was, more or less, the director of its editorial board. There is an extraordinarily great number of articles on Russia and things shamanic in the *Encyclopédie, ou Dictionnaire raisonné des sciences, des arts, et des métiers*, which appeared in seventeen volumes in Paris from 1751 to 1765. The primary sources cited in those articles range from Scheffer and Strahlenberg to Perry and Deguignes. Gmelin is very highly and often recommended. As could be expected, also mentioned frequently is Voltaire's description of Russia, *Histoire de l'empire de Russie sous Pierre le Grand*.[18]

The lengthy article on Russia discusses various ancient tribes that peopled the enormous geographical area, among them the Scythians. Its survey of religious practices includes Christianity, Islam, idolatry, and lesser forms of heathenry. An explanation is also given for the honesty and kindness explorers attributed to some of the pagans they had encountered: "It was not paganism that made them more virtuous; rather it was their pastoral life, far from soical contact, and in an age that is likened to the first era of the world, free of the great emotions so necessary for respectable people."[19] The Samoyedes, who purportedly never committed murders, robberies, or other such antisocial acts, did not, for example, even have words in their language to denote vice and virtue. Nevertheless, they retained a firm belief in their *magiciens*, who reputedly prognosticated and interceded for them with the powers of nature. Despite sustained efforts at Christianization, the sovereigns, "have not been able to destroy the superstitons of these peoples, who constantly insert into their spells the names of their idols together with the more respectable elements from Christianity."[20] The Buryats and Ostyaks are classified as barbarous worshippers of idols, while the Kamchatkans have "among them magicians, whom they call shamans."[21] Here as well as elsewhere, the Germanicized form of the word is used to name the phenomenon in Siberia—mostly spelled *schaman* in the French, although occasionally *chaman*. As for the Tatars, "They have no other priests at all, except for some shamans, whom they consult rather as sorcerers than as priests."[22] A lengthier description of Yakut customs is given:

At certain times, they make sacrifices to gods and devils. These consist of throwing the milk of a mare into a large fire, and butchering horses and sheep, which they eat while drinking brandy until they take leave of their senses. They have no other priests but *shamans*—types of sorcerers in whom they have much faith, and who deceive them through a multitude of tricks and hoaxes, by which there is but one nation rude enough to be seduced.[23]

The uninitialed separate entry on shamans represents a conservative, relatively unthreatening distillation of the available information. There are what had long since become the standard references to mind-altering substances, theatrical performance, trance, make-believe, parasitism, and incredulity due to the inherent lack of higher, rational intelligence, or what today might be called left-hemispheric brain function. This entry is worth quoting in its entirety, for it is yet another piece of evidence that the Germanicized form of the word had already established itself even in France as the generic one:

SHAMANS, noun, masc. plural (*Mod. hist.*) is the name that the inhabitants of Siberia give to impostors who perform the functions of priests, jugglers, sorcerers, and medicine men. These shamans purport to have influence over the Devil, whom they consult to predict the future, to heal illnesses, and to do tricks that seem supernatural to an ignorant and superstitious people. For this they use drums, which they beat vigorously while dancing and spinning at extraordinary speed; it is when they are disoriented from these contortions and fatigue that they pretend the Devil manifests himself to them, if he is in the proper mood. Sometimes the ceremony ends with what appears to be the stab of a knife, which increases the astonishment and reverence among the simple-minded spectators. These contortions are ordinarily preceded by the sacrifice of a dog or a horse, which they eat while swilling brandy. And the whole comedy ends with the audience giving money to the shaman, who at this point prides himself on his show of indifference comparable to other impostors of the same kind.[24]

The references to jugglers and medicine men here are apt, because these were two other eighteenth-century choices competing to become the generic word. French missionaries like Lafitau repeatedly used them in their attempts to explain to colleagues at home the phenomenon in Canada and elsewhere on the North American continent. Even if, for some reason, Diderot had not associated those words with shamanism in his earlier years, he must certainly have done so after reading volume 8 of the *Encyclopédie*. It contained two and one-half columns on "JUGGLER (*Divination*), magicians or enchanters much renowned among the savage nations of America, and who make up the profession of medicine among them."[25] The entry goes into great detail about their dealings with the spirit world, explaining that they claimed to be able to make "a kind of pact with the demons." Their intermediaries were often birds, whose language they understood and whose flying they emulated during self-induced "ecstatic transports." The spirits were supposed to help these jugglers or medicine men discover the origins and kinds of deeply concealed maladies so cures could be found. Their tutelary spirits also assisted them in prognosticating, interpreting dreams, and disentangling complicated human affairs. Success was tied to the clients' need and willingness to believe in the persuasive illusions of such practitioners.

There are many comparisons to antiquity in this entry; the most relevant one relates to the preparation and conduct of a séance. It contains residue from Herodotus and Marco Polo as well as Fontenelle and Lafitau:

> One of their most vulgar means of preparing to perform their illusions is to shut themselves up in steam rooms until they break into a sweat. Thus they do not differ at all from the Pythian priestesses such as those the poets have depicted sitting on the tripod. One sees them enter into convulsions and raptures, take on various tones of voice, and perform feats that seem beyond human powers. The language they speak in their invocations has nothing in common with any savage language; and it is probable that it consists solely of unintelligible grunts produced impromptu by an overexcited imagination, sounds that these charlatans have succeeded in passing off as a divine language. They use various tones, sometimes augmenting their voice, then feigning a thin, high-pitched voice, quite similar to that of our marionettes, and one believes that it is a spirit speaking.[26]

Nor does this entry fail to mention that a kind of natural medicine was practiced as well. Although as skeptical as most eighteenth-century Europeans about Amerindian methods of artificial resuscitation for victims of drowning and choking, its author writes that the practitioners alleviated pain and cured illnesses by confounding means of bark, herbs, plants, and drugs.

A random check of entries for other words would seem to indicate that the enlightened contributors to the *Encyclopédie* were experiencing unwittingly, perhaps, some degree of cross-pollination from the writings of exploration. The entries on enthusiasm and ecstasy stand out. They speak of releasing the natural fecundity of the imagination so that it can fly high with the kind of transport Longinus suggested. Both ancient and modern pagan priests or charlatans are cited as revealing through their grimaces and contortions the ecstatic states they achieved.[27] More important, however, stress is put on their ability to transfer that state of raised consciousness to their audiences. For example, "It is in the nature of *enthusiasm* to be communicated and reproduced; it is a lively flame which gains by degrees."[28] The example given from contemporary eighteenth-century Western European culture is, amazingly enough, theater; the entry claims that enthusiasm "passes from the souls of the actors to those of the spectators." Such transference managed to bypass human rational faculties precisely because its source lay in the soul of the actor and the spectator.[29] Throughout the *Encyclopédie*, there are references to such legendary shamans as Abaris, the Scythian priest of Apollo, well versed in the arts of healing, and to Orpheus, around whom so many modern myths had already formed.[30]

With such information circulating in France, the self-proclaimed center of the Enlightenment, it is no wonder that Diderot accepted Catherine's invitation to visit Russia during the last three months of 1773. The visit turned out to be nearly disastrous for both parties. Catherine, who had grown accustomed to the social behavior of her own German countrymen as well as the Russians, could tolerate Diderot's belching and the other sounds he emitted. But she grew to abhor the sheer physicality of his habitual back slapping, knee patting, and hand grabbing. Most of all, she disliked his freely articulated questions about Siberia and about many of the strange customs observed by explorers on the academic expeditions. She was upset when he was so bold as to submit his own questionnaire to the Academy of Sciences in St. Petersburg—her academy.[31] Diderot's staunch insistence on a response appalled her. She might have advocated universal freedom of inquiry, but she certainly did not intend to allow it when it came to matters pertaining to shamanism and the prevalence of the irrational in her realm!

Thereafter, Catherine, the levelheaded, ever-astute politician, gradually drew away from Diderot and his fellow Encyclopedists. She even began a campaign of disinformation so as to blame them for sowing the seeds of social unrest and revolution. Accordingly, she resolved that any manuscripts of Diderot that would belong to her after his death would never be made public. At one point, she wrote the following to Friedrich Melchior Grimm (1723–1807), one of the intercessors in the unintentional collusion with the German complement, especially Goethe: "Acquire for me all the works of Diderot. Of course they will not get out of my hands and will not harm anyone. Send them together with the library."[32]

The German connection here is terribly significant, although it has been largely overlooked. For the young German poets and intellectuals of the 1770s, Diderot was already a living legend. When Goethe, who happened to have overlapped with twelve Russian students in Leipzig in the 1760s, reminisced in *Aus meinem Leben, Dichtung und Wahrheit* about his own experiences of those days, he wrote, "We felt great kinship with Diderot, because in everything for which the French censured him he was truly German."[33]

When Goethe transferred to the University of Strasbourg in the 1770s, it was his good friend Herder who excitedly arrived from Paris with firsthand news about Diderot and what that particular savant was up to. En route to Russia, Diderot managed to make stopovers in places where Goethe had friends who eagerly reported the gist of their conversations. In the 1780s, Goethe kept track of Diderot via the *Correspondence littéraire*, which Grimm, whose fortunes in Russia were prospering, continued to send to the court at Gotha.[34] Through that informally published series of reports, which was like a newsletter, Goethe had already become aware of a piece about Rameau's nephew, and he recorded his comments, as he did to other works from Diderot's pen. Goethe, who had been wrestling with the contradictions of aesthetic theory since his youth, acknowledged the creative surges that came during ecstasy, no matter how that ecstasy was induced, whether by the muses, alcohol, drugs, or by stimulation of the inner ear. However, he already doubted how worthwhile such uncontrolled surges might be for actual artistic productivity. At that stage in his intellectual development, Goethe warned against anything that smacked of Romanticism, anarchy, relativism, irrationality, or shamanism. He preferred distance and discipline, while stressing the necessity of observing what was being held up as the Greek ideal by the emerging media as well as the ensconced academics.

When a copy of the manuscript of Diderot's *Neveu de Rameau* turned up in Weimar in the opening years of the nineteenth century, Goethe did not fail to give it the perusal he once promised.[35] Its importance struck him as being so unquestionable that he agreed to translate it into German. The objective was to publish, if not a dual-language edition, then one in German, quickly followed by a French one. In preparing his notes, Goethe referred to some of the same travel reports about Russia that Diderot himself must have used.[36] Diderot's work—conceived in the 1760s and revised in the 1770s, after his trip to Russia—first became public in Goethe's German translation in 1805. A manuscript in Diderot's own hand did not come to light until 1891.

Le neveu de Rameau is a satirical dialogue or dramatic conversation that touches on nearly all the burning aesthetic issues of the eighteenth century. Focusing on the creative process and the transference of its power to audiences, Diderot brilliantly synthesized his thinking on the arts with his knowledge about philosophy, science, and anthropology. Much of what he wrote was also taken up in his *Paradoxe sur le comédien*, another dialogue conceived around the same time and handled in similar ways. These dialogues juxtaposed two extremes in the theory of performance. One kind of performer upheld enough rationality to distance his own personality from the role he was playing, and thus preserve his own self, while the other kind of performer empathized so totally with the role that he got carried away by it and thereby lost his own self. In *Le neveu de Rameau*, Moi stands for down-to-earth Europeanism—that is, philosophy or truth, mathematics, rationality, coolness, calmness, common sense, and male adulthood. Lui, on the other hand, was shaped to represent things shamanic: acting or illusion, flights of fancy or genius, irrationality, heated enthusiasm, emotional agitation, frivolity, and androgynous childhood.

Diderot repeatedly used what had become the conventional information about shamanism to shape Lui's argument as well as his character. At the beginning of the dialogue, we learn that Lui is an eccentric, inherently different from other human beings. Unlike them, he is described as a case study in extreme contradictions. He exhibits very good sense at times, although he is usually given to unrepentant lunacy. The thrust of his discourse is as often lofty as it is base. Like shamans the world over, he is capable of sustained fasting, yet when the opportunity to gorge himself arises, he avails himself of that opportunity with great fervor. Throughout, he maintains extraordinary control over his own physical responses and their influence on his mind: "He is endowed with a strong constitution, a special warmth of imagination, and an unusual power of lung."[37] He also is described, like the shamans, as being double-jointed or agile enough to assume postures that resemble those of marionettes rather than human beings. In the *Paradoxe*, by way of comparison, Diderot wrote: "A great actor is also a most ingenious puppet, and his strings are held by the poet, who at each line indicates the true form he must take."[38]

The nephew shares many views with the shamanism of the travel reports. He recognizes sexuality as part of the human condition, mocking those who hypocritically uphold chastity and, as a procurer, aiding those who seek natural fulfillment. Bloodlines and ancestry are also important: "And then there is heredity. My father's blood is the same as my uncle's; my blood is like my father's. The paternal molecule was hard and obtuse, and like a primordial germ it has affected all the rest."[39] When asked about his relationship to his own son, Lui responds by fondly referring to him as a savage: "Do I love the little savage? I am crazy about him!"[40]

Like the aboriginal shamans, Rameau's nephew claims to be very valuable to society because he knows things no one else knows. Moi seems to agree when he likens Lui's activities to those performed by shamans in non-European societies: "If such a character makes his appearance in some circle, he is like a grain of yeast that ferments and restores to each of us a part of his native individuality. He shakes and stirs us up, makes us praise or blame, smokes out the truth, discloses the worthy and unmasks the rascals. It is then that the sensible man keeps his ears open and sorts out his company."[41] The nephew does not hesitate to emphasize his own unique ability to provide socially beneficial recreation: "My species is scarce, very scarce. Now that they've lost me, what do they do? They're as sad as dogs. I am an inexhaustible store of silliness. Every minute I said things that reduced them to tears from laughter. I was worth to them a whole lunatic asylum."[42]

In addition to the multiple personalities Diderot has Lui assume, he also has him admit to being "an ignoramus, a fool, a lunatic, a lazy, impudent, greedy good-for-nothing—what we Burgundians call a n'er-do-well—a blackguard, in short."[43] His assessment of Moi's reactions contains one of many pertinent double-entendres: "You've always taken an interest in me because I'm a good fellow whom you despise at bottom but who amuses you."[44] Others have to do with apes and demons and fakers. The nephew also likes to portray himself as a jester who experiences a certain something inside himself that speaks to and through him. Diderot's *Paradoxe* took up that idea and further distinguished types of men: "My friend, there are three types—Nature's man, the poet's man, the actor's man. Nature's is less great than the poet's, the poet's less great than the great actor's, which is the most exalted of all. This last climbs on the shoulders of the one before him and shuts himself up inside a great basket-work figure of which he is the soul."[45]

The important role of deception in human survival comes up again and again. Early in the dialogue, Lui categorically states that "nothing is more useful to the nations of the earth than lies, nothing more harmful than the truth."[46] His own tricks are subtle as well as not so subtle, but he refuses to consider them vile because he thinks they belong naturally to his profession.[47] As in any kind of curing or consoling, the circumstances of the case at the moment determine the strategy selected for success: "I'm never false if my interest is to speak true and never true if I see the slightest use of being false."[48]

The nephew speaks warmly of drunken orgies, with their possibilities for physical enjoyment, especially sexual release. As in native séances, during which intoxicated participants became enthralled by the shaman's tale, Diderot has him say "we will drink and make up tales and develop all sorts of whims and vices. It will be delightful."[49] Alluding to the lycanthropy and cannibalism reported about some primitive tribes, Lui states, "We devour one another like wolves when the snow has long been on the ground. Like tigers we tear apart whatever succeeds."[50] Such violence, he insists, needs to be carried over to European artistic expression in order to transform it from the deadly dullness of careful producers, like his uncle, to the truly sublime: "We want the animal cry of the passions to dictate the melodic line, and the expressive moments must come close together."[51] Lui condones wickedness and great criminality as long as they achieve sublimity, even going so far as to hope that Moi will place him "in the great tradition of the master scoundrels."[52]

A number of further correspondences with shamanism as known to the eighteenth century need to be mentioned as well. There is the reference to the process of religious conversion, whereby foreign gods are placed next to native idols. Then there are the idols that Moi notices the nephew form, seemingly unconsciously, while they speak about patricide, incest, and basic problems of human psychology: "He seemed to be kneading a ball of dough within his fingers and smiling at the ridiculous shapes he was imparting to it. This done, he made a gesture as if throwing the outlandish idol far from him."[53] Rameau's nephew helps bring this scene to its end by remarking that he felt nature had put his self into the bag of idols and that he had invented a thousand ways for regaining possession of himself.[54] Diderot also does not fail to have him mention flying high, although not high enough to reach whatever heaven was inhabited by those cranes long associated with tales of archaic Scythian shamanism. A pantomime— so often used dramatically to punctuate the end of scenes in the dialogue—has the nephew moving like an arrow, one of the shamanic vehicles that has been standard since the mythical Abaris, if not since the shamans or cave painters at Lascaux and elsewhere.

Furthermore, Diderot's dialogue demonstrates the incipient convergence in the enlightened Western European mind of the characteristics of the shaman with those of what was evolving into the genius. Both are personally difficult, yet socially necessary. Both are labeled as outcasts at best, or lunatics at worst.[55] Both ignore the rules, strictures, and obstacles set up by the more conventional brethren who outnumber them. Both are given to wild flights of fancy. Diderot even has Lui express a hope that Moi attributed to him a degree of genius. Then he has Lui state, "I agree with you. But you'd be surprised how little I think of methods and rules. The man who needs a textbook can't go far. Geniuses seldom read, and they experiment a great deal; they are their own masters. Consider Caesar, Turenne, Vauban, the Marquise de Tencin, her brother the Cardinal, and his secretary, Abbé Trublet. And then Bouret? Who ever gave Bouret lessons? Nobody. Nature creates the superior man."[56]

The influence of reports about those shamanic practices still operative in the eighteenth century would seem most evident in the various episodes of the nephew's pantomiming, portraying, making believe, or just plain playing. His soul, which in one instance is described as beginning to divide itself between opposing motives, somehow never stops doing so. The spiritual subdivision accelerates and compounds. We read of the sweat, the convulsions, and the rapture. Interesting if unsurprising parallels are to be found once again in the *Paradoxe*: "Who can tell whence these traits have their being? They are a sort of inspiration. They come when the man of genius is hovering between nature and his sketch of it, and keeping a watchful eye on both. The beauty of inspiration, the chance hits of which his work is full, and of which the sudden appearance startles himself, have an importance, a success, a sureness very different from that belonging to the first fling. Cool reflection must bring the fury of enthusiasm to its bearings."[57]

Like any successful performer, Rameau's nephew prides himself in making his audience succumb to the reality of his public performance, yet he not only cherishes but also protects the mysterious processes involved. The contagious enthusiasm that results from his performing is mentioned again and again, as are his croaking voice and his agile body. The most striking example of Diderot's absorption of the shamanic literature occurs not in the music lesson, not in the discussions of theater, not in the references to the many Parisian operatic quarrels. It occurs in the Café de la Régence when Rameau is gripped by the spirit of his uncle's work at the opera. At first, the nephew paces up and down, humming some arias. Then he begins singing louder and louder as the spirit takes greater hold of him and deprives him of his wits. He imitates the voices, the gait, and the gestures of several characters, changing his mood in quick succession.

The people in the café are joined by passers-by whom the commotion has attracted. They guffaw at first, but slowly they begin paying attention until he wins them over completely:

> But he noticed nothing, he kept on, in the grip of mental possession, an enthusiasm so close to madness that it seemed doubtful whether he would recover. He might have to be put into a cab and be taken to a padded cell. While singing fragments of Jomelli's *Lamentations*, he reproduced with incredible precision, fidelity, and warmth the most beautiful passages of each scene. That magnificent recitative in which Jeremiah describes the desolation of Jerusalem, he drenched in tears which drew

their like from every onlooker. His art was complete—delicacy of voice, expressive strength, true sorrow. He dwelt on the places where the musician had shown himself a master. If he left the vocal part, it was to take up the instrumental, which he abandoned suddenly to return to the voice, linking them so as to preserve the connection and unity of the whole, gripping our souls and keeping them suspended in the most singular state of being that I have ever experienced.[58]

This performer manages to enchant the spectators who had at first mocked him, to transmit his enthusiasm to them, and to unite them in a grand tribal totality: "He whistled piccolos and warbled traverse flutes, singing, shouting, waving about like a madman, being in himself dancer and ballerina, singer and prima donna, all of them together and the whole orchestra, the whole theater; then redividing himself into twenty separate roles, running, stopping, glowing at the eyes like one possessed, frothing at the mouth."[59] Diderot strikes at the very heart of the paradox when he writes that Rameau "was night and its gloom, shade and silence—for silence itself is depictable in sound."[60]

The description of Rameau coming out of his trancelike experience, or crashing, contains ideas that also were repeated in subsequent theoretical writings dealing with the highly sensitive, creative performing artist:

Worn out, exhausted, like a man emerging from a deep sleep or a prolonged reverie, he stood motionless, dumb, petrified. He kept looking around him like a man who has lost his way and wants to know where he is. He waited for returning strength and wits, wiping his face with an absentminded gesture. Just as a man who on waking should see a large number of people around his bed and not remember or be able to conceive what he had done, he began by asking: "What is it, gentlemen? Why do you laugh? You look surprised—what is it?" Then he added: "This, this merits the name of music. There is your true musician."[61]

Diderot's *Le neveu de Rameau* clearly shows that the performing artist was beginning to be considered the shaman of higher civilization—that is, eighteenth-century Western European civilization.

CHAPTER SIX

Herder on the Artist as the
Shaman of Western Civilization

INFORMATION about shamanism proliferated to such a great degree in the eighteenth century that Johann Gottfried Herder's (1744–1803) steadily expanding interest seems to have been inevitable. He immersed himself in the literature of travel in order to learn about the effects of geography, climate, and diet on human physiology and psychology. He also probed possible connections to mythology and comparative religions, as well as aesthetics and theories of performance. All the while he, like many of the scientists doing fieldwork, gave constant attention to methodology. That attention, in addition to his personal interaction with investigators, helped clarify aims and methods in such a way as to create a sounder scientific basis for the emergent study of man as a social being.

From early on, Herder subjected those publishing any kind of travel literature to the strictest scrutiny. In one piece, he bemoaned their lack of both wisdom and aptitude: "It is even more regrettable that travel observations are so seldom made and recorded by wise people and those with understanding of their fellow man."[1] Their unwitting eurocentricity was as worrisome to him as their lack of personal sensitivity. In another essay, he roundly criticized their failure to recognize themselves as products of a particular kind of society composed of certain belief systems that had grown out of specific local conditions of nature. He explained that natives from other parts of the world seemed strange or foolish to the European "because they have ways of thinking and tastes different from the ones his mama, his dear nurse, and his school buddies implanted in him."[2] Herder insisted the European cosmographers' projections of spurious creatures served to enrich only works of fiction, like *Gulliver's Travels*.[3] Otherwise, they mightily hindered scientific investigation. Equally harmful to the advance of knowledge were those Europeans who had no historical awareness whatsoever. Their smug self-centeredness produced the kind of feelings of superiority that admitted only their own epoch, their own taste, and their own way of doing things. Any deviation from those norms they labeled inferior or subhuman.

The worst offenders, Herder wrote, were the French. They were so convinced of their cultural perfection that they viewed anything else as representing some degree of degeneration. Herder repeatedly cited the name Fontenelle to epitomize such purblind parochialism and intellectual bigotry. In one essay about contemporary German literature, Herder went so far as to write that Fontenelle "saw nothing in his own nation, did not want to see anything, and finally, was not capable of seeing anything else even in old shepherds. He pictured what he saw and wanted to see: habits and associations and civility and courtly manners that, in the last analysis, could only please a Frenchman but must be despicable and loathsome to a Greek."[4] In other essays, Herder did more than merely question Fontenelle's credibility. He called him a flighty *bel esprit*, or he considered him a self-proclaimed arbiter of fashion, or he counted him among the monotonous "authors of poetic handbooks." Elsewhere, Herder, like Kant, characterized Fontenelle as being so deficient in both intellectual rigor and philosophical depth that he could write books for no one except frothy French females.[5]

The English fared no better when it came to sloppy scholarship, another factor Herder considered deleterious to the whole intellectual enterprise. His review of a German translation of a book dealing with observations about explorations of the Near East stated outright that the author missed the point because he worked deductively from predetermined notions. Although many travel reports had been surveyed, it had been done "according to the servile spirit of our own prejudice."[6] After recommending several significant reports that had been omitted from the discussion, Herder summarized his evaluation: "On the part of the author and translator, a tiresome contribution to the dearth of results and to the pedantic spirit of our century."[7]

Herder also disavowed Newton, Leibniz, and anything else that smacked of scientific determinism because he strongly opposed reducing perception according to theories based solely in mathematics or logic. While he did not doubt that measurements and statistics could be meaningful, he worried about their facile abuse. By definition, he thought, they allowed only for certain kinds of simplistic evidence, and, he insisted, there were many more variables to be taken into consideration. Reality for him was as heteromorphic as mankind's ability to perceive it and deal with it. Throughout his life, Herder advocated developing a methodology for advancing human knowledge that humbly took cognizance of as many variables as possible. Herder believed human psychology itself warranted closer attention. He demanded greater intellectual respect for the writings of thinkers of the past who had ventured forth to explore the universally documented mysteries as well as their seemingly magical manifestations. Withstanding pressures from what had already become hard-core mathematical, scientific professionalism, Herder, the theologian and philosopher, warmly defended the intentions of Renaissance investigators who probed into the recesses of magic in the hope of finding clues that would reveal the secrets of nature. Along with Pico della Mirandola, Agrippa von Nettesheym, and Paracelsus, he thought mythology, poetry, animism, and natural history (*Naturkunde*) had all been intertwined for eons.[8] Those in the seventeenth century who persisted with such research despite harassment also interested Herder. He occasionally cited, for example, the physician Robert Fludd (1574–1637) and the mystic Jakob Böhme (1575–1624). Herder even bestowed a degree of legitimacy on their work by continuing to support the possibility that the superstitions of the past might provide the scientific facts of the future. Herder continued to seek an acceptable holistic approach that would not only include but also explain the effects of matters having to do with diet, sexuality, spirituality, climate, and geography.

The writings that demonstrate Herder's avid theoretical concern about scientific methodology began to appear in the 1770s, just around the time he realized there was something very important to be learned from shamanism as still practiced in the more remote parts of the world. He pondered the validity of the monogenetic theory, writing in one essay, "One should not take exception to the fact that all nations stole these treasures from one people; that one must have got everything from the Orient; that all streams originate out of one great source. This hypothesis has too much that is arbitrary."[9] While seeking to identify historical cycles and philosophical correspondences, Herder emphasized the importance of induction, comparative approaches, and cultural humility, or at least restraint.

Herder himself demonstrated that intellectual stance in *Abhandlung über den Ursprung der Sprache*, the essay that won the 1770 prize granted by the Royal Academy of Sciences in Berlin. To challenge the theory of the divine origin of human language, he combined information gained from his wide reading in the literature of exploration with his knowledge of mythology, physiology, and psychology. His opening sentences set the tone: "Already as a beast the human being had language. All the intense, and the most intense among the intense, all the painful sensations of his body, all the vehement passions of his soul manifested themselves incommunicably in outcry, in tones, in wild unarticulated sounds."[10] The connection of those sounds to the excitability of the nervous system was, Herder wrote, found in all animals—

an idea similar to the *cri animal* Diderot had Rameau mention.[11] It was a law of nature. Human comprehension of that natural language decreased, however, as civilization developed a separate language of arbitrary signs. The more uncivilized, or, to use Herder's euphemism, unpolished the language was, the more it relied on natural tones. The contemporary natives of Brazil and the Caribbean, like the primordial inhabitants of Siberia, communicated through howls, grunts, yelling, and doleful accents. European researchers did not even have to go so far afield. "Our small remainder of uncivilized people in Europe, Estonians and Lapps, etc., often have sounds just as half-articulated and untransmittable through writing as the Hurons and the Peruvians."[12]

Residual traces remained even in the psyche of the most highly polished Western European: "So many sorts of sensibility lie dormant in our nature, also so many tones."[13] Consequently, the natives understood the needs and reactions of the animals they associated with most closely, like the hunter with his hounds. Explorers also often confessed feeling profoundly moved by the lamentations, whoops, and incantations of the aborigines they were observing.[14]

The language of natural tones was not, Herder maintained, the source from which the language of arbitrary signs developed. That was a language consciously invented by human beings exercising their rational faculties. They first named animals according to the sounds those animals emitted. Herder explained: "Since all nature resounds, there is nothing more natural for sensual man than that nature lives, it speaks, it acts. That primitive saw the tall tree with its magnificent top and was full of wonder: the top rustled! That is active, moving divinity! The primitive prostrates himself and worships!"[15] Herder confirmed what many modern as well as ancient writers had already said about poetry being older than prose. Most of his examples were culled from what was contained in the travel reports, but he offered others as well, namely the mystics, enthusiasts, and convulsives who combined accent and rhythm with sensual imagery and vivid metaphor to convey their nearly inexpressible experiences. Even as an individual language became more regulated, it remained, Herder insisted, "always a species of song, as the accents of so many primitives attest."[16]

As a creature dependent on family, Herder continued, man not only invented the means to communicate, but also developed applications for that means, which provided still stronger social bonds:

> In almost all small nations of all continents, as rude as they may be, there are lays about their forefathers, songs about the deeds of their ancestors that are the treasure of their language and history and poetry, their wisdom and their moral support, their instruction and their games and

dances. The Greeks sang of their Argonauts, of Hercules and Bacchus, of heroes and victors over Troy. The Celts sang of the progenitors of their tribes, of Fingal and Ossian! Among the Peruvians and North Americans, among those on the Caribbean islands and the Marianas, this linguistic source still prevails in the songs of their clans and forefathers, as do in almost all parts of the world father and mother have similar names.[17]

Herder's "Auszug aus einem Briefwechsel über Ossian und die Lieder alter Völker," which appeared in *Von deutscher Art und Kunst* in 1773, studied the implications of such methods still further. The volume was conceived around the time when Herder had excitedly arrived in Strasbourg after meetings with Diderot and others in Paris who rejected the neoclassical code upheld by the aristocratic establishment of France. The essay demonstrates Herder's attempt to peel away the numerous accretions of Western European civilization and to clarify his own position, much as the explorers did in their prefaces. He claimed to be constantly alert to possible signs of cultural bias in his own reactions to the unknown. He blamed the ethnocentricity of most intellectuals for producing misconceptions and stereotypes that then became dangerously self-perpetuating: "Woe, however, even to the philosopher of the human race and its customs to whom his own scene is the only one and who always mistakes the first as also the worst!"[18] Well aware of the long tradition of cribbing and lying among travel writers, he indicated precisely how reliable he considered the particular evidence he offered. If he assured his readers that he had had the opportunity to witness one thing, then he just as openly stated that another was secondhand or thirdhand.[19]

Herder insisted that folk poetry was not only admissible anthropological evidence, but unimpeachable as such. Those songs still performed by living people all over the planet, he argued, were vestiges of the prehistoric past that could reveal much about the pace of cultural evolution as well as about the multifarious combinations of components operative in different climates and geographical areas.[20] Such songs also seemed to contain psychological features common to mankind in general. Despite avowals of methodological openness and purity, Herder rejected erudition and theoretical abstraction as goals in themselves. He wanted to extract some practical use from the knowledge gained by studying the songs of the natural folk. He hoped they would somehow help liberate European, and more specifically German, culture from the stultification caused by authoritarian systematization and determinism.

That abiding, lifelong hope encouraged him to recommend researching travel literature for information about Amerindian song, which, he thought, represented the type of instinctual poetry produced by human beings at a certain stage in their cultural development. In an essay printed in 1795, he wrote that the customs and mores of the Five Nations constituted the best mirror for showing "how, with a particular mode of education, poetry could become so great and strong through a natural instinct without any art or rules." Of all the reports he had gotten to know, he still singled out that by Lafitau as "a compendium of the ethics and poetics of the primitives."[21] What they produced he called comparable to the Edda and to recent discoveries in Celtic and ancient Scottish.

When Herder's collection *Alte Volkslieder* appeared in 1774, it, too, was interspersed with many comments involving approaches to perception, description, and evaluation of the unknown or unfamiliar. Herder liked to stress that his age was privileged to know about many more peoples than the ancients would have dreamed possible. In addition to the usual selections from the Greeks and Romans, he included songs by peoples all over the world, from Madagascar to Lapland and from Kamchatka to Greenland. They were gleaned from explorers' reports and manuscripts as well as other publications. Their degree of trustworthiness was conscientiously mentioned in his commentary, along with bibliographical cross-references and evaluations.

The introduction to the fourth book took up ideas Herder had steadily been refining, and it articulated them with still greater precision. His main concern was how Europeans proceeded to acquaint themselves with peoples of other parts of the earth, whom he preferred to view as "our brothers in human nature." He protested that purportedly civilized Christians tended to deny them any trace of humanity and concentrated only on "what their land produces and how they can be still better subjugated, used, tormented, managed, and ruined."[22] They were not, he asserted, subhuman creatures who could be indiscriminately used as objects; they were human beings with language, souls, and feelings. That lamentable confusion persisted, according to him, because of grave methodological problems. He rejected the extrinsic approaches used by many explorers and missionaries, and what he termed the European fools racing through. The distortions they perpetrated were adumbrated by the ever-popular filtrations of travel accounts, with their "engravings of caricatures and reports that match those engravings."[23] Taken together, Herder thought, they created a totally false, yet unfortunately indelible, image in the European mind. The confusion could only be resolved by gathering and quickly disseminating more factual information about what native peoples produced.

That information was to be gained most readily, Herder believed, from factors common to unpolished nations all over the past and present world: "Language, tone, movement, portrayal, proportion, dance: and that alone which tied everything together—song." Song was such an interminably rich resource because, he wrote, "whatever their song might be, it exists, and it is for the most part a gathering point of all their knowledge, religion, spiritual stirrings, the peculiarities of their former ages, the joys and sorrows of their lives."[24]

Another of Herder's pleas to end the ongoing methodological folly revealed his fervent wish that others would continue his work and make more songs available. It also alluded to the socializing effect of song, something he rarely failed to note:

> If only the poor, miserable attempt of this book could awaken something more: that a person would produce with some completeness the whole, true natural history of nations from their own monuments. That person would collect the folk songs, mythologies, fairy tales, and biases having strong influence on their character. He would not himself speak, but rather let the sources speak. Without always asking what something would be good for, he would present it, whether good or not, without beautification. He would present it as it is, instead of embellishing it with the cape of religion or classical taste and thereby deforming it. But he would do so with fidelity, joy, and love.[25]

Herder's methodological concerns converged when he discussed those responsible for originating, performing, and promulgating songs intended to assuage personal fears and engender tribal unity. Again, he proposed that the expressively inhibited culture of Europe might learn much from studying the folk songs' naturalness, liveliness, and pertinence for survival. He viewed the Greenlanders and the Indians of the Americas as living examples of the stages in which human beings developed their societies before ultimately vanishing. Finally, their songs showed him they shared certain characteristics with the known forms of Greek civilization, in addition to Old Norse and Celtic. According to Herder, the necessary focal point was always the shaman, who was able to summon powers that were believed to control nature. No matter what the circumstances, Orpheus was and would inevitably remain the epitome of the shaman.[26] This was one of Herder's earliest applications of the Germanicized version of the Tungus word:

> Do you believe that Orpheus, the great Orpheus, eternally worthy of mankind, the poet in whose inferior remnants the entire soul of nature lives, that he was originally something other than the noblest shaman that

Thrace, at the time also northern Tatary, could have seen? And so on. If you want to get to know the Greek Tyrtaeus, you should look where there is a war celebration with martial song and the singing leader of the North Americans! Do you want to see ancient Greek comedy at its inception? It is still completely as Horace describes with the dregs and dance in the satyr plays and mummeries of those same primitives there![27]

Here and elsewhere in reference to the shaman, Herder used the German word *edel* to convey more than is rendered by the English word "noble." He meant genuinely human in the sense of humane, just, helpful, magnanimous.[28]

In another work published in 1774, *Aelteste Urkunde des Menschengeschlechts*, Herder strove to make sense of the resources from past times that had survived. Once more his consciousness of methodology and point of view was strongly apparent. The reliability of the evidence he was processing always came into question. While some was discounted as hearsay, other evidence was classified as a product of "an estimable compiler of relations."[29] Herder emphasized the fallaciousness of reductionist approaches: "So how far separate is all ancient history from the dainty fiction of the philosopher who philosophizes from one hypothesis!"[30] He accused both English and French researchers of having motives other than "the love of truth and literary justice." The former were as diverted by patriotism as the latter were by their desire to construct reality "according to Parisian footprints."[31]

Herder's intention with this work was to debunk the demystifiers, like Fontenelle and Voltaire, by uncovering shamanism as a factor crucial in the formation of all human societies. He followed in the footsteps of Justus Möser (1720–1794), who had frequently defended superstition as necessary for surviving the harsh vicissitudes of life. So fundamental was it, Möser had written, that neither the missioners, nor the explorers, nor the scientists, nor the men of the Enlightenment could manage to purge it: "The roots they were not able to destroy."[32] Similarly, Herder considered shamans responsible for creating order out of chaos so that their brethren could cope with nature as well as themselves. The shamans were the originators of magic, music, medicine, mathematics, laws or codes of behavior, writing—all the things that contributed to beneficial social frameworks. As in most human endeavors, Herder argued, the risk of failure was always high, as was the chance for fraudulence. The innumerable songs that continued to honor shamans, however, demonstrated to him the unwavering awe in which they had been held for milleniums. That in itself was enough proof to preclude classifying shamans as worthless, selfserving cheats. The rationalists of the Enlightenment were, in

Herder's opinion, reacting much as Catherine the Great did when she worked to obliterate all traces of shamanism in her empire. Incapable of dealing with a phenomenon beyond their purview, they denied the shaman's role in the history of the evolution of the human race, or they attempted to construct that history according to their own peculiar prejudices.[33]

Herder preferred the exact opposite. He expended the effort to obtain the available facts and, puzzling as they might have been, tried to do them justice according to what appeared to him to be their own assumptions. As a result, he wrote that human cave dwellers had been so sensually oriented that images and actions composed their primary as well as secondary means of communication. When they wanted to record it, they therefore could come up only with pictographs and hieroglyphs.[34] They easily remembered information conveyed concretely, vividly, and rhythmically. The earliest songs, usually performed communally, were for purification purposes or otherwise to reconcile offended spirits. Still later songs served to impress cataclysmic changes as well as the deeds of forebears on their memories, thereby giving them a certain sense of identity and continuity. Dance and mimicry were essential elements in all such performances, or sessions of acting-out, for their songs, Herder elsewhere wrote, always belonged "more to living action than to dead painting."[35]

As early mankind began devising megalithic monuments, sacred pillars, and the like, other kinds of songs were made to commemorate those events and what they stood for. Eventually, an alphabet was invented by one of their latter-day shamans, who always retained control over the magic words, charms, curses, and spells: "The entire natural language was a sacred dialect of the priests. The Nordic Edda had its own hallowed dictionary."[36] Herder often pointed out that the shamans considered mythological by his contemporary world, like Pythagoras and Orpheus, actually came chronologically very late.[37] At that, the works attributed to them were most likely written down by still later shamans or poets. Even so, Herder maintained here and also in his defense of James Macpherson's (1736–1796) Ossian, they remained genuine because they reflected the real concerns of people from earlier times.[38] Forgery was therefore neither a relevant concept nor a possibility.

Information about Orpheus enabled Herder to propose a working sketch of shamanism among peoples moving into historical times and becoming, as he was wont to call them, more polished nations. He considered all Orphic matters reverberations of barbaric echoes emanating from the Egyptian mysteries that had originated in the impenetrable past of the Orient.[39] The hymns, he explained, all dealt with cosmogony and were nothing less than "dismembered limbs of the ur-song of all beings" that happened to have been made up in Thracian caves.[40] He described them as "doxologies of ancient sacred symbols: received and disseminated vestiges of archaic fundamental ideas of natural philosophy and mythology, which were, so to speak, litanized and liturgized into hexameters."[41]

As far as the name Orpheus was concerned, Herder continued to think of it as a kind of flag deployed to stimulate culturally local memories of various shamanic achievements from the remotest European past. Using the word *Wundermann* (miracle worker), yet another eighteenth-century German synonym for shaman, Herder offered a biographical summation:

Orpheus, the prophet and lawgiver and designer of Greek antiquity— what a miracle worker! Just exactly the same as the Egyptian Hermes. Just the same titles, writings, and inventions that are ascribed to the former. The letters, the music, the lyre with seven strings, the natural history, magic, and prophecy, the astrology and cosmology, particularly, however, theology, poetry, and law—all of this is found again with Orpheus.

As it was with Hermes, so must it be with Orpheus![42]

In what were yet earlier stages of the evolution of human cultures, Herder contended, still other names were invoked. There were, for example, the Egyptian Thoth, the Phoenician Sanchuniathon, and the Persian Zoroaster.[43] Such a plethora of information about those shamans existed that Herder mused whether their ancestry could not possibly be traced nearly all the way back to Adam and the Garden of Eden.[44] He, however, did not attempt to do so.

Herder persisted in his belief that poetry, or better, performed song, touched the human psyche in such a way as to release something into the soma that subdued rage, relaxed stress, and enabled individuals to tolerate each other's whims and foibles. It is almost uncanny that the twentieth century's highly technological research into the physiological workings of the brain explains the theta waves as being induced by images, poetry, music, and performance to help regulate the body's immunological system.[45] Herder firmly believed that the shamans' performing talents had produced human civilizations and allowed them to develop. Even in the last decade of his life, Herder was associating civilization or humanity with Orpheus, the shaman.[46] In the thirty-first letter of *Briefe zu Beförderung der Humanität*, published in 1794, he maintained, "The Greeks did not have the word humanity. However, from the time Orpheus made human beings out of beasts through the sound of his lyre, the concept of this word was the art of the muses."[47] More importantly, Herder believed such shamanic talents continued to provide precisely what it was that human society needed to survive. All civilizations had shamans, as did all levels and epochs of those civilizations. Shamanism seemed to Herder to be as ubiquitous as human life itself.

With such ideas in mind, Herder expanded his investigations still further in the late 1770s. The essay that appeared in the widely circulating *Deutsches Museum* in 1777, "Von Ähnlichkeit der mittlern englischen und deutschen Dichtkunst, nebst Verschiednem, das daraus folget," compared the likes of Chaucer, Spenser, and Shakespeare with the magically empowered skalds and bards of earlier ages in northern Europe. Herder even went so far as to postulate a line of descent from the most archaic shamans of the East to those like Orpheus and then on to the Romans, and from them to the troubadours and minstrels of the European Middle Ages.[48] All their creations, he insisted, were not only aesthetic monuments but also cultural documents. In Herder's opinion, the two could not be separated. They simply belonged together: "Their songs are the archives of their people, the treasure of their knowledge and religion, their theogony and cosmogonies of the deeds of their forefathers and of the events of their history, reproduction of their heart, image of their domestic life in joy and sorrow, at their bridal bed and grave. Nature gave them one consolation against the many misfortunes that afflict them and a substitute for many of the so-called happinesses that we enjoy, that is, love of freedom, indolence, ecstasy and song."[49]

After surveying what he knew of interpretations by Gotthold Ephraim Lessing (1729–1781), Ewald Christian von Kleist (1715–1759), and Heinrich Wilhelm von Gerstenberg (1737–1823), Herder presented a summary of his own thinking about the subject at that time: "Also the Greeks were once, as it were, primitives, and even in the flowering of their most beautiful era there is much more nature than the blinking eye of the scholiast and classicist finds."[50] He bemoaned the fact that rationalistically oriented European scholars continued to overlook such obvious, generally available evidence about shamanism: "Tyrtaeus's war songs are Greek ballads, and when Arion, Orpheus, and Amphion lived, they were noble Greek shamans."[51]

Like many of his contemporaries, Herder continued to reflect on the relationship of poetry, psychology, and physiology. In *Ueber die Würkung der Dichtkunst auf die Sitten der Völker in alten und neuen Zeiten,* composed in 1778, he suggested that language was the channel used by the poet, the shaman, the mediator, the channeler, to allow human beings to experience, in their own souls, nature or those things greater than themselves. The more open—that is, physiologically receptive—

the individual, the more profound his experience would be. Collective participation increased the profundity of the poetic experience since more warmth was generated. Herder wrote, "The more it has an effect on people in crowds who receive their impressions as a community and who communicate those impressions to one another like reflected rays of sunlight, all the greater the increase in warmth and illumination springing forth."[52] Such psychological manipulation occurred more readily in cultures at their earliest stages of development when subjects were so easily manipulated. Again, he did not fail to mention the ever-present possibility of the abuse of power, in which case medicine quickly became poison.

Herder's fascination with such demonstrable experiences stimulated him to give greater attention to reincarnation and metempsychosis, or the transmigration of souls. His *Vom Erkennen und Empfinden der menschlichen Seele: Bemerkungen und Träume*, published in 1778, argued that three major sources provided information about the individual human psyche: "Biographies, observations of physicians and friends, prophecies of poets."[53] He recommended studying great poets like Homer and Shakespeare, for they seemed to possess an inherent comprehension of human beings and their imaginations, which consisted not only of images but also of unfathomable tones, words, signs, and feelings for which there were often no names. While acknowledging contemporary medical researches, he warned that psychology, especially the study of the mad, must never be divorced from physiology. He was concerned because he believed that "we feel only what our nerves give us; only thereupon and therefrom are we able to think."[54]

Herder was particularly interested in those capacities with which children were born. He maintained that at the moment of birth their dispositions and imaginations were already as inherently drafted as the future growth of their limbs and organs. He even went so far as to state that the human fetus received signals contributing to the development of its imagination while still in the maternal womb. Herder rejected the theory of tabula rasa outright, for he thought there was enough evidence proving that much was inherited, and not just from parents. He surmised—as Lessing was to do in *Die Erziehung des Menschengeschlechts* (1780)—there were always some vague transmissions from other existences: "Soft tones sound. They seem to come, as it were, from another world. Here and there stirs an impulse of reflection, passion, feeling, which prophesies a whole cosmos of slumbering forces, a complete living human being. And it is, it seems to me, the most insipid opinion that ever entered the paper head of a pedant that all human souls are the same and that they all come into the world as plain empty slates."[55] One of Herder's other statements mentioned a pool of potentialities in each and every individual. Its imagery notwithstanding, it suggested suspicions were beginning to emerge that there might be something future generations would identify as genes: "In the child there is a fountainhead of diverse lives, still only covered by vapor and haze. A bud blossoms in which the full tree, the complete flower, is embedded."[56]

Another matter broached in this essay was the tendency to associate reports about shamans with what was becoming the theory of genius. Herder humbly confessed to ignorance, "because I know nothing less on earth than what a genius is, or whether the genius may be designated a he, a she, or an it."[57] Once again he blamed France and what he thought of as its institutionalized prejudices for categorizing even newly acquired, exciting facts and manipulating them for purposes of cultural aggrandizement, so as to be able to present France as abounding in geniuses. Herder's own countrymen upset him even more by allowing themselves to be lulled so easily into accepting such nonsense that the gender and pronunciation of a word became the major concern. Herder actually lamented that "'Schenie'" had won out over "Genie."[58]

Herder's publications of the 1780s increasingly pitted the shaman, whom he considered universal and natural, against the genius, whom he continued to view as a creation of the French. If he had in the preceding decades worked to lay open the genealogy of the shaman, he now concentrated strictly on the line of descent into historical times to his present. In 1782, the influential journal *Der Teutsche Merkur*, edited by Christoph Martin Wieland (1733–1813), brought out "Das Land der Seelen, Ein Fragment." It contended that all cultures posit at certain points in their evolution a life beyond earthly existence, whether called Elysium, the Isles of the Blest, Walhalla, or Paradise. Explorers' reports supplied Herder with songs and tales exemplifying metempsychosis and round-trip journeys to those other worlds. Lafitau had recorded an Amerindian story about a young man so despondent over the premature death of his sister that he decided to rescue her from the Great Beyond. Equipped with suggestions and appurtenances from a shaman, he made the perilous voyage and gained the protection of the king of the spirit world against the threats of the queen of darkness. When the young man returned to the living, he prematurely opened the container in which he had captured his sister's spirit, and it promptly flew back, forever lost to him. Herder called him another Orpheus.[59] Tales could be found closer to home as well, especially among the inhabitants of the Baltic coast, who were notorious for having long retained their heathen beliefs. There was a haunting one from 1763 about an adolescent Lithuanian peasant girl who dreamed her way into the realm of the spirits and liked it there so much that she wanted to stay permanently. Following the advice she had received, she went into the forest on her return to the living and leaned against a tree. Shortly after her family found her, she ran away again. Three months later they noticed her at a tree and touched her, thereby consummating her permanent death.

Herder's explanation of such phenomena revealed an awareness of the underground movement as well as a startling appreciation for the influence of psychological and physiological matters, particularly sexuality:

> A belief of this type adheres to the language, customs, and myths of fore-fathers. As the only surviving national happiness of a suppressed people, the more such belief is forbidden, all the more warmly will it be propagated secretly. The thoughts of youth attach themselves to it. Solitude, particularly in the open air of meadows and groves, incubates them. And in those years when nature awakens, when with blood once restrained, once raging, objects in heaven or on earth are sought to which to fasten dusky or flowery perceptions, there are then dreams of the kind that are deceptively real, awake as well as sleeping.[60]

Herder reprinted this fragment in 1797 in *Zerstreute Blätter*, together with "Palingenesie, Vom Wiederkommen menschlicher Seelen, Mit einigen erläuternden Belegen," which was essentially a response to Lessing's essay on the education of the human race. Herder began by adapting to his own methodological stance direct quotations from Lessing that outlined the antiquity of belief in metempsychosis and reincarnation. The twelfth paragraph treated recent anthropological discoveries as a confirmation of age-old philosophical speculations: "The hypothesis is certainly ancient, not only perchance as speculation, but also much earlier still as a notion of sensual human beings."[61] More specifically, the twenty-second paragraph argued, "Before the doctrine of the transmigration of souls became speculation or system, it was popular belief, a notion of sensual people."[62] Each tribe or *Volk*, Herder maintained, had worked out the beliefs peculiar to its own survival: "So there developed a realm of shades under the grave or a paradise beyond the grave, as is shown by the Sheol and Garden of Eden of the Hebrews and, under changed circumstances, also the Hades and Elysium of the Greeks."[63] Those in nebulous climes had thought in terms of clouds, while aggressive, warlike types posited great long halls where the departed souls of heroes could be received with all their fine attributes. Still other, less tightly knit peoples, Herder continued, developed beliefs in transmigration due to the myriad possibilities of nature's great bounty. All such peoples evidenced so much empathy with animals that their songs and tales always mentioned easy transcommunication.

In paragraph twenty-one, Herder related such matters to what he had learned about shamanism:

The art of the sorcerers (shamans) consummated everything. If they were unable to retrieve the soul that had flown away (and there were also stories about this), they indeed knew to search for it and to ask for it in that animal or in this bird. The general belief of these natural peoples was that a quick thought could wander and appear and, furthermore, that the soul really departed the body in dreams and in strenuous ecstasies and performed everything the inspired one imagined. This belief even made the transmigration of the soul almost into a believed experience.[64]

He thereafter even suggested that for very happy, mellow peoples—possibly he was referring to Otaheitians—transmigration was like "an opium, which causes indifference."[65]

Inquiring intellectual that Herder was, he quickly got back to the significance of transmigration within the Pythagorean, Neoplatonic tradition. Instead of providing answers, Herder offered a startling series of further questions, one of the most striking of which had to do with the real meaning of enlightenment through the ages.[66] In answer to one, he reiterated an anecdote about how an Amerindian responded to an inquisitive missionary: "You uncivil thing! I told you a fairy tale, and you call it falsehood?"[67] The additional proofs Herder appended had to do with Kalidasa's *Shakuntala*, a work recently uncovered in Europe, and constituted a summary of his reading in the literature of travel. The conclusion was once again the following: "Conceits of this sort are not philosophy, but rather, a sensual illusion of sensual people."[68]

More than mere corroboration came in *Vom Geist der Ebräischen Poesie: Eine Anleitung für die Liebhaber derselben, und der ältesten Geschichte des menschlichen Geistes*, which was published in Dessau in 1782–1783. This work, which prefigured some of the biblical scholarship of today, revealed the increasing sophistication of Herder's ability to bring to bear information from a wide variety of fields without allowing orthodox theological concerns to present obstructions. The section on hymns of triumph stated how crises stimulated all early peoples to consult soothsayers for assistance in making decisions. Moses opposed such superstitious practices and got support; in one case, at least, during Bileam's vision, Jehovah saw fit to intervene directly. A divine emissary appeared to the entranced Bileam and scolded him for braying as nonsensically as his jackass. When ordered to say only that which the god of the Israelites put into his soul, he remained terrified and mute. Herder's analysis is worth reading in its entirety:

Also in this incident I see nothing that would be dissimilar to the soul of a shaman. One should read travel relations of all countries where shamanism still exists: with astonishment one sees what powerful conditions they are capable of. The soul wanders out of the body, which lies lifeless, and brings news about what they saw in this or that place where they were. Those are, after all, their prophecies, which the people respect and during which even the shrewdest travelers were amazed. All, of course, admired the exertion of these people to induce a powerful condition in comparison with which this vision of Bileam is child's play. Why should the divinity that now wanted to overpower the voice of this cunning prophet, who really did not move along to curse, not go the way that was most usual for him and that was the most effective for him? A horrible phenomenon must have happened to him en route: he heard and saw in a waking vision what is being told here. How petty it is of us, however, to ask whether the ass really did speak and how it spoke and whether and in which way God gave it reason and human speech organs, and so on. The ass of the vision did speak to the shaman, that is, he heard the voice and saw the appearance. It may not and should not speak to us, not even if we wanted to become shamans.[69]

Herder's most comprehensive and astute interpretation of shamanism came in *Ideen zu einer Philosophie der Geschichte der Menschheit*, which appeared in Riga and Leipzig from 1784 to 1791. This work, which constituted a supreme effort to establish fair as well as reasonable methodological parameters, summed up just about everything that the finest eighteenth-century minds—from Pallas, Gmelin, Steller, and Krascheninnikow to Lafitau, Charlevoix, Meiners, and Forster—had come to think about the phenomenon.

In the *Ideen*, Herder contended that more than three-fourths of the people on earth believed in shamans. The details of the actual practices differed, he argued, only because they were formed according to the location, climate, and particular characteristics of the people. Depending on such specifics, he referred to shamanism either as a religion or as superstition. Some versions, he wrote, were in the enlightened eighteenth century still documentable in Greenland, Lapland, and Finland, along the coast of the Arctic Ocean, in Siberia, on the continent of Africa, and throughout the Western Hemisphere.[70] In the Far East, Herder went on to explain, shamanism persisted in isolated places privately among simple people because its practice in public had been suppressed by the intrusion of more orthodox religions and more artificial political systems. It was especially evident, he wrote, on the islands of the South Seas.

According to Herder, nothing at all was accomplished by calling the shaman a trickster or a deceiver. Although in many regards shamans were, indeed, just that, it had to be realized that they themselves were of the people and that they therefore had been deceived by the traditional preconceptions of their tribal roots. Otherwise, there would have been no reason why an initiate would have endured the prolonged fasting, solitude, emotional stress, and physical exhaustion needed initially to summon his tutelary spirit. Nor would it otherwise have been reasonable for him to repeat those debilitating efforts throughout his less-than-normal life in order to intercede with the spirit world on behalf of other tribesmen.

The shaman's ability not only to reach the imagination of others but to gain complete sway over it interested Herder more than the various means employed to induce frenzy or the trance. Unlike many others who reflected on this phenomenon in the eighteenth century, Herder did not find the chanting and dancing to the tambourine, the ventriloquism, legerdemain, and other artful tricks contemptible. He did not because of what he had found to be almost a refrain running through the literature of exploration and travel:

> The most rational travelers had to be astonished at the many juggling tricks of this sort because they saw victories of the imagination that they had hardly believed possible and often did not know how to account for. After all, fancy is still the least explored and, perhaps, the least explorable of all human spiritual powers. Fancy is connected with the entire bodily structure, especially with the brain and the nerves, as so many strange illnesses show. Thus, fancy appears to be not only the bond and the basis of all finer spiritual powers, but also the juncture of the connection between mind and body, as it were, the sprouting blossom of the whole sensual organization for the further employment of the rational faculties.[71]

Furthermore, the *Ideen* evidenced Herder's awareness of the many words from non-European languages conveying some stage of the phenomenon that had already become encapsulated in the form Germanicized from the Tungus. If in one part he wrote about "the angekoks, the sorcerers, magicians, shamans, and priests," in others he referred to the lamas, mimes, minstrels, and jugglers.[72] Herder stated that such types had to have been in the line of descent to the skalds and bards of yore, who were then, in turn, the predecessors of those influential during his own day.

Those connections were confirmed in Herder's *Adrastea*, which appeared in the opening years of the nineteenth century.[73] Here Herder examined the universal significance of enthusiasm in human life. He considered being inspired or filled with the spirits as necessary and basically beneficial: "There is a tinder in us that wants to become sparks, a power that brings forth ideas and deeds."[74] Yet, if not cultivated properly, it could develop to excess and become very harmful. Continuing with the fire imagery typical in discussions of transport, ecstasy, and enthusiasm, he wrote that without proper natural controls, an all-consuming conflagration could result. What had happened in the past with prophets and poets demonstrated that to Herder, as did what was happening in the present with charismatic Christians and those who flocked to join contemporary secret societies in order to gain the kind of illumination that brought wisdom or power.[75]

Herder had come to believe that enthusiasm, shamanism, and all aspects of the irrational had to be acknowledged openly and confronted. They were natural. Whenever the natural was disavowed, or ignored, or repressed, or imprisoned by predetermined codes, whether Franco-Roman neoclassicism or any other, the eventual result could, he maintained, only be an eruption of gigantic proportions. The methodology Herder had developed over his lifetime enabled him to give a commonsensical retrospective evaluation of the Enlightenment and the French Revolution:

> It has long been said that no great, abundant good is produced without enthusiasm, just as no abomination can be imagined that fanaticism could not do. Precisely the end of our past century proved this terribly beyond any conception. After it had often been uttered and repeated that with increased, widespread enlightenment a nation, according to its character, mild, indeed, called frivolous, was capable of no fanaticism, no superstition, and no enthusiasm, that nation then broke out in a fury that laid waste to so many heads and countries of Europe. Never should one consider the tinder for enthusiasm or for fanaticism eradicated or eradicable from human nature.[76]

The legacy Herder left his own countrymen combined reverence for the arts and the sciences with involvement in the active life of service (*das thätige Leben*). Its thrust was "never anything to excess." Its motto was moderation.[77]

CHAPTER SEVEN

Mozart,
or, Orpheus Reborn

By the time Leopold Mozart (1719–1787) began demonstrating his children's prodigious gifts publicly, Europeans had already become predisposed to welcome a living Orpheus. What they had learned from the travel literature about shamans in the wild seemed to make understandable what theorists were writing about the nature of the artist. The issue that loomed largest in the popular mind of the eighteenth century was whether artists were made or born. The increasing number who held they were born saw art as more than something learned from a book of preordained rules. Sensitivity, communicative skill, and what came to be called genius seemed to be involved.

The new theory that was developing combined myths of Orpheus and reports about shamans with ideas concerning genius.[1] This combination was to remain an intellectualized abstraction only until the German musician Mozart became its focal point and helped bring it to life in the second half of the eighteenth century. Data from documents dealing with Mozart's biography reveal that those who described him, including his father and himself, relied on this Orpheus-shaman-genius combination, thereby creating a new myth of the artist as civilizer that could be understood by common people as well as by academicians and intellectuals.

Before turning to those biographical documents, I should like to survey the major issues in the evolving theory of genius. Writings on genius abounded during Mozart's lifetime. Physicians and scientists as well as literary people and theologians produced them. Some of the earliest in the German language were by Gotthold Ephraim Lessing, a free-lance writer who was a decade younger than Leopold Mozart. Lessing repeatedly defended the genius as someone who knew how to create an artistic microcosm according to internal laws that were as inscrutable as those of God himself. As early as 1749, when he was twenty years old, he wrote for a musicological journal about the wonderful self-regulating ability of the genius as far as the creative process was concerned: "A spirit whom nature determined an exemplary spirit is what he is through himself, and becomes great without rules.

He proceeds, so boldly he may proceed, safely without instruction. He draws out of himself. He is his own school and books. Whatever moves him, is moving. Whatever pleases him, is pleasing. His auspicious taste is the taste of the world. Who fathoms his worth? Only he himself can fathom it."[2]

While Lessing was comfortable with the thought that *he* was not a genius, he persisted in exploring intellectually what genius meant. First, it did not mean knowledge, erudition, observance of the rules, or what is nowadays called left-hemispheric brain function.[3] In 1767, Lessing wrote in the *Hamburgische Dramaturgie*: "Genius is allowed not to know a thousand things that every schoolboy knows. Not the acquired stores of his memory, but that which he can produce out of himself, out of his own sensibility, constitutes his richness."[4] According to Lessing, the real genius is capable of creating works that combine cause and effect in such a way that nothing is left to chance. Should that genius ignore the rules, he must have an overpowering artistic inclination to do so. Whether he creates a hybrid or not is irrelevant. What is relevant is whether it has the power to please and to continue pleasing. Elsewhere Lessing contended that critical insight was among the many gifts with which the genius was innately endowed, the reason being that, "not every judge of art is a genius, but every genius is a born critic. He has the proof of all rules within himself."[5]

German thinkers of diverse backgrounds continued to concern themselves with matters having to do with genius. As a result, genius became a shibboleth in Germany and throughout Europe. Heinrich Wilhelm von Gerstenberg was one writer who summed up its connotations as inspiration, imagination, the spark, the creation of illusion, novelty, and originality. As he further explained, there were gradations among intellectuals and wits, but none whatsoever among geniuses. An artist without great genius would simply not be an artist.[6] Gerstenberg opposed foreign rationalistic systems that reduced the arts to imitations of nature because he thought they did not account for the creative imagination of the genius.

Johann Georg Sulzer (1720–1779), though generally more conservative in his views, went still further in attempting to codify precisely what happened during the creative process. In *Allgemeine Theorie der Schönen Künste* (1773–1775), a repository of conventional wisdom about the arts, he published the following description:

All artists of any genius claim that from time to time they experience a state of extraordinary psychic intensity which makes work unusually easy, images arising without great effort and the best ideas flowing in such profusion as if they were the gift of some higher power. This is without doubt what is called inspiration. If an artist experiences this condition, his object appears to him in an unusual light; his genius, as if guided by a divine power, invents without effort, shaping his invention in the most suitable form without strain; the finest ideas and images occur unbidden in floods to the inspired poet; the orator judges with the greatest acumen, feels with the greatest intensity, and the strongest and most vividly expressive words rise to his tongue.[7]

Among the theologians was Johann Georg Hamann (1730–1788), himself considered the "Magus of the North." He agreed that cognition could not be delimited rationally: "Senses and passions speak and understand nothing but images. In images is the whole treasure of human knowledge and happiness."[8] Hamann, like the Neoplatonists of antiquity and the Renaissance, explained poetry as being the same as religion. He asserted that both were natural kinds of prophesying that—as some of those involved in psychoneuroimmunology would argue today—appealed to something intrinsic in human beings and helped heal by encouraging natural restorative functions.[9] Hamann articulated relatively clearly his belief that all our knowledge is sensuous and figurative: "Poetry is the mother tongue of the human race; just as gardening is older than agriculture, painting than writing, singing than declamation, similes than syllogisms, barter than commerce. A deeper sleep was the rest of our ancestors, and their movement a whirling, ecstatic dance."[10]

The subject of genius also attracted practicing physicians, who gave eager attention to performing artists—actors, singers, dancers, and musicians. Whenever possible, those physicians examined cranial structures, brains, and nervous systems; they also collected skulls. Often, they compared their results with what they knew about the lifestyles of their subjects. They tried to relate art and culture to health, longevity, and the so-called quality of life.

Franz Anton May (1742–1814), professor of medicine at Heidelberg and physician to the court in Mannheim, published his observations in a number of articles. Like many others interested in matters involving public health, May concentrated on the effects of sustained intellectual, spiritual, and artistic activity on the human body. He justified his research by claiming that performing artists were possible "psychiatrists" who, if cultivated, could contribute to the emotional well-being of society. While someone with the nervous system of a teamster or a woodchopper might not be effective as a performer in public, he wrote, many of those who did perform were hypersensitive, or simply high-strung. Like many of his medical colleagues, May described in terms of the female nervous system the kind of great sensi-

tivity that allowed for the production of art. There were many contemporary discussions about androgynous performers, which would
seem to be related to the descriptions about shamanism in the travel
reports.[11]

One of May's fellow physicians, and a medical researcher of some
repute, Melchior Adam Weickard (1742–1803), published a lengthy
work about the philosophical physician in the 1770s. It contained a
special section dealing with "fancy or imagination." There we find the
following entry: "A Genius, a human being with exalted imaginative
powers, must have more excitable brain fibers than other human beings. Those fibers must be set into motion quicker and more easily, so
that lively and frequent images arise."[12] Eighteenth-century physicians were wont to attribute the eccentricities of the creative person—
what others usually called craziness, madness, or otherness—to that
person's seeming need to live in a world of his or her own making.[13]

As the eighteenth century progressed, the theoretical profile of the
artist merged with the myth of Orpheus that had been evolving since
the Renaissance.[14] A good example of the tone can be found in Sir
William Temple's (1628–1699) *Essay upon the Ancient and Modern
Learning* (1690):

> What are the Charms of Musick, by which Men and Beasts, Fishes, Fowls,
> and Serpents were so frequently Enchanted, and their very Natures
> changed; By which the Passions of men were raised to the greatest height
> and violence, and then as suddenly appeased, so as they might be justly
> said to be turned into Lyons or Lambs, into Wolves or into Harts, by the
> Power and Charms of this admirable Art? 'Tis agreed by the Learned
> that the Science of Musick, so admired of the Ancients, is wholly lost in
> the World, and that what we have now is made up out of certain Notes
> that fell into the fancy or observation of a poor *Fryar* in chanting his
> Mattins. So as those Two Divine Excellencies of Musick and Poetry are
> grown in a manner to be little more, but the one Fidling, and the other
> Rhyming; and are indeed very worthy of the ignorance of the Fryer and
> the barbarousness of the *Goths* that introduced them among us.[15]

Johann Gottfried Walther (1684–1748) had the orphic power
spreading to the vegetable and mineral kingdoms to civilize the uncivilized. In his *Musikalisches Lexikon oder musikalische Bibliothek* (1732), he
gave a list of references after describing Orpheus as having been such
a good musician that "he could through his artistry and lyre draw to
himself not only human beings but also mountains, rocks, trees, wild
animals, and the like, by which quite certainly the barbaric Thracians
were meant."[16] Those who subsequently wrote on music often re-

ferred to the exaltation and transport produced by works of art that managed to take possession of the senses of the human audience.[17] This, in addition to the curative effect of music, was said to be magical or related to witchcraft.

Even Leopold Mozart himself did not fail to mention, in *Gründliche Violinschule*, Orpheus among antiquity's most noteworthy musicians. He brushed aside those who doubted the historical existence of Orpheus by stating that too many reputable authors had testified about his great achievements. Nevertheless, "that much of a fabulous character is mixed with this is quite certain; but in these fables be many truths."[18] The footnote attached to this is quite revealing. While bemoaning the contemporary lack of practical recognition for musicians, it contributed greatly to the Orphic view of the modern musician:

> At the time these men lived, learned people were deified. And precisely this is the reason why everything is so fabulous. Who knows? Perhaps the poets of future centuries will have enough material to celebrate our contemporary virtuosos in song. For it truly seems as if ancient times were returning. One is now accustomed (as one says) already in many places to deify scholars and artists with many bravos without honoring them with any other rightful and vigorous reward. But, this kind of thin encomium is also supposed to infuse the gentlemen virtuosos with divine nature and transfigure their bodies so that they can live off of heavenly conceits and never have need of earthly necessities.[19]

All such discussions about Orpheus as poet-musician-magician-seer-prophet then contributed to the rhetoric applied to specific instances as European musicians strove to liberate themselves from the professional servitude in which they were expected to perform.

In the German lands artists found it especially difficult to gain liberation. Centuries of cultural hegemony, first by the Romans, then by the Italians and the French, made the German language and its products not only despised but in some instances forbidden. German music was no less harshly received. Everything indigenous was thought to be inferior.

In 1780, Frederick the Great (1712–1786) published one of the many treatises he wrote in French. It presented his views on cultural activity in the German lands, concentrating on the literary and performing arts. Frederick aimed to show that his countrymen were so totally lacking in genius as well as taste that they could not possibly compete with the French and the Italians. German, which Frederick is said to have eschewed using, except in the stables with his horses and hounds, was "still a half-barbaric language, divided into as many different dialects as there were provinces." There were around three hundred. "What one," Frederick continued, "writes in Swabia is hardly intelligible in Hamburg, and the Austrian style is obscure for the Saxons."[20] Recalling age-old weaknesses in the Holy Roman Empire of the German Nation, he mentioned that there was no unified, umbrellalike political entity to support cultivation of a common language. Consequently there was neither a dictionary nor a canon of works establishing any linguistic norms. Nor was there an authoritative body, such as an academy, to enforce those norms. Frederick even suggested that it would be physically impossible for an author, even one of the greatest spirit (*esprit*, not *Geist*), to handle such a rude language excellently. Elsewhere, we learn his response to German performers: "A German singer? I should as soon expect to receive pleasure from the neighing of my horse!"[21] The language spoken by the subjects of his maternal grandfather and his other Hanoverian relatives fared no better: "All other languages lose, when one translates them; the English language alone gains thereby."[22]

That is, unless the translation were into German. Frederick obviously meant translation into French or Italian. The current Shakespeare craze, rampant throughout the entire Holy Roman Empire in the last quarter of the eighteenth century, was a sure indicator of the lack of genius and taste. Those "abominable plays" were not only being performed everywhere, they were also being enthusiastically received by audiences. Frederick, who warmly supported Italian opera and French spoken drama, was appalled to think that "the whole gathering finds an exceptional pleasure in witnessing these ridiculous farces, which would only be worthy of performance before the savages of Canada. I judge these pieces so severely because they transgress against all the rules of drama. These rules are not arbitrary."[23] The surest indicator of the Germans' total lack of taste, in Frederick's opinion, was their enjoyment of indigenous dramas emulating Shakespearean form and style. The worst offender was a creature by the name of Johann Wolfgang Goethe (1749–1832).

Goethe, like Moses Mendelssohn (1729–1786), Immanuel Kant (1724–1804), Friedrich Schiller (1759–1805), Christoph Willibald Gluck (1714–1787), Franz Josef Haydn (1732–1809), and other such creatures, might have had high hopes for Frederick's qualities as a political leader who could bring unity to the German lands. These men did not, however, have much confidence in his aesthetic views. What Frederick meant by "genius," "taste," and "excellence" was derived from the wearily long evolution of Franco-Roman neoclassicism. It represented the ultimate codification of creativity and critical response. Whether that code actually worked for the seventeenth-century French, the Renaissance Italians, and the ancient Romans is not important here. It simply did not work for the Germanic peoples of the eighteenth century, neither those on the European mainland nor those who had immigrated to the British isles. All those folk preferred induction to deduction. They also loved grass-roots movements. Furthermore, they required rule by precedent rather than rule by code.[24] The reason I immortalize Frederick the Great's closed mind at such length is that it illustrates the overwhelming difficulties eighteenth-century Germans faced in breaking free from the superimposed restrictions, from the predetermined forms, from the given mind-set.

The mythologization process was already in operation on the very day Mozart was born and registered as the legitimate issue of his mother and father. Since the Bavarian custom—Mozart's father was a citizen of Augsburg in Bavaria—was to record legitimate births in Latinate form, the name Johann Goldmund Wolfgang Gottlieb Mozart was inscribed as Joannes Chrysostomus Wolfgangus Theophilus Mozartus. The surname, according to the usual fashion of the times, had appeared and would continue to appear in various documents as Moser, Mozer, Mozard, Motshart, Motsart, Mozhart, and Mozzart, as well as Mozarth and Mozart.[25] It must, however, also be remembered that proud eighteenth-century German parents of sons usually wanted them to have God with them at all times. Consequently, there was a plethora of such godly names. In addition to Gottfried, Gottlieb, Gotthold, and Gottlob, there were names like Fürchtegott, Traugott, and so on. It was perhaps only possible in the 1980s that the lovely, yet dreadfully commonplace, eighteenth-century German name—Gottlieb—could make such a stir in its Latin translation, Amadeus. Woferl, Wolfgangl, Wolfgangerl, or Wolfgang Gottlieb Mozart, which is how he regularly signed his name in early documents, knew he would have to do something to make his name sound better to those imbued with power and influence who would only support things French, Italian, and Latin. Contributing to his own living legend, he seems to have decided to use the French form, Amadé, after his trip to Italy. The Italians honored Mozart with poems in the 1770s, constantly referring to him as Amadeo so as to claim him as one of their own.[26] I shall hereafter refer to him as often as possible as Wolfgang Gottlieb Mozart, in order to provide a feel for the sound of his real name, if there is such a thing.

Little Wolfgang Gottlieb Mozart quickly became the talk of all the

German lands. His father, of course, helped impress on people that his son was someone special. In 1763, for example, he gave him top billing, writing "it is astonishing and hardly believable that a child of German birth could have such a musical talent, genius, and so much spirit."[27] Even the fourteen-year-old Goethe registered his impressions about the seven-year-old virtuoso musician who performed before kings and courtesans, calling him a precious little adult, what with his big wig and even bigger sword. It is quite obvious from Goethe's reminiscences that he disliked being overshadowed. Be that as it may, genius among the Germans had to be considered suspect. Everyone in eighteenth-century Europe accepted as given that the Germans had no style, no taste, and no polish. Few contemporaries the world over wanted to give them credit for having anything like normal human intelligence. Benjamin Franklin (1706–1790), for one, went so far as to write of less-intelligent, swarthy races and to classify the Germans among them, along with the Swedes and the Africans. In embarrassingly few accounts were the Germans viewed as being artistically talented in any field whatsoever. They were generally considered hopeless in music, poetry, and the other arts.

Then, suddenly, Wolfgang Gottlieb Mozart came on the scene. Not only was he an instantaneous world-class sensation, but he also, with his father's unending assistance, managed to encourage the process of mythologization by tying in with what was currently being discussed in the theoretical writings. Whether it was sheer instinct or not—perhaps, age-old show-business savvy—Mozart knew how to play with his name as well as with the word genius so as to invent himself and control his own public image. In his correspondence with his father he referred to his own genius.[28] Mozart also knew how to tie in with what was appearing in currently salable novels. Eighteenth-century novelists were giving great notice to the evolution of the performing artist from a profligate vagabond to a trendsetter. As a result, the genius, the would-be genius, and the fraudulent genius—of whatever degree—became frequent topics in their works.

Wolfgang Gottlieb Mozart—whose reputed favorite dish was liver dumplings with sauerkraut—was so special that even the French stopped and paid attention. Friedrich Melchior Grimm was a proponent of everything Mozart stood for. Grimm reported this in his *Correspondance littéraire*, a kind of journal in which he transmitted the latest cultural news from Paris to his subscribers in the German lands and the Russia ruled by the notorious Catherine the Great. Again and again, he wrote that the Parisians were astonished by the young Mozart's musical gifts. To describe the phenomenon that was Mozart, he used words expressing the idea of genius, talent, prodigy, all precisely in the same way the theorists had used them.[29]

Gradually, Mozart became known all over the globe as "the living Orpheus," the mythological figure that the eighteenth century had come to consider the shaman par excellence. The seven-year-old Wolfgang Gottlieb was already believed to be the reincarnated enchanter of all of nature who successfully cast his spell over its innumerable creatures.[30] He was further described with other words from the realm of magic and bewitchment. Even the emperor referred to him as a little magician (*Hexenmeister*).[31] Grimm, who was associated with the circles around Diderot as well as those around Catherine, thought Mozart's musical improvisation demonstrated genuine inspiration and "a mass of enchanting ideas, which moreover he knows how to connect with taste and without confusion."[32] Because of eighteenth-century advances in anthropological information due to the ongoing worldwide voyages of exploration, those words had become relatively common. Mozart was not only a child-wonder (*Wunderkind*), a singular phenomenon, a miracle, but one who publicly performed the kind of wonders that captivated audiences and left them spellbound.[33] Some went on to surmise that Mozart had curative powers. One person wrote to a friend about experiencing Mozart's pieces: "You would have recovered your health and hearing, had you listened to them for only a quarter of an hour, for it was indescribably enchanting."[34] Even the staid and relatively objective Charles Burney (1726–1814), whose son was an explorer of some renown, had assimilated the gist of what was being reported about shamans.[35] He wrote of "the little German, whose premature and almost supernatural talents astonished us in London a few years ago, when he had scarce quitted his infant state."[36] Wolfgangerl Gottlieberl himself used this trendy vocabulary when evaluating contemporaries. He wrote his father from Mannheim on November 22, 1777, about a certain violinist that "he is no wizard, but a very sound fiddler."[37]

Until now I have not found any observers of Wolfgang Gottlieb Mozart who came right out and called him a shaman or any other of the eighteenth-century's equivalent expressions. There is one, however, who came very close—the physician Simon André Tissot (1728–1798), whose medical specialty was the nervous system. He actually had a chance to experience one of Mozart's performances, and did not hesitate to publish his reaction in an essay in 1766. In it, Tissot stated his belief that everything Mozart did revealed spirit, creativity, and "that character of force which is the stamp of genius, that variety which proclaims the fire of imagination, and that charm which proves an assured taste."[38]

"Our little Orpheus," as Tissot repeatedly called Mozart, had been "born with an exquisite ear and an organism disposed to be strongly affected by music."[39] Tissot explained that Wolfgang Gottlieb had grown up hearing nothing but great music, so his very body itself could not tolerate anything less: "Aural sensibility and justness are so keen in young Mozart that wrong, harsh or too loud notes bring tears to his eyes. His imagination is as musical as his ear, for it is always conscious of a multitude of sounds all together."[40] What Tissot could not rationalize or find an explanation for was Wolfgang Gottlieb's musical compunctions:

He was sometimes involuntarily driven to his harpsichord, as by a hidden force, and he drew from it sounds that were the living expression of the idea that had just seized him. One might say that at such moments he is an instrument at the command of music, imagining him like a set of strings, harmoniously arranged with such art that a single one cannot be touched without all others being set in motion; he plays all the images, as a Poet versifies and a Painter colours them.[41]

In his attempt to grasp what genius was, Tissot, the physician, wrote:

When I see the young Mozart jokingly create these tender and sublime symphonies which one would take for the language of immortals, every fibre of my being takes up the theme, so to speak, of immortality, just as all the powers of my spirit despair of it. Carried away by a delightful illusion, beyond the narrow sphere which confines my senses, I could almost take this child, so blest by heaven, for one of those pure spirits, who inhabit the happy realm destined for me.[42]

Wolfgang Gottlieb Mozart was the kind of unique genius, or miracle of nature, whose sensational reputation not only spread but demanded scientific verification. After all, his lifetime spanned the age that liked to think of itself as the Enlightenment. The Royal Society in London enjoyed very close ties with Continental researchers and intellectuals because of the University at Göttingen, founded by those Hanoverians who happened to become English royalty. That scientifically oriented society wanted proof of, or at least testimonials about, genius. As a result, Daines Barrington (1727–1800), a polyglot lawyer and naturalist, submitted an eye- and earwitness account in 1769. It was read to the Royal Society in 1770, but it was not published until 1771. Like so many before and after, Barrington's account struggled to articulate "genius," or "the most extraordinary musical talents," that could withstand all grueling tests as though nothing were out of the ordinary. Since so much of the theory of genius was related to the literary scene, the references to literature that Barrington made were to be expected. He recorded the following about Joannes Chrysostomus Wolfgangus Theophilus Mozart, born at Salzburg in Bavaria in 1756:

> Suppose then, a capital speech in Shakespeare never seen before, and yet read by a child of eight years old, with all the pathetic energy of a Garrick.
>
> Let it be conceived likewise, that the same child is reading, with a glance of his eye, three different comments on this speech tending to its illustration; and that one comment is written in Greek, the second in Hebrew, and the third in Etruscan characters.
>
> Let it be also supposed, that by different signs he could point out which comment is most material upon every word; and sometimes that perhaps all three are so, at others only two of them.[43]

Barrington thought Mozart otherwise comported himself like any other child of the same age. The British observer developed a sort of fondness for the Bavarian child-wonder, even wishing him as long a life as George Frederic Handel, "contrary to the common observation that such *ingenia praecocia* are generally short lived."[44] Others expressed similar worries that Mozart would burn out and die young, and thus become symbolic of his art. In this way the living legend was mythologized during his own lifetime in order to suit the theory of genius that was developing. The reciprocity noted from documented evidence is actually quite astonishing.

The many poetic tributes Mozart received from his fans often compared him to Orpheus, Apollo, and other shamans easily recognized by the eighteenth century. One written in 1770 had him competing with Orpheus's mythological scope:

> If Orpheus enraptured the forests, if Tartarus he moved,
> Now thou stealest men's hearts, child, and movest the stars.[45]

By the late 1780s many had him excelling the shamans of antiquity:

> When Orpheus' magic lute out-rings,
> Amphion to his lyre sings,
> The lions tame, the rivers quiet grow,
> The tigers listen, rocks a-walking go.
> When Mozart masterly music plays
> And gathers undivided praise,
> The quire of Muses stays to hear,
> Apollo is himself all ear.[46]

Such tributes stressed what they considered his irresistible magic to establish psychic well-being for the individual and cultural, if not political, unity for the Germans. That magic was usually depicted as a transference of power from the divine realm to the mundane. One of the most comprehensive examples was produced in 1786 by Anton Daniel Breicha (fl. 1780s), who has been identified as a physician and writer:

> Enchanted by thee I incline to refuse
> The Muses' assistance. Be thou then my Muse!
> Be thou Pindus' clear and intoxicant source!
> I heard thee, melodious thinker, and lo!
> The pow'r of thy genius soon did I know,
> Drawn on by its strong, irresistible course.
>
> 'Tis true, by thy music thou dost not move trees
> And rocks, nor ever wild beasts does it please,
> As Orpheus' did; but thou breakest the barriers,
> With more ease than he; for the souls of us mortals
> To heavenly bliss dost thou open the portals,
> For children, for maidens, for men and for warriors.
>
> When love of thy heart-melting strains is the theme
> The youth seeks his maid, and more passionate seem
> The beats of his heart in his love-laden breast.
> She beckons him on to the heavenly bliss
> Which they seal with a long and a rapturous kiss
> By the youth on the maiden's lips ardently pressed.
>
> When feverish anguish inspires thy strain
> We freeze with compassion and horror; again
> When it's playful and gay we revive with delight;
> When plaintive and gloomy, like sounds of the tomb,
> Thy mournfullest music enwraps us in gloom;
> The cords of our hearts with thy music unite.
>
> Thy fatherland, cordially grasping thy hand,
> As Germans are wont, now shall sever the band
> Of Friendship with strangers, and honour in thee
> The German Apollo. Germania's Muses
> Rejoice, and fell rivalry's furtive abuses
> Destroy their own plots and are vanquished by thee.[47]

Several years before Wolfgang Gottlieb Mozart's death, a leading musicological journal reviewed the performance career of a youngster by the name of Ludwig van Beethoven (1770–1827). In it, we see how Mozart had already become the measuring stick for geniuses. For example, we read: "This young genius [Beethoven] deserves support to enable him to travel. He would be sure to become a second Wolfgang Amadeus Mozart, if he progressed as he has begun."[48]

A journal concerned with theatrical matters also proclaimed Mozart's genius two years before he died. It went on to describe him as

> great and beautiful, full of new ideas and unexpected turns, full of art, fire, and genius. Now we are enchanted by beautiful, charming song; now we are made to smile at subtle, comic wit and fancy; now we admire the naturally conceived and superbly executed planning; now the magnificence and greatness of Art takes us by surprise. Where all this is united, it is bound to make its effect and to satisfy the sensitive hearer as well as the experienced and practised expert. Mozart is gifted with the happy genius that can blend art with nature and song with grace. Again he ventures on impetuous and fiery sallies, and how bold are his harmonies![49]

The year before Mozart died, a periodical in Berlin ratified his stature as that of an unarguably inimitable genius:

> Mozart is among those extraordinary men whose reputation will endure for centuries. His great genius embraces, so to speak, the whole extent of the art of music: it is rich in ideas; his works are a river in spate which carries along with it every stream that approaches it. None before him has surpassed him, and posterity will never deny this great man its profound reverence and admiration. To judge him one must be more than a mere connoisseur. What a masterpiece is the music of today![50]

Mozart—whether on his own account or because of the press he continued to incite—was, indeed, sought after by European patrons. Not one of them, however, managed to come through with what would have been a sufficient financial amount. Neither Joseph of Austria, nor Frederick the Great of Prussia, nor George III of England was interested enough. The powers that were in Prague also failed to make the acknowledged German genius their own. No greater success could be recorded by Potemkin, who tried to get Mozart into the Russian service and failed. But perhaps Wolfgang Gottlieb intuited Catherine's lack of musical appreciation as well as her lack of musical knowledge.

When Mozart died in 1791, he was universally mourned. A Viennese newspaper wrote of him as a human being who had "surpassed Orpheus with his playing."[51] Journalists elsewhere reiterated his ability to reach the hearts of his listeners and to transport them to other imaginative realms. In Hamburg, he was commemorated with an article distinguishing genius from mind in a way that would seem to presage the line of investigation that has subsequently tried to explain right- and left-hemispheric brain functions. Its author purportedly noticed that Mozart had begun "to compose not merely at the dictate of his *genius*, but also at that of his *mind*;—that is, he was beginning to subject his imagination to his intellect."[52] By 1794, memories of a reincarnated Orpheus were being associated with "the all-powerful and magic name of Mozart."[53]

After Mozart's death, many writers took up what the physicians had claimed about the hypersensitivity of the performing artist who was capable of creating new worlds for all of us to play in. The various aspects of play were usually stressed in one way or another. Jean Baptiste-Antoine Suard (1733–1817) did so by combining current ideas about the genius with those about the child: "Mozart was one of those extraordinary children who astonish with their premature talent; but, very different from almost all those little prodigies who, having reached maturer years, have turned out to be very ordinary men, his talent grew with his body and he became a man of genius." Suard described him as being highly irritable, melancholic, immoderate, mercurial, and careless. In sum, "Mozart was all his life a sort of child."[54] Part of a suggested epitaph even had it that "he who lies here as a child added to the wonders of the world and as a man surpassed Orpheus with his playing."[55] Mozart was so often described in this way that there developed a tendency to memorialize him as the genius who, retaining his pristine, childlike qualities, never matured according to the usual expectations of the real workaday world.

Goethe, himself tremendously well informed about exploration as well as about magic, contributed mightily to the emergent tack of Mozartian mythologization. He compared Mozart's genius to a productive kind of spiritual power capable of controlling the hidden animistic forces operative in the world. That kind of demonic savoir faire, as he mentioned on March 2, 1831 to Johann Peter Eckermann (1792–1854), an alumnus of Göttingen, could only be so closely related to music: "Music contains something demonic, for it ranks so high that no understanding can reach it, and it exudes a power that dominates everything and of which nobody can give himself an account. Religious cult can therefore not dispense with it; it is one of the best means to have a miraculous effect on man."[56]

As the mythologization process continued in the nineteenth century, ideas on genius and the child were brought together with magic, as described by explorers and as suggested by Goethe. They were ideas similar to those mentioned by Plato in the *Ion*: that the inspiration of the muse or similar spirit was transferred through a series of rings from the creator to the performing artist and then on to the audience. Michael Kelly (1762–1826), the Irish tenor, relied on that pattern, for example, when he reminisced, "All the original performers had the advantage of the instruction of the composer, who transfused into their minds his inspired meaning. I never shall forget his little animated countenance, when lighted up with the glowing rays of genius;—it is as impossible to describe it, as it would be to paint sunbeams."[57] The memoirs of those who claimed to have witnessed Mozart performances usually relied on the very rhetoric that ratified the synthesis of Orpheus-shaman-genius. One wrote: "But who could tear himself away when Mozart was improvising! The soup was allowed to grow cold and the roast to burn simply so that we could continue to listen to the magic sounds which the master, completely absorbed in what he was doing and unaware of the rest of the world, conjured from the instrument."[58] Some reported that Mozart had not wanted to be taken for a common magician merely competent in his craft. He preferred recognition for his daring flights: "His greatest torment, the one he often complained about himself, was that audiences expected from him and wished to see mechanical sorcery and juggling tightrope-walker tricks, but they were not able to follow or did not want to follow the sublime flight of his imagination and his prodigious ideas."[59] Some eyewitnesses even recorded Mozart's swift swings in mood and abrupt changes in personality. What they wrote often reflected reports about shamanic brinksmanship and the pursuit of magical possibilities to the outer reaches of madness. Caroline Pichler (1769–1843), a writer and well-known figure in Viennese cultural circles, related, for example, that she had once been practicing at the pianoforte when Mozart surprised her, "and began to improvise such wonderfully beautiful variations that everyone listened to the tones of the German Orpheus with bated breath. But then he suddenly tired of it, jumped up, and in the mad mood which so often came over him, he began to leap over tables and chairs, miaow like a cat, and turn somersaults like an unruly boy."[60]

The mythologization that commenced with the birth of Wolfgang Gottlieb and persisted throughout his life, continued to accelerate markedly after his premature death in 1791. However he was viewed, he remained good copy for the emerging media. Just about every aspect of his known biography was structured into one form or another, including children's puppet plays.[61] Among the many literary and musical artists who contributed to that continuing mythologization process, E.T.A. Hoffmann (1776–1822)—of the *Tales of Hoffmann* fame—stands out. This devoted fan was twenty years younger than Mozart, yet had so readily succumbed to the mythologization in progress that he chose to add not Gottlieb, but rather Amadeus, to his own given names. Hoffmann, who had grown up in a society bursting to the brim with explorers' reports about shamans, enchanters, and medicine men, wanted to think of Wolfgang Gottlieb Mozart as a kindred spirit. At one point, he even confessed that it was precisely Mozart who had been responsible for steering him into the depths and heights of the spirit world. And Hoffmann meant spirits![62]

While agreeing with Goethe that music transcended the immanent sphere of everyday life, Hoffmann went on to explain that those who composed music had to be enraptured spirits who understood functioning in dreams as well as in infinity. Before long, Hoffmann himself was forced to switch to the vocabulary and syntax of the nonrational and the enchanted. Again and again, he referred to the magical "breath" that attracted human beings into other realms of consciousness.[63]

Hoffmann's association of Mozart's genius with the travel reports about the phenomenal power of shamans and the like is, perhaps, best represented in "Don Juan," a tale that first appeared in Leipzig's *Allgemeine Musicalische Zeitung* on March 31, 1813, and that was later included in *Fantasiestücke in Callots Manier* (1814–1815).[64] This tale incorporated most of the shamanic phenomena known to the eighteenth century: out-of-body experiences, flight, and bilocation. It was written to criticize not only European operatic audience behavior but also production practices, and evidence would seem to indicate that it was quite successful in achieving its intended goals. Subsequent productions of Mozart's *Don Giovanni* did, indeed, include the final scenes, wherein all the characters touched by the Don came onstage again, so as to demonstrate in all three real dimensions their release from the supernatural powers.[65]

E.T.A. Hoffmann, along with many others before and after him, intuited that Mozart was, indeed, worthy of mythologization. What Mozart himself contributed to that process will remain as fascinating as what another artist of the time did to help invent his public image and to create yet more myths of the modern European shaman. That artist is Goethe, and he is the subject of the next two chapters.

CHAPTER EIGHT

Shamans Failed and Successful in Goethe

JOHANN WOLFGANG VON GOETHE (1749–1832) exhibited a great interest in wizards, heroes, and rulers from his earliest years. When he was not assuming the diabolical roles of Friedrich Gottlieb Klopstock's (1724–1803) *Messias* in surreptitious readings with playmates, he was enjoying puppet shows about exceptional kings and sorcerers who in their search for knowledge and power purportedly feared nothing, not even the wrath of the Judeo-Christian god. By the time Goethe reached his early twenties, three such major figures seemed to dominate his thoughts: Faust, Götz von Berlichingen, and Julius Caesar. The known records of their deeds and misdeeds continued to stimulate his artistic imagination throughout his life. While his thinking about Caesar never materialized into an independent literary work, Götz's autobiography served as the basis for a play published in 1773. And Faust became the subject of a lifelong dramatic project that was to make that figure into a shaman just as archetypally representative of contemporary European civilization as Orpheus was of antiquity.[1]

Goethe, the humanist and scientist, lived at the crossroads of Europe. This was true intellectually as well as geographically. News from Paris and St. Petersburg, London and Rome all managed to intersect in Weimar. The past of the ancients had finally given way to the future of the moderns so that what had once been relegated to the realm of the occult was becoming enlightened for all to see out in the open. Goethe's readings in magic and Renaissance Neoplatonism were as seriously motivated as his study of the sciences of the day. He shared his contemporaries' great concern for developing a sound methodology, although he often did not agree with their final choices.

Goethe firmly believed that mythology, poetry, and science had always been inherently interrelated, suiting the particular times and circumstances of the cultures involved. Like Herder, he maintained that "the history of the sciences is a great fugue in which the voices of the nations appear little by little."[2] Examining the seemingly hidden relationships among mythology, poetry, and science, he thought, would reveal much about the evolution of human culture and also about the appearance of science at a certain moment of a culture's development. In his opinion, history showed that there actually were

> Four epochs of the sciences:
>   childlike,
>   poetic, superstitious;
>   empirical,
>   investigative, curious;
>   dogmatic,
>   didactic, pedantic;
>   ideal,
>   methodical, mystical.[3]

Goethe refused to shun that first, childlike epoch. Consequently, he strongly advocated rigorous, open-minded analysis of magic and witchcraft. He spent much effort on what during the height of the Enlightenment were rather unfashionable areas of investigation. Like Herder, Justus Möser, and many of his associates, Goethe thought that superstition was the human being's way of coming to terms with natural phenomena that he was not yet able to perceive clearly, never mind explain. Goethe later contended in his autobiographical *Dichtung und Wahrheit* that the forms of belief and superstition remained the same with all peoples at all times.[4] He also thought his highly sophisticated, rationalistically oriented contemporaries who deprecated superstitious beliefs were worse off without them because fantasy, premonition, hunch, and coincidence could not be made to disappear: "Whereby then a particular difficulty arises for the moderns because, as much as we wish, we find no easy substitute for the wondrous creatures, gods, soothsayers, and oracles of the ancients."[5]

Goethe rejected the methodology of the third scientific epoch because he thought of it as being so dogmatic, didactic, and pedantic that it summarily excluded from investigation all subjects that happened to defy the means of explanation it could muster. He warned against accepting as absolute truth the Newtonian mechanical view of nature.[6] He thought its stress on theory and mathematics made the method more important than the subject under investigation, producing a gross distortion rather than the highly commended objectivity: "Throughout the history of scientific research one notices that observers rush too quickly from the phenomenon to theory, thereby becoming inadequate, hypothetical."[7] While mathematics was a valuable tool that could well serve the scientific enterprise, he thought it was all too often misused by careerists whom he likened to the French: "Mathematicians are a kind of Frenchman; when one talks to them, they translate it into their language, and then it is immediately something completely different."[8] Repeatedly Goethe blamed the version of the Enlightenment invented by the French for codifying Newtonianism and thereby obstructing open scientific inquiry about all matters, especially seemingly paranormal ones: "The greatest blame for disseminating and ossifying this doctrine, however, lies with the French in particular."[9] Whether in science or in the arts, they always seemed to prefer laws by code rather than laws through precedent.

The clearest statement of Goethe's aversion to Sir Isaac Newton (1642–1727) came in *Materialien zur Geschichte der Farbenlehre*. Believing that one could not understand optics without reflecting on the history of philosophy and the evolution of general science, he provided information about primordial mankind's responses to color. Goethe, the avid reader of travel literature and anthropological works, contended that such peoples always began with the sensual and proceeded to the practical. Whenever their curiosity remained unsatisfied about certain phenomena, like the rainbow, however, they posed complex riddles and solved them "through a fanciful, highly poetic symbolizing."[10] Theory, Goethe continued, only dawned with the Greeks, who represented a yet higher stage of civilization. Their magic was very different from that of subsequent ages: "Ancient magic and sorcery has style, the modern does not. Ancient magic is nature viewed humanly."[11] As a sense of history developed, the theoretical way of viewing things became more and more entrenched: "With so much light one sees no shadow, with so much clearness, no body. One does not see the forest for the trees, mankind for the people. But it appears as if each and every one were getting what they deserve and are therefore in any case content."[12] Maintaining that scientific superstitions quickly emerged to replace the folk ones, he pointed out how Roger Bacon (1216–1294) resorted to numbers as possible pathways to the ineffable. The motivation was understandable, as Goethe explained, "for superstition actually only seizes false means in order to satisfy a genuine need. It is therefore neither so reprehensible as it is considered, nor so infrequent in so-called enlightened ages and among enlightened people."[13] Knowledge was always thought to mean power and for that reason was kept secret from the masses. Those venturing beyond the boundaries of what was accepted as knowable for their times engaged in dangerous games of brinksmanship and usually suffered charges of sorcery.

Goethe's review of optical learning led him to maintain that there were two basic kinds of scientific mind: one was genial, productive, and powerful enough to create worlds out of itself, while the other was intelligent, sharp, observant, and given to collecting and experimenting. Newton, he stated, definitely belonged to the former: "First he finds his theory plausible, then he convinces himself with hastiness."[14] Instead of giving solid evidence from nature itself, Newton enunciated his aperçus as truth and demanded obedience in as strict a way as the medieval scholastics. According to Goethe's accusation, he even cultivated followers to protect his scientific reputation. The members of the French Academy who stood out in Goethe's mind as the leading missioners of "the Newtonian gospel" were Fontenelle and Voltaire, the archproponents of the Franco-Roman neoclassical code.[15]

With such a deep commitment to the inductive pursuit of knowledge about nature, it was inevitable that Goethe would come into contact with the ubiquitous shamanic research of the times. The problems in that research dovetailed with his own concerns about exploring human psychology and developing scientific methodologies that would do justice even to the awesome, the unexpected, and the heretofore unheard of. All the while, such problems and concerns were engaging his fertile artistic imagination.

As a mere schoolboy, Goethe had already been excited by the news that transdisciplinary inquiries were resulting in brand-new academic fields of study at places like the Georgia Augusta University in Göttingen. He apparently had wanted very much to attend the new university, which impressed him as well as most of his contemporaries as being at the forefront of intellectual and scientific investigations.[16] Since his conservative father refused, he was forced to go elsewhere. The young Goethe might have complied with his father's wishes, but he never relinquished his curiosity about what was happening in Göttingen. He subsequently tried to keep up with the results of the experiments and discussions that took place there.

The university in Göttingen was the one most involved with training people for expeditons into unexplored regions of the world. As a result, it was to Göttingen that alumni sent artifacts, books, manuscripts, and reports of their findings and observations. The Russian contingent, which had initially been supported by Catherine's academy in St. Petersburg, was particularly loyal. Baron Georg Thomas von Asch (1729–1807), who studied medicine in Göttingen under Haller, was its leader. His doctorate brought with it the compulsory commission in Catherine's army, which he used in order to widen his circle of contacts, thus enabling him to send all kinds of things back to Göttingen regularly from 1771 to 1806.[17]

Consequently, Baron Asch had great input with regard to the medical and anthropological work being done there. For example, within five years of the date that Prof. Johann Friedrich Blumenbach (1752–1840), the acknowledged founder of anthropology and a leading expert in travel literature, requested some Russian and Asiatic skulls of him, Baron Asch managed to send twenty-two.[18] He also sent along the remains of whatever human curiosities and monstrosities he could find. The most startlingly impressive of Asch's many missives, however, contained the complete outfit of a shaman from the Tungus that somehow failed to make it to the compulsory funeral pyre. Having been described as "probably the oldest and most beautiful piece of this kind to have reached the scientific collections of Europe," it has repeatedly appeared as an unexplained illustration in twentieth-century books and articles dealing with shamanism (plate 20).[19] The outfit had been transported by Karl Heinrich Merck (fl. 1780s) of Darmstadt, who studied medicine in Giessen and Jena before being allowed to engage his scientific wits in greater Russia, thanks to the intercession of his very influential uncle, who happened to be one of Goethe's literary friends.[20]

Goethe himself visited Göttingen in 1783, during a trip to the Harz region, and he got to know even better some of the professors, not only Blumenbach, but also Georg Christoph Lichtenberg (1742–1799), whose researches included physics and psychology. Goethe did not see the renowed shaman outfit because it only arrived around 1788. In 1801, however, when Goethe once more visited Göttingen, he was taken to what had in the meantime become a very prestigious combination museum and library.[21] He must have then seen the shaman gear, always prominently displayed, for he reported that his attention was drawn immediately to the costumes and artifacts. Like so many of his generation, he recognized the connection between the populace of the Siberian expanses and the North American aborigines. Fascinated by research into things Asiatic, he assiduously kept up-to-date with the latest projects and their findings. The Asiatic Academy proposed by Sergej Semenowitsch Uwarow (1786–1855), Russian statesman and scientist, he confessed, "enticed me into those regions where I was inclined to wander for a longer time anyhow."[22]

Blumenbach, with whom Goethe continued to correspond and collaborate, also occasionally visited Weimar.[23] In a letter Goethe wrote to Schiller on October 15, 1796, we read that Blumenbach not only stopped by but "he had a very interesting mummified head along."[24] In subsequent years, Goethe often referred to Blumenbach's interesting collection of skulls.[25] Since Blumenbach was in charge of the library in Göttingen, he allowed Goethe to borrow as many books as he deemed necessary. He also helped get Goethe elected as a scientist to the learned society centered there.

Blumenbach, who seems to have been a mover and shaker, attracted inquisitive young scientists to Göttingen and inspired them to explore

Plate 20. Raiment of Tungus Shaman.

their world. Among his many disciples were Friedrich Hornemann (1772–1800), Carsten Niebuhr (1733–1815), Ulrich Jasper Seetzen (1767–1811), Alexander von Humboldt (1769–1859), and Adalbert von Chamisso (1781–1838).[26] Many of their letters and reports were made public in the *Allgemeine geographische Ephemeriden*, which were published by the relatively well-funded and well-situated Geographical Institute in Weimar in the 1790s.[27] As the records at the Zentralbibliothek der deutschen Klassik in Weimar show, Goethe also borrowed many of the books they wrote or the ones written about them.[28] He also discussed their reports as well as other matters with some of his highly visible contemporaries involved in ethnographic research, such as Friedrich Alexander Bran (1767–1831), Johann Christian Friedrich August von Heinroth (1773–1843), Christian Keferstein (1784–1866), and Carl Friedrich Philipp von Martius (1794–1868).[29]

The Weimar library records further indicate that Goethe's command of travel literature coincided with his theatrical activities as well as his medical and anthropological studies. Among the many books he borrowed were those by Marco Polo, Adam Olearius (1603–1671), John Hawkesworth (ca. 1715–1773), Cornelis de Bruyn (1652–1726 or 1727), George Vancouver (1757–1798), and Mungo Park (1771–1806).[30] Georgi's *Beschreibung aller Nationen des Russischen Reichs*, which I have discussed at length, must have been especially valuable. Goethe frequently ordered and kept in his possession the volume of illustrations accompanying that trilingual report so as to satisfy his own interests and then eventually to help prepare for several pageants called *Maskenzüge russischer Völker*, to make Grand Duchess Maria Pavlowna (1786–1859), who had recently arrived from Russia, feel at home and wanted. Many of the illustrations depict shamans and shamankas of various tribes (see plates 12–19).[31] Another such work that Goethe often consulted was Pallas's *Bemerkungen auf einer Reise in die südlichen Statthalterschaften des Russischen Reiches a.d.J. 1793–1794*.[32] The shaman's posturings in the illustrations that Pallas provided must have at least attracted Goethe's attention, if they did not complement his creative designs (see plate 10).

Goethe continued to borrow many volumes from the libraries in Weimar. Those by his friend and colleague Herder were fetched by pages again and again. Two stood out as being most important with regard to shamanism. One was *Vom Geist der Ebräischen Poesie*, which, as I pointed out earlier, focused on the shamanic common denominator of all religions. Goethe thought so highly of it that he praised it in the notes to his *West-Östlicher Divan*, which was framed by the poetic fiction of travel to the mysterious East. It was in those notes that Goethe himself broached the subject of early religious history, maintaining, like many scholars today, that Zoroaster must have been the first responsible for forming shamanic beliefs into a cult.[33] The other of Herder's works that Goethe often borrowed was *Ideen zu einer Philosophie der Geschichte der Menschheit*, which summed up and evaluated everything that the finest eighteenth-century minds had come to think about shamanism.[34] Even if Goethe did not, contrary to many claims, help write that work, there is more than enough proof that he discussed it with Herder daily during his youth, and, furthermore, that he repeatedly borrowed the published version from the Weimar library during his mature years.[35]

While some of Goethe's other requests from the Weimar library revealed his undaunted efforts to master the Russian language, many underscored his constant reworking of past intellectual as well as personal experiences.[36] Many of those experiences bore a close resemblance to what was reported in the travel literature about the psychology of the shaman. Goethe often referred to his own clairvoyance as well as to the many rationally inexplicable things he experienced in his daily life. There was the time he reported seeing his double, as well as the time he envisioned the name Goethe on the gravestone that twenty-four years later would be for his son. He also purportedly apprehended the earthquake in Messina at the very time it occurred.[37] Most of his friends and acquaintances knew that he seriously entertained thoughts about the spirit world. He would even write to scientific colleagues like Gottfried Nees von Esenbeck (1776–1858), professor of botany in Bonn, comments such as the following: "We all walk in mysteries. We are surrounded by an atmosphere about which we still know nothing at all. We do not know what stirs in it and how it is connected with our intelligence. This much is certain, under particular conditions the antennae of our souls are able to reach out beyond their physical limitations."[38] Again and again Goethe made public his firm belief in an animistic universe constantly repeopled through the process of reincarnation. One such experience challenged the limitations of rational comprehension: "I cannot explain the significance, the power, that this woman has over me in any other way but through the transmigration of souls."[39] Another eerie experience on the trip to Italy in 1786 seems to reflect his absorption in travel literature dealing with such matters: "I enjoy everything as if I had been born and bred here and had just returned from a whaling expedition to Greenland."[40] In this regard, it is interesting to note that Goethe was known among the secret society of Illuminati under the code name Abaris, the legendary shaman who was an Apollonian priest knowledgeable in the healing arts.[41]

Such experiences seem to have gone hand in hand with Goethe's

abiding curiosity about contemporary faith healers and miracle workers. Like many observers in heretofore unexplored territories, he first
attempted to strip their activities of their theatricality and pretense.
Outright quackery, much like carnival magic, was not difficult to uncover. There were times, however, when reason had to be stretched
considerably in an attempt to understand what was operative. Of special interest during a trip to Switzerland in 1779 was Michael Schuppach, the Paracelsus-reading peasant of Emmental who had caused
such a stir in medical circles that even renowned physicians like
Haller, Tissot, and Zimmermann dignified him with notice. They condemned him as a fraud. But Goethe, forever attuned to the strange
workings of the human psyche, wondered whether or not Schuppach
might have indeed effected some kind of cure for his swarm of devoted patients, who came from all walks of life, even the aristocracy.[42]
Faith, Goethe suspected, could be a great healer.

Spiritual forces also played an important role in Goethe's conception of creativity. In a manner that resembled the Plato of the *Ion* and
also the countless observers of shamans, he described to the compan-
ion of his last years, Johann Peter Eckermann, the passivity involved in
becoming enthused—that is, filled with the spirit:

> No productiveness of the highest kind, no remarkable discovery, no great
> thought which bears fruit and has results, is in the power of any one; but
> such things are elevated above all earthly control. Man must consider
> them as an unexpected gift from above, as pure children of God, which
> he must receive and venerate with joyful thanks. They are akin to the
> demon, which does with him what it pleases, and to which he uncon-
> sciously resigns himself, whilst he believes he is acting from his own im-
> pulse. In such cases, man may often be considered as an instrument in a
> higher government of the world—as a vessel found worthy for the recep-
> tion of divine influence.[43]

Goethe thought that the more creative a human being was, the
greater the influence of the spirits would be. Such thoughts were repeatedly recorded by Eckermann: "In poetry," said Goethe, "especially in that which is unconscious, before which reason and understanding fall short, and which therefore produces effects so far
surpassing all conception, there is always something daemonic."[44] So
it was too with music and the other arts. They were dominated by
inexplicable forces from the spirit world. Superb artists were particularly susceptible to those forces. Goethe named Raphael and
Shakespeare and, as could be expected, did not fail to single out the
incomparable Mozart. Another artist whose visions and out-of-body
experiences attracted his attention was Benvenuto Cellini (1500–

1571). Goethe went so far as to translate Cellini's autobiography, which, among other things, described his purportedly easy movement between worlds and his contacts with the spirits of hell. It was published in a journal he brought out with Schiller in 1796–1797, and was then revised and annotated for separate publication in 1803.[45] Literary treatment of creative individuals with such hyperactive spiritual lives also intrigued Goethe, who, as I explained above, was instrumental in seeing to the earliest publication, albeit in German translation, of Diderot's *Neveu de Rameau*. Diderot, a role model for Herder as well as for young Goethe, had during his Russian trip visited Friedrich Heinrich Jacobi (1743–1819) in Pempelfort in 1773.[46] Jacobi, a writer of psychological novels, was such a close friend that Goethe even later housed and served as mentor to his son Max, who in turn became one of the most renowned psychiatrists of the nineteenth century.

Everything Goethe consciously and unconsciously absorbed from such social connections and scientific activities he incorporated in one way or another into his own artistic production. Shamanic research, which encompassed so many of his wide-ranging concerns, was no exception. The sheer amount of evidence precludes the possibility of an occasional coincidence. Goethe knew what there was to know about shamanism in both fact and fiction, and he regularly availed himself of that knowledge. His timeless literary creations profited the most.

An example from 1774 is *Die Leiden des jungen Werthers*. The title figure exhibits just about every one of what would have been commonly recognized as shamanic characteristics. There is the deepseated, uncontrollable urge to solitude or abnormal social relations, in addition to the kind of emotional instability characterized by habitual daydreaming, introspection, and wild swings of mood due to a particularly sensitive nervous system. Physical dysfunction manifests itself in a malaise that cannot be overcome, even with rest, relaxation, and a regulated diet. Werther's sexual immaturity is evident insofar as he is not like other eighteenth-century middle class men in the novel. He does not write his mother; he only deals with her through Wilhelm. He fixates on women who are described as "taken" or of a higher social class. He condones rape. He has a strong penchant for playing with children, especially boys. That penchant is not considered healthy by, for example, the physician whose view Werther lightly discounts for being that of "a very dogmatic marionette."[47] Werther describes that male professional's arrival by writing: "The day before yesterday the medical man came out of the city and found me on the ground among Lotte's children. As some of them were crawling around on me and others were teasing me, I was tickling them and kicking up a big fuss with them."[48]

The interest in play, games, and even dolls underscores the strong tendency to assume roles and enact them. Like a shaman, Werther carefully defines the space in which he acts out his drama as well as seeing to the costumes, properties, lighting, and timing. One need only think of his carefully staged death scene. Among the other diverse artistic aptitudes are poetic susceptibility, dancing ability, and a high enough level of musical know-how to permit tuning of the clavichord.

There are many additional elements similar to those found in contemporary eighteenth-century materials treating shamanism. Practitioners were often viewed as being parasites—necessary, yet living off the labors of their fellow tribesmen. The work ethic obviously does not govern Werther, who not only does little or nothing to earn his living, but also uses Wilhelm to convey his financial needs to his mother. He does not bother to write to her himself, but then he has long had problems dealing with women. Frequently Werther describes his existence in terms of imprisonment or entombment, like the shamans and other oracles who were subjected to the mysteries in caves and other tightly enclosed, womblike spaces.[49] When absolutely distraught, however, he reports that he, like the ancient Boeotian followers of Trophonius and others seeking metaphysical answers, wished to visit the mines. Furthermore, intuition, feelings, and hunches are much more important to him than the scientific determinism or the Newtonian view of the world that led to the rejection of midwives, herbalists, and witches, thus developing the medical profession. Werther has a strong inclination to believe in spirits and to have them animate his world. Early on, he wonders "whether deceiving spirits hover around the region, or whether it is the warm heavenly fancy in my soul that makes everything around here so paradisiacal."[50] As things continue to go relatively well, he remarks, "Not one word about the magical power of ancient music is improbable to me when simple song seizes hold of me."[51]

Trees, which have always represented the three cosmic regions— hell, earth, and heaven—through which the shaman flies, provide Werther so much consolation that he often describes them or laments their being chopped down.[52] He even dreams of gaining the wings of a bird so as to be able to transport himself through those cosmic regions. His somnambulistic leanings seem to strengthen during times of full moon, although he never fully succeeds in releasing his soul for travel through the cosmos: "And when I sometimes stop en route out of weariness and thirst, sometimes in the deep night when the full moon stands over me, I sit down on a gnarled tree in a simple wood so as to get relief for my wounded soles and then doze off in the semi-darkness in a worn-out repose."[53]

Many eighteenth-century observers credited shamans with remarkable surefootedness, even at the height of frenzy during séances in which psychotropic drugs were used. It was difficult for Christian Europeans to understand how such great physical control could be paired with ecstasy. This idea appears in Goethe's novel when the narrator recounts how Werther dealt with his frustrations immediately before committing suicide: "Afterwards one found his hat on a cliff overlooking the valley from the slope of the hill, and it is incomprehensible how he climbed it on a dark, wet night without falling."[54]

Goethe also has Werther have many strange, out-of-body experiences. Werther often refers to himself as a dreamer or as hovering above and beyond the real world. He describes the ecstasy he experienced while dancing with Lotte thus: "I was no longer a person."[55] Elsewhere, he writes "and since that time, the sun, moon, and stars can calmly run their course, I know not whether it is day or night, and the whole world disappears from around me."[56] Occasionally, Werther compares himself to those persecuted by evil spirits. He claims, "I am being played like a marionette."[57] Lotte is the only one with the power to recall him to the consciousness level of everyday, middle-class reality, but that power dwindles after she—as we have to read between the lines—consummates her marriage to Albert. Virginity, and the entire female reproductive system and its lunar cycle, were acknowledged as being magical or at least profound and inexplicable by those who believed in shamans, as well as those local eighteenth-century sovereigns who still might have demanded their first-night right. Thereafter, Werther often complains, "my soul is now dead, no longer do raptures flow from it."[58]

Werther's suicide comes after what I call his swan song during his last visit to Lotte on December 21. It happens to take place at the portentous winter solstice, which the shamanic pagans of northern Europe avidly celebrated. Her suggestions for distracting the obviously mentally disturbed young man worsen his condition instead of improving it. First, she seeks refuge by playing the clavichord. Then she asks him to read from his translation of some melancholy songs about love, valor, and crossing the Great Divide to join the ancestral spirits. They are from Ossian, the purported Celtic shaman, bard, and seer-poet, so aptly forged by Macpherson and so hotly debated by critical theorists all over Europe. Whether or not Werther is supposed to recognize them as forgeries makes no difference, since they affect his nervous system quickly and irrevocably. As soon as he takes them into his hand, "a shudder [steals] upon him," and his eyes well up with tears.[59]

Werther begins a heartfelt dramatic reading. Method actor that he is, and has always been, he empathizes with the role so completely that he gets carried away by it, transmitting his own enthusiasm to Lotte, who happens to be sitting next to him on the sofa: "The agitation of both was terrible. They felt their own misery in the fate of those noble ones, felt it together, and their tears united them. Werther's lips and eyes burned on Lotte's arm, a shiver seized her, she wanted to withdraw and all the pain and sympathy lay upon her like lead."[60] Her attempt to keep him at bay by suggesting he continue fails miserably. The power of the shamanic words—as contemporary reports repeatedly stressed—is too strong for either party to remain rational enough to resist. Werther is the first one off the sofa and onto the floor for what turns out to be a rather torrid, yet short, love scene: "Her senses became confused, she pressed his hands, pressed them against her breast, leaned towards him with a melancholy movement, and their glowing cheeks touched. The world disappeared to them. He wove his arms around her, pressed her to his breast, and covered her trembling, stammering lips with frenzied kisses. Werther!"[61] Lotte regains her middle-class senses and, suddenly realizing she is on the floor with Werther, pushes him away so she can leave. When she tells him she will never see him again, he stretches out his arms toward her. He thereupon remains immobilized, as if in a trance, on the floor with his head on the sofa for more than half an hour.

Goethe's Werther is the perfect example of an unsuccessful shaman. The eighteenth century often read that those shamanic initiates who felt called would perish if they could not cure themselves by shamanizing. Goethe must have known that, especially in the early 1770s, during the height of the so-called academic expeditions in Siberia. All the ecstatic, trancelike states that Goethe has his Werther work himself into fail to unleash the kind of poetic, musical, mimetic, and dramatic gifts that might enable him to cure his own self-induced madness and self-destructive tendencies. Nor is Werther capable of transmitting his trance to others so that something generally beneficial results for the whole tribe or society. Werther is a big loser in the game of brinksmanship, not only by falling over the brink himself, but by taking along with him everyone who has been nice to him or has cared about him.

Goethe's interest in shamanism remained so intense that what he read by the explorers, ethnographers, and anthropologists began to merge with his background in Nordic and classical mythology, and it infiltrated his poetry in various and unexpected ways. The ballad *Der*

Zauberlehrling, based on Lucian of Samosata, depicts the misuse of incantatory power, demonstrating that it is best left to those who have been called to such tasks. It represents the consequences of what was described in a song of Odin, the ancient Germanic shaman, entitled "Die Zauberkraft der Lieder" in Herder's collection of folk songs.[62] Another example is the festival play that was commissioned of Goethe by the Berlin theater in 1814 to celebrate the return of King Friedrich Wilhelm III in the company of Czar Alexander after the defeat of Napoleon. The result was *Epimenides Erwachen,* which was based on the myth of the Cretan shepherd who, after sleeping half a century, awakened as a shaman. The higher powers who initiated him see to the righting of the ignominious wrongs his people bravely endured during his long absence.[63]

There is also the textbook example of a shamanka inevitably condemned to early death because of genetic problems deriving from incest. That is the quasi-androgynous Mignon in *Wilhelm Meisters Lehrjahre,* a novel filled with all kinds of allusions to the contemporary assimilation of shamanic information. They are especially noticeable in the hero's involvement with theories of acting and drama. The description of his discovery of the world populated by Shakespeare mentions, for example,

> There are said to be certain sorcerers who by magic can entice a host of different spirits into their chamber. The conjurations are so powerful that the whole room is filled and the spirits, jostled up to the tiny magic circle that the wizard has drawn, swirl around it and float above his head, constantly changing and increasing in number. Every corner is crammed full, every shelf occupied, eggs keep expanding, and gigantic shapes shrink to toadstools. But unfortunately the necromancer has forgotten the magic word to make this flood of spirits subside.[64]

There are more than allusions when Wilhelm's wounds are later dressed "with all sorts of strange speeches, maxims and ceremonies."[65]

Wilhelm Meister, who constantly refers to the magic and sorcery of theater, encounters Mignon as an overly made-up youngster among a vagabond troupe of tightrope walkers, dancers, and jugglers (*Gaukler*). This human oddity or riddle immediately gains inexplicable power over him; his eyes and his heart are irresistibly drawn to her. Throughout the novel, her presence is termed mysterious. Wilhelm gains her unflinching loyalty after he saves her from another beating by her abusive manager, whom he buys off with thirty thalers. He thereupon expends great effort and expense trying to figure her out, even double-checking her regular early-morning attendance at mass. She, in turn, serves as a tutelary spirit (*Schutzgeist*) for his son Felix.

Though suffering from poor eye-hand coordination and the kind of convulsions and strange muscle spasms associated with epileptic seizures—so typical in the shamanic profile—Mignon is innately musical and can, for example, perfectly perform the fandango amidst eggs, but only when she chooses to do so:

> She blindfolded herself, gave a sign for the music to begin, and started to move like a wound-up mechanism, beating the time of the melody with the clap of her castanets.
>
> Nimbly and lightly she executed the dance with rapid precision, stepping so briskly and firmly between and beside the eggs that at any moment one thought she would crush one of them or dislodge it by the swiftness of her twistings and turnings. But she never touched an egg despite the variety of her steps, now short, now long, including some leaps. She finally wound her way through the rows in a half-kneeling position. She pursued her course relentlessly like clockwork and the strange music gave a new twist to the movement of the rousing dance every time it started up again. Wilhelm was absolutely transported by this strange spectacle; forgetting all his cares, he followed every step of the beloved creature, amazed to see how completely her character was manifested in the dance.[66]

At the close of book 2, Wilhelm has the opportunity to witness one of Mignon's seizures. Holding her hands to comfort her, he feels a slight twitch increase to ever greater spasms. Her inability to articulate her pain prompts him to pick her up and sit her on his lap. She holds her chest firmly before uttering a cry that is accompanied by full-blown convulsions. Then "she jumped up, and then immediately fell down in front of him, as if every limb in her body were broken. It was a terrifying sight."[67] The intensity of her convulsive movements ebbs and flows, and at one point, "her rigid limbs unfroze, her whole inner self poured itself out, and in the confusion of the moment Wilhelm feared that she might melt away in his arms so that nothing of her would remain."[68]

In the fifth book, Wilhelm's players successfully mount *Hamlet*. After the performance, the cast decides to celebrate in costume, and "it seemed as if a band of regal spirits had assembled."[69] The musical instrument Mignon plays while dancing purportedly for their amusement is the one the eighteenth century most closely associated with archaic shamanism, as it was known at the time: the tambourine. She joins with the Harper and Felix, who plays the triangle, yet another shamanic instrument easily recognized by eighteenth-century readers of travel reports, for a séance-type performance that increases in velocity and ferocity:

The children jumped and danced, and Mignon was particularly un-inhibited, more than she had ever been before. She played the tambou-rine as delicately and then as loudly as possible, sometimes lightly skim-ming her fingers over the skin, at other times beating on it with the back of her hand or her knuckles, even alternating between striking her knees or her head with the instrument, sometimes just making the bells ring, so that all sorts of sounds were enticed from this simplest of instruments.[70]

When Serlo chides the intoxicated Mignon for seating herself in the place reserved for the ghost, she casually replies that he would not do her any harm, for he was related to her: "He's my uncle."[71]

The children thereupon make believe they are puppets, a standard procedure for initiates, according to many eighteenth-century re-ports. The noises they emit—much like shamanic ventriloquism—are accompanied by spastic movements that intensify. Then we read the following:

> Mignon was almost frenetically excited and, amusing as this had been in the beginning, it became such that it had to be curbed. But admonishing her seemed to have little effect, for she now began hysterically to rush around the table, tambourine in hand, hair flying, head thrown back and her body flung into the air like one of those maenads whose wild and well-nigh impossible postures still delight us on ancient monuments.[72]

As the party begins to break up after others have performed and the ghost's scarf has been found, Wilhelm Meister suddenly feels himself being grasped painfully. What Goethe's text suggests is the kind of ritualistic sexual cannibalism connected to some versions of shaman-ism: "Mignon had been hiding, and seizing hold of him, she bit him in the arm."[73]

When a conflagration breaks out at the inn, it is Mignon who man-ages to warn Wilhelm of the grave danger. She later explains that the Harper set the fire when she thwarted his attempt to make a blood sacrifice of Felix, whom she has tried to protect all along. Her intuition is coupled with her admitted ability to hear voices and converse with the spirits, sometimes the Blessed Virgin Mary among them.

The illness consuming Mignon receives particular attention in the eighth and last book of the novel. Her cramps so adversely affect her vital signs that cardiac arrest could be the diagnosis. When the cramps abate, however, her pulse rate becomes abnormally fast. A peaceful balance of mind and body only seems to result when she portrays an angel at a birthday party, for she sings the hauntingly beautiful "So let me seem till I become" and refuses to relinquish her angelic robes.[74]

The physician, who has been keeping close watch on Mignon's behavior, reports that longing for her homeland and for Wilhelm are her only two ties to this world.[75] Since there seems to be no hope of her full recovery, he suggests doing whatever possible to bring her relief. When Wilhelm visits, she is hugging her dear Felix and is indeed at peace: "She looked like a departed spirit."[76] Although she is no longer capable of climbing and springing around, she still wishes she could reach the mountain peaks, proceeding from housetops to treetops. In true shamanic style, she envies the birds their ability to fly and nest wherever they choose.

The full story behind this poignantly enigmatic creature, who also serves as a kind of glue for the novel's plot, is told when her newly arrived uncle recognizes her corpse at her funeral. It turns out that Mignon, the child of the Harper and his sister, was never normal. She walked at a decidedly early age, moved skillfully, and sang beautifully. She also quickly learned to play the zither without any formal instruction. Although prodigiously creative as a young child, communication in words was most difficult, "and the obstacle seemed to be in its mind rather than in its speech organs."[77] Greater freedom of physical expression came with the foster care to which she was given over because of her sinful origins. Then she assumed male clothing so as to gain greater flexibility while ascending mountains and running on precarious ledges. This very young Mignon already demonstrated astounding spatial memory as well as great artistic instincts when she perfectly imitated the intricately whimsical steps of wandering performers. She was also given to periods of profound solitude, disappearing for days on end. The last time, however, the multitalented child was kidnapped and did not return. When it came to the background of his most successful shaman, Goethe purposely made many changes. That is the subject of the next chapter.

CHAPTER NINE

Faust,
the Modern Shaman

GOETHE'S *Faust* forms a fitting conclusion for this book because it is a consummate masterpiece that incorporates into the very scheme of European cultural evolution nearly everything the eighteenth century had heard or thought about shamanism. It elevates the phenomenon that had been considered diabolically aberrant, incredibly ludicrous, and then harmlessly exotic, and gives that phenomenon its significant place in the history as well as the prehistory of the West. It also magnificently brings shamanism together with philosophy, specifically Renaissance Neoplatonism. Furthermore, it synthesizes the legendary German shaman of yore with the mythical magus, thereby creating a modern emblem for enlightenment in all the possible senses of that word.

The subject of shamanism and Goethe's *Faust* deserves the sort of detailed treatment that can only come in a book. If I deny it that treatment at present, it is not because I believe there is insufficient evidence for a unifying principle long sought by scholars of various persuasions.[1] I do so merely because of the spatial constraints imposed by the framework of this book. I shall therefore limit myself here mainly to those pertinent textual matters that substantiate suggesting a new reading. Among the most important are the three opening parts, which have unfortunately not always been accorded their due by editors and critics alike.[2]

The dedicatory poem, "Zueignung," immediately constructs the tragedy, the work of art, as the realm in which knowledge of the wavering forms of the spirit world can be transmitted to audiences through the poet.[3] As in a preparatory incantation, the poet addresses those forms directly in the first stanza. Throughout his life, they repeatedly approached him, sometimes quite forcibly, and each time he tried to capture them. Feeling rejuvenated by the magic breath scenting their procession, he now, like a shaman, resolves to surrender to them so as to let them reign through him at will.

The next stanza continues to use the shamanic vocabulary to concentrate on the immediate past. It describes the wavering forms as bringing along the images of happier days, while many a beloved shade rises from the spirit world. Goethe, who suspected a connection between primeval forms of shamanism and the incipient mythology that in prehistoric times began to form the cultural basis of Europe—something he would take up in part 2 of the drama—has the poetic voice refer to an ancient myth all but incomprehensible to the present. What it evokes allows love and friendship to resurface. That then renews his grief for all those who preceded him into the Great Beyond.[4]

His songs, especially the one that will follow, are the subject of the third stanza, which seems straightforward enough until we consider that most shamanic reports equated the song with the shaman's journey to the spirit world, while viewing his musical instrument as his vehicle of transportation. The poetry of remotest antiquity had already used the song as a standard formula for that kind of trip.[5] Those who first composed the poet's audiences served as continuing echoes for that which was transmitted through him from the spirits—much like the transference through the Platonic series of rings. However, his song now resounds for unknown multitudes whose receptivity to any magic, much less the magic of art, he suspects is doubtful. Those who would continue to delight in his song, he believes, have lost their necessary communal unity and, scattered over the world, their all-important home base, or sacred ground.

The concluding stanza makes the bridge—another shamanic device—to the rest of *Faust* still stronger while simultaneously indicating that the poet is approaching the end of his own journey. Moved again by that once-conquered longing for the quiet, serious spiritual realm, his whispering song now only floats forth in uncertain tones, like those of an aeolian harp. Awe grips him, tears result, and his soul begins to feel mellow and yielding. His own passage almost complete, he bilocates for a grand overview of the work that was his life:

> what I possess seems something far away
> and what had disappeared proves real.[6]

With the normal laws of causality lifted because of the shamanic framework, real time and space categories dissolve into the hypothetical or theatrical, thus allowing for the opening scene, "Vorspiel auf dem Theater." It consists of three figures essential to the European theatrical tradition, the director, the poet, and the actor, arguing about the superiority of their own individual contributions to the whole. Their discussion then serves to expand the themes of the dedicatory poem with a major focus on creativity. The closing words of the director, who has been urging cooperation, make all of creation accessible to the fictive assembled public by reducing it to the stage set at hand with its various technical devices. They also serve to underscore the notion that shamans can find out what is going on above and below as well as on earth:

> So now upon our modest stage act out
> creation in its every aspect,
> and move with all deliberate haste
> from heaven, through the world, to hell![7]

What Goethe has done here, with the utmost efficiency, is to shift levels of reality. Brilliantly using the modern arts of performance as the shamanic medium—an idea my chapter on Herder elucidates and the section on *Wilhelm Meister* in the preceding chapter takes up—he has moved from the realm of wavering forms (*schwankende Gestalten*) to dramatic characters with living actors actually embodying those forms. Everything that follows is not only part of the trip or song, but is also a play that can be comprehended through the imagination or through a suspension of the rational faculties. In other words, this play constitutes the shaman's way of communicating to his fellow human beings the knowledge he gained from his trip or trips into other realms of existence.[8]

Goethe zeroes in still further with the "Prolog im Himmel," which comes next, for the stage is not only the emblem of the cosmos, it has become the cosmos itself. There he has the Lord go so far as to select a specific individual as the very best of what humankind has produced. Faust is to become the major player, the medium within the medium. In suggesting that Mephistopheles use his hellish gifts to attempt to derail this modern shaman and return him to the ambitious, greedy level of the shaman in German folklore and the sixteenth-century folk book (*Volksbuch*), the Lord shows that he acknowledges the forces of evil and relegates them to their rightful place in his creation. Before departing the stage, the Lord gives strong affirmation to the major themes first struck in the dedication:

> May the power of growth that works and lives forever
> encompass you in love's propitious bonds,
> and may you give the permanence of thought
> to that which hovers in elusive forms.[9]

The beginning of the first part of the tragedy immediately reveals the status of North European shamanism after centuries of the Christianization process. Would-be proponents, those who somehow feel called, have lost their natural roots, while opponents, whether religious or scientific, consider it all hocus-pocus or witchcraft. Like those eighteenth-century aborigines who complained that the missioners' teachings prohibited their direct conversation with the spirit world,

Faust is totally removed from nature in his Gothic study, struggling to contact the spirits philosophically, through books.

When it came to the background of his most successful shaman, Goethe purposely made many changes.[10] Goethe's Faust is not the ignoble peasants' son of the sixteenth-century legend that led to the popular tales containing many overtly evil shamanic aspects from European folklore. As we learn at the beginning of the tragedy, Faust's father was a medicine man, alchemist, magician, or, as he is called, *ein dunkler Ehrenmann*, who not only introduced his son to the trade but also reared him in the Christian religion.[11] He named him Heinrich, instead of Johann as in folklore.[12] He imbued him with a conscience, a sense of responsibility, and a deep concern for his fellow human beings. The melancholic youngster given to bouts of solitude observed his father's work, all the while developing a thirst for still better ways to improve mankind's plight.[13] Later, in the scene with his pedantic, yet loyal, famulus, Faust mentions the two souls in his breast while reflecting on the disparity between knowledge with a capital "k" and a small "k":

> You only know one driving force,
> and may you never seek to know the other!
> Two souls, alas! reside within my breast,
> and each is eager for a separation:
> in throes of coarse desire, one grips
> the earth with all its senses;
> the other struggles from the dust
> to rise to high ancestral spheres.
> If there are spirits in the air
> who hold domain between this world and heaven—
> out of your golden haze descend,
> transport me to a new and brighter life!
> If I but had a magic cloak
> that could bear me away to exotic places
> I'd not exchange it for the choicest garments,
> not even for the mantle of a king.[14]

It was well known from the shamanic lore of Goethe's day that there were "two souls, namely the shadow and the breath of the human being," and that one of them could exit the body at night to hunt, cavort, or whatever.[15] Faust's struggle to release his soul, however, is self-conscious and unsuccessful. The failure of the best conventional means the times could offer—the cumulative rationalistic learning of four university faculties—drives Faust to attempt suicide, which is the kind of ritualistic death and resurrection typical of shamanic initiation the world over.[16]

On returning to his study after the Easter walk among the rejuvenated citizenry, Faust notices the poodle who turns out to be Mephistopheles. It is at that point that Goethe, who constantly skirts the standard form of the Faust legend, almost rejoins it by bringing up the matter of the pact. The best-trained, most intelligent human being stands at the same kind of impasse as natural man. He momentarily feels he cannot comprehend the mysteries without help. Deprived of the knowledge natural man gains as a matter of course through his images and rituals, Faust yearns to perceive heroic victory and sexual power, claiming

> What ecstasy to feel that lofty spirit's might—
> if only, then, my soul had left this body![17]

This professor and natural philosopher who seeks the hidden meaning of life thereupon curses all appearance, "all the enticements that delude my soul with cheating visions."[18] Hoping to bring the methodology of scientific determinism in line with intuition and hunch, he has come to believe he is fully prepared to analyze rationally whatever his heretofore deadened nonrational capacities might teach him.

The Faust who emerges from this discussion with Mephisto might be discouraged, but he is not beaten. He considers the human being the most marvelous creature in the universe.[19] If magic means anything to him at this point in his development, it is still a tool for the highest realization of natural philosophy rather than for demonic power.[20] That is where Mephisto, who can only provide the latter, diverges from Faust. The clearest proof of Goethe's shamanic intent is again his alteration of the standard legend. He has Faust offer a bet rather than agree to a pact:

> If ever you, with lies and flattery,
> can lull me into self-complacency
> or dupe me with a life of pleasure,
> may that day be the last for me!
> This is my wager.[21]

The scene in Auerbach's wine cellar serves to show the audience and also Mephisto that Faust has long since progressed well beyond the juggling tricks of the transient mountebanks that would amuse a group of academic failures drinking away their lives. The kind of ecstasy available there disgusts Faust rather than enticing him to participate in orgies. The further degeneration of the shamanic presented in the witch's kitchen, yet another step away from the university, at once repulses and attracts Faust. This core of what had become folk belief nevertheless leads out of male academic life to the world of woman when its magic mirror reflects "a picture of a woman of surpassing beauty!"[22] Mirrors had long been part of shamanic paraphernalia. As a receptacle for souls, the mirror often served as a means for entering the trance state.[23] This scene also enables Faust to shed years from his looks. Furthermore, it shows that he is quite familiar with the type of séance the witch conducts, in a circle with flickering light and musical accompaniment as preparation for imbibing the magic potion. Faust states,

> The silly apparatus, the demented gestures—
> I've seen enough of such jejune deceptions
> to know that I cannot abide them.[24]

Despite his rational resolve to resist, he is so swept up that his head begins to ache from the sounds:

> What is this nonsense she's reciting?
> If this goes on my head will split.
> I seem to hear the voices of
> a hundred thousand fools in chorus.[25]

The subsequent Gretchen episode not only provides Faust with ample opportunities to experience guilt, but also, more importantly, it introduces him to the female creative sphere in ways he can begin to comprehend nonrationally as well as rationally. If he at first thought only of the ecstasy of deflowering a virgin—"She's over fourteen, isn't she!"—he ultimately comes to think of that female as embodying the love that holds the cosmos together, and he cannot get her out of his thoughts.[26] Thus what the Lord said in his closing words in the prologue will be realized.

The "Wald und Höhle" scene represents Faust's furthest remove thus far from university book-learning and mechanistic approaches to nature. It is here that he begins to perceive some absolute truths nonrationally. Since primordial days, and in most shamanic practices of the eighteenth century, the cave was associated with the mother and the forest with the Great Beyond. Both were considered replete not only with mysteries but also with the revelation of those mysteries. As so often in the eighteenth century, mythology and literature gained new significance from recent discoveries. The caves in Franconia as well as elsewhere in Germany were being systematically explored in Goethe's day, and evidence was being assembled about primordial man's spiritual beliefs as well as his coexistence with extinct mammals.[27] Even Justus Möser had posited in "Von den Mysterien und dem Volksglauben der alten Deutschen und Gallier" that the ancient Germans, like the ancient Greeks, had conducted underground services that were like plays. Möser also made connections to initiatory rites and Plato's paths to the underworld.[28] Faust's lines in the cave scene are as follows:

> And when the storm-swept forest creaks and groans,
> when, as it falls, the giant fir strips down
> and crushes neighboring boughs and trunks, and when
> the hill echoes its fall as muffled thunder,
> you guide me to the safety of a cave,
> reveal my self to me, and then my heart's
> profound and secret wonders are unveiled.[29]

Ignorant of any intrinsic human worth, Mephisto continually tries to steer Faust toward the path that the Christians interpreted as magical deception and shamanic skulduggery. This is especially true in "Walpurgisnacht," when Mephisto's very first lines offer a broomstick. It was known as early as the fifteenth century that the witches' salves rubbed on the genitals with broomsticks produced sexual ecstasy and feelings of flight.[30] Faust declines the offer, preferring to stay on his own two feet as long as possible. Whether under the influence of drugs, alcohol, stimulation of the inner ear, or autosuggestion, he, Mephisto, and a will-o'-the-wisp enter a state of altered consciousness, or, as they sing,

> It would seem we've been admitted
> to the sphere of dreams and magic.
> Guide us well, do yourself credit,
> speed us on our travels onward
> in these vast, deserted spaces![31]

Despite the feverish pitch of the orgy and the potent salve the witches mention, Faust wants to turn it all into a learning experience. Such a concentration of evil, he believes, should solve many a riddle for him. Whether or not the spirits exist is not one of them. The Proktophantasmist maintains the opposite. Goethe here satirizes the Newtonian point of view that is determined to rely on its own perceptions even when faced with the very reality that contradicts them. Proclaiming that the Enlightenment abolished all spooks, the Proktophantasmist states:

> I tell you spirits to your faces:
> my spirit won't put up with despotism—
> it is itself far too despotic.[32]

Smitten by a beautiful young witch, Faust chooses to dance with her and is on the verge of succumbing to her charms until the red mouse so typical of evil in Germanic folklore springs from her mouth.[33]

Thereupon Faust envisions the deserted, distraught Gretchen, which jolts him back to thoughts of his true mission.

After the passing revue of wavering forms that is "Walpurgisnachtstraum oder Oberons und Titanias Goldne Hochzeit, Intermezzo," Faust suffers a kind of relapse, in that he implores Mephisto to use the tactics of black magic or false shamanism to free his beloved. She senses this already as they approach her cell in the dungeon. Despite the absence of rationality brought on by her overwhelming guilt, she knows intuitively to reject all their evil magical means and place herself in the hands of God. As a result, she is saved. Furthermore, she remains in Faust's thoughts, as the Lord said, and continues to be a model for his behavior.

Part 2 of Goethe's work opens with Faust reclining on a flowering lawn while various beings from the spirit world hover above him. This is an inversion of the beginning of part 1, where he was sitting up at the desk in his Gothic study, applying his rational faculties with great discipline. The nocturnal healing session the spirits have been conducting obviously succeeds in reviving the guilt-stricken Faust, for he resolves to continue his striving, albeit with a different point of view. Instead of struggling for a head-on confrontation as before, he now resolves to seek enlightenment not from the sun itself but from its reflection.[34] The rainbow, which was endemic in most eighteenth-century manifestations of shamanism, serves as the main image in this part, which is to deal primarily in images.[35] It is here that Faust becomes more and more a performer and a showman.

The scene shifts to the imperial throne room where Mephisto, having assumed the guise of a court jester, attempts to ingratiate himself with the emperor by offering to restock the depleted treasury with gold from hidden veins in Mother Earth. The commonsense reaction of the advisers as well as the average people is negative. They suspect trickery at best, sorcery at worst. With the herald's announcement that it is time to suspend rational belief, the level of dramatic reality blurs, for so begins the carnival celebration that comprises all kinds of spooks and shenanigans. Staged as a Renaissance masque, it is more or less a purgation ritual, modernized and secularized.[36] Again there is the parade of wavering forms from European theater and mythology. Faust, as a kind of updated shaman, has the last word. The herald, who amidst all the revelry seems to take his job of keeping order very seriously, cannot distinguish invited guests from party crashers:

> But I fear that air-born spirits
> are now coming through the windows,
> and I'm helpless to protect you
> from such ghostly sorcery.[37]

This scene, which is a masque within the carnival play-within-the-play, not only has the much-desired gold miraculously portrayed, but also has the emperor so carried away by his role-playing that he actually thinks he is Pan, his disguise until the conflagration burns the masks and returns him to the appropriate level of dramatic reality. Accusations of lies and charlatanry, "Lug und Trug," accompany such goings-on. Even the herald's description of Faust's arrival includes an astonished comment about the magic of the performance: "A miracle has been performed!"[38] Faust has come dispensing wealth as Plutus, richly attired in the turban and oriental robes long associated with magicians.[39] Warding off the greedy with sparks from his wand, he forms a magic circle to protect the illusory treasure. He brings the scene to a conclusion with the traditional magician's formula:

> When demonic forces threaten,
> magic must come to our aid.[40]

The summation of action that follows in "Lustgarten" indicates that the paper money the emperor signed into law while in his trance state now floods the land and has, momentarily at least, solved the most pressing problems. This magic paper brings such joy to the court that even the treasurer relaxes his strict standards, ironically stating, "I welcome the magician as my colleague."[41]

The success with the money led Faust to promise to grant yet another of the emperor's wishes. This one involves producing Helen of Troy and Paris, not as wavering forms but as distinct forms—that is, not merely in poetic description but in actual incarnation through dramatic portrayal.[42] This is the kind of thing any successful shaman would be able to do, for he would have all the skills and arts of performance so as to divert or engage his audience's imagination.[43] The Faust of German folklore, with which Goethe was widely familiar, was known for being especially astute in matters histrionic.[44] Mephisto, with whom Faust consults in "Finstere Galerie," is, however, nonplussed by this latest wish:

> Pagans are none of my affair—
> they live in their own special hell.[45]

Since he claims he is not completely in control of all the details of ancient Greek mythology, he devilishly decides to make it up as he goes along. He suggests a perilous journey to the mothers in the great repository of forms in the ur-nothingness that can be reached by means of a key that must touch the tripod near their approach:

> all is form in transformation,
> Eternal Mind's eternal entertainment.

About them hover images of all that's been created,
but you they will not see, for they see only phantoms.[46]

Mephisto's words lull Faust into summoning his courage, obeying
what he hears, and believing what is suggested. This journey will
be the most strenuous activity to which Faust's imagination or nonrational faculties have thus far been put. Its connections to shamanic
initiation rites are more than merely superficial. The mothers who
dwell on nine hills represented cosmic creative power to believers of
Siberian shamanism, who incorporated them into much of the folk
poetry recorded by Westerners.[47]

While the court impatiently awaits Faust's highly publicized performance of a spirit scene (*Geisterszene*), Mephisto captures their attention
with some traditional fast-talking quackery.[48] His own agitation over
the delay in getting the show mounted amusingly serves to describe
the increased sense of anticipation in the audience, which, like any
group at a séance, is already prepared to see whatever the medium will
want it to see:

> In such a place, I think, spells are not needed;
> ghosts will come here without an invitation.[49]

Along with the herald, the courtiers describe the setting for the performance and thereby their own high levels of expectation. It is the
astrologer, himself aware of the techniques for working an audience,
who sees it all as the magic of theater:

> By royal command the play shall start at once.
> Become an opening, what now is wall!
> When magic operates, all things are easy;
> like jetsam swept by tides, the arras vanishes;
> the wall divides and is reversed,
> creating the effect of a deep stage
> as we seem bathed in some mysterious glow;
> I'll now climb up to its proscenium.[50]

As one who knows, he subsequently confirms the mighty power of the
imagination by stating, "let Reason be the thrall of Magic."[51] This play-
within-the-play begins as the astrologer reports that Faust is emerging
from the vault as a shaman successfully returned from his perilous
trip on behalf of the present group:

> Behold the thaumaturge, in priestly robe and wreath,
> who'll now complete his daring enterprise.
> A tripod rises with him from a cavernous hole;
> I think I now smell incense from its bowl.[52]

Faust, who has gained the tripod, the prize that allows him to transcend the limitations of time and space, sums up his purported experiences in the ur-nothingness and, addressing the mothers, refers to the shaman who endures the hardships of the trip, returns to his people, and makes it all visible:

> Some are caught up in life's propitious course;
> others, the dauntless sorcerer seeks out,
> who generously displays for all to see
> the marvels that their hearts desire.[53]

Then the astrologer once again describes the ongoing pantomime, which is accompanied by music as well as by something that looks like fog. In his opinion, it is truly a spirit masterpiece. As might be expected in a post-Fontenelle, eighteenth-century rendition of a Renaissance shamanic séance, some kind of controlled substance has been added to the smoke. It is even potent enough to have one young lady remark about how good it makes her feel, quite fervently refreshed.[54] An older woman confirms this:

> There really emanates from him a gentle breath
> that deeply stirs my soul![55]

Faust, who now considers himself initiated into the priesthood, exudes so much enthusiasm over Helen that Mephisto, who has been helping in the prompter's box, warns him to control himself and not forget the role he is playing.[56] The warning falls on deaf ears, for, whether or not pretending total emotional involvement in his role in the pantomime, Faust becomes so jealous of Paris that he touches him with the magic key after grabbing hold of Helen. The ensuing dramatic explosion leaves Faust stunned on the floor while the would-be spirits exit in the mist. This exemplifies what most eighteenth-century informants reported about the protection from touch granted the entranced shaman in the show during his séance. Insects, especially flies, were to be swatted away, which we now realize was done to maintain the suspension of disbelief or hoax among onlookers. Faust's performance has been short, yet most convincing. He has returned a shaman from a trip to the other regions, still subject to a trancelike state that will persist until a cloud brings him back to the reality of the Renaissance at the beginning of act 4. This short performance serves as a prologue for the forthcoming grand production synthesizing various modern and revived ancient theatrical forms. It states, by way of exposition, the theme or argument of Faust's search and retrieval of Helen and demonstrates, like any magic show, the dangers involved in attempting to surmount the natural barriers of time and space.

In order to avoid confusion during my discussion, I offer a brief outline of this production within the play, referring for clarity's sake to acts rather than scenic or generic divisions. Act 1 begins at the Gothic laboratory where the newly formed Homunculus, seeking incarnate being for himself, peers into Faust's imagination to describe his preoccupation with Helen's incarnation. Act 2 involves the beginning of Classische Walpurgisnacht among the witches of Thessaly. It portrays the perilous journey to find the means whereby Helen can be located. The high point then comes in act 3, which is the rest of Classische Walpurgisnacht while Faust is in the underworld. Homunculus's attempt to marry Galatea provides the opportunity for a really big show that emblematically foreshadows what is eventually to happen to the reincarnation of Helen.[57] The last acts of this production within the play form the third act of *Faust*. They take place in the Pelopennesus, act 4 dealing with Helen's need for rescue before the palace of Menelaus, and act 5 with life in Arcadia and Euphorion, the product of the marriage of Faust and Helen. An epilogue rounds off the production as Faust mounts the glory machine to disappear among the clouds while the chorus of Trojan maidens sings of breaking the spell and getting things back to normal in the spirit world.

Act 1, then, of this production within the play opens with Faust lying across an antiquated bed in his former Gothic study; his soul, at least, would seem finally to be freed to experience other times and realms. Since his initial departure, science has, to apply the terms Goethe set up elsewhere in his four epochs of science, proceeded from the empirical, investigative, and curious to the dogmatic, didactic, and pedantic.[58] Students like the Baccalaureus are boldly ratifying what was to become the Cartesian idea of "thinking is being": "There was no world before I bade it be."[59] The major professor and the principal investigator in this medievally equipped alchemical laboratory is Faust's diligent old famulus, Wagner, who remains baffled by all matters pertaining to natural origins and the relationship of the mind to the body. He has been trying to create a test-tube person, for he cannot even abide the thought of something as bestial as the sex act, suggested so wittily by Mephisto, being related to the conception of human life. Since reason knows that human beings are so superior, Wagner thinks there has to be a higher, more dignified way of generating babies. His experimentation, now in Mephisto's presence, succeeds in bringing forth Homunculus, a spirit much like a genie in a bottle, who turns out to be empowered enough to see directly into the entranced Faust's head. What that confirms is Faust's thoughts about the conception by Leda and the swan of Helen, who represents for him at this point the mysteries of birth, death, and regeneration.

Like Orpheus, and like Herder's orphic archetype among the Amerindians, Faust has spent his trance searching the nether regions for a beloved lost soul.[60] His communication of that search to his German audience at the imperial court takes the form of a grand theatrical pageant that uses, as the director of the "Vorpiel" promised, all the scenery, trapdoors, lifts, glory wagons, and machines for representing fog, waves, and clouds.[61] Although until this day not proven to its fullest, due to reverential attitudes toward the text, the pageant's stageworthiness is attested to by its incorporation of a wide array of theatrically viable techniques that are very efficient with regard to sets and props. For example, there are dramatic reports, recapitulations, simultaneous relations of telescoped events, mimetic cues in the speeches, and changes of venue described in the lines. In many ways this grand production resembles the Italian musico-dramatic works celebrating Orpheus that stand at the historical beginnings of modern opera. As the Italian Renaissance glorified the Orpheus myth with syntheses of the arts, so here Goethe has the German Renaissance celebrate its most famous shaman's perilous journey to fetch Helen of Troy.[62] He uses this to outline by means of theatrical shorthand the evolution from the archaic shamanism of prehistoric times to the mythology that little by little became the foundation of Western culture. It was a mythology that was revived by the Renaissance and then revived again in the eighteenth century and the early nineteenth century.[63]

Homunculus combines his ability to read minds with his amazing awareness of the ancient spirit world, and suggests helping Faust by attending the imminent classical Walpurgisnacht. When Mephisto, who claims ignorance about remote antiquity, becomes recalcitrant, Homunculus boldly comments,

> Romantic spectres are the only ones you know,
> but any proper ghost has to be classical.[64]

Instead of staying in northwestern Europe, they head for the southeast and the notorious witches of Thessaly, with whom Mephisto has been tantalized. The witch Erichtho, noted for her ugliness in most sources, provides the initial description for the setting of the classical Walpurgisnacht, drawing immediate attention to what is to be taken as a meteor.[65] The three aerial voyagers arrive in their glory machine amid legions from Hellenic saga, and Homunculus, who serves a function similar to that of the will-o'-the-wisp in part 1, urges Mephisto to put Faust down:

> Your cavalier,
> once you set him on the ground,

will come promptly back to life,
since he seeks his Life in the lands of myth.[66]

If he dared to go to the mothers by way of initiation in the prologue of
this production, he should now have nothing to fear. Faust, filled with
the warm glow of the spirit, claims to feel as strong as a giant. The
griffins, ants, and arimasps—collectors, guardians, and thieves of the
gold—that he encounters recall the imaginings of the ancient Scythian
shamanism reported by Herodotus.[67] The sphinxes and sirens suggest
a mythology that followed. Faust claims to have gained a new attitude
permitting perception of grand, eternal forms—something like the
wavering forms in the collective tribal memory.[68] When he consults
with the sphinx about Helen he learns that, like Mephisto, the various
mythological figures operate under certain time constraints. She exists
in a more recent level of mythology, so the sphinx recommends consulting the centaur Chiron, the instructor of the most illustrious Greek
heroes.

In searching for Chiron, the still-entranced Faust, who is neither
dreaming nor hallucinating, but rather experiencing a heightened
form of collective reality, questions, for the Renaissance audience's
sake, his own level of rationality as well as what is going on:

> This is not sleep! O may they never vanish,
> these forms beyond compare
> that I envision in a miracle
> of all-pervasive feeling!
> Can they be dreams? Or are they memories?[69]

Goethe regularly shows that these characters in the play-within-the-
play are maintaining their distance by applying the standard techniques of Romantic irony that his contemporaries were using and by
having the characters comment on their emotional interest in or distance from their individual roles and those of their colleagues.[70]

Upon mounting Chiron, Faust speaks in honor of his vast medical
knowledge:

> I here and now embrace, in body and in spirit,
> the doctor to whom every plant is known,
> who understands the virtues of each root,
> who heals the sick and eases painful wounds![71]

The centaur demonstrates his modesty when he answers that he only
cured those heroes who fell near him; others he routinely left to
"priests and simple-gathering women."[72] His further reminiscences
lead to Helen whom he also, to Faust's confused delight, admits hav-

ing carried on his back. When Faust tries to pinpoint Helen's precise age at that time—something certain to please the courtly ladies of the audience—Chiron chides him for such pedantry. His explanation provides yet another ironic twist to what not only Faust but also the Renaissance audience and we the readers are here experiencing as regards shamanic time:

> Philologists, I see,
> have led you, as they have themselves, astray.
> A woman, in mythology, is an exception
> whom poets introduce in any way they want:
> she never comes of age or ever ages;
> a form that always whets the appetite,
> when young she is abducted, in age she still is courted—
> in fine, poets ignore constraints of time.[73]

Faust tells Chiron he aspires to do what his predecessors did:

> And shall not I, sustained by poignant longing,
> endow this perfect form with life—[74]

Goethe emphasizes Faust's purported ecstatic trance here by having even the wise and just Chiron comment on the craziness of his behavior:

> In mortal realms you may just be exalted,
> but in the spirit world the way you act seems madness.[75]

Then Chiron suggests that Faust seek out the charitable prophetess and seeress Manto, who, as a disciple of Aesculapius, can recommend appropriate medication to cure his illness. Insisting that he does not wish a cure, Faust alights to find himself in front of none other than Manto, who takes him seriously because of his great audacity. She agrees to do for him what she once did for Orpheus, and she states her hope that Faust will be more successful at entering the dark passageway to Persephone and returning with the lost soul of his choice. The stage directions indicate that they are to descend. Faust will not reappear again in this act.

While Faust is offstage journeying to the underworld to reclaim Helen, Homunculus serves as a dramatic device to explore levels of time and creation, which is designed to whet the theatrical appetite of a courtly audience accustomed to elaborate pageantry and to provide no offense to their concern for artistic verisimilitude. He continues to look for ways to become a human being, eventually finding the philosophers Anaxagoras and Thales in a debate over whether fire or water is the origin of life. Mephisto, who accompanies him amid the earthquakes and other products of Mother Earth, remains somewhat unnerved by the many foreign creatures who serve as his introduction to the shamanic origins of ancient Greek mythology. The Cabiri and Telchines, both originally related to fire and the forge, dealt in magic and the mysteries. As mythological vestiges from an archaic world, they were worshiped in ceremonies considered inferior only to those of Eleusis.[76] Closest to Mephisto's heart are the incredibly ugly Phorkyads, who manage to enchant him. In the meantime, Homunculus has chosen to follow Thales's advice about seeking out the prophetic Nereus, who thereupon recommends consultation with the shapeshifting marine deity Proteus:

> Away to Proteus, the man of magic powers—
> ask him how life's achieved, how one can change his form![77]

Considered unreliable by Thales, Proteus suddenly appears unnoticed and, through tricks of shamanic ventriloquism, diversifies his presence. He is one moment a gigantic turtle and then more nobly formed the next. Fascinated by Homunculus's problem, he playfully suggests it can be solved in the sea. While Thales argues that coming to life that way will require millenniums, Proteus turns himself into a dolphin that Homunculus mounts in order to join Galatea, Nereus's beautiful sea-nymph daughter, who approaches aboard her chariot of shell, necessitating, needless to say, use of the conventional wave machine. She has come for a grand celebration of the mysteries of birth and fertility. The resultant aquatic play, combined with fireworks, prompts the sirens to sing in praise of Eros as the originator of everything. It is a fit ending to this act of the production about Faust's search for Helen. And it allows the Renaissance audience of the play, and us, to get up and stretch.

In the next act, the embodiment of Helen appears ironically wondering about the distortions in her biography as well as the reasons for her present reincarnation before the palace of Menelas. Her status seems uncertain to her, especially in light of the vast differences she notices. She feels she is queen of the place and is offended by the lack of attention bestowed on her by the ugly figure of Phorkyas, who is played, as later revealed, by Mephisto.[78] The rudeness that culminates in his casting up to her the long catalogue of her lovers causes her to faint after ironically uttering that she is becoming an idol to herself as well.[79] Her companions implore Phorkyas to be silent so she can revive before her tormented spirit once again flees her form. Helen no sooner does so than Phorkyas hatches his plot to move her into the protective arms of Faust. She and those who have come with her need to be saved from their impending sacrifice. Phorkyas agrees to do this while continuing to mouth amusing one-liners about the particular level of make-believe reality that these characters are experiencing. As the mimetic cues in his lines have him sniffing her, Helen accuses him of acting out of character:

> Do not forget
> the role you're playing; finish what you have to say![80]

She also perceptively remarks about Mephisto that she fears he "will change what's good to bad."[81]

With help from the fog machine, the set changes so fast to a whimsically built medieval structure that the spokeswoman for Helen's companions perplexedly asks how they got there so quickly without needing to walk.[82] She and the others describe the castle in detail, a device Goethe uses throughout *Faust* to set the stage, to direct the acting, or to position the players. It is an ancient technique that serves to stimulate the imagination so that the spectators believe they see along with the shaman that which is not there or not clearly represented.

Faust appears in medieval courtly garb together with Lynkeus in chains because the sheer sight of Helen induced an ecstasy in him that prevented him from properly announcing her arrival.[83] In acknowledging her plea for forgiveness, Faust waxes poetic about how quickly she has conquered the hearts of his subjects. She says she needs a man to give her identity and status. He offers to serve "as co-regent of your realm that knows no bounds."[84] She thereupon learns about rhyme, and he comments on their anticipated union in the suspended time that marks this grand synthesis of multifarious arts:

> There is no past or future in an hour like this,
> the present moment only. . . .[85]

As a shaman, he has abolished time in order to reestablish the primordial condition of which the myths speak.[86] Goethe, the director of the play within the play, continues using dramatic shorthand. The chorus, for example, relates the courting behavior of the two lovers as they sit close together, going so far as to comment discreetly:

> Majesty can allow itself
> the carefree display
> to the eyes of its people
> of its private affections and joys.[87]

Helen, who still seems unable to adjust to this puzzling reincarnation, admits,

I feel so far away and yet so near,
and only want to say: I'm here! I'm here![88]

Faust then counters that he must be dreaming in this state of suspended time and place—which is the production within *Faust*—to which she responds, ironically enough,

My life seems past, and yet is somehow new;
I know you not, a stranger, but I live in you.[89]

When Phorkyas announces the arrival of Menelas's army, Faust structures the battle with an ongoing dramatic report about the ferocity of the defending Germanic tribes. Their victory, he contends, will finally put to rest Helen's past and her somewhat sordid love life.

Arcadia, with its caves and sylvan glades, is the setting of the next scene, pastorals being something in which Renaissance audiences regularly took great joy. Music emanates from one cave, which again is used to depict the long-standing abode of mystery and revelation. Helen and Faust are experiencing divine rapture together with the issue of their union, Euphorion, whom Phorkyas first describes as "a true wingless genius," and then, as the description of him has him mature before the audience's very eyes, "a miniature Apollo."[90] Euphorion's innate desire to leave the confines of earth and to fly manifests itself early, as does his inclination to duplicate with the lyre the eternal melodies that resound in his very limbs. His shamanic tendencies are further suggested by the choral comparisons to Hermes and his games and tricks on rather powerful gods.

Faust is particularly concerned about Euphorion's antics, which Goethe has him relate with another eighteenth-century alternate word for shamanizing or conjuring, *Gaukelei*.[91] The moderation he and Helen urge remains totally ignored, for Euphorion has resolved that it is his calling to achieve the impossible. In playing the hunter, he grows wilder and wilder, prompting his parents to declare, "What disorder! What an outcry!"[92] Sensing the end, they query jointly,

Don't you care
for us at all?
Is the joy we share a dream?[93]

As Euphorion falls to their feet after he has thrown himself into the air chasing a flamelike girl, his body disappears down the trapdoor while machines allow an aureole to ascend upward like a comet. What is left onstage are his clothes and his instrument. From beneath the stage his voice plaintively begs his mother not to leave him alone in the darkness of the underworld. Helen chooses to comply. She disappears in a final embrace of her beloved Faust, leaving behind in his arms her dress and her veil, which Phorkyas urges him to hold on to. They are items comparable to the feathers, stones, or pieces of leather carried by archaic shamans who always claimed to bring something back from their trips as proof of their otherworldly experiences. The play then ends with the kind of operatic *lieto fine* perfected by Mozart, imitated by the Romantics, and often misunderstood by producers as well as audiences.[94] The players and the chorus express their relief that the magic spell has finally been broken and they can get on with the rest of their mythological lives. Most of the players are concerned only about the real mysteries, those stimulated by imbibing the products of the vine. The courtiers in the audience are thereby encouraged to engage in a gala postperformance celebration. The curtain falls, and Mephisto visibly sheds his costume of Phorkyas.

Between the acts, Faust has, with Mephisto's aid, been flitting around the world fervently searching for the solution to the mysteries. Still relying on the superstitions of the childish epoch of science while disdaining the dogmatic methodology of the subsequent epoch, he is quickly approaching the "ideal, methodical, mystical."[95] As act 4 opens, Faust alights from his cloud machine expressing his belief that that solution lies with woman and her instinctual boundless love, which creates order and peace. His speech about holding such experience fast in the memory echos the Lord's words in the prologue and concludes with a thought foreshadowing the ultimate end of the work:

> Like inward beauty of the soul the lovely form
> grows clearer, rises, not dissolving, to the ether,
> and draws away with it my best and inmost self.[96]

Such thoughts bring Faust to the resolve that he wishes to reclaim land from the sea by controlling the very forces of nature.[97]

Since a new war has just broken out, it takes Mephisto no time at all to devise a plot to comply with that wish. Together with an army of diabolical spirits and three supernaturally strong men, they will serve the emperor as hired guns. Once the battle is won, they will cut a deal for the desired section of coastline. Faust thereupon appears at the imperial camp, claiming he was sent by the sorcerer of Norcia, who felt he owed the emperor a favor for having had him released from certain death at the stake as part of his coronation festivities in Rome. To convince the emperor of the legitimacy of his offer, Faust explains that nature's workings are too overwhelming and free for simple priests to understand them as anything but magic. The battle itself is conveyed by means of dramatic report with interjections from the observers. The emperor, soon realizing that the supernatural is indeed directly involved, is soothed by Faust's description of portents and by statements like "those are after-traces of long-since vanished spirit beings."[98] Then Mephisto's trusty ravens report that things are going badly before a general arrives at the camp to confirm that disaster is at hand and to proclaim, "no lasting good can come from magic."[99] The indefatigable Mephisto, reverting to the showmanship he used in Auerbach's cellar, unleashes the imagery of ferocious water spirits to deceive the enemy:

> I see no part of these aquatic lies—
> the human eye alone can be deceived—[100]

Thereupon come the spirits of the forge—long known to have shamanic associations—with some pyrotechnics, followed by the orchestra with the noise of tumult that quickly turns into joyous military airs.

The supernatural is also sensed by some soldiers who witness the three strong men plundering the rival emperor's tent:

> It's hard to say; I lacked all strength,
> and they were somehow ghost-like, too.[101]

Now that the battle is won, the emperor also closes an eye to the magical means that were used:

> Although our battle did involve some use of tricks,
> the fact remains that we were those who did the fighting.[102]

He proceeds to reward his advisers, including Faust, with fiefs for their devoted service. The archbishop is quick to accuse the emperor of consorting with sorcerers and their satanic spirits in order to force him to do penance by granting the church in perpetuity all taxes and other monies earned from those properties. Thus does Faust come to his fiefdom.

Between acts 4 and 5, Faust's imperialistic project has progressed so quickly due to Mephisto's diabolical help that the end would seem to be in sight. The sole obstacle to its completion is the homestead of an elderly couple who are as known for the warning beacon they maintain along the ferocious coast as for the warm hospitality that derives from their conjugal love. The wanderer who appears to thank them for past favors serves as an observer of the changes that have taken place and as a listener to their tales of the mysteriously created new paradise and its godless master:

> *Marvel* is the word to use!
> Even now I'm still uneasy;
> I'm convinced that the whole business
> was not done with proper means.[103]

Flames could be seen in the night, and there were streaks of incandescence and a suspicion of human sacrifice.

Faust has become so proud of his accomplishment, "this masterpiece the human spirit has wrought," that he orders Mephisto to obtain the homestead he covets even if it means forcibly resettling its occupants.[104] A lookout then observes some sparks that ignite and intensify to a glow before turning into a destructive fire that creates a hell on earth. When Mephisto reports the three casualties, Faust shifts the guilt to him before asking what is drifting toward him, shadowlike.[105]

Four gray women appear, identifying themselves as Want, Guilt, Care, and Need. Faust, still on the balcony admiring his creation, notices three departing and immediately thinks of the kind of magic with which he has become inextricably involved. Using the subjunctive mode, Faust expresses the predicament of all human scientists seeking the answers to difficult questions:

> If I could rid my path of magic,
> could totally unlearn its incantations,
> confront you, Nature, simply as a man,
> to be a human being would then be worth the effort.[106]

He feels he was such a person before having cursed the world, along with its opinions, dreams, and appearances, in part 1. Now spooks seem to control his life. Superstition has cast its net over all of nature's manifestations, which can be interpreted only as portents. Instead of being an integral part of the group within nature, as he was before, he now feels he stands alone, intimidated by nature. In other words, having denied his natural roots as a shaman within society, he became the isolated researcher who lost his awe for nature, and in a concerted attempt to bend it to his own will, consorted with the representatives of black magic. As alchemists could be true and fraudulent, so too could shamans. In renouncing magic here, Faust renounces the showmanship, but not the science, involved in shamanism.[107]

It is at this point that the figure of Care makes her presence known. After warning her not to utter any spells, Faust offers a summation of what his life was and what he learned from it. Using the kind of understatement common to him, he tells her that he quickly stormed through, repeatedly craving, and even attaining, but never discovering what actually happens in the beyond. The greatest mysteries, he has concluded, lie in the world of immanence rather than over the rainbow or beyond the clouds. When Faust admits to being a creature of the earth, an earth that will never remain mute to those able to listen and hear, he reveals that he has emerged a modern shaman who supports scientific methodologies that allow for intuition and the

study of the seemingly supernatural without adjusting the evidence to
suit his own theories:

> let him stand firm and look at what's around him:
> no good and able man finds this world mute!
> What need has he to float into eternity—
> the things he knows are tangible!
> Let his path be this earth while he exists;
> if spirits haunt him, let him not break stride
> but, keeping on, find all life's pains and joys,
> always, in every moment, never satisfied![108]

Faust resists whatever strategy Care uses. His refusal to acknowledge
her power prompts her to breathe on him, thereby striking him blind.
Joining the ranks of so many blind seers, prophets, and shamans before him, Faust now experiences an internal light.

The tragedy of Faust's life—if not his death—is that that light does
not bring him deeper conscious insight into the impossibility of creating a human paradise on earth. Consequently, he persists in his own
personal involvement with Mephisto and the temptation that involvement engenders. He continues to avail himself of the Mephistophe-
lean black magic. He orders the completion of his land reclamation
project, still concentrating on the admirable end without concern for
the diabolical means. Since Faust is blind, he cannot know that the
sound of the work he hears is the digging of his own grave. In an aside,
Mephisto claims the waters are aligned with his forces of chaos, and all
the products of the hard work will soon be destroyed. Nevertheless,
Faust remains undaunted in his belief that he is creating a state for
millions whose freedom from destruction will require unified hard
work and constant vigilance. Thinking his life will be remembered for
eons because of his technological accomplishment, he states that he is
experiencing a foretaste of the bliss he has long sought. In spite of the
fact that the dream surely will fail, Faust has contributed mightily to
keeping alive the grand dream of improving the human condition. It
is a dream derived from respect, but, more importantly, from love for
one's fellow man. Faust dies a believer.

No sooner is he dead than Mephisto, as inured to human values as
usual and hoping for the last laugh, mocks the particular moment
chosen:

> No pleasure sates him, no success suffices,
> and so he still keeps chasing shapes that always change;
> this final, mediocre, empty moment—
> the poor wretch wants to cling to it.[109]

Mephisto thereupon prepares his cohorts to do battle for Faust's soul in a dramatized *ars moriendi*. Since he has been cheated before, he urges them to hurry and bring along the stage set depicting the jaws of hell, which were among the properties of most wandering troupes. Serving as both actor and stage director, he subsequently describes an old-fashioned roaring sea of fire and brimstone, full of the damned fighting off terrifying monsters and thin as well as fat devils. With inimitable irony, he comments that it is good for them all to try to scare the sinners, for "they think these things are only lies and figments."[110]

Strewing roses and the forgiveness of sins, the host of angels descends to escort Faust's soul upward. Mephisto's attempt to rally his cohorts fails because of the great, enveloping angelic love. Enamored of them, he one last time inverts everything:

> You call us spirits damned but prove to be
> the actual sorcerers yourselves.[111]

Mephisto, whose homosexual attraction rewards him with boils, bemoans the enormous injustice done him as Faust's immortal soul separates from his body and, with the stage machinery depicting angelic help, literally rises into the heavens—which has been the goal of the entire work.

The concluding scene depicts an ascending landscape composed of gorges, cliffs, forests, and deserts where various anchorites sing their paean to the grand love that holds all creation together. In most versions of shamanism, mountains, like ladders, bridges, and rainbows, are variants of the *axis mundi* that permitted intercourse between heaven and earth.[112] This scene, theatrically inspiring as it is, carries such a thin veneer of Christian belief that Goethe reveals what might be his inclination to accept the shamanic underpinnings of all the revealed religions, something theologians and biblical scholars nowadays discuss at great length.[113] The angels hovering on high with Faust's immortal soul proclaim that love has saved this noble member of the world of spirits from evil:

> This worthy member of the spirit world
> is rescued from the devil:
> for him whose striving never ceases
> we can provide redemption.[114]

According to the summation, which is typical of the techniques used throughout *Faust*, they rejoice in their victory over "even the old Master-Devil."[115] Some younger angels, noting in the higher mists a spiritual life (*Ein Geisterleben*) composed of those who have long since separated from earth, suggest Faust's soul begin its new existence among them. Accepting the chrysalis, these blessed boys detach the earthly flakes that surround it so as to prepare it for entrance into divine life.

The anchorite in the highest cell mentions the women who pass by, floating upward. In his rapture, he sings an unorthodox hymn of praise to Mary, virgin and mother, who sways forth:

> venerated Mother;
> one coequal to the gods;
> Queen we have elected![116]

She is surrounded by the spirits of female penitents who have all been forgiven their carnal sins because of their selfless love. Gretchen joins them describing her joy at Faust's return to her, while the blessed boys let the audience know that he is quickly outstripping them.[117] Using simultaneous reports of telescoped events, comparable to those in the scenes with Euphorion, Gretchen conveys Faust's casting-off of all earthly bonds and coming forward in youthful vigor to meet the new day. She intercedes for him:

> Grant me permission to instruct him—
> he is still dazzled by the strange new light.[118]

The response of the Mater Gloriosa is for Gretchen to ascend to still loftier spheres so that Faust's immortal spirit will follow. This apotheosis of Faust the modern shaman is not sufficient. Goethe ends his work with a masterful stroke that consolidates its unity and makes it as memorable as the Lord of the prologue predicted. He has the Chorus Mysticus ratify all the major themes woven in the work:

> All that is transitory
> is only a symbol;
> what seems unachievable
> here is seen done;
> what's indescribable
> here becomes fact;
> Woman, eternally,
> shows us the way.[119]

The wavering forms whose appearance was so transitory in the "Zueignung" became incarnate in the dramatic images that formed the shaman's communication or the play. Now they have returned to the ethereal regions whence they came, for the play is over and it is only in the cosmos itself that they can have their absolute existence or reality. Only there, in those areas beyond human ken, does the indescribable happen. The work thus gives poetic dimensions to Goethe's four stages of scientific inquiry, beginning with the early superstitious stage, progressing to the empirical, combating the dogmatic, and now arriving at the "ideal, methodical, mystical."[120] It has turned from the masculine academy and professions of the so-called civilized world in order to restore, as in the primordial creation mysteries of early human culture, a well-deserved awesomeness not only for Mother Nature, but also for woman. Male-dominated scientific determinism, with its dependence on reason alone, will never provide mankind with the ultimate explanations. Those explanations can only be sought from the mysterious wisdom that is the eternal womanly (*das Ewig-Weibliche*).

Toward a Shamanology

SHAMANISM holds such fascination for the Western imagination that much continues to be written on the subject. This plethora of information from a multitude of disciplines has, however, given rise to a number of methodological problems. The gravest, in my opinion, involve not only the way perceptions of other life-styles are arrived at, but also the very definition and use of evidence. Fact and fiction about shamanism have become so intertwined that determining where one starts and the other stops is enormously difficult. It is equally difficult to find the proper attribution for the sources of many of the illustrations designed for the popular works that helped mold the European view of things shamanic (plates 21–24). Furthermore, the mythologization inherently at work in the phenomenon of shamanism itself has not generally been well accounted for.

Compounding these problems is another closely related one: there has been precious little historical accountability. Most writers uncritically create their own profiles of the shaman from the shifting sands of what was published before them. In so doing, they almost always ignore the believers and what external pressures they might have been experiencing. Twentieth-century scholarship repeatedly supports its observations or theories by citing earlier works that happened to have been built on eighteenth-century reports. Some contemporary scholars rely on what they know about the mythologies of ancient civilizations, while others mention literary renditions that are actually interpretations of the explorers' reports. Testing the credibility of sources has, to say the least, not become a habit among those interested in shamanism.

Yet another problem related to this lack of historiography has to do with taking the product for the process. All too often today, writers surmise that shamans represent vestiges of a pristine archaic phenomenon, rather than being manifestations of changes wrought over centuries of contact with more dominant cultures at different levels of development. Hardly ever have they entertained the notion that shamanism, like the human race itself, might have evolved and survived through vital processes of trial and error. Rarely have they given believers in shamanism credit for being able to develop preservation

Plate 21. Tungus Shaman.

Plate 22. Yakut Priest.

Plate 23. Tungus Sorceress.

Plate 24. Tatar Shamanka.

strategies adapted to their needs so as to withstand natural changes over time, and to make modifications due to cultural conquest or religious conversion by more powerful peoples. Nor do they consider the ongoing mutation of Western perceptions about shamanism from something utterly diabolical to something artistic and comforting, if not healing.

Since interest in shamanism has become so wide-ranging in the closing decades of the twentieth century, it behooves us to work toward solving such methodological problems so as to establish a firmer foundation for future investigation. We must begin viewing shamanism seriously within the sociohistorical contexts in which it vanished, was assimilated, or grew and persisted. For that we are largely dependent on those who observed it in those contexts at differing times and who submitted reports about what they observed or thought they observed. Mentions of things shamanic, for example, did not suddenly erupt in any one period; they have flowed continuously throughout recorded history. That flow is what needs to be examined. Much can be learned from it, although the obstacles might be discouraging. Textual interpretation and historical analysis will be as necessary as investigative instincts and interview skills. Training in language and rhetoric will be required to comprehend not only the way informants conveyed their perceptions of the shamanic phenomenon but also the way those perceptions were translated so as to be made comprehensible to Western audiences at that exact point in their cultural evolution. If terminology has varied so greatly, it has been because of the particular power structure of the times, or more recently, because of the reigning academic disciplines staking out their demesnes.

The earliest European observers of shamanism already began raising fundamental questions that are in themselves interesting and worthy of attention. Many of them struggled with their own biases, or at least began to recognize them as such, in attempting to describe, if not explain, something strange and forbidden—whether forbidden by organized religion, government, or the ensconced scientific community. They invariably named predecessors in order to lend credibility and authority to their own reports. Those choices can be quite telling. Some of these observers of shamanism were functionaries of those who sought to exploit the unknown reaches of the world, so they emphasized hard evidence. They concentrated on medicinal plants and medical practices. Others were more interested in language and the development of myth and folklore. They wrote about oracles and cultural conformities. Still others showed concern about matters of social organization and extinction.

The study of shamanism and its reception would, I am convinced, help shed light on many still-darkened areas. It might elucidate the process whereby cultural icons have been formed in the past and are still formed. It might also illuminate the lack of psychic unity in today's world and help explain contemporary uprootedness. Moreover, it might better enable those currently involved in psychoneuroimmunology and other such fields to help comprehend what has been and continues to be involved in the survival of the human race. Perhaps it might help us all gain some respect for the natural wisdom accumulated over millenniums of existence.

Studying the West's reaction to shamanism can also reveal much about relatively recent historical developments. It can show, for example, how the Enlightenment was in part, at least, invented to rein in the ubiquitous vestiges of shamanic beliefs and practices in eighteenth-century Europe and, little by little, to purge them from the dominant historical reportage. Since the occult could not be pinned down with any precision, it escaped satisfactory rational categorization and therefore had to be suppressed. This, in turn, reveals something signficant about the development of Western science. Whatever threatened the formation of a scientific status quo was denigrated or relegated to the realm of theatrical make-believe, superstition, or old wives' tales. Those who nowadays study chaos theory and the fifth force might agree with those doing research on brain waves and imagery that the scientific establishment manages to retain control over what its consensus holds as the boundaries of acceptable inquiry. Paradigm changes are simply not frequent. In some instances, especially those in which media advertisers invoke the words "scientifically proven," science itself threatens to become the new superstition among the uninitiated who choose not to reject it for fear of being hexed.

When it comes to shamanism, even the choice of words has had an effect. Since the generic term *Schaman* was German, it related the very study of the phenomenon with pursuits more superstitious, more barbarous, and less connected to the masculine rationality that eighteenth-century French cultural politicians wanted associated with their hegemony. This, then, provides some insight into what has often been termed the German failure to embrace the Enlightenment. It also aids in understanding the demography as well as the chronology involved in the evolution of Romanticism. Illumination can be brought not only to religious and political power struggles but also to the conscious shaping of the distinctive mind-set associated with modern Europe.

The nineteenth-century reception of shamanism, which is best characterized by popularization and transformation, could also teach us much about the European middle classes. They seem to have secularized the shaman completely and absorbed him into their concept of the artist as bohemian, thereby permitting his eccentric behavior in exchange for their momentary glimpses into the world of make-believe created onstage, in the orchestra hall, or in the gallery. It is with the middle classes that the star system began to emerge, producing the kind of popular being around whom a subgroup could rally and find a socially suitable anodyne. Much still needs to be studied about the line of descent from the primordial shaman to the Roman mime and then to the medieval minstrel, the eighteenth-century performer, the nineteenth-century star, and the celebrity superstar of today. Continuing scrutiny would, I am certain, show close ties between shamanism and the empathy of the Western illusionistic or method acting that became the norm in the nineteenth century, as opposed to the distancing of the style associated with the theatrical alienation of Aristophanes, Goethe, Brecht, and the Orient.

As the nineteenth century progressed, European interest in shamanism seems to have affected other fields as well. Greek antiquity experienced increasingly incisive investigations. There was a pronounced shift from the Hellenic ideal of Johann Joachim Winckelmann to a view that demanded closer examination of mysteries and cult practices. The work of Friedrich Nietzsche, Erwin Rohde, and others among the classical philologists and archaeologists needs to be reexamined. Also in need of reexamination in this light is the emer-gence of psychiatry as a field combining art and science in the course of the nineteenth century. Those functions of the secularized shaman that did not shift to the performing artist seem to have landed with the general medical practitioner and, more and more, with the incipient psychiatrist.

The puritanical prudery of the nineteenth century that made pri-vate whatever it considered publicly reprehensible would seem to have given way to the opposite in the twentieth century. Much might be learned from the recent glorification of the shaman, whether from an aboriginal tribe or from the neoshamanism movement instigated by members of so-called higher civilization. That will surely turn out to have something to do with the shape-shifting the modern and, for that matter, the postmodern world have undergone. Perhaps the need for self-deception or the need for mythic continuity is involved.

There are innumerable questions latent in the study of shaman-ism and its reception, and the implications of those questions go on and on. If a history is beginning to form out of what has already been done, then perhaps we are witnessing the emergence of what will become a new discipline, one that in its own peculiar way will com-bine the best of the humanities with certain aspects of the social sci-ences, medicine, and the physical sciences. Perhaps it is time for a shamanology.

Unless otherwise noted, I am responsible for rendering the foreign language quotations into comprehensible English. Wherever terminology is important or questions might remain, the original citation is printed in the notes as well.

Introduction

1. For information on versions in the various Siberian languages, see Nioradze, *Der Schamanismus*, pp. 1–2. Laufer gives an overview in "Origin of the Word Shaman." Hultkrantz makes a similar attempt in "Definition of Shamanism," pp. 26–27. Tibetan manifestations are taken up by Sierksma in *Tibet's Terrifying Deities*, pp. 141–58.

2. Herodotus, *History*, 1:292–93, 301, 313, 316; Minns, *Scythians and Greeks*, pp. 86–87; Neumann, *Die Hellenen im Skythenlande*, 1:246–50.

3. Lovejoy and Boas, *Primitivism and Related Ideas in Antiquity*, pp. 288, 315–16; Dodds, *Greeks and the Irrational*, pp. 135–78; Kluckhohn, *Anthropology and the Classics*, pp. 5, 19, 23; Meuli, "Scythica"; Marett, *Anthropology and the Classics* pp. 18, 44–65, 66–92, 93–120; Rohde, *Psyche* [German ed.], 2:69–70; Kirby, "Dionysus," p. 33; Kirby, "Origin of the Mummer's Play," pp. 276–78; Kirby, "Shamanistic Origins of Popular Entertainments"; Kirby, *Ur-Drama*, pp. 1–32; Charles, "Drama in Shaman Exorcism"; Charles, "Regeneration through Drama at Death"; Röhrich, "Die Märchenforschung seit dem Jahre 1945," pp. 291–92; Campbell, *Masks of God: Primitive Mythology*, pp. 229–81; Hermanns, *Schamanen* 2:343.

4. Lévi-Strauss, *Structural Anthropology*, 1:204. Interesting comparisons can be found in the writings of George Devereux; for example, "Normal and Abnormal" in *Basic Problems of Ethnopsychiatry*, pp. 14–17, 25, 64–65. Among the pertinent works of Mircea Eliade are *Myths, Dreams and Mysteries*, p. 45, and *Shamanism*.

5. Rothenberg, *Technicians of the Sacred*, p. xxx. Rothenberg gives little or no acknowledgment to scholars who have treated the subject before him. Among those scholars are Chadwick, "Shamanism among the Tatars of Central Asia," pp. 81, 93, 102; Chadwick, *Poetry and Prophecy*, pp. 12, 54, 99; Chadwick and Zhirmunsky, *Oral Epics of Central Asia*, pp. 234–67; Hatto, *Shamanism and Epic Poetry in Northern Asia*, pp. 1–7; Mühlmann, *Die Metamorphose der Frau*, pp. 67–69; Wilhelm Muster, "Der Schamanismus und seine Spuren in der Saga," pp. 98, 139, 179–82; Lommel, *Shamanism*, pp. 25, 137; Lommel, *Schamanen und Medizinmänner*, pp. 162–206; Hoerburger, *Der Tanz mit der Trommel*, pp. 14–16; Hoerburger, "Schwert und Trommel als Tanzgeräte"; and Rouget, *Music and Trance*, pp. 125–13.

6. Rouget, *Music and Trance*, pp. xviii–xix. Of a similar methodological bent is Gruber, *Tranceformation*.

7. Beuys, *Similia similibus*, p. 203; *Kreuz + Zeichen*, pp. 6, 82–85; Bojescul,

Zum Kunstbegriff des Josef Beuys, pp. 22, 94, 118, 130, 135. Many articles on the artist as shaman have appeared in print. Those by Jack Burnham, "The Artist as Shaman," "Objects and Ritual," and "Contemporary Ritual," were brought together in the book *Great Western Salt Works.* Of pertinence are pp. 140, 143, 151, 152, and 154. See also Fried, "Art and Objecthood."

8. Beuys, *Joseph Beuys Drawings,* pp. 11–12, 14, and 18, with shaman figures or shaman-related scenes on 50, 53, 54, 62, 73, 74, 80, 102, 106, 145, and 148; Tisdall, *Joseph Beuys Coyote,* pp. 10–15. An eyewitness account was given by Prof. Ingeborg Hoesterey of Indiana University in Bloomington, in "Amerika liebt mich." The subject of shamanism is not unknown to the world of music. On September 29, 1984, Janis Mattox's computerized opera, *Shaman,* had its premiere at Stanford University. The performance involved multitrack tapes and four or so live performers. Rich, "Composer," p. 97.

9. Barthes, "Death of the Author," p. 8.

10. Derrida, *Dissemination,* p. 97. Ulmer, *Applied Grammatology,* pp. 230–41, did not add anything to our knowledge of the background of shamanism.

11. Derrida, *Dissemination,* p. 118.

12. Plato, *Republic,* p. 358.

13. Michel Benamou, "Presence and Play," in Benamou and Caramello, *Performance in Postmodern Culture,* p. 3. See Ulmer, *Applied Grammatology,* and Hassan, *Dismemberment of Orpheus,* pp. xi, 7, 10, 15. Compare also Lifton, *Broken Connection,* pp. 75–76, and *Nazi Doctors,* pp. 481–85, esp. p. 481: "All Nazi doctors, that is, were to become shamans, many of them black shamans in their ritualistic participation in killing processes in the name of healing the tribe or people."

14. Most subsequent studies of poets as shamans rely almost exclusively on Eliade's interpretation, while some include a consideration of Lommel mixed with others like Carl G. Jung and Northrop Frye. See, for example, Eastham, *Paradise and Ezra Pound*; Hutchinson, *Ecstatic Whitman*; and Spivey, *Writer as Shaman.*

15. Ersch and Gruber, *Allgemeine Encyclopädie,* 3:301, s.v. Orakel.

16. Early attention to the background of the word shaman was given in Mikhailovskii, "Shamanism in Siberia and European Russia," pp. 62–65; Gennep, *Rites of Passage,* pp. 108–9; Gennep, "De l'emploi du mot 'chamanisme,'" p. 51. Shirokogoroff, *Psychomental Complex of the Tungus,* pp. 268–71, takes up the origins of the term shaman. For a more philologically oriented study, see Lot-Falck, "A propos du terme chamane." Eliade merely states that the word shaman "was accepted by the majority of nineteenth-century Orientalists." *Shamanism,* p. 495.

17. Foucault, *Birth of the Clinic,* pp. 44–52. For discussion of Foucault, see, for example, Dreyfus and Rabinow, *Michel Foucault,* pp. 15, 64, 113. The irrational was so often condemned during the eighteenth century that many subsequent scholars have continued in a similar vein, often subscribing to some current theories that disregard what might be called the other side of the Enlightenment. McGrane, *Beyond Anthropology,* for example, is an ambitious, well-written book containing many profitable ideas. However, McGrane all too often selects evidence to accommodate his reading of Foucault's *Archaeology of*

Knowledge, thereby ignoring a wealth of readily available early reports from the field that reveal somewhat different European perceptions of belief systems in the world at large.

18. Leventhal, *In the Shadow of the Enlightenment*, provides, among other things, valuable background on "how new theories in medicine and chemistry were influenced by the continued existence of the hoary doctrines of the four elements and the four humors" (p. 2).

19. Kuhn, *Structure of Scientific Revolutions*, p. 52. Richard Bernstein subsequently argued that the very choice of a theory is "a judgmental activity requiring imagination, interpretation, the weighing of alternatives, and application of criteria that are essentially open." *Beyond Objectivism and Relativism*, p. 56.

20. Kuhn, *Structure of Scientific Revolutions*, p. 108. McGrane, on the other hand, does not seem to want to allow that there might have been intelligent, rational voices opposing Newtonianism during the eighteenth century: "Newtonian mechanics here reveals itself as the dominant metaphor in retrospectively formulating and describing 'primitive mentality'; primitive mentality is that which *lacks* Newtonian mechanism, which is ignorant of a Newtonian mechanistic vision of the general operation of the cosmos." *Beyond Anthropology*, p. 75.

21. The immediate need was for a system of classification, according to Pagden, *Fall of Natural Man*, p. 11. See also p. 200 on the increasing importance of firsthand observation.

22. Those who explored Siberia between 1725 and 1825 are listed with brief information in the first part of Kirchner, *Eine Reise durch Siberien*, pp. 9–39.

23. Sauer, *Account of a Geographical and Astronomical Expedition*, appendices 5 and 6. Discussion of the ways reports were then altered to suit prevailing political winds can be found in Masterson and Brower, *Bering's Successors*, pp. 14–15.

24. La Pérouse, *Voyage*, 1:xcix.

25. Ibid., 1:cii.

26. As quoted in the illuminating study by Keller, *Reflections*, p. 36.

27. Horkheimer and Adorno, *Dialectic of Enlightenment*, p. 4.

28. The letters that the professor of medicine Johann Friedrich Blumenbach wrote recommending Friedrich Hornemann to his friend Joseph Banks, who happened to be president of the Royal Society, and to the Association for Promoting the Discovery of the Interior Parts of Africa give some insight into the curriculum being developed for the training of explorers in Göttingen. In addition to working closely with librarians, natural historians, astronomers, geographers, mineralogists, mathematicians, and linguists, specifically Arabists, Hornemann was to study drawing and gain "some necessary practical knowledge of Domestic Medicine and Surgery." Hornemann, *Journal*, pp. 9–10.

29. Stafford, *Voyage into Substance*, pp. 116, 160, 290, 327, 395.

30. William Dean provides a handy summary in the first chapter of *History Making History*, pp. 1–22.

31. Adams, *Travelers and Travel Liars*, pp. 11, 12, 44, 142, 162. Compare also Professor Adams's most recent pioneering study, *Travel Literature and the Evolution of the Novel*. The following are of related interest: Gove, *Imaginary Voyage in Prose Fiction*, pp. x, 17, 183; Mitrovich, "Deutsche Reisende und Reiseberichte im 17. Jahrhundert"; and Stewart, *Die Reisebeschreibung*, pp. 62, 90, 180, 228, 236.

32. Köhler, *Anweisung für Reisende Gelehrte*, sig.)(3 verso.

33. See, for example, Müller, *Eröffnung eines Vorschlages Zu Verbesserung*. Donnert, *Russia in the Age of Enlightenment*, devotes an entire chapter, pp. 115–25, to publishing and the press.

34. Renaudot, *Ancient Accounts of India and China*.

35. Coxe, *Account of the Russian Discoveries*; Radishchev, *Journey from St. Petersburg to Moscow*.

36. Fischer, "Muthmassliche Gedanken von dem Ursprunge der Amerikaner"; Schlözer, *Handbuch der Geschichte*; Schlözer, *Historische Untersuchung über Russlands Reichsgrundgesetze*.

37. Benyowsky, *Memoirs and Travels*, discussed in Adams, *Travelers and Travel Liars*, pp. 81–83; Kotzebue, *Graf Benjowsky*. Compare Deguignes, *Histoire générale des Huns*, and Deguignes, *Voyages à Peking*.

38. Hamilton, *New Account of the East Indies*, 1:xii–xiii.

39. Svinine, *Sketches of Russia*.

40. Stewart, *Die Reisebeschreibung*, pp. 228–36.

41. Forster, *Karakter, Sitten und Religion*, esp. pp. 79–83 and 100; Sonntag, *Das Russische Reich*, pp. iii–iv, 59–60, 73.

42. Eckartshausen, *Aufschlüsse zur Magie*; Eckartshausen, *Entdeckte Geheimnisse der Zauberey*; Meister, *Ueber die Schwermerei*.

43. Bruzen de la Martinière, *Ceremonies et coutumes religieuses des peuples idolatres*; Bruzen de la Martinière, *Ceremonies et coutumes religieuses de tous les peuples du monde*; Porter, *Travelling Sketches in Russia and Sweden*.

44. La Créquinière, *Conformité des coutumes*; Shoberl, *Russia*; Rechberg und Rothenlöwen, *Les peuples de la Russie*; see plates 21–24 below.

45. King, *Philosophy of Medicine*, p. 18.

46. Grassl, *Aufbruch zur Romantik*, p. 133. Of similar interest might be Butler, *Myth of the Magus*, pp. 179–242.

47. Compare Burkert, *Lore and Science in Ancient Pythagoreanism*, pp. 120–65.

48. For example, Diószegi wrote in *Tracing Shamans in Siberia*, pp. 10–11: "Today, shamanism already belongs to the past. Due to the propagation of science it had to become extinct. But for the sake of science, it must not disappear without trace: for the benefit of the researchers of Comparative Ethnology, Ethnogenetics and History of Religion it is indispensable that the authentic and detailed records of this vanished world be collected without delay." Compare Ränk, "Shamanism as a Research Subject."

49. Among today's debunkers are James Randi and the Committee for Scientific Investigation of Claims of the Paranormal. See, for example, Randi's totally unhistorical *Flim Flam!* pp. 173–95, on "the medical humbugs."

50. The matter is made even more complex because many nineteenth-

century students of shamanism, recognizing the great difficulties involved in the evaluation of information, turned to legends, sagas, fairy tales, stories, and songs as their main sources. They then interwove these sources with what they purported to observe. As a result, the literature continued to inform the fieldwork. See, for example, "Aus Sibirien: Lose Blätter aus dem Tagebuche eines reisenden Linguisten" in Radloff, *Das Schamanenthum und sein Kultus*, pp. 2–3. On the other hand, Shirokogoroff, *Psychomental Complex of the Tungus*, uses notes on the earliest history of shamanism to hypothesize as to its initial form.

51. Daniel Defert states that the considerable body of literature relating to discovery, exploration, and conquest has not been viewed by anthropology as its prehistory, in "Collection of the World." Defert argues that such writings "constituted not a genre but a cultural formation, that is, an area of culture, of knowledge, and the practices which structure and are supported by it" (p. 11). It is his intention to study the organizational schemes of those writings and to "elucidate the tactics of domination to which they correspond" (p. 12).

Chapter One
The Paradigm of Permissibility, or, Early Reporting Strategies

1. Older anthropological writers generally denigrated the contributions of early travelers. Czaplicka wrote, for example, in *Aboriginal Siberia*, p. ix: "The works of early travellers which deal with the area as a whole give us nothing beyond general impressions and items of curious information." Nevertheless, she, like many of her colleagues, bases her arguments on the reports of early travelers (pp. 203, 222, 243). The same was true of Oesterreich, *Possession*, p. 295: "The travellers of the eighteenth century, the 'Age of Enlightenment,' could not do enough to show the shamans as mere charlatans or impostors. Their accounts are therefore devoid of information."

2. Lea, *Materials Toward a History of Witchcraft*, 2:434–48. Thomas wrote the following, for example, in *Religion and the Decline of Magic*, p. 229: "Indeed in the sixteenth century the influence was as much the other way around. Instead of the village sorcerer putting into practice the doctrines of Agrippa or Paracelsus, it was the intellectual magician who was stimulated by the activities of the cunning man into a search for the occult influences which he believed must have underlain them. The period saw a serious attempt to study long-established folk procedures with a view to discovering the principles on which they rested." On the other hand, Ladurie agrees with those who consider European witchcraft a vestige of primordial shamanic practices. *Jasmin's Witch*, pp. 5, 8, 10, 61, 62. He speculates, "It is also possible that the eighteenth century, while retaining a respectable contingent of witches (though now less persecuted), was a time that engendered less tension and popular frustration, such as could give rise to witchcraft, than had been the case in the seventeenth century, with its great waves of impoverishment, economic stagnation and general crisis" (p. 6). Ginzburg chose to treat popular beliefs transformed under inquisitorial pressure so as to result in traditional characteristics of witchcraft, in *Night Battles*.

3. I use the word "paradigm" here in the traditional sense. It would be tempting to speculate about applying to shamanic reportage the concept of paradigm articulated by Kuhn in 1962, that is, "that some accepted examples of actual scientific practice—examples which include law, theory, application, and instrumentation together—provide models from which spring particular coherent traditions of scientific research." *Structure of Scientific Revolutions*, p. 10. If I do not do so, it is because I believe the history of shamanism needs much additional research and contemplation before its relationship to possible revolutions can be commonly acknowledged. For discussion of Kuhn's work among the social scientists, see, for example, Marcus and Fischer, *Anthropology as Cultural Critique*, p. x. Dreyfus and Rabinow discuss Foucault's relationship to Kuhn and the concept of paradigm in *Michel Foucault*, pp. 197–202.

4. See, for example, the account Hans Staden published in 1556—translated into English in 1559—*Wahrhaftige Historia*, pp. 51–54.

5. Guerra, *Pre-Columbian Mind*, pp. 133–34, 180, 191. See also, Anderson, *Peyote*, pp. 2–8.

6. Cabeza de Vaca, *Journey*, pp. 106–7. Hans Schadewaldt mentions Cabeza de Vaca in his survey, *Der Medizinmann bei den Naturvölkern*, pp. 46–47. See also Guerra, *Pre-Columbian Mind*, pp. 65–66.

7. Einhorn, *Ueber die religiösen Vorstellungen*, p. 18.

8. Ibid., p. 53. Page references will henceforth be given in parentheses in the text whenever possible.

9. Struys, *Perillous and most Unhappy Voyages*, p. 117. According to Adelung, *Kritisch-Literärische Übersicht*, 2:344, Struys had a meager amount of formal education; consequently his work, which originally appeared in Amsterdam in 1676, contained much that was trivial and incorrect.

10. Tooke, *View of the Russian Empire*, 1:562.

11. Adelung, *Kritisch-Literärische Übersicht*, 1:32–33 and 2:338–40.

12. Ibid., 1:33 lists 1672 as the initial publication date, contrary to the standard bibliographic works, including the *National Union Catalogue*, which all agree on 1692. A second edition was dated 1705, and a reprint of that edition was issued in 1785 with a new introduction. There was much contemporary speculation that publication was suppressed and then delayed on orders from Peter the Great. Ibid., 1:34.

13. Witsen, *Noord en Oost Tartaryen*, 2:636, 662–63. Mikola recently prepared and published an abridged German translation, *N. Witsens Berichte über die uralischen Völker*. See, for example, pp. 11, 49, 68, 100.

14. Adelung, *Kritisch-Literärische Übersicht*, 2:400 dates the first edition 1698. I used the 1716 edition at the Newberry Library. A French edition, *Etat présent de la Grande Russia*, appeared in Brussels in 1717. There is a copy of it at the Bavarian State Library in Munich. Compare Latourette, *History of the Expansion of Christianity*, vol. 3: *Three Centuries of Advance, A.D. 1500–A.D. 1800*, pp. 367–71.

15. For information on other such publications about America, see Sabin, Eames, and Vail, *Dictionary of Books Relating to America*.

16. Wafer, *New Voyage and Description*, p. 273.

17. La Hontan, *New Voyages to North-America*, 2:49–50.

18. Adelung, *Kritisch-Literärische Übersicht*, 1:88–93 and 100–116.

19. Hakluyt, *Principal Navigations*, 1:141–42. Compare comments about commercial needs in Hodgen, *Early Anthropology*, pp. 211–12.

20. Polo, *Description of the World*, 1:283–85. One such eighteenth-century commendation of Marco Polo's *Beobachtungsgeist* can be found in the invaluable bibliography *Versuch einer Litteratur deutscher Reisebeschreibungen*, p. 374.

21. William N. Fenton and Elizabeth L. Moore, introduction to Lafitau, *Customs of the American Indians*, 1:xxxiii, xci, and 95 n. 2.

22. Thwaites, *Jesuit Relations*, 72:324–26; Marshall and Williams, *Great Map of Mankind*, pp. 32, 83.

23. Lockman, *Travels of the Jesuits*, 1:viii–ix.

24. Shea, *Discovery and Exploration*, p. 17. Compare Quaife, *Western Country in the Seventeenth Century*, pp. 46–51.

25. *Travels of Several Learned Missioners*, p. 37.

26. The method of seeking conformities has been discussed in Hodgen, *Early Anthropology*, pp. 298, 337, 346. See also McGrane, *Beyond Anthropology*, pp. 20–21, 68.

27. *Travels of Several Learned Missioners*, p. 29.

28. Ibid., p. 30.

29. Ibid., pp. 48–49.

30. Hennepin, *New Discovery*, 1:464–65.

31. Porta, *Natural Magick*, p. 407.

32. See Flaherty, "Sex and Shamanism in the Eighteenth Century," pp. 261–80.

33. Burton, *Anatomy of Melancholy*, 1:254.

34. Scheffer, *Lappland*. Scheffer's full title translates into English as "Lapland; that Is, a New and Reliable Description of Lapland and Its Inhabitants, Which Tells of Many Heretofore Unknown Matters about the Lapps' Origins, Their Superstitions, Magical Arts, Diet, Clothing, and Activities, as Well as about the Animals and Metals of Their Country, and Which Provides Sundry Illustrations."

35. Fontenelle, *History of Oracles*, p. 103. Horst Kirchner discusses caves and cave paintings in "Ein archäologischer Beitrag," pp. 254–62.

Chapter Two
Eighteenth-Century Observations from the Field

1. Berchtold, *Essay*, 1:14.

2. With regard to medicine, compare Foucault, *Birth of the Clinic*, p. 89.

3. Meikle (1730–1799), *Traveller*, p. 14.

4. Hodgen pointed out that the range of human customs had already been delimited and formularized into ten categories by the late seventeenth century. *Early Anthropology*, pp. 167–68. Compare also Stafford, *Voyage*, pp. 40–41, 46.

5. Darnell, *Readings in the History of Anthropology*, p. 80.

6. Hodgen, *Early Anthropology*, p. 191.

7. *Observations on the Present State of Denmark, Russia, and Switzerland*, p. 280.

8. I cannot agree with Hodgen's claim that the scholarship of the early Enlightenment was "supposedly original but actually imitative." *Early Anthropology*, pp. 490–91. It seems to me that those scholars were, more often than not, testing the waters, so to speak.

9. Pearce, *Savagism and Civilization*, p. 15, singles out stress on the negative aspects.

10. See Stocking, *Victorian Anthropology*, esp. chapter 3: "Travelers and Savages: The Data of Victorian Ethnology (1830–1858)," pp. 79–109.

11. See, for example, Stuck, *Verzeichnis*, 1:iv, vi, xi; *Versuch einer Litteratur deutscher Reisebeschreibungen*, pp. 1–17, 394–98. There were also the collections of chronicles and historical data; for example, Müller, *Eröffnung eines Vorschlages Zu Verbesserung*.

12. The methodology these explorers developed was often thrown into question by those who remained behind. A prime example from 1800 was Degérando, "Considerations on the Various Methods to Follow in the Observation of Savage People," in *Observation of Savage Peoples*, pp. 59–104. His text was to guide members of the Societé des Observations de l'Homme who were about to voyage to Australia. Degérando outlined what he considered their eight basic faults, which involved incompleteness, lack of authenticity, lack of order, false analogy, linguistic limitation, partiality, failure to report on native languages, and neglect of traditions and ceremonies (pp. 64–69). The topics he tried to make programmatic are less impartial and more eurocentric than many of the earlier eighteenth-century ones.

13. Stafford, *Voyage*, pp. 46–52.

14. Bell, *Travels*, 1:xiv-xv. Bell's work appeared in French translation in 1766, Dutch in 1769–1770, and German in 1787. Compare Adams, *Travelers and Travel Liars*, pp. 1–11.

15. Bell, *Travels*, 1:207; compare also 2:146.

16. For an eighteenth-century discussion of his methodological concerns, see Messerschmidt, "Nachricht," pp. 98–99.

17. Messerschmidt, *Forschungsreise durch Sibirien*, 1:59–60.

18. Donnert, *Russia in the Age of Enlightenment*, pp. 96–97, stated that the entire report did not appear until the 1962–1977 edition.

19. Ibid., p. 97.

20. Strahlenberg, *An Histori-Geographical Description of the North and Eastern Part of Europe and Asia; But more particularly of Russia, Siberia, and Great Tartary; Both in their Ancient and Modern State: Together with An entire New Polyglot-Table of the Dialects of 32 Tartarian Nations: And a Vocabulary of the Kalmuck-Mungolian Tongue; As Also, A Large and Accurate Map of those Countries; and Variety of Cuts, representing Asiatick-Scythian Antiquities.*

21. Moore, *Travels into the Inland Parts of Africa*, p. 87, and Marshall and Williams, *Great Map of Mankind*, pp. 234–35.

22. Donnert, *Russia in the Age of Enlightenment*, pp. 99–100, discusses the team members.

23. Steller, *Beschreibung*, pp. 284–85.

24. The effects of climate on the nervous system and the susceptibility to

superstition gradually became considerations in the last quarter of the eighteenth century because of works on the subject like Falconer's *Remarks*, esp. pp. 130–59. By the middle of the nineteenth century, climate and location had formed the basis for theories concerning "arctic hysteria" as a source for shamanism. Eliade mentions this in his chapter on shamanism and psychopathology in *Shamanism*, pp. 23–24.

25. Krascheninnikow, *History of Kamtschatka*, p. 208.

26. The father, Hans Poulsen Egede (1686–1758), was bishop in Greenland. He wrote several works on his mission, which were translated from Danish into German and English. His sons subsequently wrote continuations.

27. Donnert, *Russia in the Age of Enlightenment*, pp. 99–100, 109.

28. Wo Russlands breites Reich sich mit der Erde schliesset,

Und in den letzten West des Morgens March zerfliesset;

Wohin kein Vorwitz drang; wo Thiere fremder Art,

Noch ungenannten Völkern dienten;

Wo unbekanntes Erzt sich künftgen Künstlern spart,

Und nie besehne Kräuter grünten;

Lag eine neue Welt, von der Natur versteckt,

Biss Gmelin sie entdeckt.

29. Lafitau's awareness of the methodological errors of his predecessors is discussed by Pagden in *Fall of Natural Man*, p. 184. Lafitau, Pagden maintains, realized "that all cultures are systems of symbolic representaions which constitute the means of communication between individuals within societies" (p. 199).

30. Fenton, "J.-F. Lafitau."

31. Manuel, in *Eighteenth Century Confronts the Gods*, stated, "From the travel literature, particularly the recent work of the Jesuit Lafitau, Vico learned that the American Indians animated and called gods whatever power in nature surpassed their feeble understanding" (p. 156). I have not been able to find any direct references to it, although Vico generally relies very heavily on travelers' reports, often unquestioningly so. For example, see Vico, *New Science*, pars. 334, 337, 517.

32. Lafitau, *Customs of the American Indians*, 1:95 (113). The page numbers in the text refer first to the English edition above and then to the French edition mentioned in the text. Compare Dodds, *Greeks and the Irrational*, pp. 70, 72, and chapter 5: "The Greek Shamans and the Origins of Puritanism," pp. 135–78.

33. Vico, *New Science*, pars. 100, 375, 517.

Chapter Three
Interaction, Transformation, and Extinction

1. For information on the various detachments of explorers and their relationship to the project as a whole, see Donnert, *Russia in the Age of Enlightenment*, pp. 110–11.

2. Falk, *Beyträge*, 2:459–60.

3. Lepechin, *Tagebuch*, 1:44–45.

4. Donnert, *Russia in the Age of Enlightenment*, p. 111.

5. This work was often cited by subsequent writers on the subject of shamanism; see, for example, Mikhailovskii, "Shamanism in Siberia and European Russia," pp. 81–82.

6. Compare, for example, Huet, *Traité de l'origine des Romans*.

7. Pallas, *Reise durch verschiedene Provinzen*, 3:65. Later observers in the field continued to associate the shamans' activities with storytelling and mythologizing. Sarytschew, for example, wrote in *Achtjährige Reise im nordöstlichen Sibirien*, 1:31: "Diese ihnen zugeschriebene Gewalt über die Geister hat ihnen auch das Recht gegeben, verschiedene Mährchen und Albernheiten zum Niessbrauch der abergläubischen Unwissenheit auszudenken, damit diese um desto gläubiger werden."

8. Both were published in St. Petersburg, the *Bemerkungen* in 1775 and the *Beschreibung* in four parts in 1776, 1777, and 1780.

9. Georgi thus contributed to the perception that became more prevalent in the course of the nineteenth century and that came to be labeled "arctic hysteria." See Shirokogoroff, *Psychomental Complex of the Tungus*, pp. 252–54.

10. Georgi's firsthand experiences in the field made his writing on belief systems a far cry from earlier interpretations, like Hume's *Natural History of Religion* (1757), that considered polytheism or idolatry the most ancient religion, yet concluded that "men have a natural tendency to rise from idolatry to theism, and to sink again from theism into idolatry" (pp. 23; cf. 46).

11. For my biographical discussion, I am indebted to Uhlig, *Georg Forster*, pp. 2–14, and Saine, *Georg Forster*, pp. 9–55.

12. Forster, *Geschichte der Reisen*, 3:62. See also his reviews of travel literature, for example, in *Sämmtliche Schriften*, 5:317–400.

13. Forster, *Geschichte der Reisen*, 3:69.

14. Ibid., pp. 63–65. Compare West, "Limits of Enlightenment Anthropology."

15. For examples, see Manuel, *Eighteenth Century Confronts the Gods*, p. 42, and Eliade, *Myths, Dreams, and Mysteries*, p. 39. Eliade contended that the concept of the noble savage was created and promulgated by the sixteenth, seventeenth, and eighteenth centuries "as a criterion for their moral, political and social disquisitions."

16. Forster, "Über die Pygmäen," in *Werke*, 7:119–20.

17. Ibid., pp. 27–28.

18. As with many members of eighteenth-century expeditions and authors of travel reports, there is very little biographical information available about Martin Sauer. He did not gain entry into the British, French, German, Austrian, or Swiss dictionaries of national biography, although his travel account did manage to get listed in Brunet's *Manuel*, Graesse's *Tresor*, and *A Dictionary of Books Relating to America* by Sabin, Eames, and Vail. In the article under Billings in the *Dictionary of National Biography*, we read that Sauer was conscientious in fulfilling his assigned duties, but that he greatly disliked Billings for all his personal weaknesses and public cruelties.

Sauer's dedication and preface, in addition to occasional remarks throughout his account, provide some biographical information, although it is more perplexing than intellectually satisfying. Sauer dedicated his account to Joseph Banks (1743–1820), who, among other things, was at the time president of the illustrious Royal Society of London. In Sauer's preface, we read, "I was personally acquainted with Doctor Pallas and Mr. Billings, both of whom requested that I would accompany the Expedition as Private Secretary and Translator; and on receiving the promise of permission to publish my remarks upon my return, I agreed," which would lead us to believe Sauer was a resident of St. Petersburg (pp. ix–x). While mentioning the health reasons for his return from the Billings expedition, he gave thanks to certain people who offered him assistance. They all happened to be English. Nevertheless, Sauer writes not of his return to England, as one might expect, but rather of "my arrival in London" (p. xi). Another strange statement is that he felt incapable of "saying whether the computed distances are geographical or German miles; both measures having been used by the original journalists" (p. xiii). Yet another comes at the very end of Sauer's account, where we read: "The other remarks made by the writer of the journal that I have translated, are such as I have already taken notice of" (p. 330).

The person who translated Sauer's account into French in 1802, a certain J. Castéra, mentioned in the "Avertissement du Traducteur" that he was "un Anglais." M. C. Sprengel, Sauer's German translator, reported in *Reise nach den Nordlichen Gegenden vom Russischen Asien und America*, the eighth volume of the series Bibliothek der neuesten und wichtigsten Reisebeschreibungen, published in 1803, only that Sauer had accompanied Billings everywhere as "Secretär und Journalist" (p. viii). Donnert, *Russia in the Age of Enlightenment*, p. 112, considered him an Englishman.

19. Translations appeared in German, French, and Dutch before the turn of the nineteenth century.

20. A German translation appeared in 1803, followed by one in French in 1804.

Chapter Four
Shamanism among the Medical Researchers

1. Foucault, *Birth of the Clinic*, p. 96, wrote, "Medicine as an uncertain kind of knowledge is an old theme to which the eighteenth century was especially sensitive."

2. Sierke's title might sound very promising, but it represents little more than the kind of standard debunking that evolved in the eighteenth century: *Schwärmer und Schwindler*; he concentrated on Emanuel Swedenborg, Franz Anton Mesmer, Johann Joseph Gassner, Johann Georg Schrepfer, and Cagliostro. On the other hand, compare N. O. Brown, *Hermes the Thief*, pp. 17–18.

3. Translated in Rather, *Mind and Body*, pp. 20–21.

4. Ibid., p. 128.

5. Ibid., pp. 174–75.

6. Ibid., p. 184.

7. Ibid., p. 110.

8. Ibid., p. 114.

9. Ibid., p. 113.

10. Tissot, *Life of J. G. Zimmermann*, p. 15.

11. Zimmermann, *Über Friedrich den Grossen* and *Fragmente über Friedrich den Grossen*.

12. Zimmermann, *Solitude*, 2:98–99.

13. Frank, *System*. The page numbers given in the text refer to the enlarged edition, vols. 1–4 (Mannheim, 1804), vol. 5 (Tübingen, 1813), vols. 6.1–6.2 (Vienna, 1817), vol. 6.3 (Vienna, 1819).

14. Jung-Stilling, *Theorie der Geister-Kunde*.

Chapter Five
The Impact of Russia on Diderot and *Le neveu de Rameau*

1. See, for example, Flögel, *Geschichte der komischen Literatur*, 1:99, 124, 224–27, 318–21, and 4:22–27.

2. Denis Diderot's *Neveu de Rameau* has been subjected to innumerable interpretations, each different and each valuable in its own way. In the nineteenth century, for example, Hegel insisted that it represented a dialectic between the old honest consciousness and the modern alienated or disintegrated one. Nietzsche thereupon saw it as the confrontation of philosophy or rational thought (the Apollonian) with music, intuition, or emotion (the Dionysian). The twentieth century has not hesitated to make its views known as well. Trilling wrote, "Rameau represents what lies, dangerous but wholly necessary, beneath the reasonable decorum of social life." "The Legacy of Freud." For Trilling, so deeply influenced by late nineteenth-century thought, Lui or Rameanu's nephew was Freud's id, while Moi or the narrator was Freud's ego. Compare also Sherman, "The *Neveu de Rameau* and the Grotesque," and Mall, "*Le Neveu de Rameau* and the Idea of Genius," pp. 28, 31–35. On the other hand, Leo Spitzer articulated yet another juxtaposition. He wrote that Diderot was treating a theory of mimesis or imitation vis-à-vis a theory of expression. Spitzer even went on to interpret the operatic scene at the Café de la Régence as one of incantation, claiming that it is like a lullaby, a stimulant that becomes a soporific and causes the automaton to run down. Compare Roach, "Diderot and the Actor's Machine," pp. 64–65. See also de Fontenay, *Diderot*, pp. 200–209, and Kouidis, "*The Praise of Folly*." Michel Foucault preferred to claim that Diderot's text showed that irrationality had resurfaced among eighteenth-century Western Europeans because Diderot had chosen to take or mistake a madman for a social individual. *Madness and Civilization*, pp. 99–100. For Donald O'Gorman, however, it represented the debate between Enlightenment views and enthusiasm, that is, the rational versus the irrational, in *Diderot the Satirist*, pp. 128, 152, 189, 215–16. Herbert Josephs preferred to see Diderot's *Neveu de Rameau* as a satire against society and against the author himself, in *Diderot's Dialogue*, p. 113. John Neubauer has recently gone on record as insisting that Diderot used this piece "to show by means of the incongruity between the music theory and the performance that the text radically diffuses the self." *Emancipation of Music from Language*, pp. 114–20. Friedrich Plotkin,

who once called it a "somewhat baffling dialogue," summed up what all the interpreters wrote and offered an assessment I do not consider incorrect: "They have generally grasped the underlying significance of Diderot's famous dialogue: that it prefigures the passing of 'the Age of Reason,' and the emergence of a new spirit that has somewhat loosely been identified as 'Romanticism.'" "Diderot's Nephew."

3. Cronin, *Catherine*, p. 223, and Flaherty, "Catherine the Great and Men."

4. See, for example, Lechner, "Gotthilf Heinrich von Schubert's Einfluss," p. 3. The scholarly blocking-out of concern for the occult during the Enlightenment is everywhere evident. A good example is Briggs, *Pale Hecate's Team*, p. 15: an "abrupt change of heart in the eighteenth century caused the belief [in witchcraft] to be esteemed as no more than a barbarous superstition. By the end of the eighteenth century witchcraft had become, with armour, secret passages and family curses, a pleasant piece of Gothic machinery."

5. Catherine II, *Memoirs*, pp. 152–53; Gooch, *Catherine the Great*, p. 34.

6. Guerra, *Pre-Columbian Mind*, pp. 4–5.

7. Catherine used strong words to combat "the French traveller's malicious misrepresentations of all matters, as well as his dislike to whatever bears the apellation of Russian." *Antidote*, p. iii. She also points out his failure to deal in a scholarly fashion with Gmelin and other established scientific writers (pp. 4–5, 87). For discussion, see Cronin, *Catherine*, pp. 230–31.

8. Diderot, *Encyclopédie*, 16:253–61.

9. Jessen, *Katharina II*, p. 325.

10. Compare Fitzgerald Molloy's emphasis on the use of theater to influence public opinion, in *Russian Court*, 2:422. Karlinsky, *Russian Drama*, pp. 86–88, treats Catherine's dramatic writings within the historical framework of Russian drama.

11. Jessen, *Katharina II*, p. 331.

12. Ibid., p. 343.

13. Catherine II, *Der sibirische Schaman*, p. 11. Page references given in the text refer to this edition, which I consulted at the Firestone Library of Princeton University. It is an especially rare copy, made even more so by the handwriting on the flyleaf that indicates it was the presentation copy given by Catherine to Zimmermann on January 30, 1787.

14. Lentin, "Catherine the Great and Diderot."

15. Mohrenschildt, *Russia*, pp. 23, 48.

16. Lentin, "Catherine the Great and Diderot," p. 315.

17. Schlösser, *Rameaus Neffe*, pp. 1–3, 11, 29.

18. Voltaire treats the beliefs of various peoples, concentrating on the Samoyedes, Ostyaks, and Kamchatkans. "La Russie sous Pierre le Grand," pp. 370, 374.

19. Diderot, *Encyclopédie* (1765), 14:444.

20. Ibid. (1765), 14:604.

21. Ibid. (1765), 9:110.

22. Ibid. (1765), 15:923.

23. Ibid. (1765), 8: 436.

24. Ibid. (1765), 14:759.

25. Ibid. (1765), 8:875. Compare also (1756), 6:878, s.v. Floride.

26. Ibid. (1765), 8:875.

27. Ibid. (1755), 5:719.

28. Ibid. (1755), 5:722.

29. Ibid. Compare also (1756), 6:324–25, s.v. Extase.

30. Ibid. (1756), 10:276, and (1765), 16:278.

31. Lentin, "Catherine the Great and Diderot," pp. 319–20.

32. Oustinoff, "Notes on Diderot's Fortunes," 121–22.

33. Goethe, *From My Life*, 1:361; Goethe, *Gedenkausgabe*, ed. Beutler, 10:534. References to this work will be cited as *Gedenkausgabe*.

34. Schlösser, *Rameaus Neffe*, pp. 87, 89, 96. See also Mortier, *Diderot in Deutschland*, pp. 87, 124. It is more than merely interesting that the correspondence warmly recommended the history of Russia by Levesque, *Historical & Literary Memoirs*, pp. 25–30. The edition of Levesque's *Histoire de Russie* available to me at the Newberry Library was the fourth. The fourth section of volume 7, pp. 159–91, contains a rather thorough summary of information on the subject: "Du Chamanisme, Religion fort ancienne et très-répandue dans le nord de l'Asie." The footnote on p. 191 indicates Levesque's research involvement at least since the 1780s.

35. Mortier, *Diderot in Deutschland*, pp. 219–26.

36. Schlösser, *Rameaus Neffe*, pp. 107–15, 187, 208. Also see Josephs, *Diderot's Dialogue*, p. viii.

37. Diderot, *Rameau's Nephew*, trans. Barzun and Bowen, p. 8. The original French given here in the notes is from *Oeuvres*, ed. Billy pp. 395–96: "Il est doué d'une organisation forte, d'une chaleur d'imagination singulière, et d'une vigueur de poumons peu commune." References to *Rameau's Nephew* will be cited as Barzun and Bowen; references to *Oeuvres* will be cited as Billy.

38. Diderot, *Paradox*, trans. Pollock, p. 46. References to this work will be cited as Pollock. The original French given here in the notes is from Billy, p. 1035: "Un grand comédien est un autre pantin merveilleux dont le poète tient la ficelle, et auquel il indique à chaque ligne la véritable forme qu'il doit prendre."

39. Barzun and Bowen, p. 73. "Et puis c'est qu'il y avait quelque chose de race. Le sang de mon père et le sang de mon oncle est le même sang; mon sang est le même que celui de mon père, la molécule première s'est assimilé tout le rest." Billy, p. 459.

40. Barzun and Bowen, p. 73. "Si je l'aime le petit sauvage? J'en suis fou." Billy, p. 459.

41. Barzun and Bowen, p. 9. "S'il en paraît un dans une compagnie, c'est un grain de levain qui fermente et qui restitue à chacun une portion de son individualité naturelle. Il secoue, il agite, il fait approuver ou blâmer, il fait sortir la vérité, il fait connaître les gens de bien, il démasque les coquins; c'est alors que l'homme de bon sens écoute et démêle son monde." Billy, pp. 396–97.

42. Barzun and Bowen, p. 54. "Je suis rare dans mon espèce, oui, très rare. A présent qu'ils ne m'ont plus; que font-ils? Ils s'ennuient comme des chiens.

Je suis un sac inépuisable d'impertinences. J'avais à chaque instant une boutade qui les faisait rire aux larmes; j'étais pour eux les Petites-Maisons tout entières." Billy, p. 441. Compare the twentieth-century interpretation of the shaman as a socially useful parasite in Maddox, *Medicine Man*, p. 128.

43. Barzun and Bowen, p. 18. "Un ignorant, un sot, un fou, un impertinent, un paresseux, ce que nos bourguignons appellent un fieffé truand, un escroc, un gourmand." Billy, pp. 405–6.

44. Barzun and Bowen, p. 18. "Vous avez toujours pris quelque intérêt à moi, parce que je suis un bon diable que vous méprisez dans le fond, mais qui vous amuse." Billy, p. 405.

45. Pollock, p. 67. "Mon ami, il y a trois modèles, l'homme de la nature, l'homme du poète, l'homme de l'acteur. Celui de la nature est moins grand que celui du poète, et celui-ci moins grand encore que celui du grand comédien, le plus exagéré de tous. Ce dernier monte sur les épaules du précédent, et se renferme dans un grand mannequin d'osier dont il est l'âme." Billy, p. 1054.

46. Barzun and Bowen, p. 12. "Rien n'était plus utile aux peuples que le mensonge, rien de plus nuisible que la vérité." Billy, p. 399.

47. "Elles sont d'usage dans mon état." Billy, p. 419.

48. Barzun and Bowen, p. 47. "Jamais faux, pour peu que j'aie intérêt d'être vrai; jamais vrai pour peu que j'aie intérêt d'être faux." Billy, p. 434.

49. Barzun and Bowen, p. 34. "Nous nous enivrerons, nous ferons des contes, nous aurons toutes sortes de travers et de vices. Cela sera délicieux." Billy, p. 422.

50. Barzun and Bowen, p. 48. "Nous dévorons comme des loups, lorsque la terre a été longtemps couverte de neige; nous déchirons comme des tigres tout ce qui réussit." Billy, p. 435.

51. Barzun and Bowen, p. 71. "C'est au cri animal de la passion à dicter la ligne qui nous convient. Il faut que ces expressions soient pressées les unes sur les autres." Billy, p. 457.

52. Barzun and Bowen, p. 63. "Sur la ligne des grands vauriens." Billy, p. 449.

53. Barzun and Bowen, p. 79. "Il semblait pétrir entre ses doigts un morceau de pate, et sourire aux formes ridicules qu'il lui donnait. Cela fait, il jeta la pagode hétéroclite loin de lui." Billy, p. 464.

54. "Je sentis que nature avait mis ma légitime dans la bourse des pagodes, et j'inventai mille moyens de m'en ressaisir." Billy, p. 465.

55. Compare what Diderot wrote in the *Paradoxe*: "Dans la grande comédie, la comédie du monde, celle à laquelle j'en reviens toujours, toutes les âes chaudes occupent le théâtre; tous les hommes de génie sont au parterre. Les premiers s'appellent des fous; les seconds, qui s'occupent à copier leurs folies, s'appellent des sages." Billy, p. 1009.

56. Barzun and Bowen, p. 45. "Il est vrai; mais vous ne soupçonnez pas combien je fais peu de cas de la méthode et des préceptes. Celui qui a besoin d'un protocole n'ira jamais loin; les génies lisent peu, pratiquent beaucoup et se font d'eux-mêmes. Voyez César, Turenne, Vauban, la marquise de Tencin,

son frère le cardinal, et le secrétaire de celui-ci, l'abbé Trublet. Et Bouret? Qui est-ce qui a donné des leçons à Bouret? Personne. C'est la nature qui forme ces hommes rares-là." Billy, pp. 432–33.

57. Pollock, p. 17. "On ne sait d'où. ces traits viennent; ils tiennent de l'inspiration. C'est lorsque, suspendus entre la nature et leur ébauche, ces génies portent alternativement un oeil attentif sur l'une et l'autre; les beautés d'inspiration, les traits fortuits qu'ils répandent dans leurs ouvrages, et dont l'apparition subite les étonne eux-mêmes, sont d'un effet et d'un succès bien autrement assurés que ce qu'ils y ont jeté de boutade. C'est au sang-froid à tempérer le délire de l'enthousiasme." Billy, p. 1008.

58. Barzun and Bowen, p. 69. "Lui n'apercevait rien; il continuait, saisi d'une aliénation d'esprit, d'un enthousiasme si voisin de la folie qu'il est incertain qu'il en revienne, s'il ne faudra pas le jeter dans un fiacre et le mener droit aux Petites-Maisons. En chantant un lambeau des *Lamentations* de Jomelli, il répétait avec une précision, une vérité et une chaleur incroyables les plus beaux endroits de chaque morceau; ce beau récitatif obligé où le prophète peint la désolation de Jérusalem, il l'arrosa d'un torrent de larmes qui en arrachèrent de tous les yeux. Tout y ètait, et la délicatesse du chant, et la force de l'expression, et la douleur. Il insistait sur les endroits où le musicien s'était particulièrement montré un grand maître. S'il quittait la partie du chant, c'était pour prendre celle des instruments qu'il laissait subitement pour revenir à la voix, entrelaçant l'une à l'autre de manière à conserver les liaisons et l'unité du tout; s'emparant de nos âmes et les tenant suspendues dans la situation la plus singulière que j'aie jamais éprouvée." Billy, p. 455. A similar example is to be found in the *Paradoxe*: "A great actor is neither a pianoforte, nor a harp, nor a spinnet, nor a violin, nor a violoncello; he has no key peculiar to him; he takes the key and the tone fit for his part of the score, and he can take up any. I put a high value on the talent of a great actor; he is a rare being—as rare as, and perhaps greater than, a poet." Pollock, p. 46. "Un grand comédien n'est ni un pianoforte, ni une harpe, ni un clavecin, ni un violon, ni un violoncelle; il n'a point d'accord qui lui soit propre; mais il prend l'accord et le ton qui conviennent à sa partie, et il sait se prêter à toutes. J'ai une haute idée du talent d'un grand comédien: cet homme est rare, aussi rare et peut-être plus que le grand poète." Billy, pp. 1034–35.

59. Barzun and Bowen, p. 69. "Il sifflait les petites flûtes, il reculait les traversières, criant, chantant, se démenant comme un forcené, faisant lui seul les danseurs, les danseuses, les chanteurs, les chanteuses, tout un orchestre, tout un théâtre lyrique, et se divisant en vingt rôles divers, courant, s'arrêtant avec l'air d'un énergumène, éteincelant des yeux, écumant de la bouche." Billy, pp. 455–56.

60. Barzun and Bowen, p. 70. "C'était la nuit avec ses ténèbres; c'était ombre et le silence, car le silence même se peint par des sons." Billy, p. 456.

61. Barzun and Bowen, p. 70. "Épuisé de fatigue, tel qu'un homme qui sort d'un profond sommeil ou d'une longue distraction, il resta immobile, stupide, étonné. Il tournait ses regards autour de lui comme un homme égaré qui cherche à reconnaître le lieu où il se trouve; il attendait le retour de ses forces

et de ses esprits; il essuyait machinalement son visage. Semblable à celui qui verrait à son réveil son lit environné d'un grand nombre de personnes dans un entier oubli ou dans une profonde ignorance de ce qu'il a fait, il s'écria dans le premier moment: 'Hé bien, Messieurs, qu'est-ce qu'il y a? D'où viennent vos ris et votre surprise? Qu'est-ce qu'il y a?' Ensuite il ajouta: 'Voilà ce qu'on doit appeler de la musique et un musicien.'" Billy, p. 456.

Chapter Six
Herder on the Artist as the Shaman of Western Civilization

1. "Ueber die verschiedenen Religionen," Herder, *Sämmtliche Werke*, ed. Suphan, 32:147. References to this edition will be cited as Suphan, by volume and page numbers.

2. Ibid., 32:19.

3. Herder wrote, for instance, that "alle diese Nationen gehören zu den Kaklogalliniern, Liliputtern und Huynhuyms, in die Welt, die Swift erschaffen." Ibid., 32:21.

4. "Ueber die neuere Deutsche Litteratur, Eine Beilage zu den Briefen, die neueste Litteratur betreffend." Ibid., 1:345.

5. Ibid., 1:394, 545.

6. Ibid., 5:449.

7. Ibid., 5:451.

8. Herder, *Kritische Wälder*, in Suphan 3:260–64.

9. Herder, "Versuch einer Geschichte," in Suphan, 32:94. According to the editorial comment, it never appeared in print.

10. Suphan, 5:5.

11. Billy, p. 457. See chapter 5 above.

12. Suphan, 5:12.

13. Ibid., 5:7.

14. Ibid., 5:16.

15. Ibid., 5:53.

16. Ibid., 5:58.

17. Ibid., 5:122–23.

18. Ibid., 5:168, 197.

19. Ibid., 5:170, 172.

20. Ibid., 5:167, 187. Herder argued much as Rothenberg was to do in *Technicians of the Sacred* almost two centuries later. For Rothenberg's position, see the Introduction, above.

21. Herder, "Fragment über die beste Leitung," Suphan, 9:542.

22. Suphan, 25:81.

23. Ibid.

24. Ibid., 25:82. Compare Herder's insistent analysis: "In den sogenannten Pöbelvorurtheilen, im Wahn, der Mythologie, der Tradition, der Sprache, den Gebräuchen, den Merkwürdigkeiten des Lebens aller Wilden ist mehr Poesie und Poetische Fundgrube, als in allen Poetiken und Oratorien aller Zeit." Ibid., 25:88.

25. Ibid., 25:83.

26. The role of Orpheus in eighteenth-century thought has been generally neglected because of suppositions about the purported antimythological stance of the men of the Enlightenment. Strauss, for example, wrote in *Descent and Return*, p. 3, that the rationalistic eighteenth century attempted to demythologize thinking totally while the Romantics, especially Novalis, the Schlegels, and Schelling, "were intoxicated with mythological and symbolic thinking." The first "modern" he takes up is Novalis.

27. Suphan, 25:84. Ernest Theodore Kirby has written extensively on this aspect of the subject without accounting for Herder. See Kirby, "Dionysus"; "Origin of the Mummers' Play"; "Shamanistic Origins of Popular Entertainments"; and *Ur-Drama*, esp. chaps. 1 and 5.

28. Adelung, *Grammatisch-kritisches*, pt. 1, col. 1636, s.v. edel, wrote that the word was most often used figuratively to mean "(1) rechtmässig, echt. . . . (2) Vorzüglich, das Beste in seiner Art. . . . Die Edlen des Volkes, in der biblischen und höhern Schreibart, die vornehmsten, die würdigsten Personen in einem Staate, nicht allein dem Stande, sondern auch der Tugend, der Denkungsart nach."

29. Suphan, 6:492.

30. Ibid., 6:392.

31. Ibid., 6:493.

32. Möser, "Schreiben an den Herrn Vicar in Savoyen," in *Sämmtliche Werke*, ed. Abeken, Möser, and Nicolai, 5:247.

33. Suphan, 6:284–85.

34. What recent researchers have concluded is notable; see, for example, Rudy, "Die Pictographie," p. 103.

35. Suphan, 6:288, 32:110.

36. Ibid., 6:369. Herder remained fascinated by the implications of the invention of alphabets—that is, systems that facilitated recording abstract signs. In his late years in Weimar, he even penned an outline for an essay, "Vom Einfluss der Schreibekunst ins Reich der menschlichen Gedanken." Ibid., 32:517–18. Herder's fascination was shared by other eighteenth-century Germans who were reading travel literature and who knew their Plato, especially the *Phaedrus*, wherein Socrates bemoaned the ruin of memory through discovery of the art of writing. Immanuel Kant stands out among them. He took up the issue in his anthropological lectures, which unfortunately scholarship has relegated to the realm of his extracurricular activities.

37. Suphan, 6:285. Another essay that shows Herder's thinking on the subject is *Erläuterungen zum Neuen Testament aus einer neueröfneten Morgenländischen Quelle*, published in 1775. Ibid., 7:338–39. Compare Mircea Eliade on Orpheus and Pythagoras, in *Geschichte der religiösen Ideen*, 1:160–71.

38. Suphan, 32:110.

39. Standard eighteenth-century mythological dictionaries always mentioned the Asiatic origins of Orpheus. In Hederich, *Gründliches mythologisches Lexicon*, he was called, among other things, a civilizing poet and an Egyptian *Hexenmeister* (col. 1812). Interesting for comparison with Herder's interpretation is the following comment: "Weil nun hieselbst alles noch roh und unwis-

send gewesen, so konnte er sich durch seine Beredtsamkeit, Musik und andere Künste gar leicht in eine solche Achtung setzen, dass er hernach für einen Fürsten und König gehalten worden, zumal er noch dazu mit einigen schwarzen Künsten soll haben umgehen, und also die dummen Leute desto eher zu allem, was er gewollt, bewegen können" (col. 1819).

40. Suphan, 6:398.

41. Ibid., 6:357.

42. Ibid., 6:397–98.

43. Ibid., 6:403, 424, 453.

44. Ibid., 6:463.

45. Achterberg, *Imagery in Healing*, p. 29, and also pp. 75–87 and p. 100. See also part 2 of Doore, *Shaman's Path*, pp. 88–175.

46. Two excellent studies deal with the historical development of the threefold role of Orpheus as mythical magician-theologian-civilizer: Lee, "Orpheus and Euridice," and Warden, *Orpheus*.

47. Suphan, 17:150.

48. Ibid., 9:531. This remains a topic of great interest to medievalists of the late twentieth century; see, for example, Kabell, "Skalden und Schamanen."

49. Suphan, 9:532.

50. Ibid., 9:534.

51. "Edle griechische Schamanen," ibid. The note Ronald Taylor provided about Herder's use of the word "shaman" in this passage indicated nothing more than "Buddhist priests with healing powers." *Romantic Tradition in Germany*, p. 19; cf. p. 25.

52. Suphan, 8:340.

53. Ibid., 8:180.

54. Ibid., 8:190.

55. Ibid., 8:226.

56. Ibid., 8:227.

57. Ibid., 8:221–22.

58. Ibid., 8:222.

59. Ibid. 16:334.

60. Ibid., 16:336.

61. Ibid., 16:343.

62. Ibid., 16:347.

63. Ibid., 16:343.

64. Ibid., 16:346.

65. Ibid., 16:348.

66. Ibid., 16:355–56.

67. Ibid., 16:357.

68. Ibid., 16:363.

69. Ibid., 12:159.

70. Ibid., 13:242, 305–6.

71. Ibid., 13:307–8.

72. Ibid., 14:23, 57, 100; also, 8:399–400.

73. Ibid., 24:29–30.

74. Ibid., 24:149.

75. See also Herder's unpublished manuscript dealing with the meretricious influences of secret societies: "Glaukon und Nicias, Gespräche," ibid., 15:165–78.

76. Ibid., 24:151. Compare Judith Devlin's recent study of the irrational in post-revolutionary France, *Superstitious Mind*, esp. pp. 215–30.

77. Suphan, 24:152–53.

Chapter Seven
Mozart, or, Orpheus Reborn

1. Fetzer, *Romantic Orpheus*, pp. 179–80, argues that revival of interest in the Orpheus myth began with the Romantics who sought the reintegration of poetry and music into life.

2. Lessing's contribution, entitled "Über die Regeln der Wissenschaften zum Vergnügen; besonders der Poesie und Tonkunst," first appeared in Marpurg, *Der Critische Musicus an der Spree*. The original German is as follows:

> Ein Geist, den die Natur zum Mustergeist beschloss,
> Ist, was er ist, durch sich; wird ohne Regeln gross.
> Er geht, so kühn er geht, auch ohne Weiser sicher.
> Er schöpfet aus sich selbst. Er ist sich Schul' und Bücher
> Was ihn bewegt, bewegt; was ihn gefällt, gefällt.
> Sein glücklicher Geschmack ist der Geschmack der Welt.
> Wer fasset seinen Werth? Er selbst nur kann ihn fassen.

It is also available in Lessing, *Werke*, ed. Petersen and Olshausen 1:185–86, lines 165–71. References to this work will be cited as Petersen-Olshausen. For a survey of discussions on genius in German culture, specifically Lessing, see Schmidt, *Genie-Gedankens*, 2:69–95.

3. See, for example, Ehrenwald, *Anatomy of Genius*, pp. 5–7.

4. *Hamburgische Dramaturgie*, no. 34 (August 25, 1767), in Petersen-Olshausen, 5:152–53. For his treatment of related issues, see nos. 30 (August 11, 1767) and 48 (October 13, 1767).

5. *Hamburgische Dramaturgie*, no. 96 (April 1, 1768), Petersen-Olshausen, 5:390.

6. Gerstenberg, *Briefe über Merkwürdigkeiten der Literatur*, pp. 215, 232.

7. Translated in le Huray and Day, *Music and Aesthetics*, p. 130.

8. Hamann, "Aesthetica in nuce," 2:197. Schmidt, *Genie-Gedanken*, takes up Hamann on pp. 96–119.

9. Hamann, *Tagebuch eines Christen*, 1:241.

10. Hamann, "Aesthetica in nuce," 2:197.

11. For questions about eighteenth-century perceptions of androgyny and artistic performance, see Flaherty, "Sex and Shamanism in the Eighteenth Century." May was so concerned about such matters that he followed up with a series of lectures on personal and public hygiene in the concert hall of the Mannheim theater. They eventually appeared in print as *Medicinische Fastenpredigten*.

12. Weickard, *Der Philosophische Arzt*, 1:284: "Ein Genie, ein Mensch von erhöhter Einbildungskraft muss beweglichern Hirnzasern, als ein anderer haben. Die Zasern müssen geschwinder und leichter erschüttert werden, so dass lebhafte und häufige Vorstellungen entstehen können." See Meusel, *Das gelehrte Teutschland*, 8:387–89. See also Historische Kommission, *Allgemeine Deutsche Biographie*, 41:485.

13. A good example can be found in Hoffbauer, *Psychologische Untersuchungen*, pp. 58–59.

14. Rogerson, *"Ut musica poesis,"* pp. 141–42.

15. Spingarn, *Critical Essays*, 3:56. For a discussion of British and German musical criticism, see Cowart, *Origins of Modern Musical Criticism*, pp. 115–39.

16. Walther, *Musikalisches Lexicon*, p. 454.

17. Wessel, *"Affektenlehre* in the Eighteenth Century," pp. 18, 44.

18. L. Mozart, *Treatise*, p. 120. L. Mozart, *Gründliche Violinschule*, p. 15.

19. Ibid. L. Mozart, *Treatise*, p. 20.

20. Frederick the Great, *De la littérature allemande*, pp. 4–5.

21. Burney, *Eighteenth-Century Musical Tour*, p. 167. The singer purportedly in question was Gertrude Elizabeth Schmeling (1749–1830), known by her husband's name as La Mara.

22. Frederick the Great, *De la littérature allemande*, ed. Geiger, 17.

23. Ibid., p. 23.

24. I took up that subject in *Opera in the Development of German Critical Thought*, pp. 37–66, 281–300.

25. Deutsch, *Mozart*, pp. 3, 5–9.

26. Deutsch, *Mozart*, pp. 103–5, and Goetz, *Mozart*, p. 25.

27. W. A. Mozart, *Mozart*, 1:76.

28. Ibid., p. 427.

29. Leitzmann, *Mozarts Persönlichkeit*, pp. 18–19, 30–31. Goetz, *Mozart*, pp. 33–34, provides, for example, the following German version of the December 1, 1763 issue of the *Correspondance littéraire*: "Noch unglaublicher aber ist es, dass er eine ganze Stunde lang phantasieren kann, wobei er sich Visionen voll entzückender Motive hingibt, die er mit gutem Geschmack und mit Sinn und Verstand wiederzugeben weiss. . . . Das Wunderkind verdreht einem richtig den Kopf." See also Eisen, "Contributions."

30. Deutsch, *Mozart*, p. 28.

31. Nissen, *Biographie*, p. 29.

32. Deutsch, *Mozart*, p. 26.

33. Ibid., p. 295.

34. Ibid., p. 193.

35. Burney, *General History*, 1:279, 286. The music literature of the day had generally absorbed much from the reports about other parts of the world. Johann Nikolaus Forkel, for example, wrote in the preface to the first volume of his *Allgemeine Geschichte der Musik*, published in 1788, that cultural differences wrought musical differences and that Europeans should show concern for the young, whether individuals, tribes, or nations. He repeatedly referred to Siberia, the South Seas, and the Near East (pp. xiv–xv, 140–41). Further

examples can be found in Schusky, *Das deutsche Singspiel*, pp. 3–4, 27–28, 65, 78.

36. Deutsch, *Mozart*, p. 140, from Burney, *Present State of Music*.

37. W. A. Mozart, *Mozart*, 2:138, no. 377: "Er ist meinethalben kein hexen-meister, aber ein sehr solider geiger."

38. Tissot's "Discours XVI" appeared in the journal *Aristide ou le citoyen* (Lausanne, October 11, 1766). English translations are available in Deutsch, *Mozart*, pp. 61–66, and King, *Mozart in Retrospect*, pp. 132–37. The quotation is from Deutsch, *Mozart*, 61. The role of music as a medium of communication in shamanism has long been recognized. Chadwick, *Poetry and Prophecy*, is a classic in this field of research. See esp. p. 14.

39. Chadwick, *Poetry and Prophecy*, p. 63. Nettl, *Mozart und der Tanz*, p. 8, pointed out that Mozart was not only a naturally gifted dancer, but also that he possessed the kind of physical agility that enabled him to excel at billiards and other social games. Tissot's reference to Mozart's ear obviously struck a chord with those who came later. The biography prepared by Constanze Mozart and her second husband, Georg Nicolaus von Nissen, *Biographie*, contained a comparative illustration of Mozart's ear and a normal ear across from p. 586.

40. Deutsch, *Mozart*, p. 64.

41. Ibid.

42. Ibid., p. 66.

43. Ibid., p. 97.

44. Ibid., p. 100

45. Antonio Maria Meschini, in Deutsch, *Mozart*, p. 103. Compare the one from 1768 by Christoph Zabuesing, in Nissen, *Biographie*, pp. 153–54.

46. Joseph Hurdalek, in Deutsch, *Mozart*, p. 304.

47. Ibid., pp. 282–83. Meusel, *Das gelehrte Teutschland*, 1:421.

48. Deutsch, *Mozart*, p. 213. *Magazin der Musik*, ed. Karl Friedrich Cramer (Hamburg, March 2, 1783).

49. Deutsch, *Mozart*, pp. 344–45. *Dramaturgische Blätter*, ed. Adolf Franz Friedrich Ludwig von Knigge (Hanover, 1789).

50. Deutsch, *Mozart*, p. 372. *Chronik von Berlin* (October 2, 1790).

51. Deutsch, *Mozart*, p. 431. *Wiener Zeitung* (December 31, 1791).

52. Deutsch, *Mozart*, p. 464. *Hamburgische Theaterzeitung* (July 7, 1792).

53. Deutsch, *Mozart*, pp. 472–73.

54. Ibid., pp. 497–98.

55. Ibid., p. 431.

56. This translation is from Neubauer, *Emancipation*, p. 129, which first alerted me to the passage. The original is available in Eckermann, *Gespräche mit Goethe*, in *Gedenkausgabe*, 24:472.

See also Deutsch, *Mozart*, p. 673 (March 11, 1828), "Denn was ist Genie anders als jene produktive Kraft," and p. 450 (February 14, 1831), "Aber freilich, eine Erscheinung wie Mozart bleibt immer ein Wunder, das nicht weiter zu erklären ist." Furthermore, compare Orel, "Mozart auf Goethes Bühne."

57. Deutsch, *Mozart*, p. 533; Kelly, *Reminiscences*.

58. Doris Stuck, in Deutsch, *Mozart*, p. 569.

59. Leitzmann, *Mozarts Persönlichkeit*, p. 117.

60. Ibid., p. 557. Her memoirs, *Denkwürdigkeiten aus meinem Leben, 1769–1843*, were published in Vienna in 1844.

61. One of the most important contributions to the subsequent mythologization was the biography by Georg Nicolaus von Nissen that was edited and seen through the press by his widow, Constanze Mozart von Nissen. For bibliographical information about how that process manifested itself in literary writings about Mozart, see Böhme, *Mozart in der schönen Literatur*, pp. 203–4. Böhme provided an update with "Mozart in der schönen Literatur, II." The recent work of H. C. Robbins Landon has been devoted to stripping the myth of its many trappings in order to uncover the true facts about Mozart's life. In *1791: Mozart's Last Year*, p. 124, Landon acknowledges the mythologization process and laments how difficult it has become "to separate fact from fiction."

62. King, *Mozart in Retrospect*, p. 21. The Mozartian interest of the Romantics and those who followed them would support Fetzer's contention *Romantic Orpheus*, p. 180.

63. See Engel, "Mozart in der philosophischen und ästhetischen Literatur." Of related interest might be Sir Walter Scott's attribution of Hoffmann's stance to opium abuse rather than insight or sensitivity, in "On the Supernatural," p. 97.

64. The particular E.T.A. Hoffmann tale in question is, for example, available in the original German in *Dichtungen*, ed. Harich, 1:139–56.

65. Allanbrook discusses the operatic convention of the happy ending in *Rhythmic Gesture in Mozart*, p. 324.

Chapter Eight
Shamans Failed and Successful in Goethe

1. In his conversations with Eckermann, Goethe mentioned some implications of the Orpheus myth for his corpus. On March 15, 1831, for example, it was *Novelle. Gedenkausgabe*, vol. 24: *Gespräche mit Goethe in den letzten Jahren seines Lebens*, p. 479. Compare Burkert, *Lore and Science*, pp. 120–65, and Spaethling, *Music and Mozart*, esp. pp. 130–31. Sewell, *Orphic Voice*, p. 176, contends that Herder was part of Goethe's Orphic education. The Goethean work she selects as her example is *Urworte: Orphisch*.

2. Goethe, *Maximen und Reflexionen*, in *Goethes Werke*, ed. Trunz et al., 12:418, l. 391. References to this edition will be cited as Hamburger Ausgabe.

3.   Vier Epochen der Wissenschaften:
> kindliche,
> poetische, abergläubische;
> empirische,
> forschende, neugierige;
> dogmatische,
> didaktische, pedantische;
> ideele,
> methodische, mystische.

Ibid., p. 419, no. 399.

4. Zastrau, *Goethe Handbuch*, vol. 1, col. 15. This section also provides a survey of Goethe's utterances on superstition.

5. "Über epische und dramatische Dichtung," in *Gedenkausgabe*, 14:369; Grumach, *Goethe und die Antike*, 2:700.

6. For a general introduction, see Grünthal, "Ueber die historischen Wurzeln," pp. 8–10. The research of Margaret C. Jacob would seem to support Goethe's contention. She writes, for example, "The simplistic assumption that at every turn the Newtonian natural philosophy fostered the intellectual revolution which is at the foundation of so much modern thought and belief requires serious evaluation and modification. The ideological dimension of Newtonianism, once understood, forces that reevaluation." "Newtonianism," p. 11.

7. Goethe, *Maximen und Reflexionen*, Hamburger Ausgabe, 12:440, l. 547.

8. Ibid., p. 455, l. 652. Cottrell, *Goethe's "Faust,"* pp. 87–88 and 128–29, cites such physicists as Walter Heitler and Werner Heisenberg to show that contemporary scientists have come to appreciate the methodology Goethe espoused, especially that involving the effect of the researcher on the results of his research.

9. Goethe, "Analyse und Synthese," Hamburger Ausgabe, 13:51.

10. Hamburger Ausgabe, 14:11.

11. Grumach, *Goethe und die Antike*, 2:700: Riemer 28.8.1808, Gespräche 1:534.

12. Ibid. p. 47.

13. Ibid., p. 63.

14. Ibid., p. 142.

15. Ibid., pp. 183–86, 190–91.

16. *Gedenkausgabe*, vol. 10: *Dichtung und Wahrheit*, pt. 2, bk. 6, p. 266: "Bei diesen Gesinnungen hatte ich immer Göttingen im Auge. Auf Männern, wie Heyne, Michaelis und so manchem andern ruhte mein ganzes Vertrauen; mein sehnlichster Wunsch war, zu ihren Füssen zu sitzen und auf ihre Lehren zu merken. Aber mein Vater blieb unbeweglich."

17. Buchholz, pp. 16, 27–39.

18. Buchholz, *Asch*, p. 101.

19. *CIBA-Zeitschrift* 4 (October 1936): 1322; Schmid, *Goethe und die Naturwissenschaften*, ed. Abderhalden, pp. 66, 490. References to this bibliography will be cited as Abderhalden. With regard to Blumenbach, see Plischke, *Die Ethnographische Sammlung*, and Quantz, "Beitrag," pp. 289–304.

20. Buchholz, *Asch*, pp. 73–74.

21. Ibid, p. 102. I am indebted to Dr. Manfred Urban, Akademischer Direktor, Institut und Sammlung für Völkerkunde der Universität Göttingen, for allowing me to see "Das alte Fremdenbuch des academischen Museums," the book of visitors' autographs that dates from 1808. It contains the signatures of several of Goethe's friends and associates.

22. *Gedenkausgabe*, vol. 11: *Tag- und Jahreshefte oder Annalen als Ergänzung meiner sonstigen Bekenntnisse*, p. 853; see also, Zastrau, *Goethe Handbuch*, vol. 1, cols. 407–9, esp. 409.

23. Abderhalden, pp. 66, 67, 490.

24. *Gedenkausgabe*, vol. 20: *Briefwechsel mit Friedrich Schiller*, no. 225: Goethe's letter to Schiller, October 15, 1796, p. 253.

25. Ibid., no. 821: Goethe's letter to Schiller, July 12, 1801, p. 866.

26. Plischke, *Blumenbachs Einfluss*, p. 10.

27. See, for example, "Übersicht der Geographischen Verlags-Werke."

28. See Keudell, *Goethe*, for example, p. 35, nos. 194 and 195. I was privileged to use the annotated copy at the Zentralbibliothek der deutschen Klassik in Weimar.

29. Abderhalden, pp. 491, 522, 532, 544.

30. Keudell, *Goethe*, pp. 2, 35, 36, 139, 154.

31. Ibid., no. 641, p. 104, and handwritten references on the interleaf.

32. This work, published in Leipzig in 1799, was reviewed anonymously in the *Allgemeine geographische Ephemeriden* 5 (Weimar, 1800): 55–82.

33. Hamburger Ausgabe, vol. 2: *Noten und Abhandlungen zu besserem Verständnis des West-Östlichen Divans*, pp. 128 and 135.

34. See chapter 6 above.

35. Abderhalden, p. 71; Keudell, *Goethe*, no. 72, p. 13, and no. 552, p. 91. In *Zur Morphologie* (1817), for example, Goethe reported, "meine mühselige, qualvolle Nachforschung ward erleichtert, ja versüsst, indem Herder die Ideen zur Geschichte der Menschheit aufzuzeichnen unternahm. Unser tägliches Gespräch beschäftigte sich mit dem Uranfängen der Wasser-Erde, und der darauf von altersher sich entwickelnden organischen Geschöpfe." Hamburger Ausgabe, 13:63.

36. Keudell, *Goethe*, lists Johann Heym's grammar and bilingual dictionary, p. 61, nos. 350 and 351. Propper, "Miszellen." Abderhalden, pp. 74, 491, 522, 527, 532, and 544, provides information about Goethe's association with ethnographers as well as his familiarity with their work.

37. *Gedenkausgabe*, vol. 24: Eckermann, *Gespräche mit Goethe*, November 13, 1823, pp. 70–71.

38. July 23, 1820, as quoted in Dankert, *Der Mythische Urgrund*, p. 87.

39. Goethe's letter to Wieland (April 1776); Dankert, *Der Mythische Urgrund*, p. 163.

40. Goethe, *Italian Journey*, p. 22. *Gedenkausgabe*, vol. 11: *Italienische Reise, Annalen*, September 11, 1786, p. 28.

41. My attention was drawn to the code name by Wilson, "Weimar Politics," p. 165.

42. Bode, *Goethes Schweizer Reisen*, pp. 100–101.

43. Goethe, *Conversations*, pp. 309–10. *Gedenkausgabe*, March 11, 1828, 24:678–79.

44. Goethe, *Conversations*, p. 527. *Gedenkausgabe*, March 8, 1831, 24:472; see also, December 6, 1829, pp. 373–74.

45. *Die Horen*; see *Tag- und Jahreshefte 1796*, Hamburger Ausgabe, 10:447.

46. Schlosser, *Rameaus Neffe*, p. 87.

47. "Eine sehr dogmatische Dratpuppe." Goethe, *Die Lieden des jungen Werthers*, pp. 48–49.

48. "Vorgestern kam der Medikus hier aus der Stadt hinaus zum Amtmanne und fand mich auf der Erde unter Lottens Kindern, wie einige auf

mir herumkrabelten, andere mich nekten und wie ich sie küzzelte, und ein grosses Geschrey mit ihnen verführte." Ibid., p. 48.

49. For example, p. 19. See Dankert, *Der Mythische Urgrund*, p. 106.

50. "Ob so täuschende Geister um diese Gegend schweben, oder ob die warme himmlische Phantasie in meinem Herzen ist, die mir alles rings umher so paradisisch macht." Goethe, *Die Lieden des jungen Werthers*, p. 10.

51. "Kein Wort von der Zauberkraft der alten Musik ist mir unwahrscheinlich, wie mich der einfache Gesang angreift." Ibid., p. 67.

52. Ibid., pp. 52, 140, 149. Compare Kihm, "Zur Symbolik der Schamanismus," pp. 128–29.

53. "Und wenn ich für Müdigkeit und Durst manchsmal unterwegs liegen bleibe, manchmal in der tiefen Nacht, wenn der hohe Vollmond über mir steht, im einsamen Walde auf einem krumgewachsnen Baum mich sezze, um meinen verwundeten Solen nur einige Linderung zu verschaffen, und dann in einer ermattenden Ruhe in dem Dämmerscheine hinschlummre!" Goethe, *Die Lieden des jungen Werthers*, p. 101.

54. "Man hat nachher den Huth auf einem Felsen, der an dem Abhange des Hügels in's Thal sieht gefunden, und es ist unbegreiflich, wie er ihn in einer finstern feuchten Nacht ohne zu stürzen erstiegen hat." Ibid., p. 208.

55. "Ich war kein Mensch mehr." Ibid., p. 38.

56. "Und seit der Zeit können Sonne, Mond und Sterne geruhig ihre Wirthschaft treiben, ich weis weder dass Tag noch dass Nacht ist, und die ganze Welt verliert sich um mich her." Ibid., p. 45.

57. "Ich werde gespielt wie eine Marionette." Ibid., p. 125.

58. "Das Herz ist jezo todt, aus ihm fliessen keine Entzükkungen mehr." Ibid., p. 157.

59. "Ein Schauer überfiel ihn." Ibid., p. 192.

60. "Die Bewegung beyder war fürchterlich. Sie fühlten ihr eigenes Elend in dem Schicksal der Edlen, fühlten es zusammen, und ihre Thränen vereinigten sie. Die Lippen und Augen Werthers glühten an Lottens Arme, ein Schauer überfiel sie, sie wollte sich entfernen und es lag all der Schmerz, der Antheil betäubend wie Bley auf ihr." Ibid., pp. 205–6.

61. "Ihre Sinnen verwirrten sich, sie drukte seine Hände, drukte sie wider ihre Brust, neigte sich mit einer wehmüthigen Bewegung zu ihm, und ihre glühenden Wangen berührten sich. Die Welt vergieng ihnen, er schlang seine Arme um sie her, presste sie an seine Brust, und dekte ihre zitternde stammelnde Lippen mit wüthenden Küssen. Werther!" Ibid., pp. 206–7.

62. Suphan, 25:472–76.

63. Act 1, scene 3, ll. 79–99.

64. Goethe, *Wilhelm Meister's Apprenticeship*, trans. Blackall, 9:108. References to this work will be cited as Blackall. "Man erzählt von Zauberern, die durch magische Formeln eine ungeheure Menge allerlei geistiger Gestalten in ihre Stube herbei ziehen. Die Beschwörungen sind so kräftig, dass sich bald der Raum des Zimmers ausfüllt, und die Geister, bis an den kleinen gezogenen Kreis hinangedrängt, um denselben und über dem Haupt des Meisters in ewig drehender Verwandlung sich bewegend vermehren. Jeder Winkel ist

vollgepfropft, und jedes Gesims besetzt. Eier dehnen sich aus, und Riesenge-stalten ziehen sich in Pilze zusammen. Unglücklicherweise hat der Schwarz-künstler das Wort vergessen, womit er diese Geisterflut wieder zur Ebbe bringen könnte." *Gedenkausgabe*, 7:198.

65. Blackall, p. 169. "Unter allerlei wunderlichen Reden, Zeremonien und Sprüchen." *Gedenkausgabe*, 7:303.

66. Blackall, pp. 64–65. "Sie verband sich die Augen, gab das Zeichen, und fing zugleich mit der Musik, wie ein aufgezogenes Räderwerk, ihre Bewe-gungen an, indem sie Takt und Melodie mit dem Schlage der Kastagnetten begleitete.

"Behende, leicht, rasch, genau führte sie den Tanz. Sie trat so scharf und so sicher zwischen die Eier hinein, bei den Eiern nieder, dass man jeden Augenblick dachte, sie müsse eins zertreten oder bei schnellen Wendungen das andre fortschleudern. Mit nichten! Sie berührte keines, ob sie gleich mit allen Arten von Schritten, engen und weiten, ja sogar mit Sprüngen, und zuletzt halb kniend sich durch die Reihen durchwand.

"Unaufhaltsam, wie ein Uhrwerk, lief sie ihren Weg, und die sonderbare Musik gab dem immer wieder von vorne anfangenden und losrauschenden Tanze bei jeder Wiederholung einen neuen Stoss. Wilhelm war von dem son-derbaren Schauspiele ganz hingerissen; er vergass seiner Sorgen, folgte jeder Bewegung der geliebten Kreatur, und war verwundert, wie in diesem Tanze sich ihr Charakter vorzüglich entwickelte." *Gedenkausgabe*, 7:123.

67. Blackall, pp. 81–82. "Sie fuhr auf, und fiel auch sogleich wie an allen Gelenken gebrochen vor ihm nieder. Es war ein grässlicher Anblick!" *Gedenkausgabe*, 7:153.

68. Blackall, p. 82. "Ihre starren Glieder wurden gelinde, es ergoss sich ihr Innerstes, und in der Verirrung des Augenblickes fürchtete Wilhelm, sie werde in seinen Armen zerschmelzen, und er nichts von ihr übrig behalten." *Gedenkausgabe*, 7:153.

69. Blackall, p. 196. "Es schien, als wenn eine königliche Familie im Geister-reiche zusammen käme." *Gedenkausgabe*, 7:348.

70. Blackall, p. 197. "Die Kinder sprangen und sangen fort, und besonders war Mignon ausgelassen, wie man sie niemals gesehen. Sie schlug das Tam-burin mit aller möglichen Zierlichkeit und Lebhaftigkeit, indem sie bald mit druckendem Finger auf dem Felle schnell hin und her schnurrte, bald mit dem Rücken der Hand, bald mit den Knöcheln darauf pochte, ja mit ab-wechselnden Rhythmen das Pergament bald wider die Knie, bald wider den Kopf schlug, bald schüttelnd die Schellen allein klingen liess, und so aus dem einfachsten Instrumente gar verschiedene Töne hervorlockte." *Gedenk-ausgabe*, 7:350.

71. Blackall, p. 197. "Er ist mein Oheim." *Gedenkausgabe*, 7:350.

72. Blackall, pp. 197–98. "Mignon ward bis zur Wut lustig, und die Ge-sellschaft, so sehr sie anfangs über den Scherz gelacht hatte, musste zuletzt Einhalt tun. Aber wenig half das Zureden, denn nun sprang sie auf und raste, die Schellentrommel in der Hand, um den Tisch herum. Ihre Haare flogen, und indem sie den Kopf zurück und alle ihre Glieder gleichsam in die Luft

warf, schien sie einer Mänade ähnlich, deren wilde und beinah unmögliche Stellungen uns auf alten Monumenten noch oft in Erstaunen setzen." *Gedenkausgabe,* 7:350–51.

73. Blackall, p. 198. "Mignon hatte sich versteckt gehabt, hatte ihn angefasst und ihn in den Arm gebissen." *Gedenkausgabe,* 7:351. Also compare Flaherty, "Sex and Shamanism."

74. Blackall, p. 316. "So lasst mich scheinen, bis ich werde." *Gedenkausgabe,* 7:553–54.

75. "Das einzige Irdische an ihr." *Gedenkausgabe,* 7:560.

76. Blackall, p. 322. "Sie sah völlig aus wie ein abgeschiedner Geist." *Gedenkausgabe,* 7:564.

77. Blackall, p. 359. "Und es schien das Hindernis mehr in seiner Denkungsart als in den Sprachwerkzeugen zu liegen." *Gedenkausgabe,* 7:628.

Chapter Nine
Faust, the Modern Shaman

1. I would not be so presumptuous as to try to pass off my findings as the fruit of independent research done in a vacuum. I am deeply indebted to that long line of scholars who, having spent their lives studying Goethe's text, clarified the philosophical and mythological sources of many passages and left clues for subsequent generations to pursue. My greatest debt is to Harold Jantz. What I absorbed about Renaissance magic, mythology, and Neoplatonism from his seminars at the Johns Hopkins University, as well as from *Goethe's Faust as a Renaissance Man, The Mothers in "Faust,"* and *The Form of "Faust"* is greater than I can detail here.

I am also deeply indebted to Atkins, *Goethe's "Faust," A Literary Analysis* whose interpretation of part 2 as a series of dream-plays, pp. 119–20, gave me the courage to continue looking for semblances of séance and trance. His discussion of the text's suggestion of various dramatic forms was equally helpful. To distinguish it from his translation of *Faust,* which is cited in the text, I shall refer to it as Atkins, *Literary Analysis.* Another study from which I profited greatly is Jane K. Brown's recent *Goethe's "Faust," The German Tragedy,* although I strongly disagree with her overall evaluation of the role of magic as entirely symbolic or as authorial artifice (pp. 23, 65, 85, 86, 123, 136, 238, and 251). Theories of drama unfortunately becloud the multifarious aspects of theatrical magic inherent in contemporary acting theory.

2. In a recent article, Jost Schillemeit, for example, still sees one of them as having been written for another work, "Das *Vorspiel auf dem Theater* zu Goethes *Faust.*"

3. Cottrell, *Goethe's "Faust,"* p. 74, sees it, interestingly enough, as an inner monologue: "We are inside the poet's mind and all is in flux."

4. Gearey, *Goethe's "Faust,"* p. 98, alerted me to *Dichtung und Wahrheit,* book 13, where Goethe describes his habit of communing with nonpresent voices. I cite from *Gedenkausgabe,* 10:630: "Er pflegte nämlich, wenn er sich allein sah, irgendeine Person seiner Bekanntschaft im Geiste zu sich zu rufen. Er bat sie, nieder zu sitzen, ging an ihr auf und ab, blieb vor ihr stehen, und verhandelte

mit ihr den Gegenstand der ihm eben im Sinne lag. Hierauf antwortete sie gelegentlich, oder gab durch die gewöhnliche Mimik ihr Zu- oder Abstimmen zu erkennen."

5. Meuli, "Scythica," p. 172: "Nun ist die Seelenreise das Hauptstück der Tätigkeit des Schamanen, so durchaus identisch mit seinem Lied, dass der Ausdruck für 'Fahrt' in der Schamanenpoesie eine ganz geläufige Formel für 'Lied, Gesang' geworden ist."

6. Goethe, *Faust I and II*, ed. and trans. Atkins, 2:1. References to this work will be cited as Atkins.

Was ich besitze, seh' ich wie im Weiten,
Und was verschwand, wird mir zu Wirklichkeiten.

Hamburger Ausgabe, 3:9, l. 31.

7. Atkins, p. 7.

So schreitet in dem engen Bretterhaus
Den ganzen Kreis der Schöpfung aus
Und wandelt mit bedächt'ger Schnelle
Vom Himmel durch die Welt zur Hölle.

Hamburger Ausgabe, 3:15, l. 239.

8. Benjamin Bennett, whose reading is vastly different from mine, prefers to employ the term phrenographic, that is, "the use of the whole visible stage to represent the interior of a single mind," in *Goethe's Theory of Poetry*, p. 69; see also p. 114.

9. Atkins, p. 11.

Das Werdende, das ewig wirkt und lebt,
Umfass' euch mit der Liebe holden Schranken
Und was in schwankender Erscheinung schwebt,
Befestiget mit dauernden Gedanken.

Hamburger Ausgabe, 3:19, l. 346.

10. Mason, *Goethe's "Faust,"* p. 7, views this as part of a "paradoxical process." The older generation of German writers no sooner flung Faust "out the front door of the temple of German literature and culture than the younger generation of writers set about bringing him in again at the back door." I believe their reading of travel literature with its many shamanic reports may have had something to do with this.

11. Hamburger Ausgabe, 3:39, l. 1034. In "Der Verfasser teilt die Geschichte seiner botanischen Studien mit," which was published in *Zur Morphologie* (1817), Goethe describes his increasing interest in the pharmacological value of plants with mention of the long tradition handed down from fathers to sons: "In jenen Waldgegenden hatten sich nämlich, von den dunkelsten Zeiten her, geheimnisvoll nach Rezepten arbeitende Laboranten angesiedelt und vom Vater zum Sohn manche Arten von Extrakten und Geisten bearbeitet, deren allgemeiner Ruf von einer ganz vorzüglichen Heilsamkeit durch emsige Balsamträger erneuert, verbreitet und genutzt ward." Hamburger Ausgabe, 13:151.

12. Claudia Kniep argues interestingly that the puppet-play tradition taught Goethe to think of Faust's monogram as H. F. since the warning "Homo fuge" was contained in the bloody writing. "'Blut ist ein ganz besondrer Saft.'"

13. Atkins, *Literary Analysis*, has pointed out many of Goethe's divergences, e.g., pp. 62, 65, 90, 192, 218.

14. Atkins, pp. 30–31.

> Du bist dir nur des einen Triebs bewusst;
> O lerne nie den andern kennen!
> Zwei Seelen wohnen, ach! in meiner Brust,
> Die eine will sich von der andern trennen;
> Die eine hält, in derber Liebeslust,
> Sich an die Welt mit klammernden Organen;
> Die andre hebt gewaltsam sich vom Dust
> Zu den Gefilden hoher Ahnen.
> O gibt es Geister in der Luft,
> Die zwischen Erde' und Himmel herrschend weben,
> So steiget nieder aus dem goldnen Duft
> Und führt mich weg, zu neuem, buntem Leben!
> Ja, wäre nur ein Zaubermantel mein
> Und trüg' er mich in fremde Länder!
> Mir sollt' er um die köstlichen Gewänder,
> Nicht feil um einen Königsmantel sein.

Hamburger Ausgabe, 3:41, l. 1110.

15. Klemm, *Allgemeine Cultur-Geschichte der Menschheit* 2:309: "Zwei Seelen, nämlich den Schatten und den Odem des Menschen." Bennett, *Goethe's Theory of Poetry*, p. 125, derives the two souls from Schiller's form and matter drives.

16. Goethe has Faust choose to decant the poison from the vial to a crystal chalice, something that had so long been associated with German shamanic practices that the very vocabulary—beaker, *becher, coclearius, koukelari, gaukeln*—was affected. See Grimm, *Deutsche Mythologie*, 2:867: "Eine art weissagungen geschah mit dem becher."

17. Atkins, p. 41.

> O wär' ich vor des hohen Geistes Kraft
> Entzückt, entseelt dahingesunken!

Hamburger Ausgabe, 3:53, l. 1577.

18. Atkins, p. 41. "Was die Seele Mit Lock- und Gaukelwerk umspannt." Hamburger Ausgabe, 3:54, l. 1588.

19. As Jantz pointed out, *Renaissance Man*, pp. 41–45, there are affinities to Pico della Mirandola, *On the Dignity of Man*. For example, Pico wrote (pp. 3–4) "that man is the intermediary between creatures, that he is the familiar of the gods above him as he is lord of the beings beneath him; that by the acuteness of his senses, the inquiry of his reason and the light of his intelligence, he is the interpreter of nature, set midway between the timeless unchanging and the

flux of time; the living union (as the Persians say), the very marriage hymn of the world, and, by David's testimony but little lower than the angels."
20. Compare Pico della Mirandola, *On the Dignity of Man*, pp. 53–54.
21. Atkins, p. 44.

> Kannst du mich schmeichelnd je belügen,
> Dass ich mir selbst gefallen mag,
> Kannst du mich mit Genuss betrügen,
> Das sei für mich der letzte Tag!
> Die Wette biet' ich!

Hamburger Ausgabe, 3:57, l. 1694.
22. Atkins, p. 62. "Das schönste Bild von einem Weibe!" Hamburger Ausgabe, 3:78, l. 2436.
23. Compare Eliade, *Shamanism*, p. 154.
24. Atkins, p. 65.

> Das tolle Zeug, die rasenden Gebärden,
> Der abgeschmackteste Betrug,
> Sind mir bekannt, verhasst genug.

Hamburger Ausgabe, 3:82, l. 2533.
25. Atkins, p. 66.

> Was sagt sie uns für Unsinn vor?
> Es wird mir gleich den Kopf zerbrechen.
> Mich dünkt, ich hör' ein ganzes Chor
> Von hunderttausend Narren sprechen.

Hamburger Ausgabe, 3:83, l. 2573.
26. Atkins, p. 67. "Ist über vierzehn Jahr doch alt." Hamburger Ausgabe, 3:85, l. 2627. Compare Eliade, *Shamanism*, p. 78: "An important division of the 'mythology of woman' is devoted to showing that it is always a feminine being who helps the hero to conquer immortality or to emerge victorious from his initiatory ordeals."
27. Haddon, *History of Anthropology*, p. 81. Stafford, *Voyages*, p. 116, discusses eighteenth-century artistic interest in caves and grottoes.
28. Möser, *Sämtliche Werke*, Historisch-Kritische Ausgabe, 2:402. Compare Eliade, *Shamanism*, p. 51, for an interpretation of caves in paleolithic religions.
29. Atkins, p. 83.

> Und wenn der Sturm im Walde braust und knarrt,
> Die Riesenfichte stürzend Nachbaräste
> Und Nachbarstämme quetschend niederstreift,
> Und ihrem Fall dumpf hohl der Hügel donnert,
> Dann führst du mich zur sichern Höhle, zeigst
> Mich dann mir selbst, und meiner eignen Brust
> Geheime tiefe Wunder öffnen sich.

Hamburger Ausgabe, 3:103, l. 3228. Atkins, *Literary Analysis*, discusses the occurrence of caves throughout the text, concluding "this symbol now represents life creating and life created," p. 218. As mentioned above, the rediscovery of many primeval caves in the eighteenth century stimulated much speculation about the life-styles of their inhabitants. Recent interest in caves has manifested itself in various ways in Western Europe. One example is Graichen, *Das Kultplatzbuch*.

30. Lea, *Materials*, 1:177. A discussion of Hieronymus Cardanus's writing on the subject can be found in Leuner, "Die toxische Ekstase," p. 89. Compare also Grimm, *Mythologie*, 2:878, 880.

31. Tr. Atkins, p. 99.

> In die Traum- und Zaubersphäre
> Sind wir, scheint es, eingegangen.
> Führ' uns gut und mach' dir Ehre,
> Dass wir vorwärts bald gelangen
> In den weiten, öden Räumen!

Hamburger Ausgabe, 3:122, l. 3871.

32. Atkins, p. 106.

> Ich sag's euch Geistern ins Gesicht,
> Den Geistesdespotismus leid' ich nicht;
> Mein Geist kann ihn nicht exerzieren.

Hamburger Ausgabe, 3:130, l. 4165. Atkins, *Literary Analysis*, pp. 92–93, views the Proktophantasmist as an "exponent of German Enlightenment." J. Brown, *Goethe's "Faust,"* p. 125, points out the double irony but is too quick to find it merely absurd.

33. Atkins, 131. Bächtold-Stäubli and Hoffmann-Krayer, *Handwörterbuch*, vol. 6, s.v. Maus, cols. 40–41.

34. "Am farbigen Abglanz haben wir das Leben." Hamburger Ausgabe, 3:149, l. 4727.

35. J. Brown, *Goethe's "Faust,"* pp. 138–39, sees the rainbow as "a symbol that is simultaneously nature and art, Puck and Ariel"; also, p. 143. Bennett, *Goethe's Theory of Poetry*, on the other hand, considers it at one point a metaphor for what Faust has done, specifically with Gretchen, p. 95, and at another point, "the affirmed illusoriness of culture," p. 120. See also p. 188.

36. Atkins, *Literary Analysis*, pp. 118–23. Compare Eliade, *Myth of the Eternal Return*, pp.34–35.

37. Atkins, p. 142.

> Doch ich fürchte, durch die Fenster
> Ziehen luftige Gespenster,
> Und von Spuk und Zaubereien
> Wüsst' ich euch nicht zu befreien.

Hamburger Ausgabe, 3:171, l. 5500.

38. Atkins, p. 146. "Ein Wunder ist es, wie's geschah." Hamburger Ausgabe, 3:176, l. 5688.

39. Atkins, *Literary Analysis*, p. 124.
40. Atkins, p. 153.

> Drohen Geister, uns zu schädigen,
> Soll sich die Magie betätigen.

Hamburger Ausgabe, 3:184, l. 5985.

41. Atkins, p. 157. "Ich liebe mir den Zaubrer zum Kollegen." Hamburger Ausgabe, 3:189, l. 6142.
42. "In deutlichen Gestalten." Hamburger Ausgabe, 3:190, l. 6186.
43. Compare my discussion of Burton, *Anatomy of Melancholy*, 1:205 above. Shamanic trance, along with mesmerism and other such phenomena, had become increasingly fashionable dramatic subjects by the middle of the eighteenth century. I have, for example, already treated the work of Catherine the Great. Compare Gearey, *Goethe's "Faust,"* p. 48: "The Faust of the legend was a scholar, but he was not less but more than an artist: he was able to bring to life what he imagined, not as art, but in the real world." Gearey equates poetry and magic on pp. 55 and 88.
44. Baron points out in *Doctor Faustus*, p. 61, that such leading intellectuals of the German Renaissance as Trithemius and Mutianus Rufus believed Faust was "a theatrical boasting deceiver."
45. Atkins, p. 159.

> Das Heidenvolk geht mich nicht an,
> Es haust in seiner eignen Hölle.

Hamburger Ausgabe, 3:191, l. 6209.

46. Atkins, p. 161.

> Gestaltung, Umgestaltung,
> Des ewigen Sinnes ewige Unterhaltung.
> Umschwebt von Bildern aller Kreatur;
> Sie sehn dich nicht, denn Schemen sehn sie nur.

Hamburger Ausgabe, 3:193, l. 6287.

47. Chadwick, *Shamanism among the Tatars*, p. 96. Compare Neumann, *Great Mother*, chapter 9, "The Primordial Goddess," esp. pp. 94–96. As far as the mothers in Faust are concerned, Atkins, *Literary Analysis*, pp. 133–34, calls this "first and foremost a brilliant improvisation." Jantz, *Mothers*, pp. 47–49, explicates the Renaissance iconography of creative females and discusses Goethe's familiarlity with Western myths about the magna mater. He argues, p. 81, that Goethe created the myth of the mothers out of his cumulative experience. Strauss, *Descent and Return*, pp. 25–26, prefers to interpret these scenes as part of the Orphic tradition, asserting that even the word priesthood, which is later used, was dear to them.
48. Atkins, p. 162. Hamburger Ausgabe, 3:194. Ida H. Washington has convincingly shown that Mephisto's earthy vulgarity, like his many disguises, stems from the Aristophanic tradition. "Mephistopheles as an Aristophanic Devil."
49. Atkins, p. 163.

Hier braucht es, dächt' ich, keine Zauberworte;
Die Geister finden sich von selbst zum Orte.

Hamburger Ausgabe, 3:196, l. 6375.
50. Atkins, p. 164.

Beginne gleich das Drama seinen Lauf,
Der Herr befiehlt's, ihr Wände tut euch auf!
Nichts hindert mehr, hier ist Magie zur Hand:
Die Teppiche schwinden, wie gerollt vom Brand;
Die Mauer spaltet sich, sie kehrt sich um,
Ein tief Theater scheint sich aufzustellen,
Geheimnisvoll ein Schein uns zu erhellen,
Und ich besteige das Proszenium.

Hamburger Ausgabe, 3:196–97, l. 6391.
51. Atkins, p. 164. "Durch magisch Wort sei die Vernunft gebunden."
Hamburger Ausgabe, 3:197, l. 6416.
52. Atkins, pp. 164–65.

Im Priesterkleid, bekränzt, ein Wundermann
Der nun vollbringt, was er getrost begann
Ein Dreifuss steigt mit ihm aus hohler Gruft,
Schon ahn' ich aus der Schale Weihrauchduft.

Hamburger Ausgabe, 3:197, l. 6421.
53. Atkins, p. 165.

Die einen fasst des Lebens holder Lauf,
Die andern sucht der kühne Magier auf;
In reicher Spende lässt er, voll Vertrauen,
Was jeder wünscht, das Wunderwürdige schauen.

Hamburger Ausgabe, 3:198, l. 6435. Goethe's changing of the word "Dichter" to "Magier" would seem to indicate that he wanted to clarify Faust's position as the modern shaman. This serves to support the Jantz contention, in *Mothers*, pp. 64, that the magus is "the creative master of forms, the artist poet." This would not contradict Atkins's idea: "His current role of magician-priest is an extension of that showman-poet which he first consciously essayed in Masquerade." *Literary Analysis*, p. 138.
54.   Zum Weihrauchsdampf was duftet so gemischt,
Das mir das Herz zum innigstens erfrischt?

Hamburger Ausgabe, 3:199, l. 6473.
55. Atkins, p. 166.

Fürwahr! Es dringt ein Hauch tief ins Gemüte,
Er kommt von ihm!

Hamburger Ausgabe, 3:199, l. 6475.
56. "So fasst Euch doch und fallt nicht aus der Rolle." Hamburger Ausgabe, 3:200, l. 6501. Jantz, *Mothers*, p. 55, suggests this represents "the

mysteries and initiation," and, p. 67, writes that Goethe incorporated elements from Pausanias's description of the descent into the den of Trophonius. See my discussion of *Werther* in chapter 8 as well as my discussion of Einhorn and then Fontenelle in chapter 1.

57. Atkins, *Literary Analysis*, pp. 157–58, contends as follows: "Classical Walpurgisnight, then, is the first half of a double dream-play representing a victory of Faust over Mephistopheles. In form a series of carnival-like episodes (the scene Pharsalian Fields) that culminate in a grand *trionfo* (the scene Rocky Inlets of the Aegean Sea), the pattern is that of Masquerade, but its execution is unfettered by any physical or occasional limitations other than those inherent in the fiction of a witches' Sabbath." Gearey, *Goethe's "Faust,"* pp. 202–3, writes, "The play generally will become less and less the imitation of an action presumed to be read, and more the projection of images intended to make visible to the hero, no less than to the audience, the great forces by which they have been invisibly and collectively formed."

58. See my discussion in chapter 8.

59. Atkins, p. 174. "Die Welt, sie war nicht, eh' ich sie erschuf." Hamburger Ausgabe, 3:208, l. 6794.

60. J. Brown, *Goethe's "Faust,"* p. 180, comments on the Orpheus relationship without taking it further: "Faust has already donned his role as poet in Act I; as poet—a second Orpheus in this context—Faust creates a Helen apart from himself."

61. Scholars have overlooked neither the operatic features of the Helen episode nor the musico-dramatic possibilities of part 1. Most recently there has been Schimpf, *"Faust als Melodrama?"*

62. Jantz, *Mothers*, pp. 51–52, pointed out that Goethe clearly wanted the association of Faust and Orpheus noticed. I believe the text indicates it was much stronger than that.

63. For Bennett's interpretation of mythology and myth, see *Goethe's Theory of Poetry*, pp. 145, 161.

64. Atkins, p. 178.

> Romantische Gespenster kennt ihr nur allein;
> Ein echt Gespenst, auch klassisch hat's zu sein.

Hamburger Ausgabe, 3:213, l. 6946.

65. J. Brown, *Goethe's "Faust,"* p. 172, interprets her as mediating the transformation of the historical world into a poetic one.

66. Atkins, p. 181.

> Setz ihn nieder,
> deinen Ritter und sogleich
> Kehret ihm das Leben wieder,
> Denn er sucht's im Fabelreich.

Hamburger Ausgabe, 3:216, l. 7052.

67. Books 3 and 4. Atkins, *Literary Analysis*, p. 161.

68. "Gestalten gross, gross die Erinnerungen." Hamburger Ausgabe, 3:220, l. 7190.

69. Atkins, p. 186.

> Ich wache ja! O lasst sie walten,
> Die unvergleichlichen Gestalten,
> Wie sie dorthin mein Auge schickt.
> So wunderbar bin ich durchdrungen!
> Sind's Träume? Sind's Erinnerungen?

Hamburger Ausgabe, 3:222–23, l. 7271.

70. I take up this question in "Empathy and Distance." A few examples are Ludwig Tieck's *Die verkehrte Welt: Ein Historisches Schauspiel in fünf Aufzügen* (1798), August Wilhelm Schlegel's *Ehrenpforte und Triumphbogen für den Theater-Präsidenten von Kotzebue bei seiner gehofften Rückkehr in's Vaterland, Mit Musik* (1800), and E.T.A. Hoffmann's *Seltsame Leiden eines Theater-Direktors* (1819) and *Prinzessin Brambilla, Ein Capriccio nach Jakob Callot* (1821).

71. Atkins, p. 188.

> Den Arzt, der jede Pflanze nennt,
> Die Wurzeln bis ins tiefste kennt,
> Dem Kranken Heil, dem Wunden Linderung schafft,
> Umarm' ich hier in Geist- und Körperkraft!

Hamburger Ausgabe, 3:224, l. 7345.

72. Atkins, p. 188. "Den Wurzelweibern und den Pfaffen." Hamburger Ausgabe, 3:225, l. 7352.

73. Atkins, p. 190.

> Ich seh', die Philologen,
> Sie haben dich so wie sich selbst betrogen.
> Ganz eigen ist's mit mythologischer Frau,
> Der Dichter bringt sie, wie er's braucht, zur Schau:
> Nie wird sie mündig, wird nicht alt,
> Stets appetitlicher Gestalt,
> Wird jung entführt, im Alter noch umfreit;
> Gnug, den Poeten bindet keine Zeit.

Hamburger Ausgabe, 3:227, l. 7426.

74. Atkins, p. 190.

> Und sollt' ich nicht, sehnsüchtiger Gewalt,
> Ins Leben ziehn die einzigste Gestalt?

Hamburger Ausgabe, 3:227, l. 7438.

75. Atkins, p. 190.

> Mein fremder Mann! als Mensch bist du entzückt;
> Doch unter Geistern scheinst du wohl verrückt.

Hamburger Ausgabe, 3:227, l. 7446.

76. Lindsay, *Clashing Rocks*, pp. 195–96. See also Eliade, *Forge and the Crucible*, pp. 102–3.

77. Atkins, p. 207.

> Hinweg zu Proteus! Fragt den Wundermann
> Wie man entstehn und sich verwandeln kann.

Hamburger Ausgabe, 3:247, l. 8152.

78. Wolfgang Schadewaldt came close to explicating this intricately interwoven play of image and reality when he gave the following interpretation: "Vom Blendwerk der Magie bleibt alles umspielt, es ist keine Frage, Mephisto *spielt* die Schaffnerin Phorkyade, ja er spielt sie. Denn alles ist irgendwie auch wieder wie ein aufgeführtes Spiel, das schliesslich mit dem Todessturz des Sohnes, dem die Mutter in den Tod folgt, grässlich zerreisst." "Faust und Helena," p. 30. More recently David Barry has argued about the uncanny reading effect this episode produces. "Turning the Screw on Goethe's Helena," p. 268. I agree with Jane Brown's view that this is all Renaissance pastiche. *Goethe's "Faust,"* pp. 198, 210.

79. Ich als Idol, ihm dem Idol verband ich mich.
   Es war ein Traum, so sagen ja die Worte selbst.
   Ich schwinde hin und werde selbst mir zum Idol.

Hamburger Ausgabe, 3:267, l. 8879.

80. Atkins, p. 229.

> Du fällst
> Ganz aus der Rolle; sage mir das letzte Wort!

Hamburger Ausgabe, 3:273, l. 9047.

81. Atkins, p. 229. "Gutes wendest du zum Bösen um." Hamburger Ausgabe, 3:274, l. 9073.

82. "Schnell und sonder Schritt." Hamburger Ausgabe, 3:276, l. 9144.

83. Discussion of Lynkeus the lynx-eyed man as well as hypotheses about the shamanic origins of the classical myths can be found in Lindsay, *Clashing Rocks,* pp. 89–90, 118–21.

84. Atkins, p. 236. "Als Mitregenten deines Grenzunbewussten Reichs." Hamburger Ausgabe, 3:282, l. 9362.

85. Atkins, p. 237.

> Nun schaut der Geist nicht vorwärts, nicht zurück,
> Die Gegenwart allein—.

Hamburger Ausgabe, 3:283, l. 9381.

86. Eliade, *Shamanism*, p. 171.

87. Atkins, p. 237.

> Nicht versagt sich die Majestät
> Heimlicher Freuden
> Vor den Augen des Volkes
> Übermütiges Offenbarsein.

Hamburger Ausgabe, 3:284, l. 9407.

88. Atkins, p. 237.

> Ich fühle mich so fern und doch so nah,
> Und sage nur zu gern: Da bin ich! da!

Hamburger Ausgabe, 3:284, l. 9411.

89. Atkins, p. 237.

> Ich scheine mir verlebt und doch so neu,
> In dich verwebt, dem Unbekannten treu.

Hamburger Ausgabe, 3:284, l. 9415.

90. Atkins, pp. 242–43. "Ein Genius ohne Flügel" and "ein kleiner Phöbus." Hamburger Ausgabe, 3:290, ll. 9603, 9620.

91. Atkins, p. 246. Hamburger Ausgabe, 3:294.

92. Atkins, p. 246. "Welch ein Unfug! welch Geschrei!" Hamburger Ausgabe, 3:295, l. 9789.

93. Atkins, p. 249.

> Sind denn wir
> Gar nichts dir?
> Ist der holde Bund ein Traum?

Hamburger Ausgabe, 3:298, l. 9881.

94. Allanbrook, *Rhythmic Gesture*, p. 324: "The *lieto fine* ('happy ending') was of course habitual in the late eighteenth century; somehow, no matter what the depredations, proper orders were reestablished and their restoration celebrated. This celebration ought not to be considered the result of 'mere convention'; it emanates from a distinct point of view which, eschewing satirical or tragical exaggerations of the way the world is, chooses to assert instead the goods of continuity and order, and the equilibrium of good sense. It is a little-remarked habit of much late eighteenth-century opera to make mention somewhere in the happy closing chorus of its musical nature—to call attention to the fact that the participants are singing. This custom may have to do with the fact that many operas were *feste teatrali* commissioned to honor a royal wedding or other ceremony, and were thus in themselves celebratory."

95. See chapter 8.

96. Atkins, p. 254.

> Wie Seelenschönheit steigert sich die holde Form,
> Löst sich nicht auf, erhebt sich in den Äther hin
> Und zieht das Beste meines Innern mit sich fort.

Hamburger Ausgabe, 3:304, l. 10064.

97. I have not been able to find any textual evidence to agree with Jane Brown that it is appropriate to read acts 4 and 5 "as a commentary on the aftermath of the French Revolution." *Goethe's "Faust,"* p. 224.

98. Atkins, p. 267. "Das sind die Spuren Verschollner geistiger Naturen." Hamburger Ausgabe, 3:319, l. 10598.

99. Atkins, p. 269. "Das Gaukeln schafft kein festes Glück." Hamburger Ausgabe, 3:322, l. 10695.
100. Atkins, p. 270.

> Ich sehe nichts von diesen Wasserlügen,
> Nur Menschenaugen lassen sich betrügen.

Hamburger Ausgabe, 3:323, l. 10734.
101. Atkins, p. 273.

> Ich weiss nicht, mir verging die Kraft,
> Sie waren so gespensterhaft.

Hamburger Ausgabe, 3:326, l. 10835.
102. Atkins, p. 273.

> Hat sich in unsern Kampf auch Gaukelei geflochten,
> Am Ende haben wir uns nur allein gefochten.

Hamburger Ausgabe, 3:327, l. 10857.
103. Atkins, p. 280.

> Wohl! ein Wunder ist's gewesen!
> Lässt mich heut noch nicht in Ruh;
> Denn es ging das ganze Wesen
> Nicht mit rechten Dingen zu.

Hamburger Ausgabe, 3:335, l. 11111.
104. Atkins, p. 284. "Des Menschengeistes Meisterstück." Hamburger Ausgabe, 3:339, l. 11248.
105. "Was schwebet schattenhaft heran?" Hamburger Ausgabe, 3:342, l. 11383.
106. Atkins, p. 288.

> Könnt ich Magie von meinem Pfad entfernen,
> Die Zaubersprüche ganz und gar verlernen,
> Stünd' ich, Natur, vor dir ein Mann allein,
> Da wär's der Mühe wert, ein Mensch zu sein.

Hamburger Ausgabe, 3:343, l. 11404.
107. Dieckmann holds, "He is wrong to recoil from the magic in his path. The demonic forces *are* life, his life." *Goethe's "Faust,"* p. 78. Gearey, on the other hand, contends that the renunciation speech does not mean rejection of the imaginative faculty, so that "Not to think, but to be, will come to claim priority." *Goethe's "Faust,"* p. 88.
108. Atkins, p. 289.

> Er stehe fest und sehe hier sich um;
> Dem Tüchtigen ist diese Welt nicht stumm.
> Was braucht er in die Ewigkeit zu schweifen!
> Was er erkennt, lässt sich ergreifen.

Er wandle so den Erdentag entlang;
Wenn Geister spuken, geh' er seinen Gang,
Im Weiterschreiten find er Qual und Glück,
Er, unbefriedigt jeden Augenblick.

Hamburger Ausgabe, 3:344–45, l. 11445.
109. Atkins, p. 292.

Ihm sättigt keine Lust, ihm gnügt kein Glück,
So buhlt er fort nach wechselnden Gestalten;
Den letzten, schlechten, leeren Augenblick,
Der Arme wünscht ihn festzuhalten.

Hamburger Ausgabe, 3:349, l. 11587.
110. Atkins, p. 294. "Sie halten's doch für Lug und Trug und Traum."
Hamburger Ausgabe, 3:351, l. 11655.
111. Atkins, p. 297.

Ihr scheltet uns verdammte Geister
Und seid die wahren Hexenmeister.

Hamburger Ausgabe, 3:354, l. 11780.
112. Eliade, *Shamanism*, pp. 492–93.
113. Atkins, for one, observes, "And so, the stage picture notwithstanding, it is clear that the heaven to which Faust imagines himself being transported is to be no more Christian and conventional than was that of the Prologue in Heaven." *Literary Analysis*, p. 259. Compare also pp. 17 and 39. On p. 264, he likened it to "a Catholicized Arcadia" and wrote, p. 276, one could note "in man's imperfect striving for natural truths a universlly shared pattern of religious experience." See also Mason, *Goethe's "Faust,"* pp. 360, 373. This complex issue, like many I have raised, cannot be given its due here. The evidence would indicate, however, that it should be studied at length soon.
114. Atkins, p. 301.

Gerettet ist das edle Glied
Der Geisterwelt vom Bösen,
Wer immer strebend sich bemüht,
Den können wir erlösen.

Hamburger Ausgabe, 3:359, l. 11934.
115. Atkins, p. 301. "Der alte Satansmeister." Hamburger Ausgabe, 3:359, l. 11951.
116. Atkins, p. 303.

Mutter, Ehren würdig,
Uns erwählte Königin
Göttern ebenbürtig.

Hamburger Ausgabe, 3:361, l. 12010.
117. Atkins, *Literary Analysis*, p. 266, considers them "counterparts of Homunculus by virtue of their insubstantiality and power of levitation."

118. Atkins, p. 305.

> Vergönne mir, ihn zu belehren,
> Noch blendet ihn der neue Tag.

Hamburger Ausgabe, 3:363, l. 12092.
119. Atkins, p. 305.

> Alles Vergängliche
> Ist nur ein Gleichnis;
> Das Unzulängliche,
> Hier wird's Ereignis;
> Das Unbeschreibliche,
> Hier ist's getan;
> Das Ewig-Weibliche
> Zieht uns hinan.

Hamburger Ausgabe, 3:364, l. 12104.
120. See my discussion above. Cottrell, *Goethe's "Faust,"* p. 127, observes, "Goethe virtually turns the epistemological basis of science inside-out."

Bibliography

Primary Works

Acerbi, Giuseppe. *Travels through Sweden, Finland, and Lapland, to the North Cape in the Years 1798 and 1799.* 2 vols. London, 1802.

Adelung, Friedrich von. *Catherinens der Grossen Verdienste um die vergleichende Sprachenkunde.* St. Petersburg, 1815.

Adelung, Johann Christoph. *Grammatisch-kritisches Wörterbuch der Hochdeutschen Mundart.* 4 vols. Leipzig, 1793–1801.

Algarotti, Francesco. *Saggio di Lettere sopra la Russia.* 2d ed. Paris, 1763.

Bartram, William. *Travels through North and South Carolina, Georgia, East and West Florida, the Cherokee Country, the Extensive Territories of the Muscogulges or Creek Confederacy, and the Country of the Chactaws, Containing an Account of the Soil and Natural Productions of those Regions; together with Observations on the Manners of the Indians.* Philadelphia, 1791. Reprint. London, 1792.

Bayle, Pierre. *Dictionnaire historique et critique.* 4 vols. Rotterdam, 1697.

Bell, John. *Travels from St. Petersburg in Russia, to Diverse Parts of Asia.* 2 vols. Glasgow, 1763.

Benyowsky, Mauritius Augustus de. *Memoirs and Travels.* 2 vols. London, 1790.

Berchtold, Leopold. *Essay to direct and extend the Inquiries of Patriotic Travellers; with further Observations on the Means of preserving the Life, Health, & Property of the unexperienced in their Journies by Land and Sea. Also a Series of Questions, interesting to Society & Humanity, necessary to be proposed for Solution to Men of all ranks & Employments, & of all Nations and Governments, comprising the most serious Points relative to the Objects of all Travels, To which is Annexed a List of English and foreign Works intended for the Instruction and Benefit of Travellers, & a Catalogue of the most interesting European Travels which have been published in different Languages from the earliest Times, down to September 8th 1787.* 2 vols. London, 1789.

Beuys, Joseph. *Beuys zu Ehren: Zeichnungen, Skulpturen, Objekte, Vitrinen, und das Environment "Zeige deine Wunde" von Joseph Beuys, Gemälde, Skulpturen, Zeichnungen, Aquarelle, Environments, und Video-Installationen von 70 Künstlern.* Ed. Armin Zweite. Munich, 1986.

——. *Joseph Beuys Drawings.* City Art Gallery, Leeds; Kettle's Yard Gallery, Cambridge; Victoria and Albert Museum, London. London, 1983.

——. *Kreuz + Zeichen: Religiöse Grundlagen im Werk von Joseph Beuys.* Suermondt-Ludwig-Museum und Museumsverein. Aachen, 1985.

——. *Moderna Museet.* Moderna Museets Utstallningskatalog, 90. Stockholm, 1971.

——. *Similia similibus: Joseph Beuys zum 60. Geburtstag.* Ed. Johannes Stüttgen. Cologne, 1981.

Bossu, Jean-Bernard. *Travels through that Part of North America formerly called Louisiana.* London, 1771.

Boulanger, Nicolas-Antoine. *L'antiquité dévoilée par ses usages, ou examen critique des principales opinions, cérémonies & institutions religieuses & politiques des différens peuples de la terre.* 3 vols. Amsterdam, 1766.

Bruzen de la Martinière, Antoine Augustin. *Ceremonies et coutumes religieuses des peuples idolatres, représentées par des figures dessinées de la main de Bernard Picart avec une explication Historique, & quelque dissertations curieuses.* 2 vols. Amsterdam, 1735.

―――. *Ceremonies et coutumes religieuses de tous les peuples du monde, représentées par des figures dessinées de la main de Bernard Picart.* 5 vols. Amsterdam, 1723–1737.

Burney, Charles. *An Eighteenth-Century Musical Tour in Central Europe and the Netherlands.* Vol. 2 of *Dr. Burney's Tours in Europe,* ed. Percy A. Scholes. London, New York, Toronto, 1959.

―――. *A General History of Music from the Earliest Ages to the Present Period.* Ed. Frank Mercer. New York, 1935. Reprint. 1957.

―――. *Present State of Music in France and Italy.* London, 1771.

Burton, Robert. *The Anatomy of Melancholy: What it is, with all the kinds, causes, symptomes, prognostickes & severall cures of it.* Ed. Holbrook Jackson. 3 vols. Oxford, 1628. Reprint. New York, 1977.

Cabeza de Vaca, Alvar Nuñez. *The Journey of Alvar Nuñez Cabeza de Vaca and His Companions from Florida to the Pacific, 1528–1536.* Trans. Fanny Bandelier. New York, 1922.

Catherine II, Empress of Russia. *The Antidote; Or an Enquiry into the Merits of a Book, Entitled: A Journey into Siberia, Made in MDCCLXI in Obedience to an Order of the French King, and Published, with Approbation, by the Abbé Chappe d'Auteroche, of the Royal Academy of Sciences: In which many essential Errors and Misrepresentations are pointed out and confuted; and many interesting Anecdotes added, for the better Elucidation of the several Matters necessarily discussed: by a Lover of Truth.* London, 1772.

―――. *Documents of Catherine the Great: The Correspondence with Voltaire and the Instruction of 1767 in the English Text of 1768.* Ed. W. F. Reddaway. Cambridge, 1931.

―――. *Drey Lustspiele wider Schwärmerey und Aberglauben.* Ed. Friedrich Nicolai. Berlin and Stettin, 1789.

―――. *Erinnerungen der Kaiserin Katharina II.* Ed. Alexander Herzen and G. Kuntze. Memoirenbibliothek, 2d ser., vol. 13. Stuttgart, 1907.

―――. *The Memoirs of Catherine the Great.* Ed. Dominique Maroger, trans. Moura Budberg. New York, 1961.

―――. *Der sibirische Schaman, ein Lustspiel.* St. Petersburg, [1786] 1787.

Chappe d'Auteroche, Jean. *A journey into Siberia, made by order of the King of France.* London, 1770.

―――. *Voyage en Sibérie, fait par ordre du roi en 1761; contenant les moeurs, les usages des Russes, et l'etat actuel de cette puisance; la description géographique & le nivillement de la route de Paris à Tobolsk.* 2 vols. in 3. Paris, [1761] 1768.

Choris, Louis. *Voyage pittoresque autour du monde, avec des portraits des sauvages d'Amerique, d'Asie, d'Afrique, et des Iles du Grand Océan; des paysages, des vues maritimes, et plusieurs objets d'histoire naturelle; accompagné de descriptions de mammifères et oiseaux par M. le Baron Cuvier et M. A. de Chamisso, et d'observations sur les crânes humaines par M. Le Docteur Gall.* Paris, 1820–1821.

Court de Gébelin, Antoine. *Monde primitif.* 9 vols. Paris, 1773–1782.

Coxe, William. *Account of the Russian Discoveries between Asia and America, To which are added, The Conquest of Siberia, and the History of the Transactions and Commerce between Russia and China.* London, 1780.

Cranz, David. *Historie von Grönland, enthaltend die Beschreibung des Landes und der Einwohner und insbesondere die Geschichte der dortigen Mission der Evangelischen Brüder zu Neu-Herrenhut und Lichtenfels.* Barby, 1765.

————. *The History of Greenland: Including an Account of the Mission Carried on by the United Brethren in that Country.* 2 vols. London, 1820.

Defoe, Daniel. *Robinson Crusoe: An Authoritative Text, Backgrounds and Sources, Criticism.* Ed. Michael Shinagel. New York, 1975.

Degérando, Joseph-Marie. *The Observation of Savage Peoples.* Trans. F.C.T. Moore, with a preface by E. E. Evans-Pritchard. London, 1969.

Deguignes, Joseph. *Histoire générale des Huns, des Turcs, des Mogols, et des autres Tartares occidentaux, &c. avant et depuis Jesus Christ jusqu'à present.* 5 vols. Paris, 1756–1758.

————. *Voyages à Peking, Manille et L'Isle de France, faits dans l'intervalle des années 1784 à 1801.* 3 vols. Paris, 1808.

Deutsch, Otto Erich, ed. *Mozart: A Documentary Biography.* Trans. Eric Blom, Peter Branscombe, and Jeremy Noble. 2d ed. Stanford, 1966.

Diderot, Denis. *Le neveu de Rameau.* In *Oeuvres*, pp. 395–474.

————. *Oeuvres.* Ed. André Billy. N.p. [Gallimard], 1951.

————. *The Paradox of Acting.* Trans. Walter Herries Pollock. New York, n.d.

————. *Paradoxe sur le comédien.* In *Oeuvres*, pp. 1003–58.

————. *Rameau's Nephew and Other Works.* Trans. Jacques Barzun and Ralph H. Bowen. Garden City, N.Y., 1956.

Diderot, Denis, et al., eds. *Encyclopédie, ou Dictionnaire raisonné des sciences, des arts, et des métiers.* 17 vols. Paris, 1751–1765.

Dupuis, Charles. *Origine de tous les cultes, ou Religion universelle.* 3 vols. Paris, 1795.

Eckartshausen, Karl von. *Aufschlüsse zur Magie aus geprüften Erfahrungen über verborgene philosophische Wissenschaften und verdeckte Geheimnisse der Natur.* 4 vols. Munich, 1788–1792.

————. *Entdeckte Geheimnisse der Zauberey zur Aufklärung des Volks über Aberglauben und Irrwahn.* Munich, 1790.

Eckermann, Johann Peter. *Gespräche mit Goethe in den letzten Jahren seines Lebens.* In Goethe, *Gedenkausgabe*, 24.

Egede, Poul Hansen. *Nachrichten von Grönland, Aus einem Tagebuche, geführt von 1721 bis 1788.* Copenhagen, 1790.

Einhorn, Paul. *Ueber die religiösen Vorstellungen der alten Völker in Liv- und Ehstland: Drei Schriften von Paul Einhorn und eine von Johann Wolfgang Böckler, aufs neue wieder abgedruckt mit einer seltenen Nachricht Friedrich Engelken's über den grossen Hunger 1602.* Riga, 1857. Reprint. Hanover, 1968.

Engel, Samuel. *Geographische und Kritische Nachrichten und Anmerkungen über die Lage der nördlichen Gegenden von Asien und Amerika, nach den allerneuesten Reisebeschreibungen.* Mietau, Hasenpoth, Leipzig, 1772.

Ersch, Johann Samuel, and Johann Georg Gruber. *Allgemeine Encyclopädie der Wissenschaften und Künste.* 3 pts. 167 vols. Leipzig, 1818–1889.

Falconer, William. *Remarks on the Influence of Climate, Situation, Nature of Country, Population, Nature of Food, and Way of Life, on the Disposition and Temper, Manners and Behavior, Intellects, Laws and Customs, Form of Government, and Religion, of Mankind.* London, 1781.

Falk, Johann Peter. *Beyträge zur Topographischen Kenntnisz des Russischen Reichs.* 2 vols. St. Petersburg, 1785–1786.

Fischer, H. "Muthmassliche Gedanken von dem Ursprunge der Amerikaner." *Neue Nordische Beyträge zur physikalischen und geographischen Erd- und Völkerbeschreibung, Naturgeschichte und Oekonomie* 3 (St. Petersburg and Leipzig, 1782): 289–322.

Flögel, Karl Friedrich. *Geschichte der komischen Literatur.* 4 vols. Liegnitz and Leipzig, 1784–1787. Reprint. Hildesheim and New York, 1976.

Fontenelle, Bernard Le Bovier de. *Histoire des oracles.* Paris, 1687.

———. *Histoire des oracles.* Ed. Louis Maigron. Paris, 1971.

———. *The History of Oracles, and the Cheats of the Pagan Priests In two Parts.* Trans. Aphra Behn. London, 1688.

Forkel, Johann Nikolaus. *Allgemeine Geschichte der Musik.* Die grossen Darstellungen der Musikgescichte in Barock und Aufklärung, 8. Ed. Othmar Wesseley. Graz, 1967.

Forster, Georg. *Geschichte der Reisen, die seit Cook an der Nordwest- und Nordost-Küste von Amerika und in dem nördlichsten Amerika selbst von Meares, Dixon, Portlack, Coxe, Long u.a.m. unternommen worden sind.* 3 vols. Berlin, 1791.

———. *A Journey from Bengal to England, through the Northern Part of India, Kashmire, Afghanistan, and Persia, and into Russia, by the Caspian Sea.* 2 vols. London, 1798.

———. *Sämmtliche Schriften.* Ed. G. G. Gervinus. 9 vols. Leipzig, 1843.

———. *A Voyage round the World, in His Britannic Majesty's Sloop, Resolution, commanded by Capt. James Cook, during the Years 1772, 3, 4, and 5.* 2 vols. London, 1777.

———. *Werke: Sämtliche Schriften, Tagebücher, Briefe.* Ed. Deutsche Akademie der Wissenschaften zu Berlin. 18 vols. Berlin, 1958–.

Forster, Johann Georg Adam. *Entdeckungsreise nach Tahiti und in die Südsee: 1772–1775.* Alte abenteuerliche Reiseberichte. Tübingen, 1979.

Forster, Johann Reinhold. *Karakter, Sitten und Religion einiger merkwürdigen Völker.* Halle, 1793.

Frank, Johann Peter. *System einer vollständigen medicinischen Polizey.* New ed. 6 vols. in 8. Mannheim, Tübingen, and Vienna, 1804–1819.

Frederick the Great of Prussia. *De la littérature allemande.* Ed. Ludwig Geiger. Deutsche Litteraturdenkmale des 18. und 19. Jahrhunderts. 2d ed. Berlin, 1902. Reprint. Darmstadt, 1969.

Georgi, Johann Gottlieb. *Bemerkungen einer Reise im Russischen Reich im Jahre 1772.* 2 vols. St. Petersburg, 1775.

————. *Beschreibung aller Nationen des Russischen Reichs, ihrer Lebensart, Religion, Gebräuche, Wohnungen, Kleidungen und übrigen Merkwürdigkeiten.* 4 pts. with suppl. St. Petersburg, 1776–1780.

Gerstenberg, Heinrich Wilhelm von. *Briefe über die Merkwürdigkeiten der Literatur.* Ed. Alexander von Weilen. Deutsche Litteraturdenkmale des 18. und 19. Jahrhunderts, 29–30. Stuttgart, 1890. Reprint. Nendeln, Liechtenstein, 1968.

Giovanni da Pian del Carpine. *Relation du voyage de Jean du Plan Carpin, cordelier, qui fut envoyé en Tartarie par le pape Innocent IV. l'an 1246.* In *Recueil de voyages au Nord, contenant divers mémoires très utiles au commerce & à la navigation,* ed. Jean Frédéric Bernard, 7:330–424. 10 vols. Amsterdam, 1725–1738.

Gmelin, Johann Georg. *Reise durch Sibirien, von dem Jahr 1733 bis 1743.* 4 vols. Göttingen, 1751–1752.

Goethe, Johann Wolfgang von. *Aus meinem Leben, Dichtung und Wahrheit.* In *Gedenkausgabe,* 10:11–852.

————. *Briefwechsel mit Friedrich Schiller.* In *Gedenkausgabe,* 20.

————. *Conversations of Goethe with Eckermann and Soret.* Trans. John Oxenford. Rev. ed. London, 1898.

————. *Des Epimenides Erwachen.* In Hamburger Ausgabe, 5:366–99.

————. *Faust I and II.* Ed. and trans. Stuart Atkins. Cambridge, Mass., 1984.

————. *From My Life, Poetry and Truth.* Trans. Robert R. Heitner, ed. Thomas P. Saine and Jeffrey L. Sammons. 2 vols. New York, 1987.

————. *Gedenkausgabe der Werke, Briefe und Gespräche.* Ed. Ernst Beutler. 24 vols., 3 suppl. vols. Zurich and Stuttgart, 1948–1971.

————. *Goethes Faust: Der Tragödie erster und zweiter Teil, Urfaust.* In Hamburger Ausgabe, 3.

————. *Goethes Werke: Textkritisch durchgesehen und mit Anmerkungen versehen.* Hamburger Ausgabe. Ed. Erich Trunz et al. 14 vols. Hamburg, 1948–1966.

————. *Italian Journey (1786–1788).* Trans. W. H. Auden and Elizabeth Mayer. San Francisco, 1982.

————. *Italienische Reise.* In *Gedenkausgabe,* 11:7–613.

————. *Das Leben von Benvenuto Cellini.* In *Gedenkausgabe,* 15:413–925.

————. *Die Leiden des jungen Werthers.* Leipzig, 1744. Reprint. Dortmund, 1978.

————. *Materialien zur Geschichte der Farbenlehre.* In Hamburger Ausgabe, 14:7–269.

————. *Maximen und Reflexionen.* In Hamburger Ausgabe, 12:365–547.

————. *Die Metamorphose der Pflanzen.* In Hamburger Ausgabe, 13:64–101.

————. *Noten und Abhandlungen zu besserem Verständnis des West-Östlichen Divans.* In Hamburger Ausgabe, 2:126–267.

————. *Tag- und Jahreshefte oder Annalen als Ergänzung meiner sonstigen Bekenntnisse.* In *Gedenkausgabe,* 11:615–956.

————. *West-Östlicher Divan.* In Hamburger Ausgabe, 2:7–270.

————. *Wilhelm Meister's Apprenticeship.* Trans. Eric A. Blackall with Victor Lange. New York, 1989.

————. *Wilhelm Meisters Lehrjahre.* In *Gedenkausgabe,* 7.

————. *Zur Farbenlehre.* In Hamburger Ausgabe, 13:314–523.

Goethe, Johann Wolfgang von. *Zur Morphologie.* In Hamburger Ausgabe, 13:53–250.

———, trans. *Rameaus Neffe: Ein Dialog von Diderot.* In *Gedenkausgabe,* 15:927–1079.

Goetz, Wolfgang, ed. *Mozart: Sein Leben in Selbstzeugnissen, Briefen und Berichten.* Berlin, 1941.

Grimm, Friedrich Melchior. *Correspondance littéraire, philosophique, et critique, adressée à un souverain d'Allemagne.* 16 vols. Paris, 1812–1813.

———. *Correspondance littéraire, philosophique, et critique.* Ed. Maurice Tourneux. 16 vols. Paris, 1877–1882.

———. *Historical & Literary Memoirs and Anecdotes, Selected from the Correspondence of Baron de Grimm and Diderot with the Duke of Gotha, between the years 1770 and 1790.* 2 vols. London, 1814.

Grimm, Jacob. *Deutsche Mythologie.* 4th ed. 2 vols. Berlin, 1876. Reprint. Darmstadt, 1965.

Güldenstädt, Johann Anton. *Reisen durch Russland und im Caucasischen Gebürge.* St. Petersburg, 1781.

Hakluyt, Richard, ed. *The Principal Navigations, Voyages, Traffiques & Discoveries of the English Nation* [1598]. New York, 1965.

Hamann, Johann Georg. "Aesthetica in nuce, Eine Rhapsodie in Kabbalistischer Prose." In *Sämtliche Werke,* pp. 195–217.

———. *Sämtliche Werke.* Ed. Josef Nadler. 6 vols. Vienna, 1949–1957.

———. *Tagebuch eines Christen.* In *Sämtliche Werke,* 1:5–349.

Hamilton, Alexander. *A New Account of the East Indies, being the Observations and Remarks of Capt. Alexander Hamilton, Who spent his Time there From the Year 1688 to 1723 Trading and Travelling, by Sea and Land, to most of the Countries and Islands of Commerce and Navigation, between the Cape of Good-hope, and the Island of Japon.* 2 vols. Edinburgh, 1727.

Hederich, Benjamin. *Gründliches mythologisches Lexicon.* Ed. Johann Joachim Schwabe. Rev. and enlarged ed. Leipzig, 1770. Reprint. Darmstadt, 1967.

Hennepin, Louis. *A New Discovery of a Vast Country in America.* Ed. Reuben Gold Thwaites. 2 vols. Chicago, 1903.

Herder, Johann Gottfried. *Abhandlung über den Ursprung der Sprache.* In Suphan, 5:1–154.

———. *Adrastea.* In Suphan, 24:1–464.

———. *Aelteste Urkunde des Menschengeschlechts.* In Suphan, 6:193–511.

———. *Alte Volkslieder.* In Suphan, 25:1–126.

———. "Auszug aus einem Briefwechsel über Ossian und die Lieder alter Völker." *Von deutscher Art und Kunst.* In Suphan, 5:159–207.

———. *Briefe zu Beförderung der Humanität.* In Suphan, 17:1–414.

———. *Erläuterungen zum Neuen Testament aus einer neueröfneten Morgenländischen Quelle.* In Suphan, 7:335–470.

———. "Fragment über die beste Leitung eines jungen Genies zu den Schätzen der Dichtkunst." In Suphan, 9:541–44.

———. "Glaukon und Nicias, Gespräche." In Suphan, 15:165–78.

———. *Herders Sämmtliche Werke.* Ed. Bernhard Suphan. 33 vols. Berlin, 1877–1913. Reprint. Hildesheim and New York, 1978.

————. *Ideen zu einer Philosophie der Geschichte der Menschheit.* In Suphan, 13:1–442.

————. *Kritische Wälder, Oder Betrachtungen, die Wissenschaft und Kunst des Schönen betreffend, nach Massgabe neuerer Schriften.* In Suphan, 3:1–480.

————. "Das Land der Seelen: Ein Fragment." In Suphan, 16:333–40.

————. "Palingenesie, Vom Wiederkommen menschlicher Seelen, Mit einigen erläuternden Belegen." In Suphan, 16:341–67.

————. *Ueber die neuere Deutsche Litteratur, Eine Beilage zu den Briefen, die neueste Litteratur betreffend.* In Suphan, 1:131–531.

————. *Ueber die Würkung der Dichtkunst auf die Sitten der Völker in alten und neuen Zeiten.* In Suphan, 8:334–436.

————. "Versuch einer Geschichte der lyrischen Dichtkunst." In Suphan, 32:85–140.

————. "Vom Einfluss der Schreibekunst ins Reich der menschlichen Gedanken." In Suphan, 32:517–18.

————. *Vom Erkennen und Empfinden der menschlichen Seele: Bemerkungen und Träume.* In Suphan, 8:165–235.

————. *Vom Geist der Ebräischen Poesie: Eine Anleitung für die Liebhaber derselben, und der ältesten Geschichte des menschlichen Geistes.* In Suphan, 12:1–308.

————. "Von Ähnlichkeit der mittlern englischen und deutschen Dichtkunst, nebst Verschiednem, das daraus folget." In Suphan, 9:522–35.

Herodotus. *The History.* Trans. George Rawlinson, ed. E. H. Blakeney. 2 vols. London and New York, 1926. Reprint. 1949.

Hoffbauer, Johann Christoph. *Psychologische Untersuchungen über den Wahnsinn, die übrigen Arten der Verrückung und die Behandlung derselben.* Halle, 1807.

Hoffmann, E.T.A. "Don Juan." *Fantasiestücke in Callots Manier.* In *Dichtungen und Schriften sowie Briefe und Tagebücher.* Ed. Walther Harich, pp. 139–56. 15 vols. Weimar, 1924.

Holmberg, Heinrich Johann. *Ethnographische Skizzen über die Völker des russischen Amerika.* Acta Societatis Scientiarum Fennicae, pp. 282–422. Helsingfors, 1855–1862.

Hornemann, Friedrich. *The Journal of Friedrich Hornemann's Travels from Cairo to Murzuk in the Years 1797–1798.* Vol. 1 of *Missions to the Niger,* ed. E. W. Boville. Works Issued by the Hakluyt Society, 2d ser., no. 123. Cambridge, 1964.

Huet, Pierre Daniel. *Traité de l'origine des Romans.* 1670. Trans. Eberhard Werner Happel, 1682. Facsimile reprint. Stuttgart, 1966.

Hufeland, Christoph Wilhelm. *Gemeinnützige Aufsätze zur Beförderung der Gesundheit und des Wohlseyns.* Vienna, 1797.

————. *Ideen über Pathogenie und Einfluss der Lebenskraft auf Entstehung und Form der Krankheiten als Einleitung zu pathologischen Vorlesungen.* Jena, 1795.

————. *Die Kunst das menschliche Leben zu verlängern.* Jena, 1797.

Hume, David. *The Natural History of Religion* [1757]. Ed. H. E. Root. Stanford, 1956.

Hurd, Richard, ed. *Dialogues on the Uses of Foreign Travel; Considered as Part of*

An English Gentleman's Education: Between Lord Shaftesbury and Mr. Locke. London, 1764.

Jung-Stilling, Johann Heinrich. *Theorie der Geister-Kunde, in einer Natur- Vernunft- und Bibelmäsigen Beantwortung der Frage: Was von Ahnungen, Gesichten und Geistererscheinungen geglaubt und nicht geglaubt werden müsse.* Frankfurt and Leipzig, 1802.

Kant, Immanuel. *Anthropologie in pragmatischer Hinsicht.* Ed. J. H. von Kirchmann. Berlin, 1872.

Kelly, Michael. *Reminiscences of Michael Kelly.* 2d ed. London, 1826.

Klemm, Gustav. *Allgemeine Cultur-Geschichte der Menschheit.* 10 vols. Leipzig, 1843–1852.

Köhler, Johann David. *Anweisung für Reisende Gelehrte, Bibliothecken, Münz-Cabinette, Antiquitäten-Zimmer, Bilder-Säle, Naturalien- und Kunst-Kammern, u.d.m. mit Nutzen zu besehen.* Frankfurt and Leipzig, 1762.

Kolb, Peter. *Caput Bonae spei Hodierum, das ist Vollständige Beschreibung des afrikanischen Vorgebürges der Guten Hoffnung* [1719]. Schriftenreihe der Volkshochschule der Stadt Marktredwitz, 22. Marktredwitz, 1975.

Kotzebue, August Friedrich Ferdinand von. *Graf Benjowsky oder die Verschwörung auf Kamtschatka, Schauspiel in fünf Aufzügen.* Leipzig, 1795.

Krascheninnikow, Stephan. *Beschreibung des Landes Kamtschatka.* Trans. Johann Tobias Köhler. Lemgo, 1766.

———. *Explorations of Kamchatka, North Pacific Scimitar.* Trans. E.A.P. Crownhart-Vaughan. Portland, Or., 1972.

———. *The History of Kamtschatka, and the Kurilski Islands, with the countries adjacent; illustrated with maps and cuts.* Trans. James Grieve, M.D. Gloucester, 1764.

Labat, Jean-Baptiste. *Nouveau voyage aux Isles de l'Amérique.* The Hague, 1724.

La Créquinière, de. *Conformité des coutumes des Indiens orientaux, avec celles des Juifs & des autres peuples de l'antiquité.* Brussels, 1704.

Lafitau, Jospeh François. *Allgemeine Geschichte der Länder und Völker von America.* Trans. Johann Friedrich Schröter, with an introduction by Siegmund Jacob Baumgarten. 2 vols. Halle, 1752–1753.

———. *Customs of the American Indians Compared with the Customs of Primitive Times.* Trans. and ed. William N. Fenton and Elizabeth L. Moore. 2 vols. Toronto, 1974.

———. *Moeurs des sauvages ameriquains, comparées aux moeurs des premièrs temps.* 2 vols. Paris, 1724.

La Hontan, Louis Armand, baron de. *New Voyages to North-America, Giving a Full Account of the Customs, Commerce, Religion, and Strange Opinions of the Savages of that Country, With Political Remarks upon the Courts of Portugal and Denmark, and the Present State of the Commerce of those Countries.* 2d ed. 2 vols. London, 1735.

Langsdorff, Georg Heinrich von. *Bemerkungen auf einer Reise um die Welt, in den Jahren 1803–1807.* Frankfurt am Main, 1812.

———. *Voyages and Travels in Various Parts of the World during the Years 1803, 1804, 1805, 1806, and 1807.* 2 vols. London, 1813–1814. Reprint. Amsterdam and New York, 1968.

La Pérouse, Jean François de Galaup. *The Voyage of La Pérouse Round the World, in the Years 1785, 1786, 1787, and 1788, with the Nautical Tables.* 2 vols. London, 1798.

Le Huray, Peter, and James Day, eds. *Music and Aesthetics in the Eighteenth and Early Nineteenth Centuries.* Cambridge Readings in the Literature of Music. Cambridge, London, and New York, 1981.

Le Jeune, Paul. *Relation of What Occurred in New France in the Year 1635.* In Thwaites, *Jesuit Relations.* vol. 8 [1897].

———. *Relation of What Occurred in New France in the Year 1636.* In Thwaites, *Jesuit Relations.* vol. 10 [1897].

Leitzmann, Albert. Ed. *Mozarts Persönlichkeit: Urteile der Zeitgenossen gesammelt und erläutert.* Leipzig, 1914.

Lepechin, Ivan Ivanovich. *Tagebuch der Reise durch verschiedene Provinzen des Russischen Reiches in den Jahren 1768 und 1769.* Trans. Christian Heinrich Hase. 3 vols. Altenburg, 1774–1783.

Lesseps, Mathieu de. *Journal historique du voyage de M. de Lesseps, Consul de France, employé dans l'expédition de M. le comte de la Pérouse, en qualité d'interprète du Roi; Depuis l'instant où il a quitté les frégates Françoises au port Saint-Pierre & Saint-Paul du Kamtschatka, jusqu'à son arrivée en France, le 17 octobre 1788.* 2 vols. Paris, 1790.

Lessing, Gotthold Ephraim. *Die Erziehung des Menschengeschlechts.* In Petersen-Olshausen, 6:64–83.

———. *Hamburgische Dramaturgie.* In Petersen-Olshausen, 5.

———. "Über die Regeln der Wissenschaften zum Vergnügen; besonders der Poesie und Tonkunst." In Petersen-Olshausen, 1:182–87.

———. *Werke.* Ed. Julius Petersen and Waldemar von Olshausen. 30 vols. Berlin, Leipzig, Vienna, Stuttgart, 1925–1935. Reprint. Hildesheim and New York, 1970.

Levesque, Pierre-Charles. *Histoire de Russie, et des principales nations de l'Empire Russe.* 4th ed. 8 vols. and atlas. Paris, 1812.

———. *Historical & Literary Memoirs and Anecdotes, Selected from the Correspondence of Baron de Grimm and Diderot with the Duke of Saxe-Gotha between the years 1770 and 1790.* London, 1814.

Lisiansky, Urey Fedorovich. *A voyage round the world in the years 1803, 4, 5, & 6, performed, by order of his imperial majesty Alexander the First, Emperor of Russia, in the Ship Neva.* London, 1814.

Lockman, J., ed. *Travels of the Jesuits, into Various Parts of the World.* 2 vols. London, 1743.

Lorant, Stefan. *The New World: The First Pictures of America made by John White and Jacques le Moyne and engraved by Theodore de Bry.* Rev. ed. New York, 1965.

Marpurg, Friedrich Wilhelm, ed. *Der Critische Musicus an der Spree.* Berlin, 1749–1750. Reprint. Hildesheim and New York, 1970.

May, Franz Anton. *Medicinische Fastenpredigten oder Vorlesungen über Körper-und Seelen Diätetik zur Verbesserung der Gesundheit und Sitten.* Mannheim, 1793.

Meikle, James. *The Traveller; Or, Meditations on Various Subjects, Written on board a Man of War, To which is added, Converse with the World Unseen, To which is prefixed, The Life of the Author.* 2d American ed. Albany, 1812.

Meister, Leonhard. *Ueber die Schwermerei.* 2 vols. Bern, 1775–1777.

Messerschmidt, Daniel Gottlieb. *Forschungsreise durch Sibirien, 1720–1721.* Ed. E. Winter and N. A. Figurovskij. 5 vols. Quellen und Studien zur Geschichte Osteuropas, 8. Berlin, 1962–1977.

———. "Nachricht von D. Daniel Gottlieb Messerschmidts siebenjahriger Reise in Sibirien." *Neue Nordische Beyträge zur physikalischen und geographischen Erd- und Völkerbeschreibung, Naturgeschichte und Oekonomie* 3 (St. Petersburg and Leipzig, 1782): 97–158.

Meusel, Johann Georg. *Das gelehrte Teutschland oder Lexikon der jetzt lebenden teutschen Schriftsteller.* 5th ed. 23 vols. Lemgo, 1796–1834.

Milton, John. *Moscovia: Or, Relations of Moscovia, As far as hath been discover'd by English Voyages; Gather'd from the Writings of several Eye-witnesses; And of other less-known Countries lying Eastward of Russia as far as Cathay, lately discovered at several times by Russians* [1682]. In *The Works of John Milton,* ed. Frank Allen Patterson, 10:327–82. New York, 1932.

Montesquieu, Charles Louis Secondat, baron de la Brède et de. *The Spirit of the Laws: A Compendium of the First English Edition.* Ed. David Wallace Carrithers. Berkeley, 1977.

Moore, Francis. *Travels into the Inland Parts of Africa: Containing a Description of the Several Nations for the space of Six Hundred Miles up the River Gambia; their Trade, Habits, Customs, Language, Manners, Religion, and Government, the Power, Dispositon and Characters of some Negro Princes; with a particular Account of Job Ben Solomon, a Pholey, who was in England in the Year 1733, and known by the Name of the African, To which is added, Capt. Stibb's Voyage up the Gambia in the Year 1723, to make Discoveries.* London, 1738.

Möser, Justus. *Sämmtliche Werke.* Ed. Bernard Rudolf Abeken, Johanne Wilhelmine Juliane Möser, and Friedrich Christoph Nicolia. Rev. and enlarged ed. 10 vols. Berlin, 1842–1843.

———. *Sämmtliche Werke.* Historisch-Kritische Ausgabe, ed. Akademie der Wissenschaften zu Göttingen. 14 vols. Oldenburg, Berlin, Hamburg, 1943–1988.

———. "Schreiben an den Herrn Vikar in Savoyen, abzugeben bey dem Herrn Johann Jacob Rousseau." In Historisch-Kritische Ausgabe, 3:15–33.

Mozart, Leopold. *Gründliche Violinschule.* 3d ed., rev. Augsburg, 1787. Facsimile reprint, ed. Hans Joachim Moser. Leipzig, 1956.

———. *A Treatise on the Fundamental Principles of Violin Playing.* Trans. Editha Knocker. London, New York, and Toronto, 1951.

Mozart, Wolfgang Amadeus. *Mozart: Briefe und Aufzeichnungen.* Ed. Wilhelm H. Bauer and Otto Erich Deutsch. 7 vols. Basel, London, and New York, 1962–1975.

Müller, Gerhard Friedrich. *Eröffnung eines Vorschlages Zu Verbesserung der Russischen Historie durch den Druck einer Stückweise herauszugebenden Sammlung von allerley zu den Umständen und Begebenheiten dieses Reichs gehörigen Nachrichten.* 2 vols. St. Petersburg, 1732–1733.

Neueste Beschreibung von Alt und Neu Groen-Land. Nuremberg, 1679.

Neville, Henry. *The Isle of Pines.* London, 1668.

Nissen, Georg Nikolaus von. *Biographie W. A. Mozart's, Nach Originalbriefen,*

Sammlungen alles über ihn Geschriebenen, mit vielen neuen Beylagen, Steindrücken, Musikblättern und einem Fac-Simile. Leipzig, 1828.

Nuñez Cabeza de Vaca, Alvar. *The Journey of Alvar Nuñez Cabeza de Vaca and His Compaanions from Florida to the Pacific, 1528–1536*. Trans. Fanny Bandelier. New York, 1922.

Nynauld, Jean de. *De la lycanthropie, transformation, et extase des sorciers*. Paris, 1615.

Observations on the Present State of Denmark, Russia, and Switzerland, In a Series of Letters. London, 1784.

Pallas, Petrus Simon. *Bemerkungen auf einer Reise in die südlichen Statthalterschaften des Russischen Reiches a.d.J. 1793–1794*. Leipzig, 1799.

———. *Reise durch verschiedene Provinzen des Russischen Reichs*. 3 vols. St. Petersburg, 1771–1776.

Perry, John. *The state of Russia under the present Czar, In relation to the several great and remarkable things he has done, as to his naval preparations, the regulating his army, the reforming his people, and the improvement of his country, Particularly those works on which the author was employ'd, with the reasons of his quitting the czar's service, after having been fourteen years in that country, Also an account of those Tartars, and other people who border on the eastern and extreme northern parts of the czar's dominions, their religion, and manner of life; with many other observations, To which is annex'd, a more accurate map of the czar's dominions, than has hitherto been extant*. London, 1716.

Pichler, Caroline. *Denkwürdigkeiten aus meinem Leben, 1769–1843*. Vienna, 1844.

Pico della Mirandola, Giovanni. *On the Dignity of Man*. Trans. A. Robert Caponigri. South Bend, 1956.

Plato. *The Republic and Other Works*. Trans. B. Jowett. Garden City, 1960.

Polo, Marco. *The Description of the World*. Ed. A. C. Moule and Paul Pelliot. 2 vols. London, 1938. Reprint. New York, 1976.

Porta, Giambattista della. *Natural Magick* [1658]. Facsimile reprint. The Collector's Series in Science, ed. Derek J. Price. New York, 1957.

Porter, Robert Ker. *Travelling Sketches in Russia and Sweden During the Years 1805, 1806, 1807, 1808*. 2d ed. 2 vols. London, 1813.

Purchas, Samuel. *Purchas His Pilgrimage, Or Relations of the World and the Religions Observed in all Ages and Places Discovered, from the Creation unto this Present, In foure Partes: This First containeth A Theologicall and Geographicall Historie of Asia, Africa, and America, with the Ilands Adjacent, Declaring the Ancient Religions before the Floud, the Heathnish, Jewish, and Saracenicall in all Ages since, in those parts professed, with their severall Opinions, Idols, Oracles, Temples, Priestes, Fasts, Feasts, Sacrifices, and Rites Religious: Their beginnings, Proceedings, Alterations, Sects, Orders and Successions, With briefe Descriptions of the Countries, Nations, States, Discoveries, Private and Publike Customs, and the most Remarkable Rarities of Nature, or Humane Industrie, in the same*. London, 1613.

———. *Purchas his Pilgrimage or Relations of the World and the Religions*. London, 1626.

Quaife, Milo Milton, ed. *The Western Country in the Seventeenth Century: The Memoirs of Lamothe Cadillac and Pierre Liette*. Chicago, 1947.

Radishchev, Aleksandr Nikolaevich. *A Journey from St. Petersburg to Moscow* [1790]. Trans. Leo Wiener, ed. Roderick Page Thaler. Cambridge, Mass., 1958.

Raspe, Rudolf Erich. *Baron Munchausen's Narrative of His Marvellous Travels and Campaigns In Russia.* Oxford, Cambridge, and London, 1785.

Rather, L. J. *Mind and Body in Eighteenth-Century Medicine: A Study Based on Jerome Gaub's De regimine mentis.* Berkeley and Los Angeles, 1965.

Rechberg und Rothenlöwen, Karl von. *Les peuples de la Russie, ou description des moeurs, usages et costumes des diverses nations de l'Empire de Russie, accompagnée de figures coloriées.* 2 vols. Paris, 1812–1813.

Renaudot, Eusebius, trans. *Anciennes relations des Indes et de la Chine, de deux voyageurs Mahométans, qui y allèrent dans le neuvième siècle, traduites d'arabe.* Paris, 1718.

———. *Ancient Accounts of India and China, By Two Mohammedan Travellers, Who went to those Parts in the 9th Century; Translated from the Arabic.* London, 1733.

Richter, Wilhelm Michael. *Geschichte der Medicin in Russland.* 3 vols. Moscow, 1813–1817. Reprint. Leipzig, 1965.

Romans, Bernard. *A Concise Natural History of East and West Florida.* Ed. Rembert W. Patrick. New York, 1775. Facsimile reprint. Gainesville, 1962.

Sarytschew, Gawrila André Jewitsch. *Achtjährige Reise im nordöstlichen Sibirien, auf dem Eismeere und dem nordöstlichen Ozean.* Trans. Johann Heinrich Busse. 2 vols. Leipzig, 1805–1806.

Sauer, Martin. *An Account of a Geographical and Astronomical Expedition to the Northern Parts of Russia, for ascertaining the degrees of latitude and longitude of the mouth of the river Kovima; of the whole coast of the Tshutski, to East Cape; and of the islands in the Eastern Ocean, stretching to the American coast; Performed, By Command of Her Imperial Majesty Catherine the Second, Empress of All the Russias, by Commodore Joseph Billings, In the Years 1785, &c to 1794; The whole narrated from the original papers by Martin Sauer, Secretary to the expedition.* London, 1802.

———. *Reise nach den Nordlichen Gegenden vom Russischen Asien und America.* Trans. and ed. M. C. Sprengel. Bibliothek der neuesten und wichtigsten Reisebeschreibungen, ed. M. C. Sprengel, vol. 8. Weimar, 1803.

———. *Voyage fait par ordre de l'impératrice de Russie Catherine II, dans le nord de la Russie asiatique.* Trans. and ed. J. Castéra. 2 vols. Paris, 1802.

Scheffer, Johann. *Lappland, Das ist: Neue und wahrhafftige Beschreibung von Lappland und dessen Einwohnern, worin viel bisshero unbekandte Sachen von der Lappen Ankunft, Aberglauben, Zauberkünsten, Nahrung, Kleidern, Geschäfften, wie auch von den Thieren und Metallen so es in ihrem Lande giebet, erzählet, und mit unterschiedlichen Figuren fürgestellet worden.* Frankfurt am Main and Leipzig, 1675.

Schlözer, August Ludwig, trans. *Handbuch der Geschichte des Kaisertums Russland vom Anfange des Stats, bis zum Tode Katharina der II Aus dem Russischen übersetzt.* Göttingen, 1802.

———. *Historische Untersuchung über Russlands Reichsgrundgesetze.* Gotha, 1777.

Schusky, Renate, ed. *Das deutsche Singspiel im 18. Jahrhundert: Quellen und*

Zeugnisse zu Ästhetik und Rezeption. Gesamthochschule Wuppertal, Schriften-reihe Literaturwissenschaft, 12. Bonn, 1980.

Scott, Sir Walter. "On the Supernatural in Fictitious Composition and Particu-larly on the Works of Ernest Theodore William Hoffmann." *Foreign Quar-terly Review* (July–November 1827): 60–98.

Shea, John Gilmary, ed. *Discovery and Exploration of the Mississippi Valley: With the Original Narratives of Marquette, Allouez, Membré, Hennepin, and Anastase Douay.* New York, 1852.

Shoberl, Frederic. *Russia, being a description of the Character, Manners, Customs, Dress, Diversions, and other Peculiarities of the Different Nations, inhabiting the Russian Empire.* 4 vols. The World in Miniature. London, 1822.

Sonnini de Manoncourt, Charles Nicolas Sigisbert. *Travels in Upper and Lower Egypt undertaken by Order of the Old Government of France.* Trans. Henry Hunter. 3 vols. London, 1799.

Sonntag, Carl Gottlob. *Das Russische Reich, oder Merkwürdigkeiten aus der Ge-schichte, Geographie und Naturkunde aller der Länder, die jetzt zur Russischen Monarchie gehören.* Riga, 1791.

Spingarn, J. E., ed. *Critical Essays of the Seventeenth Century.* 3 vols. Bloomington and London, 1957.

Staden, Hans. *Wahrhaftige Historia und Beschreibung einer Landschaft der wilden nacketen grimmigen Menschenfresserleuten in der neuen Welt Amerika gelegen.* Ed. Gertrud Tudsen. Die Umwelt des Auslandsdeutschen in Südamerika, ser. 1, vol. 4. Buenos Aires, 1934.

Stavorinus, John Splinter. *Voyages to the East Indies.* Trans. Samuel Hull Wilcocke. 3 vols. London, 1798. Reprint. 1969.

Steller, Georg Wilhelm. *Beschreibung von dem Lande Kamtschatka, dessen Ein-wohnern, deren Sitten, Nahmen, Lebensart und verschiedenen Gewohnheiten.* Ed. J. B. Scherer. Frankfurt and Leipzig, 1774.

———. *Beschreibung von dem Lande Kamtschatka.* Quellen und Forschungen zur Geschichte der Geographie und Reise, ed. Hanno Beck, vol. 10. Stuttgart, 1974.

Strahlenberg, Philipp Johann Tabbert von. *An Histori-Geographical Description of the North and Eastern Part of Europe and Asia; But more particularly of Russia, Siberia, and Great Tartary; Both in their Ancient and Modern State: Together with An entire New Polyglot-Table of the Dialects of 32 Tartarian Nations: And a Vocab-ulary of the Kalmuck-Mongolian Tongue; As Also, A Large and Accurate Map of those Countries; and Variety of Cuts, representing Asiatick-Scythian Antiquities.* London, 1736.

Stuck, Gottlieb Heinrich. *Verzeichnis von aeltern und neuern Land- und Reise-Beschreibungen, Ein Versuch eines Hauptstücks der geographischen Litteratur mit einem vollstaendigen Realregister und einer Vorrede von M. Johann Ernst Fabri, Inspector der Koeniglichen Freytische und Secretair der Hallischen Naturfor-schenden Gesellschaft.* 2 vols. Halle, 1784–1787.

Struys, Johann Jansen. *The Perillous and most Unhappy Voyages.* Trans. John Morrison. London, 1683.

Sulzer, Johann Georg. *Allgemeine Theorie der Schönen Künste.* 2 vols. Leipzig, 1773–1775.

Svinine, Paul. *Sketches of Russia.* London, 1814.

Swift, Jonathan. *Gulliver's Travels: A Facsimile Reproduction of a Large-Paper Copy of the First Edition, 1726, Containing the Author's Annotations.* Intro. Colin Mc-Kelvie. Delmar, N.Y., 1976.

Temple, William. *Essay upon the Ancient and Modern Learning* [1690]. In Spingarn, *Critical Essays,* 3:32–72.

Thwaites, Reuben Gold, ed. *The Jesuit Relations and Allied Documents: Travels and Explorations of the Jesuit Missionaries in New France, 1610–1791, The Original French, Latin, and Italian Texts, with English Translations and Notes.* 73 vols. Cleveland, 1896–1901.

Tissot, Simon André. "Discours XVI." In *Aristide ou le Citoyen.* Lausanne, October 11, 1766.

———. *The Life of J. G. Zimmermann.* London, 1797.

Tooke, William. *View of the Russian Empire during the Reign of Catharine the Second, and to the Close of the Present Century.* 3 vols. London, 1799.

The Travels of Several Learned Missioners of the Society of Jesus, into Divers Parts of the Archipelago, India, China, and America. London, 1714.

Trenchard, John. *The Natural History of Superstition.* London, 1709.

"Übersicht der Geographischen Verlags-Werke des F.S. priv. Industrie-Comptoirs zu Weimar." In *Allgemeine geographische Ephemeriden,* pp. 357–65. Weimar, 1800.

Versuch einer Litteratur deutscher Reisebeschreibungen, sowohl Originale als Uebersetzungen; wie auch einzelner Reisenachrichten aus den berühmtesten deutschen Journalen, Mit beigefügten kurzen Recensionen, Notizen von ihren Verfassern und Verlegers-Preisen, In alphabetischer Ordnung nach den Ländern chronologisch bearbeitet. Prague, 1793.

Vico, Giambattista. *The New Science.* 3d ed. [1744]. Trans. Thomas Goddard Bergin and Max Harold Fisch. Ithaca and London, 1984.

Voltaire, François Marie Arouet de. *Histoire de l'empire de Russie sous Pierre le Grand, par l'auteur de l'histoire de Charles XII.* Geneva, 1759–1763.

———. *Russia under Peter the Great.* Trans. M.F.O. Jenkins. Rutherford, 1983.

———. "La Russie sous Pierre le Grand" [selections]. In *Oeuvres Historiques,* ed. René Pomeau, pp. 369–76. Paris, 1957.

Wafer, Lionel. *A New Voyage and Description of the Isthmus of America* [1699]. 3d ed. enlarged. London, 1729.

Waitz, Theodor. *Anthropologie der Naturvölker.* 6 vols. Leipzig, 1859–1872.

Walther, Johann Gottfried. *Musikalisches Lexikon oder musikalische Bibliothek.* Leipzig, 1732. Facsimile reprint, ed. Richard Schaal. Documenta Musicologica, ser. 1, no. 3. Kassel and Basel, 1953.

Weber, Henry. *Popular Romances: Consisting of Imaginary Voyages and Travels.* Edinburgh, 1812.

Weickard, Melchior Adam. *Der Philosophische Arzt.* Rev. and enlarged ed. 3 vols. Frankfurt am Main, 1790–1799.

Witsen, Nicolas. *Noord en Oost Tartaryen: Behelzende eene Beschryving van verscheidene Tartersche en Nabuurige Gewesten, in de noorder en oostelykste deelen van Aziën en Europa; zedert naauwkeurig onderzoek van veele jaaren, en eigen ondervinding ontworpen, beschreven, geteekent, en in 't licht gegeven.* 2d ed. 2 vols. Amsterdam, 1785.

———. *N. Witsens Berichte über die uralischen Völker.* Trans. and abridged Tibor Mikola. Studia Uralo-Altaica. Szeged, 1975.

Zapf, Georg Wilhelm. *Zauberbibliothek.* Augsburg, 1776.

Zedler, Johann Heinrich. *Grosses vollständiges Universal-Lexicon aller Wissenschafften und Künste, welche bisshero durch menschlichen Verstand und Witz erfunden und verbessert worden.* 64 vols. Halle, 1732–1750.

Zimmermann, E.A.W. von. *Taschenbuch der Reisen oder unterhaltende Darstellung der Entdeckungen des 18ten Jahrhunderts, in Rücksicht der Länder, Menschen und Productenkunde, Für jede Klasse von Lesern.* 18 vols. Leipzig, 1801–1807.

Zimmermann, Johann Georg. *Aphorisms and Reflections on Men, Morals, and Things.* London, 1800.

———. *Fragmente über Friedrich den Grossen.* Leipzig, 1790.

———. *Solitude.* Trans. Simon André Tissot. London, 1804.

———. *Über Friedrich den Grossen und meine Unterredung mit ihm kurz vor seinem Tode.* Leipzig, 1788.

———. *Von der Erfahrung in der Arzneykunst.* 2 vols. Zurich, 1763–1764.

Secondary Works

Abrams, Meyer H. *Natural Supernaturalism: Tradition and Revolution in Romantic Literature.* New York, 1971.

Achterberg, Jean. *Imagery in Healing: Shamanism and Modern Medicine.* Boston and London, 1985.

Adams, Percy G. *Travelers and Travel Liars, 1660–1800.* Berkeley and Los Angeles, 1962.

———. *Travel Literature and the Evolution of the Novel.* Lexington, Ky., 1983.

Adelung, Friedrich von. *Kritisch-Literärische Übersicht der Reisenden in Russland bis 1700, deren Berichte bekannt sind.* 2 vols. St. Petersburg, 1846. Reprint. Amsterdam, 1960.

Allanbrook, Wye. *Rhythmic Gesture in Mozart: "Le Nozze di Figaro" and "Don Giovanni."* Chicago and London, 1983.

Altner, Günter. "Goethe as a Forerunner of Alternative Science." In Amrine, *Goethe and the Sciences,* pp. 341–50.

Amrine, Frederick, Francis J. Zucker, and Harvey Wheeler, eds. *Goethe and the Sciences: A Reappraisal.* Boston Studies in the Philosophy of Science, 97. Dordrecht, Boston, Lancaster, and Tokyo, 1987.

Anderson, Edward F. *Peyote: The Divine Cactus.* Tucson, 1980.

Angelino, Henry, and Charles L. Shedd. "A Note on Berdache." *American Anthropologist* 57 (1955): 121–26.

Atkins, Stuart. *Goethe's "Faust": A Literary Analysis.* Cambridge, Mass., 1958.

Atkinson, Geoffroy. *The Extraordinary Voyage in French Literature before 1700.* Columbia University Studies in Romance Philology and Literature. New York, 1920.

———. *The Extraordinary Voyage in French Literature from 1700 to 1720.* Paris, 1922.

Bachofen, Johann Jakob. *Das Mutterrecht, eine Untersuchung über die Gynaikokratie der alten Welt nach ihrer Religion und rechtlichen Natur*. Stuttgart, 1861.

Bächthold-Stäubli, Hanns, and E. Hoffmann-Krayer, eds. *Handwörterbuch des deutschen Aberglaubens*. 10 vols. Berlin and Leipzig, 1927–1942. Reprint. Berlin and New York, 1987.

Baron, Frank. *Doctor Faustus, From History to Legend*. Munich, 1978.

Barnstone, Willis. *The Poetics of Ecstasy: Varieties of Ekstasis from Sappho to Borges*. New York and London, 1983.

Barry, David. "Turning the Screw on Goethe's Helena." *German Life and Letters*, n.s. 39 (July 1986): 268–78.

Barthes, Roland. "The Death of the Author." Trans. Richard Howard. In *The Discontinuous Universe, Selected Writings in Contemporary Consciousness*, ed. Sallie Sears and Georgianna W. Lord, pp. 7–12. New York, 1972.

Bastian, Adolf. *Der Mensch in der Geschichte: Zur Begründung einer psychologischen Weltanschauung*. 2 vols. Leipzig, 1860.

Bates, Alfred. *The Drama: Its History, Literature, and Influence on Civilization*. London, 1903.

Benamou, Michel, and Charles Caramello, eds. *Performance in Postmodern Culture*. Madison, 1977.

Benjamin, Walter. *The Origin of German Tragic Drama*. London, 1977.

Bennett, Benjamin. *Goethe's Theory of Poetry: "Faust" and the Regeneration of Language*. Ithaca and London, 1986.

Benot, Yves. *Diderot: De l'athéisme à l'anticolonialisme*. Paris, 1970.

Bernhagen, W. "Johann Leonhard Frisch und seine Beziehungen zu Russland." In *Die deutsch-russische Begegnung und Leonhard Euler*, pp. 112–24. Quellen und Studien zur Geschichte Osteuropas, 1. Berlin, 1958.

Bernstein, Richard J. *Beyond Objectivism and Relativism: Science, Hermeneutics, and Praxis*. Philadelphia, 1983.

Binns, J. W. "Women or Transvestites on the Elizabethan Stage? An Oxford Controversy." *Sixteenth-Century Journal* 5 (1974): 95–120.

Birdsell, Joseph B. "The Problem of the Early Peopling of the Americas as Viewed from Asia." In *Papers on the Physical Anthropology of the American Indian*, ed. William S. Laughlin, pp. 1–69. New York, 1951.

Bitterli, Urs. *Die "Wilden" und die "Zivilisierten": Grundzüge einer Geistes- und Kulturgeschichte der europäisch-überseeischen Begegnung*. Munich, 1976.

Black, J. L. "G. F. Müller and the Russian Academy of Sciences Contingent in the Second Kamchatka Expedition, 1733–1743." *Canadian Slavonic Papers* 25 (June 1983): 235–52.

Bleibtreu-Ehrenberg, Gisela. "Homosexualität und Transvestition im Schamanismus." *Anthropos* 65 (1970): 189–228.

———. *Mannbarkeitsriten: Zur institutionellen Päderastie bei Papuas und Melanesiern*. Frankfurt am Main, Berlin, and Vienna, 1980.

———. "Der Schamane als Meister der Imagination oder Die hohe Kunst des Fliegenkönnens." In Duerr, *Alcheringa*, 49–71.

———. "Sexuelle Abartigkeit im Urteil der abendländischen Religions-, Geistes-, und Rechtsgeschichte im Zusammenhang mit der Gesellschaftsentwicklung." Ph.D. diss. Bonn, 1970.

————. *Tabu Homosexualität: Die Geschichte eines Vorurteils.* Frankfurt am Main, 1978.

————. *Der Weibmann: Kult, Geschlechtswechsel im Schamanismus—Transvestition bei Naturvölker.* Frankfurt am Main, 1984.

Blodgett, Jean. *The Coming and Going of the Shaman: Eskimo Shamanism and Art.* Winnipeg, 1978.

Boas, Franz. *The Mind of Primitive Man.* New York, 1931.

Bode, Wilhelm. *Goethes Schweizer Reisen.* Leipzig, 1922.

Böhme, Erdmann Werner. *Mozart in der schönen Literatur (Drama, Roman, Novelle, Lyrik), eine motivgeschichtliche Abhandlung mit über 500 Werke umfassenden Bibliographie.* Greifswald, 1932.

————. "Mozart in der schönen Literatur, II. Teil: Ergänzungen und Fortsetzung." In *Mozart-Jahrbuch 1959,* pp. 165–87. Salzburg, 1960.

Böhme, Gernot. "Is Goethe's Theory of Color Science?" In Amrine, *Goethe and the Sciences,* pp. 147–73.

Bojescul, Wilhelm. *Zum Kunstbegriff des Joseph Beuys.* Kultur- Literatur- Kunst, ed. Jürgen Klein, 1. Essen, 1985.

Bonin, Werner F. *Lexikon der Parapsychologie.* Bern, Munich, Darmstadt, 1976.

Bouteiller, M. *Chamanisme et guérison magique.* Paris, 1950.

Bremner, Geoffrey. *Order and Change: The Pattern of Diderot's Thought.* Cambridge, New York, and Melbourne, 1983.

Briggs, Katharine Mary. *Pale Hecate's Team: An Examination of the Beliefs on Witchcraft and Magic among Shakespeare's Contemporaries and His Immediate Successors.* London, 1962.

Brown, Jane K. *Goethe's "Faust," The German Tragedy.* Ithaca and London, 1986.

Brown, Norman Oliver. *Hermes the Thief: The Evolution of a Myth.* Madison, 1947.

Brunet, Jacques Charles. *Manuel du libraire et de l'amateur de livres.* 5th ed., rev. and enlarged. 9 vols. Paris, 1860–1890.

Buchholz, Arnold. *Die Göttinger Russlandsammlungen Georgs von Asch, Ein Museum der russischen Wirtschaftsgeschichte des 18. Jahrhunderts.* Giessen, 1961.

Bullough, Vern L. *Sex, Society, and History.* New York, 1976.

Burkert, Walter. *Lore and Science in Ancient Pythagoreanism.* Trans. Edwin L. Minar, Jr. Cambridge, Mass., 1972.

Burnham, Jack. "The Artist as Shaman." *Arts Magazine* 47 (May–June 1973): 42–45.

————. "Contemporary Ritual: A Search for Meaning in Post-Historical Terms." *Arts Magazine* 47 (March 1973): 38–41.

————. "Denis Oppenheimer: The Artist as Shaman." *Arts Magazine* 47 (May–June 1973): 42–45.

————. *Great Western Salt Works: Essays on the Meaning of Post-Formalist Art.* New York, 1974.

————. "Objects and Ritual: Towards a Working Ontology of Art." *Arts Magazine* 47 (December–January 1973): 28–32.

Burns, E. *Theatricality: A Study of Convention in the Theatre and in Social Life.* London, 1972.

Buschan, Georg. *Über Medizinzauber und Heilkunst im Leben der Völker*. Berlin, 1941.

Butler, E. M. *The Myth of the Magus*. Cambridge, 1948.

Campbell, Joseph. *The Masks of God: Occidental Mythology*. New York, 1964. Reprint. New York, 1976.

——. *The Masks of God: Oriental Mythology*. New York, 1962. Reprint. New York, 1976.

——. *The Masks of God: Primitive Mythology*. New York, 1959. Reprint. New York, 1976.

Cartwright, Michael. "Diderot and the Idea of Performance." In *Studies in Eighteenth-Century French Literature Presented to Robert Niklaus*, ed. J. M. Fox, M. H. Waddicor, and D. A. Watts, pp. 31–42. Exeter, 1975.

Castaneda, Carlos. *Journey to Ixtlan: The Lessons of Don Juan*. New York, 1972.

——. *A Separate Reality: Further Conversations with Don Juan*. New York, 1971.

——. *Tales of Power*. New York, 1974.

——. *The Teachings of Don Juan: A Yaqui Way of Knowledge*. New York, 1968.

Cawley, Robert Ralston. *Unpathed Waters: Studies in the Influence of the Voyagers on Elizabethan Literature*. Princeton, 1940.

——. *The Voyagers and Elizabethan Drama*. Boston, 1938.

Chadwick, Nora Kershaw. *Poetry and Prophecy*. Cambridge, 1942.

——. "Shamanism among the Tatars of Central Asia." *The Journal of the Royal Anthropological Institute of Great Britain and Ireland* 66 (January–June 1936): 75–112.

Chadwick, Nora Kershaw, and Victor Zhirmunsky. *Oral Epics of Central Asia*. Cambridge, 1969.

Charles, Lucile Hoerr. "The Clown's Function." *Journal of American Folklore* 58 (January–March 1945): 25–34.

——. "Drama in First-Naming Ceremonies." *Journal of American Folklore* 64 (January–March 1951): 11–35.

——. "Drama in Shaman Exorcism." *Journal of American Folklore* 66 (January–March 1953): 95–122.

——. "Growing up through Drama." *Journal of American Folklore* 59 (July–September 1946): 247–62.

——. "Regeneration through Drama at Death." *Journal of American Folklore* 61 (April–June 1948): 151–74.

Chekov, Michael. *To the Actor: On the Technique of Acting*. New York, 1953.

Ciarlo, J. A. "Ascensionism in Fantasy and Action: A Study of the Motivation to Fly." Ph. D. diss., Cambridge, Mass., 1964.

Clifford, James. *The Predicament of Culture: Twentieth-Century Ethnography, Literature, and Art*. Cambridge, Mass., 1988.

Closs, Alois. "Die Ekstase des Schamanen." *Ethnos* 34 (1969): 70–89.

Cole, Garold L. *Travels in America from the Voyages of Discovery to the Present: An Annotated Bibliography of Travel Articles in Periodicals, 1955–1980*. Norman, 1984.

Conant, Martha Pike. *The Oriental Tale in England in the Eighteenth Century*. Columbia University Studies in English and Comparative Literature. New York, 1908. Reprint. 1966.

Cottrell, Alan P. *Goethe's "Faust": Seven Essays.* University of North Carolina Studies in the Germanic Languages and Literatures, 86. Chapel Hill, 1976.

Cowart, Georgia. *The Origins of Modern Musical Criticism: French and Italian Music, 1600–1750.* Studies in Musicology, 38. Ann Arbor, 1981.

Crawley, Ernest. *Dress, Drinks, and Drums: Further Studies of Savages and Sex.* Ed. Theodore Bestermann. London, 1931.

Crocker, Lester G. *Diderot's Chaotic Order: Approach to Synthesis.* Princeton, 1974.

Cronin, Vincent. *Catherine, Empress of All the Russias.* New York, 1978.

Crossley, Robert. "Ethereal Ascents: Eighteenth-Century Fantasies of Human Flight." *Eighteenth-Century Life* 7 (January 1982): 54–64.

Cunningham, D. J. "Anthropology in the Eighteenth Century." *The Journal of the Royal Anthropological Institute* 38 (January–June 1908): 10–35.

Cutner, Herbert. *A Short History of Sex-Worship.* London, 1940.

Czaplicka, Marie Antoinette. *Aboriginal Siberia: A Study in Social Anthropology.* Oxford, 1914.

Dankert, Werner. *Goethe: Der Mythische Urgrund seiner Weltschau.* Berlin, 1951.

Darnell, Regna. *Readings in the History of Anthropology.* New York, Evanston, San Francisco, and London, 1974.

Darnton, Robert. "The High Enlightenment and the Low-Life of Literature in Pre-Revolutionary Times." *Past and Present* 51 (May 1971): 81–115.

Dean, William. *History Making History: The New Historicism in American Religious Thought.* State University of New York Series in Philosophy. Albany, 1988.

Defert, Daniel. "The Collection of the World: Accounts of Voyages from the Sixteenth to the Eighteenth Centuries." Trans. Marie J. Diamond. *Dialectical Anthropology* 7 (1982): 11–20.

De Fontenay, Elisabeth. *Diderot: Reason and Resonance.* Trans. Jeffrey Mehlman. New York, 1982.

DeMille, Richard. *Castaneda's Journey: The Power and the Allegory.* Santa Barbara, 1980.

———. *The Don Juan Papers: Further Castaneda Controversies.* Santa Barbara, 1980.

Derrida, Jacques. *Dissemination.* Trans. Barbara Johnson. Chicago, 1981.

———. *Of Grammatology.* Trans. Gayatri Chakravorty Spivak. Baltimore and London, 1976.

Devereux, George. *Basic Problems of Ethnopsychiatry.* Trans. Basia Miller Gulati and George Devereux. Chicago and London, 1980.

Devlin, Judith. *The Superstitious Mind: French Peasants and the Supernatural in the Nineteenth Century.* New Haven and London, 1987.

De Woskin, Kenneth J., trans. *Doctors, Diviners, and Magicians of Ancient China.* New York, 1983.

Dieckmann, Liselotte. *Goethe's "Faust": A Critical Reading.* Englewood Cliffs, 1972.

Diószegi, Vilmos. *Tracing Shamans in Siberia: The Story of an Ethnographical Research Expedition.* Trans. Anità Rojkay Babó. Oosterhut, The Netherlands, 1968.

Dobkin de Rios, Marlene. *Visionary Vine: Psychedelic Healing in the Peruvian Amazon.* San Francisco, 1972.

Dodds, Eric Robertson. *The Greeks and the Irrational.* Sather Classical Lectures, 25. Berkeley and Los Angeles, 1951.

Donnelly, Alton S. *The Russian Conquest of Bashkiria, 1552–1740: A Case Study in Imperialism.* New Haven, 1968.

Donnert, Erich. *Russia in the Age of Enlightenment.* Leipzig, 1986.

Doore, Gary, ed. *Shaman's Path: Healing, Personal Growth, and Empowerment.* Boston and London, 1988.

Dreyfus, Hubert L., and Paul Rabinow. *Michel Foucault: Beyond Structuralism and Hermeneutics.* 2d ed. Chicago, 1983,

Drury, Nevill. *Don Juan, Mescalito, and Modern Magic: The Mythology of Inner Space.* London, Boston, Melbourne, and Henley, 1978.

Duchet, Michèle. *Anthropologie et histoire au siècles des lumierès: Buffon, Voltaire, Rousseau, Helvétius, Diderot.* Paris, 1971.

Duerr, Hans Peter, ed. *Alcheringa oder die beginnende Zeit: Studien zu Mythologie, Schamanismus und Religion, Mircea Eliade zum 75. Geburtstag.* Frankfurt am Main and Paris, 1983.

Eastham, Scott. *Paradise and Ezra Pound: The Poet as Shaman.* Lanham, Md., 1983.

Edsman, Carl Martin. "A Swedish Female Folk Healer from the Beginning of the Eighteenth Century." In Edsman, *Studies in Shamanism,* pp. 120–65.

——, ed. *Studies in Shamanism Based on Papers Read at the Symposium on Shamanism Held at Åbo on the 6th to 8th of September, 1962.* Stockholm, 1962.

Ehrenreich, Barbara, and Deirdre English. *Witches, Midwives, and Nurses: A History of Women Healers.* Glass Mountain Pamphlet no. 1. 2d ed. New York, 1973.

Ehrenwald, Jan. *Anatomy of Genius: Split Brains and Global Minds.* New York, 1984.

Eisen, Cliff. "Contributions to a New Mozart Documentary Biography." *Journal of the American Musicological Society* 39 (Fall 1986): 617–18.

Eisler, Robert. *Man into Wolf: An Anthropological Interpretation of Sadism, Masochism, and Lycanthropy.* London, 1948. Reprint. Santa Barbara, 1978.

Eliade, Mircea. *The Forge and the Crucible.* Trans. Stephen Corrin. New York, 1971.

——. *Geschichte der religiösen Ideen.* Trans. Elizabeth Darlap, Adelheid Müller-Lissner, Werner Müller, and Günther Lanczkowska. 3 vols. Freiburg, Basel, and Vienna, 1978–1981.

——. *The Myth of the Eternal Return; or, Cosmos and History.* Trans. Willard R. Trask. Princeton, 1974.

——. *Myths, Dreams, and Mysteries: The Encounter between Contemporary Faiths and Archaic Realities.* Trans. Philip Mairet. The Library of Religion and Culture, ed. Benjamin Nelson. London and New York, 1960. Reprint. New York, 1975.

——. *Occultism, Witchcraft, and Cultural Fashions: Essays in Comparative Religions.* Chicago and London, 1976.

————. "Recent Works on Shamanism: A Review Article." *History of Religions* 1 (1961): 152–86.

————. *Shamanism: Archaic Techniques of Ecstasy.* Trans. Willard R. Trask. Rev. and enlarged ed. Princeton, 1974.

Embacher, Friedrich. *Lexikon der Reisen und Entdeckungen.* Amsterdam, 1961.

Engel, Hans. "Mozart in der philosophischen und ästhetischen Literatur." In *Mozart-Jahrbuch 1953*, pp. 67–69. Salzburg, 1954.

Engemann, Walter. "Das ethnographische Weltbild Voltaires: Ein Beitrag zur Geschichte der Völkerkunde und der Entdeckungen." *Zeitschrift für Ethnologie* 61 (1929): 263–77.

Fairchild, Hoxie Neale. *The Noble Savage: A Study in Romantic Naturalism.* New York, 1928. Reprint. 1961.

Faivre, J. P. "Savants et navigateurs: Un aspect de la cooperation international entre 1750 et 1840." *Cahiers d'histoire mondiale* 1 (1966): 98–124.

Fellows, Otis. "The Theme of Genius in Diderot's *Neveu de Rameau.*" *Diderot Studies* 2 (1952): 168–99.

Fenton, William N. "J.-F. Lafitau (1681–1746), Precursor of Scientific Anthropology." *[Southwestern Journal of Anthropology] Journal of Anthropological Research* 25 (1969): 173–87.

Fetzer, John F. *Romantic Orpheus: Profiles of Clemens Brentano.* Berkeley, Los Angeles, and London, 1974.

Findeisen, Hans. *Okkulte Begebnise im schamanistischen Raum.* Augsburg, 1956.

————. *Die 'Schamanenkrankheit' als Initiation, Eine völker- und sozialpsychologische Untersuchung.* Abhandlungen und Aufsätze aus dem Institut für Menschen- und Menschheitskunde, 45. Augsburg, 1957.

————. *Schamanentum.* Stuttgart, 1957.

Finney, Gretchen Ludke. "Music and Ecstasy: A Religious Controversy." In *Musical Backgrounds for English Literature: 1580–1650*, pp. 47–75. New Brunswick, 1962.

Flaherty, Gloria. "Catherine the Great and Men." *Lessing Yearbook* 18 (1986): 141–50.

————. "Empathy and Distance: Romantic Theories of Acting Reconsidered." *Theatre Research International* 15 (1990): 127–43.

————. *Opera in the Development of German Critical Thought.* Princeton, 1978.

————. "Sex and Shamanism in the Eighteenth Century." In Rousseau and Porter, *Sexual Underworlds*, pp. 261–80.

Foucault, Michel. *The Archaeology of Knowledge and the Discourse on Language.* Trans. A. M. Sheridan Smith. New York, 1972.

————. *The Birth of the Clinic: An Archaeology of Medical Perception.* Trans. A. M. Sheridan Smith. New York and London, 1973. Reprint. New York, 1975.

————. *The History of Sexuality.* Trans. Robert Hurley. 2 vols. New York, 1978–1985.

————. *Madness and Civilization: A History of Insanity in the Age of Reason.* Trans. Richard Howard. New York, 1965.

Frank, Jerome D. *Persuasion and Healing: A Comparative Study of Psychotherapy.* Rev. ed. New York, 1974.

Fried, Michael. "Art and Objecthood." *Artforum* (Summer 1967): 12–23.

Furst, Peter, ed. *Flesh of the Gods: The Ritual Use of Hallucinogens*. New York, 1972.

Fussell, G. E., and Constance Goodman. "Travel and Topography in Eighteenth-Century England: A Bibliography of Sources for Economic History." *The Library, A Quarterly Review of Bibliography*, ser. 4, no. 10 (1929–1930): 84–120.

Gage, Matilde Joslyn. *Woman, Church, and State: A Historical Account of the Status of Woman through the Christian Ages, with Reminiscences of the Matriarchate*. Chicago, 1893.

Garrard, John Gordon, ed. *The Eighteenth Century in Russia*. Oxford, 1973.

Gaster, Theodore. *Thespis, Ritual, Myth, and Drama in the Ancient Near East*. New York, 1950. Reprint. 1975.

Gearey, John. *Goethe's "Faust": The Making of Part I*. New Haven and London, 1981.

Geertz, Clifford. "From the Natives' Point of View: On the Nature of Anthropological Understanding." In *Meaning in Anthropology*, ed. K. Basso and H. Selby, pp. 221–37. Albuquerque, 1976.

Gennep, Arnold van. "De l'emploi du mot 'chamanisme.'" *Revue historique des religions* 47 (1903): 51–57.

———. *The Rites of Passage*. Trans. Monika B. Vizedom and Gabrielle L. Caffee, intro. Solon T. Kimbal. London, 1960.

Gernet, Louis. *The Anthropology of Ancient Greece*. Trans. John Hamilton, S.J., and Blaise Nagy. Baltimore and London, 1968.

Gerold, Karl Gustav. *Herder und Diderot: Ihr Einblick in die Kunst*. Frankfurter Quellen und Forschungen zur germanischen und romanischen Philologie, 28. Frankfurt am Main, 1941. Reprint. Hildesheim, 1974.

Gimbutas, Marija. *The Goddesses and Gods of Old Europe, 6500–3500 B.C.: Myths and Cult Images*. Rev. ed. Berkeley and Los Angeles, 1982.

Ginzburg, Carlo. *The Night Battles: Witchcraft and Agrarian Cults in the Sixteenth and Seventeenth Centuries*. Trans. John Tedeschi and Anne Tedeschi. Baltimore, 1983.

Goldberg, B. J. *The Sacred Fire: The Story of Sex in Religion*. New York, 1958.

Gooch, G. P. *Catherine the Great and Other Studies*. 1954. Reprint. Hamden, 1966.

Gove, Philip Babcock. *The Imaginary Voyage in Prose Fiction: A History of Its Criticism and a Guide for Its Study, with an Annotated Checklist of 215 Imaginary Voyages from 1700 to 1800*. New York, 1941.

Graesse, Johann Georg Theodor. *Trésor de livres rares et précieux*. 7 vols. Dresden, 1859–1869.

Graichen, Gisela. *Das Kultplatzbuch: Ein Führer zu den alten Opferplätzen, Heiligtümern und Kultstätten in Deutschland*. Hamburg, 1988.

Grassl, Hans. *Aufbruch zur Romantik: Bayerns Beitrag zur deutschen Geistesgeschichte, 1765–1785*. Munich, 1968.

Gruber, Elmar. *Tranceformation: Shamanismus und die Auflösung der Ordnung*. Basel, 1982.

Grumach, Ernst. *Goethe und die Antike: Eine Sammlung*. 2 vols. Berlin, 1949.

Grünthal, Ernst. "Ueber die historischen Wurzeln von Goethes naturwissenschaftlicher Denkweise." *Berner Beiträge zur Geschichte der Medizin und der Naturwissenschaften.* Ed. E. Hintzsche and W. Rytz, 10 (1949): 8–10.

Guerra, Francisco. *The Pre-Columbian Mind: A Study into the Aberrant Nature of Sexual Drives, Drugs Affecting Behaviour, and the Attitude towards Life and Death, with a Survey of Psychotherapy, in Pre-Columbian America.* London and New York, 1971.

Gunther, Erna. *Indian Life on the Northwest Coast of North America as Seen by the Early Explorers and Fur Traders during the Last Decades of the Eighteenth Century.* Chicago and London, 1972.

Hammond, William A. "The Disease of the Scythians (morbus feminarum) and Certain Analogous Conditions." *The American Journal of Neurology and Psychiatry* 1 (1882): 339–55.

Harner, Michael J. *The Way of the Shaman: A Guide to Power and Healing.* New York, 1980.

———, ed. *Hallucinogens and Shamanism.* London, Oxford, and New York, 1973. Reprint. 1981.

Hassan, Ihab. *The Dismemberment of Orpheus: Toward a Postmodern Literature.* 2d ed., enlarged. Madison and London, 1982.

———. *Paracriticisms: Seven Speculations of the Times.* Urbana, 1975.

Hatto, A. T. *Shamanism and Epic Poetry in Northern Asia.* London, 1970.

Hegel, Georg Wilhlem Friedrich. *Phenomenology of Spirit.* Trans. Arnold Vincent Miller. Oxford, 1977.

Heissig, Walther. "A Mongolian Source to the Lamist Suppression of Shamanism in the Seventeenth Century." *Anthropos* 48 (1953): 1–29, 493–536.

Herdt, Gilbert H. *Guardians of the Flutes: Idioms of Masculinity.* New York, 1981.

Hermanns, Matthias. "Medizinmann, Zauberer, Schamane, Künstler in der Welt der frühen Jäger." *Anthropos* 61 (1966): 883–89.

———. *Schamanen—Pseudoschamanen, Erlöser und Heilbringer: Eine vergleichende Studie religiöser Urphänomene.* 3 vols. Wiesbaden, 1970.

Herzog, Rolf. "Die Völker des Lenagebietes in den Berichten der ersten Hälfte des 18. Jahrhunderts." Ph.D. diss. Göttingen, 1949.

Historische Kommission bei der Bayerischen Akademie der Wissenschaften. *Allgemeine Deutsche Biographie.* 56 vols. Leipzig, 1875–1912. Reprint. Berlin, 1971.

Hodgen, Margaret T. *Early Anthropology in the Sixteenth and Seventeenth Centuries.* Philadelphia, 1971.

Hoerburger, Felix. "Schwert und Trommel als Tanzgeräte." *Deutsches Jahrbuch für Volkskunde* 1 (1955): 240–45.

———. *Der Tanz mit der Trommel.* Quellen und Forschungen zur musikalischen Folklore, 2. Regensburg, 1954.

Hoesterey, Ingeborg. "Amerika liebt mich: Die erste Aktion von Joseph Beuys in den USA." *Der Tagesspiegel,* Berlin, June 8, 1974.

Hoppàl, Mihály, ed. *Shamanism in Eurasia.* Forum, 5. Aachen, 1984.

Horkheimer, Max, and Theodor W. Adorno. *Dialectic of Enlightenment.* Trans. John Cumming. New York, 1988.

Hovorka, Oskar von, and Adolf Kronfeld. *Vergleichende Volksmedizin*. 2 vols. Stuttgart, 1908–1909.

Hubbard, David G. *The Skyjacker: His Flights of Fantasy*. New York, 1971.

Hultkrantz, Äke. "A Definition of Shamanism." *Temenos: Studies in Comparative Religion* 9 (1973): 25–37.

———. *The North American Indian Orpheus Tradition: A Contribution to Comparative Religion*. The Ethnographical Museum of Sweden, monograph ser., 2. Stockholm, 1957.

———. *The Religions of the American Indians*. Trans. Monica Setterwall. Berkeley, Los Angeles, and London, 1979.

Hutchinson, George B. *The Ecstatic Whitman: Literary Shamanism and the Crisis of the Union*. Columbus, 1986.

Jacob, Margaret C. "Newtonianism and the Origins of the Enlightenment: A Reassessment." *Eighteenth Century Studies* 11 (Fall 1977): 1–25.

Jacobs, Sue-Ellen. "Berdache: A Brief Review of the Literature." *Colorado Anthropologist* 1 (1968): 25–40.

Jantz, Harold. *The Form of "Faust": The Work of Art and Its Intrinsic Structures*. Baltimore and London, 1978.

———. *Goethe's Faust as a Renaissance Man: Parallels and Prototypes*. Princeton, 1954. Reprint. New York, 1974.

———. *The Mothers in "Faust": The Myth of Time and Creativity*. Baltimore, 1969.

Jenkins, Linda Walsh. "Sex Roles and Shamans." In *Women in American Theater, Careers, Images, Movements: An Illustrated Anthology and Sourcebook*, ed. Helen Krich Chinoy and L. W. Jenkins, pp. 12–18. New York, 1981.

Jessen, Hans, ed. *Katharina II. von Russland*. Düsseldorf, 1970.

Josephs, Herbert. *Diderot's Dialogue of Language and Gesture: Le Neveu de Rameau*. Columbus, 1969.

Kabell, Aage. "Skalden und Schamanen." *FF [Folklore Fellows] Communications*, 96 (1980): 1–44.

Kakar, Sudhir. *Shamans, Mystics, and Doctors: A Psychological Inquiry into India and Its Healing Traditions*. Boston, 1982.

Kapelrud, Arvid S. "Shamanistic Features in the Old Testament." In Edsman, *Studies in Shamanism*, pp. 90–96.

Kapferer, Bruce. *A Celebration of Demons*. Bloomington, 1983.

———. "Mind, Self, and Demon in Demonic Illness: The Negation and Reconstruction of Self." *American Ethnologist* 6 (February 1979): 110–33.

Karlinsky, Simon. *Russian Drama from Its Beginnings to the Age of Pushkin*. Berkeley, Los Angeles, and London, 1985.

Keller, Evelyn Fox. *Reflections on Gender and Science*. New Haven and London, 1985.

Keudell, Elise von. *Goethe als Benutzer der Weimarer Bibliothek*. Ed. Werner Deetjen. Weimar, 1931.

Kihm, Walter. "Zur Symbolik im Schamanismus." Ph.D. diss., Freiburg, 1974.

King, A. Hyatt. *Mozart in Retrospect: Studies in Criticism and Bibliography*. London, New York, and Toronto, 1955.

King, Francis. *Sexuality, Magic, and Perversion*. London, 1971.

King, Lester S. *The Philosophy of Medicine: The Early Eighteenth Century.* Cambridge, Mass., and London, 1978.

Kirby, Ernest Theodore. "Dionysus: A Study of the Bacchae and the Origins of Drama." Ph.D. diss., Pittsburgh, 1972.

————. "The Origin of the Mummers' Play." *Journal of American Folklore* 84 (July–September 1971): 275–88.

————. "The Shamanistic Origins of Popular Entertainments." *The Drama Review* 18 (March 1974): 5–15.

————. *Ur-Drama: The Origins of Theatre.* New York, 1975.

Kirchner, H. "Ein archäologischer Beitrag zur Urgeschichte des Schamanismus." *Anthropos* 47 (1952): 244–86.

Kirchner, Walther, ed. *Eine Reise durch Sibirien im achtzehnten Jahrhundert: Die Fahrt des Schweizer Doktors Jakob Fries.* Veröffentlichungen des Osteuropa-Instituts München, ed. Hans Koch, 10. Munich, 1955.

Kittredge, G. L. *Witchcraft in Old and New England.* New York, 1919. Reprint. 1956.

Kjerbühl-Petersen, Lorenz. *Die Schauspielkunst: Untersuchungen über ihr Wirken und Wesen.* Stuttgart, Berlin, Leipzig, 1925.

Kluckhohn, Clyde. *Anthropology and the Classics.* Providence, 1961.

Knapp, Bettina. *Theatre and Alchemy.* Detroit, 1980.

Kniep, Claudia. "'Blut ist ein ganz besondrer Saft': Warum heisst Goethes Faust Heinrich?" *Wirkendes Wort: Deutsche Sprache in Forschung und Lehre* 35 (March–April 1985): 85–88.

Knoll-Greiling, Ursula. "Berufung und Berufungserlebnis bei den Schamanen." *Tribus* 2–3 (1953): 227–38.

Kocher, Paul H. *Christopher Marlowe: A Study of His Thought, Learning, and Character.* Chapel Hill, 1946. Reprint. New York, 1962.

König, Herbert. "Schamane und Medizinmann." *CIBA Zeitschrift* 4 (1936): 1294–1301.

Köpping, Klaus-Peter. "Schamanismus und Massenekstase: Besessenheitskulte im modernen Japan und im antiken Griechenland." In Duerr, *Alcheringa*, pp. 74–107.

Kouidis, Apostolos P. "*The Praise of Folly*: Diderot's Model for *Le Neveu de Rameau*." In *Studies on Voltaire and the Eighteenth Century*, ed. Hayden Mason, pp. 244–46. Oxford, 1980.

Krauss, Werner. *Zur Anthropologie des achtzehnten Jahrhunderts: Die Frühgeschichte der Menschheit im Blickpunkt der Aufklärung.* Munich, 1979.

Krieg, Margaret B. *Green Medicine: The Search for Plants that Heal.* New York, 1966.

Kris, Ernst. "Approaches to Art." In *Psychoanalysis Today*, ed. Sandor Lorand, pp. 360–62. New York, 1944.

Kris, Ernst, and Otto Kurz. *Die Legende vom Künstler: Ein geschichtlicher Versuch.* Vienna, 1934.

Krohn, Alan. *Hysteria: The Elusive Neurosis.* Psychological Issues, 12, nos. 1–2. New York, 1978.

Krupnick, Mark, ed. *Displacement: Derrida and After.* Bloomington, 1983.

Kümmel, Werner Friedrich. *Musik und Medizin: Ihre Wechselbeziehungen in Theorie und Praxis von 800 bis 1800.* Freiburg and Munich, 1977.

Kuhn, Thomas. *The Structure of Scientific Revolutions.* 2d ed., enlarged. Chicago, 1970.

La Barre, Weston. *The Ghost Dance.* Garden City, 1970.

Ladurie, Emmanuel Le Roy. *Jasmin's Witch.* Trans. Brian Pearce. New York, 1987.

Landon, H. C. Robbins. *1791: Mozart's Last Year.* New York, 1988.

Lane, Yoti. *The Psychology of the Actor.* New York, 1960.

Larsen, Stephen. *The Shaman's Doorway: Opening the Mythic Imagination to Contemporary Consciousness.* New York, 1976.

Laski, Marghanita. *Ecstasy: A Study of Some Secular and Religious Experiences.* Bloomington, 1961.

Latourette, Kenneth Scott. *A History of the Expansion of Christianity.* 7 vols. New York, 1937–1945.

Laufer, Berthold. "Origin of the Word Shaman." *American Anthropologist,* n.s. 19 (July–September 1917): 361–71.

Lea, Henry Charles. *Materials Toward a History of Witchcraft.* Ed. Arthur C. Howland and George Lincoln Burr. 3 vols. Philadelphia, 1939. Reprint. New York and London, 1957.

Lechner, Wilhelm. "Gotthilf Heinrich von Schubert's Einfluss auf Kleist, Justinus Kerner, und E.T.A. Hoffmann: Beiträge zur deutschen Romantik." Ph.D. diss., Münster, 1911.

Lee, M. O. "Orpheus and Euridice: Myth, Legend, Folklore." *Classica et Mediaevalia* 26 (1965): 402–12.

Leitzmann, Albert, ed. *Mozarts Persönlichkeit: Urteile der Zeitgenossen gesammelt und erläutert.* Leipzig, 1914.

Lentin, A. "Catherine the Great and Diderot." *History Today* 22 (May 1972): 313.

LeShan, Lawrence. *The Medium, the Mystic, and the Physicist.* New York, 1966.

Leutz, Grete. *Das klassische Psychodrama.* Berlin, 1974.

Leventhal, Herbert. *In the Shadow of the Enlightenment: Occultism and Renaissance Science in Eighteenth-Century America.* New York, 1976.

Lévi-Strauss, Claude. *The Savage Mind.* Chicago, 1966.

———. *Structural Anthropology.* Trans. Claire Jacobson and Brooke Grundfest Schoepf. 2 vols. New York and London, 1963.

Lewin, Louis. *Phantastica: Narcotic and Stimulating Drugs, Their Use and Abuse.* Trans. P.H.A. Wirth. New York, 1964.

Lewis, I. M. *Ecstatic Religion: An Anthropological Study of Spirit Possession and Shamanism.* Harmondsworth, 1971.

Licht, Hans. *Sexual Life in Ancient Greece.* Trans. J. H. Freese, ed. Lawrence H. Dawson. London, 1932. Reprint. 1971.

Lifton, Robert Jay. *The Broken Connection: On Death and the Continuity of Life.* New York, 1979.

———. *The Nazi Doctors: Medical Killing and the Psychology of Genocide.* New York, 1986.

Lindsay, Jack. *The Clashing Rocks: A Study of Early Greek Religion and Culture and the Origins of Drama.* London, 1965.

Lommel, Andreas. *Schamanen und Medizinmänner: Magie und Mystik früher Kulturen.* 2d ed., rev. and enlarged. Munich, 1980.

————. *Shamanism: The Beginnings of Art.* Trans. Michael Bullock. New York and Toronto, 1967.

Lorant, Stefan. *The New World: The First Pictures of America made by John White and Jacques Le Moyne and engraved by Theodore de Bry With Contemporary Narratives of the French Settlements in Florida, 1562–1565, And the English Colonies of Virginia.* Rev. ed. New York, 1965.

Lot-Falck, Éveline. "A propos du terme chamane." *Études mongoles* 8 (1977): 7–18.

Lovejoy, Arthur O., and George Boas. *Primitivism and Related Ideas in Antiquity.* Baltimore, 1935. Reprint. New York, 1965.

Lurie, Nancy Oestreich. "Winnebago Berdache." *American Anthropologist* 55 (1953): 708–12.

MacAloon, John J., ed. *Rite, Drama, Festival, Spectacle: Rehearsals toward a Theory of Cultural Performance.* Philadelphia, 1984.

McGrane, Bernard. *Beyond Anthropology: Society and the Other.* New York, 1989.

Madariaga, Isabel de. *Russia in the Age of Catherine the Great.* New Haven and London, 1981.

Maddox, John Lee. *The Medicine Man: A Sociological Study of the Character and Evolution of Shamanism.* New York, 1923. Reprint. 1977.

Mall, James. "*Le Neveu de Rameau* and the Idea of Genius." *Eighteenth-Century Studies* 11 (Fall 1977): 26–39.

Manning, Clarence A. *Russian Influence on Early America.* New York, 1953.

Manuel, Frank Edward. *The Eighteenth Century Confronts the Gods.* Cambridge, Mass., 1959.

Marcus, George E., and Michael M. J. Fischer. *Anthropology as Cultural Critique: An Experimental Moment in the Human Sciences.* Chicago and London, 1986.

Marett, Robert Ranulph, ed. *Anthropology and the Classics: Six Lectures Delivered before the University of Oxford by Arthur J. Evans, Andrew Lang, Gilbert Murray, F. B. Jevons, J. L. Myres, and W. Ward Fowler.* Oxford, 1908. Reprint. New York, 1966.

Marr, George Simpson. *Sex in Religion: A Historical Survey.* London, 1936.

Marshall, P. J., and Glyndwr Williams. *The Great Map of Mankind: Perception of New Worlds in the Age of the Enlightenment.* Cambridge, Mass., 1982.

Mason, Eudo C. *Goethe's "Faust": Its Genesis and Purport.* Berkeley and Los Angeles, 1967.

Masterson, James R., and Helen Brower. *Bering's Successors, 1745–1780: Contributions of Peter Simon Pallas to the History of Russian Exploration toward Alaska.* Seattle, 1948.

Meuli, Karl. *Kalewala, Altfinnische Volks-und Heldenlieder.* Basel, 1940.

————. "Scythica." *Hermes: Zeitschrift für klassische Philologie* 70 (1935; reprint. 1967): 121–76.

Mikhailovskii, V. M. "Shamanism in Siberia and European Russia, being the second part of 'Shamanstvo'" [1892]. Trans. Oliver Wardrop. *The Journal of the Anthropological Institute of Great Britain and Ireland* 24 (1895): 62–100, 126–58.

Minns, Ellis H. *Scythians and Greeks: A Survey of Ancient History and Archaeology on the North Coast of the Euxine from the Danube to the Caucasus.* Cambridge, 1913.

Mitrovich, Mirco. "Deutsche Reisende und Reiseberichte im 17. Jahrhundert: Ein Kultur Historischer Beitrag." Ph.D. diss., Urbana, 1963.

Mohrenschildt, Dimitri S. von. *Russia in the Intellectual Life of Eighteenth-Century France.* New York, 1936. Reprint. New York, 1972.

Molloy, Fitzgerald. *The Russian Court in the Eighteenth Century.* 2 vols. London, 1905.

Moreno, Jakob. *Angewandte Psychodrama.* Paderborn, 1972.

Mortier, Roland. *Diderot in Deutschland, 1750–1850.* Trans. Hans G. Schürmann. Stuttgart, 1967.

Mühlmann, Wilhelm E. "Hyperboräische Eschatologie." In *Chiliasmus und Nativismus*, ed. W. E. Mühlmann, pp. 197–221. Berlin, 1964.

———. *Die Metamorphose der Frau: Weiblicher Schamanismus und Dichtung.* 2d ed., rev. Berlin, 1984.

Müller, Friedrich. *Allgemeine Ethnographie.* Vienna, 1873.

Muster, Wilhelm. "Der Schamanismus bei den Etruskern." In *Frühgeschichte und Sprachwissenschaft*, pp. 60–77. Vienna, 1948.

———. "Der Schamanismus und seine Spuren in der Saga, im deutschen Brauch, Märchen und Glauben." Ph.D. diss., Graz, 1947.

Myres, John Linton. "Herodotus and Anthropology." In Marett, *Anthropology and the Classics*, pp. 152–68.

Nettl, Paul. *Mozart und der Tanz: Zur Geschichte des Balletts und Gesellschaftstanzes.* Zurich and Stuttgart, 1960.

Neubauer, John. *The Emancipation of Music from Language: Departure from Mimesis in Eighteenth-Century Aesthetics.* New Haven and London, 1986.

Neumann, Erich. *The Great Mother: An Analysis of the Archetype.* Trans. Ralph Manheim. Bollingen Series, 47. 2d ed. Princeton, 1963.

Neumann, Karl. *Die Hellenen im Skythenlande: Ein Beitrag zur alten Geographie, Ethnographie, und Handelsgeschichte.* Berlin, 1855.

Nicholson, Shirley, ed. *Shamanism: An Expanded View of Reality.* Wheaton, 1987.

Nioradze, Georg. *Der Schamanismus bei den sibirischen Völkern.* Stuttgart, 1925.

Oesterreich, Traugott Konstantin. *Possession, Demoniacal and Other, among Primitive Races, in Antiquity, the Middle Ages, and Modern Times.* Trans. D. Ibberson. London and New York, 1930. Reprint. Secaucus, 1974.

O'Gorman, Donald. *Diderot the Satirist: "Le Neveu de Rameau" and Related Works, An Analysis.* University of Toronto Romance Studies, 17. Toronto and Buffalo, 1971.

Oldenbourg, Zoé. *Catherine the Great.* Trans. Anne Carter. New York, 1965.

Olsen, Dale Alan. "Music and Shamanism of the Winikina-Waro Indians: Songs for Curing and Other Theurgy." Ph.D. diss., Los Angeles, 1973.

Orel, Alfred. "Mozart auf Goethes Bühne." In *Mozart-Jahrbuch 1953*, pp. 87–89. Salzburg, 1954.

Oustinoff, Pierre C. "Notes on Diderot's Fortunes in Russia." *Diderot Studies* 1 (1949; reprint 1971): 121–42.

Pagden, Anthony. *The Fall of Natural Man: The American Indian and the Origins of Comparative Ethnology.* Cambridge, New York, and Melbourne, 1982.

Park, Willard Z. *Shamanism in Western North America: A Study in Cultural Relationships.* Northwestern University Studies in the Social Sciences, 2. Evanston and Chicago, 1938.

Parssinen, Terry M. *Secret Passions, Secret Remedies: Narcotic Drugs in British Society, 1820–1930.* Philadelphia, 1983.

Pearce, Roy Harvey. *Savagism and Civilization: A Study of the Indian and the American Mind.* Berkeley, Los Angeles, and London, 1988.

Perkins, Jean. *The Concept of the Self in the French Enlightenment.* Histoire des idées et critique littéraire, 94. Geneva, 1969.

Pfeiffer, John E. *The Creative Explosion: An Inquiry into the Origins of Art and Religion.* Ithaca, 1982.

Plischke, Hans. *Die Ethnographische Sammlung der Universität Göttingen, ihre Geschichte und ihre Bedeutung.* Göttingen, 1931.

———. *Johann Friedrich Blumenbachs Einfluss auf die Entdeckungsreisenden seiner Zeit.* Abhandlungen der Gesellschaft der Wissenschaften zu Göttingen, Philologisch-Historische Klasse, ser. 3, no. 20. Göttingen, 1937.

———. "Zur Geschichte der Reisebeschreibungen: Ein kulturgeschichtlich-bibliographischer Überblick." *Völkerkunde: Beiträge zur Erkenntnis von Mensch und Kultur* 3 (1926–1927): 24–32.

Plotkin, Friedrich. "Diderot's Nephew and the Mimics of the Enlightenment." *Centennial Review* 13 (Fall 1969): 410.

Powley, Edward Harrison. "Turkish Music: An Historical Study of Turkish Percussion Instruments and Their Influence on European Music." Master's thesis, Rochester, 1968.

Propper, Maximilian von. "Miszellen: 1. Goethes Anlauf, sich mit der russischen Sprache zu befassen; 2. Alt-Weimar im Spiegel jugendlicher Einfalt (Aus einem unveröffentlichten Brief Maria Pawlownas); Zu einer hässlichen Goethe-Legende." *Goethe-Jahrbuch* 97 (1979): 235–43.

Quantz, Hermann. "Beitrag zur Geschichte des Blumenbachschen Museums in Göttingen im 19. Jahrhundert und besonders seiner Ethnographischen Sammlung unter Ernst Ehlers." In *Göttinger Völkerkundliche Studien*, ed. H. Plischke, pp. 289–304. Leipzig, 1939.

Radloff, Wilhelm. *Aus Sibirien: Lose Blätter aus dem Tagebuche eines reisenden Linguisten.* 2 vols. Leipzig, 1884.

———. *Das Schamanenthum und sein Kultus: Eine Untersuchung.* Leipzig, 1885.

Raeff, Marc. *Catherine the Great: A Profile.* New York, 1972.

———. *Imperial Russia, 1682–1825: The Coming of Age in Modern Russia.* Borzoi History of Russia, ed. Michael Cherniavsky, vol. 4. New York, 1971.

Randi, James. *Flim Flam! The Truth about Unicorns, Parapsychology, and Other Delusions.* New York, 1980.

Ränk, Gustav. "Shamanism as a Research Subject: Some Methodological Viewpoints." In Edsman, *Studies in Shamanism*, pp. 15–22.

Rich, Alan. "A Composer Whose Computer Music Has a Magical Twist." *Smithsonian* (December 1984): 97–104.

Riha, Thomas, ed. *Readings in Russian Civilization*. Chicago and London, 1964.

Roach, Joseph R. "Diderot and the Actor's Machine." *Theatre Survey: The American Journal of Theatre History* 22 (May 1981): 51–68.

Rodgers, Gary Bruce. *Diderot and the Eighteenth-Century French Press*. Studies on Voltaire and the Eighteenth Century, vol. 107. Banbury, Oxfordshire, 1973.

Rogerson, Brewster. "*Ut musica poesis*: The Parallel of Music and Poetry in Eighteenth-Century Criticism." Ph.D. diss., Princeton, 1945.

Rohde, Erwin. *Psyche: The Cult of Souls and Belief in Immortality among the Greeks*. New York, 1925.

————. *Psyche: Seelenkult und Unsterblinchkeitsglaube der Griechen*. 2d ed. 2 vols. Leipzig and Tübingen, 1898. Reprint. Darmstadt, 1980.

Röhrich, Lutz. "Die Märchenforschung seit dem Jahre 1945." *Deutsches Jahrbuch für Volkskunde* 2 (1956): 274–319.

Rosenfeld, G. "Justus Samuel Scharschmidt und seine Bedeutung für die deutsche Russlandkunde am Anfang des 18. Jahrhunderts." *Zeitschrift für Geschichtswissencahft* 2 (1954): 866–902.

Rothenberg, Jerome. "New Models, New Visions: Some Notes toward a Poetics of Performance." In Benamou and Carmello, *Performance in Postmodern Culture*, pp. 11–17.

————. ed. *Technicians of the Sacred: A Range of Poetries from Africa, America, Asia, Europe, and Oceania*. 2d ed., rev. and enlarged. Berkeley, Los Angeles, and London, 1985.

Rouget, Gilbert. *Music and Trance: A Theory of the Relations between Music and Possession*. Trans. Gilbert Rouget and Brunhilde Biebuyck. Chicago and London, 1985.

Rousseau, G. S., and Roy Porter, eds. *Sexual Underworlds of the Enlightenment*. Manchester, England, 1987.

Rudy, Z. "Die Piktographie mit besonderer Berücksichtigung der Völkerschaften Sibiriens." *Anthropos* 61 (1966): 98–128.

Runeberg, Arne. *Witches, Demons, and Fertility Magic: Analyses of Their Significance and Mutual Relations in Welt-European Folk Religion*. Helsinki, 1947. Reprint. 1979.

Sabin, Joseph, Wilberforce Eames, and R.W.G. Vail. *A Dictionary of Books Relating to America, from Its Discovery to the Present Time*. 29 vols. New York, 1868–1936.

Sachs, Curt. *Handbuch der Musikinstrumentenkunde*. Kleine Handbücher der Musikgeschichte nach Gattungen, 12. Leipzig, 1920.

————. *The History of Musical Instruments*. New York, 1940.

Saine, Thomas. *Georg Forster*. New York, 1972.

Salmen, Walter. *Der fahrende Musiker im europäischen Mittelalter*. Kassel, 1960.

Sárosi, Bálint. *Zigeunermusik*. Trans. Imre Ormay. Budapest, Zurich, Freiburg, 1977.

Schadewaldt, Hans. *Der Medizinmann bei den Naturvölkern.* Stuttgart, 1968.

Schadewaldt, Wolfgang. "Faust und Helena: Zu Goethes Auffassung vom Schönen und der Realität des Realen im Zweiten Teil des 'Faust.'" *Deutsche Vierteljahrsschrift für Literaturwissenschaft und Geistesgeschichte* 30 (1956): 1–40.

Schechner, Richard. *Between Theater and Anthropology.* Philadelphia, 1985.

Schillemeit, Jost. "Das *Vorspiel auf dem Theater* zu Goethes *Faust:* Entstehungszusammenhänge und Folgerungen für sein Verständnis." *Euphorion* 80 (1986): 149–57.

Schimpf, Wolfgang. "*Faust* als Melodrama? Überlegungen zu einer Bühnenfassung von 1819." *Euphorion* 81 (1987): 347–53.

Schlösser, Rudolf. *Rameaus Neffe: Studien und Untersuchungen zur Einführung in Goethes Übersetzung des Diderotschen Dialogs.* Forschung zur neueren Literaturgeschichte, 15. Berlin, 1900.

Schmid, Günther. *Goethe und die Naturwissenschaften: Eine Bibliographie.* Ed. Emil Abderhalden. Halle, Saale, 1940.

Schmidt, Jochen. *Die Geschichte des Genie-Gedankens, 1750–1945.* 2 vols. Darmstadt, 1985.

Schmidt, Leopold. "Der Herr der Tiere in einigen Sagenlandschaften Europas und Eurasiens." *Anthropos* 47 (1952): 509–38.

Schröder, Dominik. "Zur Struktur des Schamanismus." *Anthropos* 50 (1955): 848–81.

Schullian, Dorothy, and Max Schoen. *Music and Medicine.* Freeport, 1948. Reprint. 1971.

Schwab, Raymond. *The Oriental Renaissance: Europe's Discovery of India and the East, 1680–1880.* Trans. Gene Patterson-Black and Victor Reinking. New York, 1984.

Scurla, Herbert, ed. *Jenseits des Steinernen Tores: Entdeckungsreisen deutscher Forscher durch Sibirien im 18. und 19. Jahrhundert.* 2d ed. Berlin, 1965.

———. *Reisen in Nippon, Berichte deutscher Forscher des 17. und 19. Jahrhunderts aus Japan: Engelbert Kaempfer, Georg Heinrich von Langsdorff, Philipp Franz von Siebold.* Berlin, 1968.

Seiden, Milton F. "Jean-François Rameau and Diderot's Neveu." *Diderot Studies* 1 (1949; reprint 1971): 143–91.

Sewell, Elizabeth. *The Orphic Voice: Poetry and Natural History.* New Haven, 1960.

Sharon, Douglas. *Wizard of the Four Winds: A Shaman's Story.* New York, 1978.

Sherman, Carol. "The *Neveu de Rameau* and the Grotesque." *Romance Notes* 16 (Autumn 1974): 103–8.

Shirokogoroff, Sergei Mikhailovich. *Psychomental Complex of the Tungus.* London, 1935. Reprint. New York, 1980.

Shroder, Maurice Z. *Icarus: The Image of the Artist in French Romanticism.* Harvard Studies in Romance Languages, 17. Cambridge, Mass., 1961.

Sierke, Eugen. *Schwärmer und Schwindler zu Ende des achtzehnten Jahrhunderts.* Leipzig, 1874.

Sierksma, Fokke. *Tibet's Terrifying Deities: Sex and Aggression in Religious Acculturation.* Trans. G. E. Van Baaren-Pape. Rutland, Vt., and Tokyo, 1966.

Slotkin, James Sydney, ed. *Readings in Early Anthropology.* Chicago, 1965.

Smiley, Joseph Royall. *Diderot's Relations with Grimm.* Illinois Studies in Language and Literature, 34. Urbana, 1950.

Smith, Marian. "Shamanism in the Shaker Religion of Northwest America." *Man* 54 (1954): 119–22.

Sonnenschein, David. "Homosexuality as a Subject of Anthropological Inquiry." *Anthropological Quarterly* 39 (1966): 73–82.

Spaethling, Robert. *Music and Mozart in the Life of Goethe.* Columbia, S.C., 1987.

Spitzer, Leo. "The Style of Diderot." In *Linguistics and Literary History: Essays in Stylistics,* pp. 135–91. Princeton, 1948.

Spivey, Ted Ray. *The Writer as Shaman: The Pilgrimages of Conrad Aiken and Walker Percy.* Macon, Ga., 1986.

Spoerri, T., ed. *Beiträge zur Ekstase.* Bibliotheca Psychiatrica et Neurologica, 134. Basel and New York, 1968.

Stafford, Barbara. *Voyage into Substance: Art, Science, Nature, and the Illustrated Travel Account, 1760–1840.* Cambridge, Mass., and London, 1984.

Stauder, Wilhelm. *Alte Musikinstrumente in ihrer vieltausendjährigen Entwicklung und Geschichte.* Braunschweig, 1973.

Stewart, William E. *Die Reisebeschreibung und ihre Theorie im Deutschland des 18. Jahrhunderts.* Literatur und Wirklichkeit, ed. Karl Otto Conrady, 20. Bonn, 1978.

Stocking, George W., Jr. *Victorian Anthropology.* New York and London, 1987.

Strauss, Walter A. *Descent and Return: The Orphic Theme in Modern Literature.* Cambridge, Mass., 1971.

Taylor, Ronald. *The Romantic Tradition in Germany: An Anthology with Critical Essays and Commentaries.* London, 1970.

Thomas, Keith Vivian. *Religion and the Decline of Magic.* New York, 1971.

Tirén, Karl. *Die Lappische Volksmusik, Aufzeichnungen von Juoikos-Melodien bei den Schwedischen Lappen.* Ed. Ernst Manker. Nordiska Museet: Acta Lapponica, 3. Stockholm, 1942.

Tisdall, Caroline. *Joseph Beuys Coyote.* Munich, 1980.

Traister, Barbara Howard. *Heavenly Necromancers: The Magician in English Renaissance Drama.* Columbia, Mo., 1984.

Trilling, Lionel. "The Honest Soul and the Disintegrated Consciousness." In *Sincerity and Authenticity,* pp. 26–113. Reprint. New York and London, 1980.

———. "The Legacy of Freud." *Kenyon Review* 2 (Spring 1940): 153–55.

Turner, Victor. "Frame, Flow, and Reflection: Ritual and Drama as Public Liminality." In Benamou and Caramello, *Performance in Postmodern Culture,* pp. 33–55.

Uhlig, Ludwig. *Georg Forster: Einheit und Mannigfaltigkeit in seiner geistigen Sicht.* Tübingen, 1965.

Ulmer, Gregory L. *Applied Grammatology, Post(e)-Pedagogy from Jacques Derrida to Joseph Beuys.* Baltimore and London, 1985.

Valentin, Erich. "Das magische Zeichen: Mozart in der modernen Dichtung." In *Mozart-Jahrbuch 1956,* pp. 7–8. Salzburg, 1957.

Veeser, H. Aram, ed. *The New Historicism.* New York and London, 1989.

Wagar, Warren. *Terminal Visions: Literature of Last Things.* Bloomington, 1982.

Waley, Arthur. *The Nine Songs: A Study of Shamanism in Ancient China.* London, 1955.

Waliszwski, Kazimierz. *The Story of a Throne (Catherine II of Russia).* 2 vols. 1895. Reprint. Freeport, 1971.

Walker, Benjamin. *Sex and the Supernatural: Sexuality in Religion and Magic.* New York, Evanston, San Francisco, and London, 1973.

Warden, John, ed. *Orpheus: The Metamorphosis of a Myth.* Toronto, Buffalo, and London, 1982.

Wardman, H. W. "Enthusiasm: The Enlightenment, the Revolution, and After." *European Studies Reivew* 6 (1976): 45–60.

Washington, Ida. "Mephistopheles as an Aristophanic Devil." *Modern Language Notes* 101 (April 1986): 659–69.

Wasson, R. Gordon. *Soma: Divine Mushroom of Immortality.* New York, 1968.

Wasson, R. Gordon, Albert Hofmann, and Carl A. P. Ruck. *The Road to Eleusis: Unveiling the Secret of the Mysteries.* New York, 1978.

Weigle, Marta. *Spiders and Spinsters: Women and Mythology.* Albuquerque, 1982.

Wessel, Frederick. "The *Affektenlehre* in the Eighteenth Century." Ph.D. diss., Bloomington, 1955.

West, Hugh. "The Limits of Enlightenment Anthropology: Georg Forster and the Tahitians." *History of European Ideas* 10 (1989): 147–60.

White, Hayden. *Metahistory: The Historical Imagination in Nineteenth-Century Europe.* Baltimore and London, 1973.

Wiener, Leo. *An Anthology of Russian Literature.* 2 vols. New York, 1902–1903. Reprint. New York, 1967.

Wilbert, Johannes. "Magico-Religious Use of Tobacco among South American Indians." In *Spirits, Shamans, and Stars: Perspectives from South America,* ed. D. L. Bowman and R. A. Schwarz, pp. 13–25. The Hague, 1979.

———. *Tobacco and Shamanism in South America.* New Haven and London, 1987.

Wilson, W. Daniel. "Weimar Politics in the Age of the French Revolution: Goethe and the Spectre of Illuminati Conspiracy." In *Goethe Yearbook: Publications of the Goethe Society of North America,* ed. Thomas P. Saine, 5:163–86. Columbia, S.C., 1990.

Winter, E. *Halle als Ausgangspunkt der deutschen Russlandskunde im 18. Jahrhundert.* Veröffentlichungen des Institutes für Slawistik, 2. Berlin, 1953.

Zastrau, Alfred. *Goethe Handbuch: Goethe, seine Welt und Zeit in Werk und Wirkung.* 2d ed., rev. and enlarged. Vol. 1 and vol. 4. Stuttgart, 1955–1961.

Zolla, Elémire. *The Writer and the Shaman: A Morphology of the American Indian.* Trans. Raymond Rosenthal. New York, 1969.